MEDIAEVAL
GARDENS

Mediaeval Gardens

JOHN HARVEY

B. T. Batsford Ltd · London

© John Harvey 1981
First published 1981

First paperback edition 1990

All rights reserved. No part of this publication may be reproduced, in any form or by any means, without permission from the Publisher

ISBN 0 7134 2396 X

Typeset by Keyspools Ltd., Golborne, Lancs.
and printed in Great Britain by
Courier International Ltd,
Tiptree, Essex
for the publishers
B. T. Batsford Ltd.
4 Fitzhardinge Street
London W1H 0AH

BY THE SAME AUTHOR

Henry Yevele
Gothic England
The Plantagenets
Dublin
Tudor Architecture
The Gothic World
English Mediaeval Architects
A Portrait of English Cathedrals
The Cathedrals of Spain
Catherine Swynford's Chantry
(Lincoln Minster Pamphlet)
The Master Builders
The Mediaeval Architect
Conservation of Buildings
Early Gardening Catalogues
Man the Builder
Cathedrals of England and Wales
Early Nurserymen
Sources for the History of Houses
Mediaeval Craftsmen
York
The Black Prince and His Age
The Perpendicular Style
The Georgian Garden (Dovecote Press)
Restoring Period Gardens (Shire)

Bibliographies
English Cathedrals – A Reader's Guide
(*National Book League*)
Conservation of Old Buildings
(*Ancient Monuments Society*)
Early Horticultural Catalogues – A Checklist to 1850
(*University of Bath Library*)

Revised Muirhead's Blue Guides
Northern Spain
Southern Spain

Edited with translation
William Worcestre: Itineraries (1478–1480)

Frontispiece:
1 The large painting of Falconry at the Court of Philip the Good, Duke of Burgundy, a copy after a lost original of 1442, gives a detailed picture of a 'Pleasance in the Marsh' such as those recorded at Hesdin in Artois and at Kenilworth Castle in Warwickshire. This 'Gloriette', set in a lake provided with swans and other waterfowl, also serves as a perch for peacocks. The grounds, with specimen trees, picnic table and drinking fountain, are clearly the result of deliberate planting

Contents

Acknowledgments vi
List of Illustrations vii
Note on the revised edition ix
Preface x

Introduction 1

CHAPTER ONE
THE LEGACY OF CLASSICAL GARDENING 18

CHAPTER TWO
BEFORE THE MILLENNIUM: AD 500–1000 25

CHAPTER THREE
GARDENS OF SOUTHERN EUROPE 37

CHAPTER FOUR
GARDENS UNDER THE NORMANS 52

CHAPTER FIVE
GARDENS OF THE HIGH MIDDLE AGES 74

CHAPTER SIX
THE GARDEN AND ITS PLANTS 94

CHAPTER SEVEN
INTRODUCTIONS – THE PLANTER'S PALETTE 120

EPILOGUE
THE END AND A NEW BEGINNING 134

Bibliography and Abbreviations 144
Notes to the Text 148
ADDENDA 154
APPENDIX ONE
Some Royal Gardeners 155
APPENDIX TWO
Friar Henry Daniel, Botanist and Gardener 159
APPENDIX THREE
Plants of the Middle Ages: a Dated List 163
Index 181

Acknowledgments

THE AUTHOR AND PUBLISHERS gratefully acknowledge the financial assistance of the Trustees of the Crompton Bequest in respect of part of the cost of the illustrations; they express their special gratitude to Miss Verena Smith for her generous gift of the three photographs reproduced as fig. 63; and to Mr Anthony Huxley for the kind loan of a number of prints and colour transparencies; and would like to thank the following for permission to reproduce the photographs included in this book:
the Dean and Chapter of Canterbury Cathedral for Pl. I; the President and Fellows of Corpus Christi College, Oxford for 28; the Rt Hon the Earl of Oxford and Asquith for 79, 81; the Rt Hon the Lord St Oswald for 16; the Master and Fellows of Trinity College, Cambridge, for 37; Archivo Mas, Barcelona, for Pl. VII A and 43; Bayerische Staatsgemäldesammlungen, München, for 24, 49; Biblioteca Nazionale Marciano, Venezia (Foto Toso) for 23, 34; Bibliothèque Nationale, Paris, for Pl. VII B, 4, 17, 20, 47, 56, 57, 66, 83; Bibliothèque Royale Albert Ier, Bruxelles, for 42, 59, 62, 74, 75, 76; Bodleian Library, Oxford, for Pl. III A, 5, 21, 25, 28, 30, 38; British Library for Pl. III B, 6, 7, 8, 9, 10, 19, 22, 26, 27, 29, 31, 32, 33, 35, 36, 40, 46, 54, 55, 58, 60, 61, 65, 67, 68; Syndics of the Cambridge University Library for 14, 37; Château de Versailles (Photographie Giraudon) for 1; Country Life, London, for 77, 80; Fitzwilliam Museum, Cambridge, for 82; Foundation Johan Maurits van Nassau, The Hague (Foto A. Dingjan) for 2; Gemäldegalerie, Berlin (West), (Foto Jörg P. Anders) for 15, 39; church of St Bavo, Ghent (Copyright A.C.L., Bruxelles) for 3; Angelo Hornak for Pl. I; Institut Royal du Patrimoine Artistique, Bruxelles (Copyright A.C.L.) for 51, 53; Metropolitan Museum of Art, New York (Gift of J. Pierpont Morgan, 1917) for 50; Musée d'Art Religieux et d'Art Mosan, Liège (Copyright A.C.L.) for 51; Musée Royal des Beaux-Arts, Anvers (Copyright A.C.L., Bruxelles) for Pl. VIII; 3, 12; Musées Royaux des Beaux-Arts de Belgique, Bruxelles (Copyright A.C.L.) for 52; Musées Nationaux, Paris, for 48, 73; Museo Provinciale d'Arte, Trento (concessione della Provincia Autoname di Trento) for 70; Museu Nacional de Arte Antiga, Lisbõa, for 44; Museum Solothurn (Swiss Institute for Art Research, Zürich) for 72; Österreichische Nationalbibliothek, Wien (Bild-Archiv) for 13; Palazzo Medici Riccardi, Firenze (Foto Scala) for Pl. II; Photographie Giraudon, Paris, for Pl. IV, 1; Pierpont Morgan Library, New York, for 64; Pinacoteca di Brera, Milano, for 71; Royal Academy of Arts Photo Studios Ltd for 16; St Germain-en-Laye (Bibliothèque Municipale; Photo: Bibliothèque Nationale, Paris) for 69; Städelsches Kunstinstitut, Frankfurt-am-Main, for Pl. V; Stiftsbibliothek, St Gallen (Carsten Seltrecht foto) for 18; University Library, Utrecht, for 11; Victoria and Albert Museum Library (Photo: Sally Chappell) for 45; and Wallraf-Richartz Museum, Köln, for Pl. VI; figs. 78, 79, 81, are from photographs specially taken for this book by the author.

List of Illustrations

The colour plates are numbered in Roman capitals, I–VIII; black-and-white photographs in bold Arabic numerals, 1–83.

COLOUR PLATES

Between pages 114 and 115

I Canterbury Cathedral: west window. Figure of Adam in stained glass, c 1178 (Copyright Angelo Hornak)
II Florence: Palazzo Medici. Wall painting of landscape, part of Procession of the Magi, by Benozzo Gozzoli, c 1460
IIIA King and Queen playing chess in a garden, by Johannes, c 1400 (Bodleian Library, MS Bodley 264, f 258)
IIIB Narcissus at the spring in a walled garden. *Roman de la Rose*, French, c 1400 (British Library, Egerton MS 1069, f 1)
IV *Très Riches Heures* de Jean de Berri: miniatures by Pol de Limbourg, 1410–15 (Musée Condé, Chantilly, MS 65)
A Paris: garden of the royal palace (calendar for June)
B Château de Dourdan and park (calendar for April) (Copyright Photographie Giraudon)
V The Garden of Paradise, by a Rhenish master, c 1410–20 (Städelsches Kunstinstitut, Frankfurt-am-Main)
VI The Madonna in the Rose Arbour, by Stefan Lochner, c 1440 (Wallraf-Richartz Museum, Cologne)
VIIA Garden detail from The Virgin with Angels, by a follower of Hans Memling, c 1490 (Granada, Capilla Real)
VIIB Maugis and La Belle Oriande in a garden. *Roman de Renaud de Montauban*, c 1475 (Paris, MS Arsenal 5072, f 71v)
VIII The Festival of the Guild of Archers, by the Master of Frankfort, 1493 (Musée Royal des Beaux-Arts, Antwerp, No. 529)

BLACK AND WHITE ILLUSTRATIONS

1 Falconry at the Court of Philip the Good. Copy after an original of c 1442 (Château de Versailles, photo Giraudon)
2 Forest scenes on the wings of a triptych, by Gerard David, c 1490 (Mauritshuis, The Hague, No. 843)
3 Ghent: St Bavo. The Adoration of the Lamb, by Hubert and Jan van Eyck, 1432 (Church of St Bavo, Ghent)
A Central panel, part
B Right-hand outer panel
4 Window-box, from a miniature in the *Térence des Ducs*, c 1405 (Paris, MS Arsenal 664, f 47)
5 Beating turf with a mallet, from Crescentiis, Italian, c 1450 (Bodleian Library, MS Canon Misc 482, f 62v)
6 Richard II yielding the Crown, from a French chronicle, c 1440 (British Library, Harley MS 4380, f 184v)
7 The game of bowls, c 1280 (British Library, Royal MS 20 D. iv, f 187)
8 Planting vines from baskets. French version of Crescenzi, c 1485 (British Library, Add MS 19720, f 27)
9 The Castle of Roses. *Roman de la Rose*, French, c 1485 (British Library, Harley MS 4425, f 39)
10 Monk in a tree house. Italian, c 1400 (R. Forrer, *Unedirte Miniaturen des Mittelalters*, II, pl. 56)
11 A castle garden. Augustine, *De civitate dei*. South Netherlands, c 1475–86 (Utrecht University Library, MS Tiele 42, f 11v)
12 The Madonna of the Fountain, by Jan van Eyck, 1439 (Antwerp, Musée Royal des Beaux-Arts, No. 411)
13 Emilia in her garden. *Livre du Cuer d'Amours espris*, c 1465 (Vienna, Österreichische Nationalbibliothek, Cod. 2617, f 53)
14 Landscape with planted trees. *Les Douze Dames de Rhetorique*, by Jean Robertet of Bruges, c 1470–80 (Cambridge University Library, MS Nn. 3.2)
15 Gardens in background of the Enthroned Madonna, by Quentin Massys, c 1520 (Gemäldegalerie, Berlin-West, No. 561)
16 Vase of flowers from the painting of Sir Thomas More and his family attributed to Hans Holbein the younger, c 1528 (The Rt Hon the Lord St Oswald, Nostell Priory)
17 The poet Petrarch dreaming in a trellised arbour, c 1502 (Bibliothèque Nationale, Paris, MS fr. 594, f 3)
18 Plan of an ideal monastery, c 816 (Stiftsbibliothek St Gallen, Cod. 1092)
19 David and Bathsheba. *Liber Humanae Salvationis*, German, late 14th century (British Library, Add. MS 38119, f 1v)
20 Guillaume de Machault writing his poems in a walled garden, c 1360 (Bibliothèque Nationale, MS fr. 1586, f 30v)
21 The dreamer in a garden. *Somnium Viridarii*, French, c 1445 (Bodleian Library, MS Bodley 338, f 1)
22 Tafalla: garden architecture of the royal palace, c 1405; drawings of 1865 made before destruction.
A Mirador (gazebo-gloriet) and watercourse
B Banquet pavilion, with Mirador in background
C Stone seat
D Stone throne
(P. de Madrazo, *Navarra y Logroño*, 1886, III, 257, 259–60)
23 Garden beds, shrubs and pot-plants. *Grimani Breviary*, Flemish, c 1510 (Venice, Biblioteca Nazionale Marciana)
24 Railed flower-benches from Virgin and Child.

School of Stefan Lochner, c 1440 (Munich, Alte Pinakothek, WAF 506)
25 Sports garden with archery butts, c 1465 (Bodleian Library, MS Douce 93, f 101)
26 Transport of a carnation plant. Book of Hours, Flemish, c 1500 (British Library, Add. MS 38126, f 110)
27 Vine-dressing in Anglo-Saxon times. *Utrecht Psalter*, English c 1000 (British Library, Harley MS 603, f 54v)
28 Gardener and rural labourers in Henry I's dream. *Chronicle of Florence and John of Worcester*, English, c 1130–40 (Corpus Christi College, Oxford, MS 157, p. 382)
29 Vines growing on posts and rails. French, c 1325 (British Library, Add. MS 17333, f 27v)
30 St Elizabeth teaching the Baptist in a Rose Arbour. Late 15th century (Bodleian Library, MS Douce 31, f 232v)
31 Flowery meads with shrubbery and flower-bed. Address to Robert of Anjou, King of Naples, from Prato (i.e. 'meadow') in Tuscany, c 1335 (British Library, Royal MS 6 E. ix, f 15v)
32 Nobles in a garden by a marble fountain. *Cocharelli MS*, North Italian, late 14th century (British Library, Egerton MS 3781, f 1r)
33 The 'City of Babylon' and Balsam Garden. Romances given to Queen Margaret of Anjou, 1445 (British Library, Royal MS 15 E. vi, f 4v)
34 The Garden Enclosed. *Grimani Breviary*, Flemish, c 1510 (Venice, Biblioteca Nazionale Marciana)
35 Fencing a newly laid-out garden. French version of Crescenzi, c 1485 (British Library, Add. MS 19720, f 27)
36 Picking fruit in the Orchard. French version of Crescenzi, c 1485 (British Library, Add. MS 19720, f 117)
37A Plan of water-supply of Canterbury Cathedral and priory, English, c 1165
B Detail of the 'Herbarium' (Trinity College, Cambridge, from the *Edwin Psalter*)
38 Foxglove and Chamomile, from the Bury St Edmunds *Herbal*, English, c 1120 (Bodleian Library, MS Bodley 130, f 44)
39 Virgin and Child with Saints in a Rose pergola. German, c 1470 (Gemäldegalerie, Berlin-West, No. 1235)
40A Plan of Windsor with the Castle and Park, by John Norden, 1607
B Detail of the Castle, Garden and Orchard (British Library, Harley MS 3749, ff 5v–5)
41 The Madonna of the Rose Bower, by Martin Schongauer, 1473 (St Martin's Church, Colmar)
42 Saints Cosmas and Damian in a lordly garden. *Hennessy Book of Hours of the Virgin*, by Simon Bening, c 1510 (Bibliothèque Royale, Brussels, MS II. 158, f 175v)
43 The Virgin with Angels in a garden pavilion, painted for Queen Isabella of Spain by a follower of Hans Memling, c 1490 (Granada, Capilla Real)
44 Mystical Marriage of St Catherine, by the Master of the 'Virgo inter Virgines', c 1490 (Museu Nacional de Arte Antiga, Lisbon)
45 Calendar for April, showing gardening, from the destroyed *Turin Hours*, Flemish, c 1400 (P. Durrieu, *Heures de Turin*, 1902, pl. iv)
46 Lovers in a garden, from the poems of Christine de Pisan, French, c 1415 (British Library, Harley MS 4431, f 376)
47 Garden scenes from the *Hours of Queen Anne of Brittany*, by Jean Bourdichon, 1501–07
A Calendar for May, with benched ornamental tree
B Calendar for April, ladies in a castle herber
C Pruning with a billhook (Bibliothèque Nationale, Paris, MS lat. 9474, ff 8, 7, 6)
48 Terrace garden, from the Madonna with Chancellor Rollin, by Jan van Eyck, c 1425 (Musée du Louvre, Paris, No. 1271)
49 Terrace garden, from the Virgin and Child with St Luke, by Rogier van der Weyden, 1450 (Munich, Alte Pinakothek, HG. 1188)
50 Castle garden, from The Annunciation, by a follower of Rogier van der Weyden, c 1460 (Metropolitan Museum of Art, New York, Gift of J. Pierpont Morgan, 1917, 17.190.7)
51 Terrace garden, from the Virgin and Child by the Master of St Gudule, c 1470–90 (Musée d'Art Religieux et d'Art Mosan, Liège)
52 Castle garden, from The Unjust Sentence of the Emperor Otho III, by Dirk Bouts, 1468 (Brussels, Musée Royal des Beaux-Arts)
53 Roof and balcony gardens, from Portrait of a Man, by Jan Mostaert, c 1510 (Brussels, Musée Royal des Beaux-Arts)
54 Suburban villa gardens on the Giudecca, Venice, from the bird's-eye plan by Jacopo de' Barbari, 1500
55A Flower garden, from the French version of Crescenzi, c 1485
B Detail of trained carnations (British Library, Add. MS 19720, f 214)
56 A garden of the Duke of Burgundy, from *L'instruction d'un jeune Prince*, Flemish, c 1470 (Bibliothèque de l'Arsenal, Paris, MS 5104, f 14v)
57 Garden with 'Gloriette', from the *Roman de Renaud de Montauban*, 1468–70 (Bibliothèque de l'Arsenal, Paris, MS 5072, f 270v)
58 Garden and shrubbery seen from a pavilion, from *Tractie de Conseil*, French, c 1500 (British Library, Royal MS 19 A. vi, f 110)
59 Bacchus and drinkers, scene in the Park of Hesdin. *Epitre d'Othéa à Hector*, by Jean Miélot, 1461 (Bibliothèque Royale, Brussels, MS 9392, f 24v)
60 Courtly company in a garden. *Roman de la Rose*, Flemish, c 1485 (British Library, Harley MS 4425, f 12v)
61 Courtly dance in a garden. *Roman de la Rose*, Flemish, 1485 (British Library, Harley MS 4425, f 14v)
62 King René d'Anjou writing in his garden pavilion. *Hours of Isabella of Portugal*, French, c 1480 (Bibliothèque Royale, Brussels, MS 10308, f 1)
63A Benched fruit-tree. Woodcut in a Book of Hours by Theilman Kerver, Paris, 1503
B, C Carved pillar of the same subject, Boxgrove Priory, Sussex, De la Warr tomb, 1532 (Copyright photographs, Miss Verena Smith)
64 Gardeners at work. French version of Crescenzi, Flemish, c 1460 (Pierpont Morgan Library, New York, M. 232, f 157)
65 Gardeners at work. Book of Hours, Flemish, c 1490, from calendar for March (British Library, Add. MS 18852, f 3v)
66 Old man digging in a herber. *Valerius Maximus*, French, c 1470 (Bibliothèque de l'Arsenal, Paris, MS 5196, f 357v)
67 Two ladies gardening. *De Lof der Vrouwen*, Dutch, 1475 (British Library, Add. MS 20698, f 17)
68 Digging with a long-handled spade. French version of Crescenzi made in Bruges for Edward IV, c 1480 (British Library, Royal MS 14 E. vi, f 208)
69 St Mary Magdalene and Christ as the Gardener. Book of Hours, French, c 1500 (St Germain-en-Laye, Bibliothèque Municipale, MS 1)
70A Courtly gathering in a rose garden. Wall-

painting of 'Sol in Gemini', Italian, c 1415–20
B Detail of rose-bush (Trent, Castello, Torre del Aquilo)
71 The Madonna in the Rose Arbour, with pot of columbines, by Bernardino Luini, c 1510 (Milan, Pinacoteca di Brera, No. 289)
72 The Virgin and the Strawberries, by an Upper Rhenish master, c 1410–20 (Museum Solothurn, No. A 32)
73 Rose of gold and enamel, c1309. Given by Pope Clement V to the Prince-Bishop of Basel (Musée de Cluny, Paris, No. 2351)
74 Garden with a peacock and pot of carnations. *Histoire de Charles Martel*, by Loyset Liédet, 1470 (Bibliothèque Royale, Brussels, MS 6, f 9)
75 Garden with figures of royal beasts. *Histoire de Charles Martel*, by Loyset Liédet, 1470 (Bibliothèque Royale, Brussels, MS 9, f 7)
76 A royal garden party disturbed: Pepin kills a lion. *Histoire de Charles Martel*, by Loyset Liédet, 1470 (Bibliothèque Royale, Brussels, MS 7, f 59v)
77 Thornbury Castle, Gloucestershire. Interior of the Garden Gallery walls, 1511–20 (Copyright *Country Life*)
78 Westminster, Jewel Tower, moat, and Abbey garden wall, 1365 and earlier (Copyright the author)
79 Mells Manor House, Somerset: site of mound at north-west angle of garden, c 1520 (Copyright the author)
80 Mells Manor House: buttressed garden wall, c 1520 (Copyright *Country Life*)
81 Mells Manor House: doorway into garden, c 1520 (Copyright the author)
82 Buttressed garden walls and planted trees, from a Book of Hours, c 1500 (Fitzwilliam Museum, Cambridge, MS 294, f 34v)
83 Henri d'Albret, King of Navarre, plucks a daisy in the royal gardens at Alençon, 1526 (Bibliothèque de l'Arsenal, Paris, MS 5096, f 1)

MAPS AND PLANS

Map of Western Europe 19
Map of Britain to show gardens and planting 55
Plan of Gloucester with Kingholm and Lanthony 83
Plan of Peterborough Abbey and the Abbot's Garden 85
Plan of Kenilworth Castle and Pleasance 107
For Windsor Castle and Park, see 40

NOTE ON THE REVISED EDITION

Since this book was first published in 1981, further research has thrown light on many details: the more important of these will be found in the Addenda, page 154. Attention is also directed to the following articles:

'Queen Eleanor of Castile as a Gardener', *The Garden History Society: Newsletter* 5, Summer 1982, 3–4.
'Al-Biruni and oriental plants in AD 1050', ibid., *Newsletter 8*, Summer 1983, 4–5.
'Vegetables in the Middle Ages', *Garden History*, XII no. 2, Autumn 1984, 91–9.
'The First English Garden Book: Mayster Jon Gardener's Treatise and its background', ibid., XIII no. 2, Autumn 1985, 83–101.
The Oxford Companion to Gardens (1986), articles on *Carolingian Gardens; England: Medieval Gardens; Medieval Garden; Pleasance.*
'The Square Garden of Henry the Poet', *Garden History*, XV no. 1, Spring 1987, 1–11.
'Henry Daniel: a Scientific Gardener of the 14th century', ibid., XV no. 2, Autumn 1987, 81–93.
'Parks, Gardens and Landscaping', in M. A. Aston ed., *The Mediaeval Landscape of Somerset* (Somerset County Council, 1988), 98–107.
'The Fromond List of Plants', *Garden History*, XVII no. 2, Autumn 1989, 122–34.

Preface

THE TERM 'MEDIAEVAL GARDENS' MAY, to some students of large-scale landscape, seem almost self-contradictory. The word 'garden' itself has come to take on an extended meaning, including the whole grounds of Versailles or Chatsworth, Heidelberg or Studley Royal, rather than the basic sense of the yard or garth where plants are grown. Regardless of period or style, small gardens tend to be overlooked, and experts have even been heard to say of a very lovely garden at one of the oldest inhabited houses in this country: 'But it isn't a garden'. It had never been 'landscaped', in it the family planted and tended trees, vegetables and flowers for their utility and beauty, in it they could enjoy afternoon tea or sit in contemplation. To designers of the grandiose 'architectural' composition, such a garden may seem merely contemptible; yet they should bear in mind, not only that great oaks from little acorns grow, but that small is beautiful.

Gardens of the Middle Ages were indeed, for the most part, on a scale overshadowed by the mighty projects of the Renaissance. They consisted of an internal courtyard or patio **19**, as today in Spain, or of a square enclosure with a side of 100 feet or less. Yet within this small compass, and still further circumscribed by traditions of planning and treatment, it was possible for the gardeners of the time to achieve superlative quality. Their 'palette' of known plants was an extremely restricted one, peculiarly limited in its flowering season, but they were able to provide in a high degree that recreative function which is the peculiar product of good gardening.

Modern conditions of urban life have recently highlighted the virtues of even smaller gardens, in window boxes **4** or in hanging baskets. It is nonsense to deny to any such manifestations the name of garden, and we must likewise be wary of decrying mediaeval horticulture on the ground that it was on a small scale, had few species of plants, and was not organized on a scientific basis of any kind. Rather we should make the effort to penetrate the veil of obscurity which divides us from the period before the Renaissance and appreciate another facet of the amazing culture which gave to the world the Gothic cathedrals and the many thousands of parish churches scattered through the whole of western Europe. To do this it is necessary to accept the existence of a completely different set of values from those of the modern world in which we live. Fundamentally the Middle Ages exemplified a human society based upon transcendental and spiritual motives. Material values were firmly kept in second place and, while it was held that a man might legitimately seek his livelihood, he must not exalt pecuniary interest above his honour or the good of his soul. The fact that many men, and women, fell short of these ideals does not change the fact that the ideals were firmly placed in the forefront of society.

In such a society the garden clearly held an important place. The European Middle Ages were more, not less, akin to the civilizations of the East than the modern age after the Italian Renaissance. Ancient Egypt, Babylonia, India, China and Japan, as well as pre-Columbian Mexico, were all cultures with a philosophical and aesthetic interest in plants and gardens, and a similar outlook can be discerned as the savagery of the Dark Ages gave way to the

2 The scenic beauty of forests, recognized in Gerard David's wings of a triptych (*c* 1490), was already appreciated much earlier, and trees were planted with aesthetic aims at least as early as the eleventh century

profoundly integrated civilization which we call mediaeval. It is true that the age was not primarily concerned with observation, with representational portrayal of natural species, or with 'perspective views' of landscape. For those trained in the post-Renaissance tradition of 'scientific' optical perspective and of aesthetic individualization it is indeed difficult to grasp the mediaeval viewpoint, one not fixed in a determined position but in continuous motion.

Other difficulties stand in the way of adequate recognition of mediaeval gardening as an art. By far the greatest is the total disappearance of pleasure gardens of the period. Unlike architecture, of which many representative structures survive, gardens have entirely perished, unless we count a handful of long-lived trees and a few stone walls. Secondly, we do not even have pictures of these lost gardens, but only generalized ideal or imaginary views, most of them of very late date. Here again is a sharp contrast: the study of buildings erected in the same centuries is supplemented by many graphic records made after 1550, of earlier structures now gone. Although hardly any recognizable representations of specific churches, castles or houses (any more than of gardens) were actually contemporary with the works, an interest in the correct portrayal of architecture came soon enough to save many from total oblivion. Nothing of the kind happened to preserve for us records of the mediaeval gardens known to have existed. Finally the small scale of the typical *hortus conclusus* militates against its acceptance as a major art form. Yet nobody would dream of suggesting that painting did not exist then because no easel pictures were produced; nor, even had all wall-paintings disappeared, would the art of miniature illumination be dismissed for lack of size.

We must, however, consider whether the small enclosed garden was indeed the only aesthetic expression in this field during the period. Gardening in the wider sense includes not only the large-scale layouts since the Renaissance, but the ancient walled 'paradises' of the East. It has been generally assumed that, in contradistinction to current usage both earlier and later, the landscape in the Middle Ages was untouched by hand. All woodland is said to have been virgin forest, invaded by carpenters who sought out suitable trees as wild products, not as plants sown, tended and pruned by man. It is unlikely that this wholly negative picture of the landscape was true for the whole of western Europe and for the five centuries 1000–1500. Are we to suppose that the grandly composed landscape of the Van Eycks' *Adoration* at Ghent 3 was purely a work of imagination? Surely it must, along with glimpses of the same sort in many other paintings and illuminations, reflect the actual existence of large areas of parkland which owed much to human interference? 1, 2, 14, 33–5, 42–4

The problem has been still further complicated by the suggestion, made by Mr Miles Hadfield in his authoritative *History of British Gardening*, that England was even more backward in aesthetic horticulture than France and Flanders. He points to the fact that, whereas exquisite continental miniatures of late mediaeval gardens exist, English counterparts of such scenes are not found. Yet this argument cuts both ways. It is equally true that there are Netherlandish paintings and illuminations, as far back as the fourteenth century, showing individual buildings in recognizable detail; but that no such English paintings have survived. The fact is that, because of the survival of the buildings themselves, we know that Lincoln Cathedral is just as real as that of Antwerp and that Windsor Castle and Westminster Palace flourished as much under Edward III and Richard II as did the Louvre or Vincennes so meticulously recorded by Pol de Limbourg in the *Très Riches Heures*. The addiction to the accurate portrayal of man's surroundings simply happens to have sprung up in the region of the Netherlands and, surprisingly, not to have produced early imitators in England, despite geographical proximity and very close interchanges in trade and art.

National differences in gardening, as in architecture and the other arts, there certainly were, though we can hardly hope to discover the precise distinctions between the mediaeval gardens of England, France, Germany and greater Flanders. Along with Italy, the Iberian Peninsula, and at least the southern parts of the Scandinavian realms, these constituted

3A

3B

3 The magnificent scenery of the Van Eycks' 'Adoration of the Lamb', including palms to identify the Gothic city as Jerusalem, is in the main based upon the great parks of the Burgundian realm, with deliberately planted specimen trees, copses and shrubs in a managed landscape
A The enormous sweep of the hillside in the great central panel is probably directly derived from some planned vista now lost.
B The outer right panel, behind a throng of pilgrims, shows rolling open grassland planted with carefully placed shrubs, clumps and specimen trees, among them conspicuously a cypress and a palm. The principle of variation in colour of foliage was evidently already recognized, and we know that exotics including the cypress were being grown in England even fifty years before

Western Europe (see map, p. 19). In spite of national antipathies and more or less continuous warfare, all of these lands owed spiritual allegiance to Rome and shared Latin as a common language of the learned, with French for purposes of courtly conversation and trade. As in other fields, there was a common cultural background transcending the regional distinctions between one country and the next. Apart from the range of plants grown, largely determined by climate, it seems that national distinctions in gardening were comparatively slight. Germany certainly favoured the linden or lime-tree as the shade tree *par excellence* for recreational gardens; England, helped by its rainy weather, was able to specialize in magnificent lawns for the game of bowls 7; France – northern France – cultivated the splendid evergreen rosemary long before it was carried to Britain. The biggest contrast, both climatic and cultural, was that between North and South of the Pyrenees. Spain and Portugal, as inheritors of the Moors with their scientific knowledge of horticulture, were in a different position from the rest of Europe. In another way Italy, also penetrated by the Arab world through Sicily and slowly recovering the knowledge of classical times, presented an individual picture distinct from that north of the Alps.

* * *

Much has already been written on the subject of mediaeval horticulture, notably in English, French and German; but out of a large output there seem only to have emerged two books devoted to the subject. The earlier, a worthy pioneer, was the slight but scholarly study of Alexander Kaufmann, *Der Gartenbau im Mittelalter* (Berlin, 1892). Based largely on literary sources, not German alone but European in scope, Kaufmann's work is fundamental. The same cannot be said of the text of *Mediaeval Gardens*, published posthumously from the collections of Sir Frank Crisp (1924). Crisp's enormous body of illustrations is, however, of considerable utility in spite of defective references and the fact that a high proportion consists of plans and views of Renaissance gardens included to show the continuance (as Crisp believed) of mediaeval gardening traditions. For more satisfactory treatment of the period it is necessary to go to periodical literature and to chapters in general histories of gardening or in books of related scope.

Among the most helpful early works were Richard Pulteney's *Historical and Biographical Sketches of the Progress of Botany in England* (1790), and the splendid edition and annotated translation of the Arabic 'Book of Agriculture' (c 1180) by J. A. Banqueri, canon of Tortosa, issued in two sumptuous volumes of Arabic text and Spanish version on facing pages in 1802. This work by Ibn al-'Awwam, though not the earliest, is the most comprehensive of all the great post-classical treatises produced on European soil. Serious study of mediaeval gardening received a new impetus with the publication of the St Gall monastic plan by F. Keller (Zürich, 1844) and the English study of it by Robert Willis published in 1848 (*Archaeological Journal*, Vol. V). The same volume contained a notable article by T. Hudson Turner on early horticulture in this country. Further research on the subject was done by Thomas Wright (*A History of Domestic Manners . . .*, 1862) and later by Percy Newberry whose articles in the *Gardener's Chronicle* for 1889 provided a basis for the detailed treatment of the period (76 pages) in Alicia Amherst's classic *A History of Gardening in England* (1895).

In the meantime the Spanish antiquary Pedro de Madrazo had in 1865 recorded the surviving remains of the two great castle gardens at Tafalla and Olite in Navarre, just before their destruction (published in his *Navarra y Logroño*, 1886). In France the outstanding student was Charles Joret, whose immense and detailed study of the rose (*La Rose*, 1892) also covers a wide field of detailed research into mediaeval gardening. Additional material for France was included by Georges Riat in *L'art des Jardins* (1900), but this was thrown into the shade as a work of historical scholarship by the detailed chapters on the woods, orchards and gardens of Normandy in Léopold Delisle's magistral *Etudes sur la Condition de la Classe Agricole et l'Etat de l'Agriculture en Normandie au Moyen-Age* (1851), probably the one entirely satisfactory source-book on the subject. Were it not for the scanty survival of Scottish records, the same might be said of the notable *A History of Gardening in Scotland* (1935) by E. H. M. Cox.

Valuable material was included by Marie Luise Gothein in her massive *Die Geschichte der Gartenkunst* (1914), overshadowed by the Great War, but achieving world fame in 1928 when the English translation appeared as *A History of Garden Art*. Regrettably devoid of detailed references, Gothein's work set a bad example to horticultural scholars all too often followed as, though with mitigations, by Eleanour Sinclair Rohde (e.g. in the important mediaeval section of *The Story of the Garden*, 1932). More recent general histories in English have followed Crisp's dictum that 'England ... was far behind other European countries', and the great outpouring of twentieth-century histories in other languages has started with the Renaissance. To this generalization one major exception must be made: the meticulously detailed and amply referenced section on mediaeval gardening (58 pages) in Herman Fischer's *Mittelalterliche Pflanzenkunde* (Munich, 1929). This, though now 50 years old, remains the one modern authority to lay adequate stress upon the evidence for aesthetic horticulture before 1500, tracing the relevant chapters of Petrus de Crescentiis (*Ruralium Commodorum Liber*, issued in manuscript *c* 1305) back to their origin in the (unacknowledged) work of Albertus Magnus fifty years before.

* * *

So far as the present study is based upon original sources it is a by-product of more than forty years of reading mediaeval building accounts and related records, mostly English. In all times and places, building and gardening have gone hand in hand, and much of the detailed evidence for gardening operations is contained in rolls and books of miscellaneous character concerned with 'works'. It has to be admitted that, obscure as the subject of mediaeval architecture may seem, that of gardening is still more so. The sources of all kinds do, it is true, suffice to prove conclusively that there were extensive gardens throughout western Europe in the period between 1000 and 1500, and that many of them were pleasure gardens or had recreation as a major purpose alongside utilitarianism. In a few cases the evidence goes beyond this, and we can reconstruct at least in outline the size and general form of quite large and complex grounds going far beyond the limits of the enclosed garden which is all that is commonly seen in contemporary paintings and illuminations (i.e. of *c* 1400–1500).

* * *

Since the paintings and miniatures cannot directly illustrate the whole of the text, the plates and their captions must be regarded as complementary and to some extent independent. Most of what we know of the precise forms of design used in the Middle Ages comes from the pictures of only the final 150 years. For comparison a number of particularly detailed views (Plates **42–62**) have been brought together to show the many variations of treatment even in the relatively small herbers which provided the main opportunity for the display of flowering plants, shrubs and specimen trees.

In the text, quotations of any length have been indented to avoid the repeated use of quotation marks; those from Latin and foreign languages are in modern English translation. Citations from works in English have been modernized in spelling and in punctuation but in no other way, except for occasional retention of the original spelling when only a few words appear in the text. The original spelling is also retained in all passages from Chaucer's poetic works. Modern scientific names of plants have been supplied in parenthesis ( ), mainly in agreement with those used in the *Dictionary of Gardening* of the Royal Horticultural Society (see Appendix, p. 163, for details).

This book owes a great debt to many generous helpers, but first to my mother, who awoke my interest in gardens at an early age; next to two leading members of the London Natural History Society: Lawrence J. Tremayne (1873–1959); and Herman Spooner (1878–1976) who, among much else, had been the chief compiler of the famous *Hortus Veitchii* (1906). More immediately I here record my thanks to John Sales, who suggested the book, and to Richard Gorer who has given me repeated help over botanical and horticultural problems; both of them have read the text in draft and have made most valuable suggestions. For much vitally important information in various fields and especially for enlightening references to the literature and records of the subject I express my gratitude to Miss F. E. Crackles; to L. S. Colchester, Ray Desmond, and Michael McGarvie; Professor R. B. Dobson, Professor Paul D. A. Harvey, and Dr C. H. Talbot; as well as to the past and present editors of the Medieval Latin Dictionary, Ronald E. Latham and Dr D. R. Howlett, and Miss Joyce Batty, whose assistance has been fundamental.

Among the very large number of others to whom I tender my warm thanks I would mention F. Alan Aberg, J. Roy Armstrong, Mrs Mavis Batey, C. James Bond, Dr W. Brogden, Professor Christopher Brooke, Professor R. Allen Brown, Dr R. W. Dunning, Mr Peter J. Gwyn, Dr George A. Holmes, Henry R. Hurst, Dr A. C. Jones, William Kellaway, Dr C. H. Lawrence, Ken Lemmon, Dr K. G. T. McDonnell, Donald F. Mackreth, Sir Robert Mackworth-Young, Nicholas H. MacMichael, Mrs Janet Martin, Mrs Frances Neale, Dr David Palliser, Professor R. B. Pugh, Oliver Rackham, Alan M. Rome, Trevor Rowley, Dr Xavier de Salas, Mrs Kay Sanecki, Lord and Lady Saye and Sele, Rob Scaife, Dr Christopher Thacker, Graham S. Thomas, Dr William Urry, Professor Richard Vaughan, Mrs G. A. Ward, Dom Aelred Watkin, and Paul V. Waton. Among the institutions which have been particularly helpful I must thank the authorities and staff at the British Museum and British Library, the Bodleian Library, Cambridge University Library, the Guildhall Library and London Corporation Records Office, the London Library, the Libraries of the Society of Antiquaries, the Society of Genealogists, the Linnean Society, the Warburg Institute, and Lambeth Palace Library, as well as several local libraries and especially Mrs Bane and the staff of the Frome Library; the Public Record Office and several county and other record offices; and finally the Warden and Fellows of Winchester College, with two successive Archivists, Peter Gwyn and Dr Roger Custance, and the Fellows' Librarian, Paul Yeats-Edwards.

I am grateful to my publishers and in especial to Paula Shea and Tim Auger, as well as to Miss Mimi Rolbant and Mrs Clare Sunderland for their work in collecting the illustrations. My thanks to the Trustees of the Crompton Bequest go beyond the formal acknowledgment of my gratitude made elsewhere. Adequate illustration of a book of this character is now excessively costly and, as on previous occasions, their financial assistance has been of vital importance to the work.

In conclusion I wish to emphasize the debt owed by all students in this field to the Garden History Society. Not only does the congenial companionship of its members greatly facilitate research but its journal *Garden History* has for the first time established a suitable medium for the publication of the results. I count myself singularly fortunate in that my text of Friar Henry Daniel's horticultural treatise on Rosemary – the earliest known book on gardening in English – should have been accepted for publication in 1972 in the first issue of Volume One. Last, but very far from least, it gives me great pleasure to record how much this book, like others before it, owes to my wife, who has shared in all stages of its preparation and read the proofs.

Frome 1981 John H. Harvey

Introduction

IT HAS LONG BEEN FASHIONABLE to derive the history of gardening from the story of Eden in the second chapter of Genesis. Without attempting to go back to origins, we may accept that horticulture has been fundamental to the development of civilization. The utilitarian (dietetic and medicinal) employment of plants to sustain and preserve life and health has always been inevitable, but has not necessarily involved the practice of gardening in those human cultures which were content to gather wild foods and herbs. Nomadic peoples moving from place to place to pasture their flocks would have at best only temporary gardens for taking a single rapid crop. In such circumstances there could be hardly a trace of aesthetic motives. The contemplation of art and nature together, promoted by gardens of the higher kind, is a sophisticated refinement of settled society. It is, in fact, when we reflect on the meaning of civilization as the art of living in cities that we approach an understanding of the real significance of the garden. As a relief from the oppressive world of city life and work, the garden joins the sheltering house to form the home, precisely for those who are to some extent cut off from nature.

All the great phases of European gardening have been closely associated with urban culture. It is hardly necessary to stress the intimate links between horticulture and social history in the great cities of the ancient Mediterranean, in Rome the preponderant city of the Empire, or later in Toledo, Seville, Granada, Montpellier, Paris, Vienna, Antwerp and London. In recent centuries the growth of population has produced a counter-flow outwards from the overgrown town to parks and gardens which provide at least a semblance of the country. Inflated site values work progressively against the integration of houses and gardens in towns and are moving towards an opposition between the concepts of urban and rural life. The Middle Ages, apart from their historical position, are also central in their balance between the extremes of the ancient and the modern outlook.

Even in much earlier periods, however, an opposition between town and country has existed. In the ancient civilizations of the Near East the 'countryside' was largely a wilderness; but in it were oases depending upon natural springs of water. These could be improved by the hand of man, enclosed within a wall, and irrigated to produce a park or, in the familiar term derived through Greek from the Old Persian, a paradise. Such a park, whether used as a game preserve or not, is distinct from a garden, but the two share certain constants: the cultivation of plants, the inclusion of water, and the factor of deliberate design. It is because of these common factors that the concept of modern gardening has been enlarged to include landscaping and aesthetic arboriculture. Within the last five centuries, and largely through the impulse of the Italian Renaissance **Pl.II**, the garden has become progressively identified with the large-scale 'amenity park'. As we saw at the start, this identification has been carried to the point of absurdity when it leads to the rejection of the small 'homely' garden as no garden at all.

It is time, therefore, to take stock and to define more precisely what we mean by 'gardens' in historical perspective, and what was understood in the Middle Ages to belong to gardening.

For the purposes of this book, gardening is used to mean the culture of plants of any kind, regardless of motive and of the type of plant grown. A garden, then, embraces the purely utilitarian kitchen garden producing vegetables, flavourings and salads; the orchard planted with trees bearing fruits and nuts of different kinds and often of outstanding visual beauty as well; the physic garden of medicinal herbs brought under cultivation for convenience or introduced from abroad; and also the planting of trees in rows 14, groves or parks with a view to pleasure or recreation wholly or in part.

At this point we reach a problem of vital importance: to what extent were mediaeval gardens directed to aesthetic ends? Alicia Amherst, in her classic book written 85 years ago, stated that 'the kitchen garden was in most cases the only one attached to a house. The idea of a garden, solely for beauty and pleasure, was quite a secondary consideration.' Much more recently Oliver Rackham, in *Trees and Woodland in the British Landscape*, has laid down that there is 'no exception to the general medieval practice of multiple uses for the same piece of land' and that deer in parks were 'not always in practice the predominant objective.' Both of these dicta are acceptable as far as they go: if the garden included herbs which happened to be beautiful it could serve an aesthetic as well as a material purpose; if the game preserve could also yield valuable timber and coppice wood, so much the better. We must beware of interpreting these negative statements as implying that aesthetic motives did not exist. It is worth bearing in mind that not so long ago it was widely believed that mediaeval buildings were only beautiful by accident, before adequate research had shown that both castle and cathedral were intended not merely to be functional, but to look impressive or lovely.

This multi-purpose aspect of the mediaeval garden is closely linked to the optical viewpoint of the artist of the time, not fixed but in continuous motion, as has already been said (p. xii). The various motives involved were not mutually exclusive, but complementary. This is not to say, however, that we need literally accept that there was no such thing in the Middle Ages as an ornamental pleasure garden. We shall see, on the contrary, that there was both a theory and a practice of planting gardens for their beauty, and that this was associated with the state of the economy. The penurious subsistence of the earlier Dark Ages could not support many or extensive pleasure gardens; a period of prosperity (even if only for the fortunate few) such as the epoch of demesne farming in England for the century-and-a-half between Henry II and Edward III, produced the wherewithal for surplus investment: in buildings, in works of art generally, and in gardens, fish-ponds and parks. In times of recession and political chaos, such as the sixty years of Lancastrian usurpation from 1400 to 1460, there is less evidence for recreational gardening.

The ultimate reasons for fluctuation were not by any means all political; beneath the economic recession there might lie natural changes of climate. Sir Harry Godwin in *The History of the British Flora* suggests in round figures the dates 1150–1300 for an early mediaeval Warm Epoch and 1550–1700 for a Little Ice Age. Professor J. C. Russell considers that this chilly period had already set in just after 1300, pointing out that in 1303 and in 1306–7 the Baltic was frozen over to its southern limits. This hardening of the natural environment led in some parts of Europe to a fall in population, but in Britain it seems to be notably associated with a falling off in the acreage of vineyards. Grapevines were still grown for ornamental purposes on a large scale, and for the production of dessert grapes in the South, but from the fifteenth century until the middle of the twentieth (with its rise in temperatures) the idea of even southern England as a wine country met with progressive discouragement.

Here again we must not lay all the responsibility on the climate, for it is obvious that the period of English political ascendancy in south-western France brought home-grown wines into direct competition with the best vintages of Europe. Those who had a palate, and could afford to please it, imported from Bordeaux rather than maintain a body of experts to grow and harvest wine grapes north of the Channel. In this field it is probably unrealistic to expect that England could ever be a major producer of wine, and it is no shame to acknowledge the superior endowments of Gascony or the Rhineland. In other directions it is less easy to accept the long-standing legend of English inferiority. Sir Frank Crisp considered that the English were 'far behind other European countries'; the late Edward Hyams wrote that 'in England gardening remained very backward'; Miles Hadfield suspects that monastic gardening in the British Isles 'was generally a second-rate version of contemporary continental gardening'. Is this pessimistic outlook really justified? Probably not.

It seems likely in any case that the quality of gardening, like that of architecture, was influenced to a considerable extent by the personal taste of the king and of a small number of courtiers, nobles and churchmen; and also by England's political prestige at a given time. We know that Henry III visited his brother-in-law St Louis and would have liked to bring back the Sainte-Chapelle in a cart. Although he could not do that, he was able to produce by his lavish patronage a great deal of English Gothic building of very high quality at Westminster Abbey and elsewhere. It is unlikely that his many gardens would lag very far behind those of Paris, especially under the pressure of his queen, Eleanor of Provence, for whom he certainly introduced many appurtenances of comfortable life from glazed windows to adequate sanitation. Henry's son, Edward I, the acknowledged leader of the West, when just back from contact with the refinements of Palestine and nearly two years spent at the courts of Sicily, Italy and France, set about making important gardens in the Palace of Westminster and the Tower of London 6. There is no reason to think that these were not among the very finest royal gardens of the time in the whole of western Europe.

Turning from mere probabilities to established fact, let us consider what is known of horticulture in the West, and especially in England, from various sources. It is convenient at this stage to deal only with the period before about 1310, and this for two main reasons. On the continent the year 1305 saw the completion of the one major book largely concerned with gardens, the *Ruralium Commodorum Liber* of the Bolognese lawyer Petrus de Crescentiis (Pietro de' Crescenzi, 1230–1320); while in England the long reign of Edward I came to an end in 1307, ushering in twenty years of political instability. The climate was deteriorating, famine ensued throughout Europe in 1315, and the age of high agricultural profits was over. There are three main types of source: firstly the serious treatises of scientific or encyclopaedic character which embodied the highest learning of the time; secondly, objective descriptions of actual gardens, or archival sources concerning them; and thirdly, literary and poetic material. This last body of information, heavily drawn upon in most of the earlier histories, is the least reliable; for all that, it cannot be altogether discounted or regarded as merely fabulous.

The first outstanding source for England is Aelfric's vocabulary of AD 995. This has been disregarded as including many names of plants and trees that could not then have been in cultivation, but closer inspection shows this adverse verdict to be unjustified. Concerned with the teaching of Latin, Aelfric listed words of general use in the daily conversation of the schools of Anglo-Saxon England. His lists of herbs and trees gave just over 200 names, but of these not more than nine can be regarded as unlikely to have been grown in the greater monastic gardens, and several of these are not certainly identifiable: *colochintida*, 'wylde cyrfet'; *collocasia*, 'harewinta'; *papirus*, 'duthhamor'; *mandragora*, 'eordhaeppel'; *ficus*, 'ficbeam'; *palma*, 'palmtwig', *uel* 'palm'; *olea, oliua*, 'elebeam'; *oleaster*, 'unwaestmbaere elebeam'; *cedrus*, 'cederbeam'. In the case of palm it is obvious that Aelfric means the ecclesiastical palm-branch (which might be of willow, yew or box), not the palm-tree; the fig, olive, oleaster and cedar would all be well known to pilgrims and of scriptural interest, while the fig at least was introduced to England later in the Middle Ages. So, apparently, was the mandrake, though we cannot be sure that Aelfric was right in equating it with the English name 'earth-apple'. Besides plant-names, Aelfric gives us 'luffendlic stede' (lovely place) as the English of *amenus locus*, an important aesthetic implication; and translates the Old English 'wyrttun' (garden) as *botanicum uel uiridarium*. This word *viridarium*, which became *verger* in French, an orchard of fruit-trees, has important horticultural overtones.

In his valuable history of Dutch gardening, Van Sypesteyn had already pointed out in 1910 that the mediaeval equivalent of the later pleasure garden was the *vergier* or orchard, for taking the fresh air, enjoying shade in summer and the like; and that it was often surrounded by walls, hedges and moats **11, 42, 62**. We shall see later many instances of this, and it is essential to recognize at the outset that a verbal distinction is often (though not invariably) made between *pomerium*, the utilitarian orchard, and *viridarium* (also sometimes *virgultum* and *virectum*) the pleasure ground; as between *gardinum*, a kitchen garden, and *herbarium* which was always a specialized form of garden: for medicinal herbs, or for flowers, on a limited scale and usually laid with green turf. *Hortus* or *ortus* remained a common generic word for garden grounds of all kinds, and *ortolanus* was frequent usage for a gardener, alongside *gardinarius*.

Soon after Aelfric, Notker (Labeo) of St Gall referred to flower gardens where roses, marigolds and violets grow, but we reach a quite modern sophistication early in the twelfth century with Hugh of St Victor (c 1078–d.1141). Hugh, born in Saxony but later domiciled in Marseilles and for much of his life in Paris, described a garden (*ortus*) as ditched about, beautified with the adornment of trees, delightful with flowers, pleasant with green grass, offering the benefit of shade, agreeable with the murmur of a spring, filled with divers fruits, praised by the song of birds (*arborum distinctus ornatus, floribus jucundus, gramine viridante suavis . . . umbrarum amoenitatem praestans, murmure fontis delectabilis, fructibus variis refectus, volucrum cantu laudabilis*). Towards the end of the century the Englishman Alexander Neckam (1157–1217), to whose extensive treatment of gardens and plants, both in prose and verse, we must return, wrote of the Rose, fitly clad in blushing purple, the glory and glad honour of the garden when in bloom

> *Et rosa, purpureo vestita rubore decenter,*
> *Vernans est horti gloria, laetus honos.*

Bartholomew de Glanville, better known as Bartholomew the Englishman (c 1200–c 1260), completed about 1240 one of the most widely used encyclopaedias of the whole Middle Ages, devoting the 17th Book to plants. What is here apposite is that among his definitions of the several meanings of *virgultum* he tells us: 'And sometime an herber is yclept *virgultum*, (*viridarium*) or *viretum*, and is a green place and merry with green trees and herbs.' The translation is that finished in 1399 by John Trevisa (c 1340–1402), with spelling modernized. Trevisa brings in the word 'herber' as something well understood in his day to be equivalent to *viridarium*, which he omits from the three terms given in the Latin text. Since the earlier meaning was certainly not that of the more modern arbour or bower, even though overlapping these, it will be convenient to use 'herber' throughout this book as the translation of the mediaeval Latin *herbarium*. In most cases the context indicates the shade of meaning emphasized: close garden with lawn, flower garden, or garden of medicinal herbs.

Bartholomew's definition of a herber concludes with: 'as is said tofore *de orto*. Look *in litera* O'; but neither the Latin text nor Trevisa's complete (and excellent) translation contains the

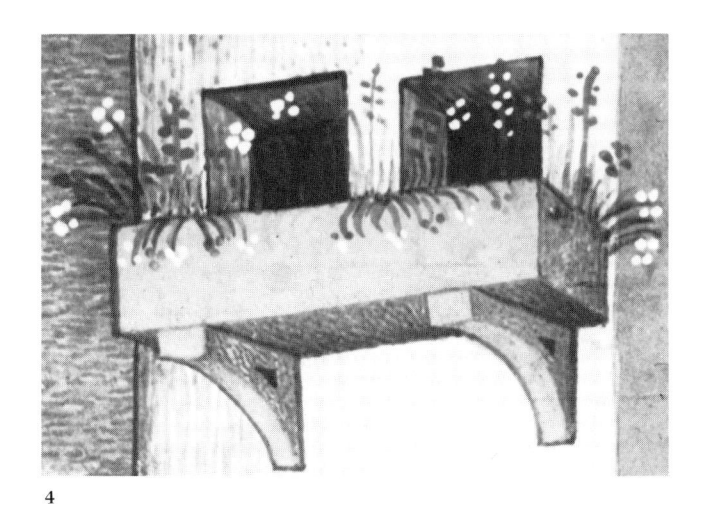

4 The window-box of flowers is a very old form of garden, as is shown by this French miniature of the opening of the fifteenth century   5 The importance of beating a lawn to compress the turf was successively insisted upon by Bartholomew de Glanville, Albert the Great, and Crescenzi. The process is here shown in an initial letter from an Italian copy (from Bologna) of Crescenzi's Latin text   6 This French illumination, though later than the event, gives a virtually contemporary view of the interior of an English royal palace, when Richard II yielded the Crown to Henry IV in 1399. The wall tapestry of fruit trees and garden plants in pots indicates the importance at the time of ornamental horticulture as a theme   7 An English drawing (c 1280) shows a game of bowls in progress in the time of Edward I. This is perhaps the earliest view implying the provision of a large and truly levelled lawn, such as that in the Palace of Westminster being rolled in 1259

section *De Orto*. Presumably it existed in Bartholomew's own manuscript, and we must suspect that it provided some of the material for the next and more detailed description, by Albertus Magnus. Albert, Count of Bollstädt, was born about 1206 at Lauingen in Swabia, studied at Padua and entered the Dominican Order; he died in 1280. In his treatise *On Vegetables and Plants* of about 1260 he added to the sections on utilitarian culture a chapter on pleasure gardens of such importance that it must be quoted in full:

On the planting of pleasure gardens (*viridariorum*)

> There are, however, some places of no great utility or fruitfulness but designed for pleasure, which are rather lacking in cultivation and on that account cannot be reckoned with any of the said lands: for these are what are called pleasure gardens. They are in fact mainly designed for the delight of two senses, viz. sight and smell. They are therefore provided rather by removing what especially requires cultivation: for the sight is in no way so pleasantly refreshed as by fine and close grass kept short.
>
> It is impossible to produce this except with rich and firm soil; so it behoves the man who would prepare the site for a pleasure garden, first to clear it well from the roots of weeds, which can scarcely be done unless the roots are first dug out and the site levelled, and the whole well flooded with boiling water so that the fragments of roots and seeds remaining in the earth may not by any means sprout forth. Then the whole plot is to be covered with rich turf of flourishing grass, the turves beaten down with broad wooden mallets 5 and the plants of grass trodden into the ground until they cannot be seen or scarcely anything of them perceived. For then little by little they may spring forth closely and cover the surface like a green cloth.
>
> Care must be taken that the lawn is of such a size that about it in a square may be planted every sweet-smelling herb such as rue, and sage and basil, and likewise all sorts of flowers, as the violet, columbine, lily, rose, iris and the like. So that between these herbs and the turf, at the edge of the lawn set square, let there be a higher bench of turf flowering and lovely; and somewhere in the middle provide seats so that men may sit down there to take their repose pleasurably when their senses need refreshment. Upon the lawn too, against the heat of the sun, trees should be planted or vines trained, so that the lawn may have a delightful and cooling shade, sheltered by their leaves. For from these trees shade is more sought after than fruit, so that not much trouble should be taken to dig about and manure them, for this might cause great damage to the turf. Care should also be taken that the trees are not too close together or too numerous, for cutting off the breeze may do harm to health. The pleasure garden needs to have a free current of air along with shade. It also needs to be considered that the trees should not be bitter ones whose shade gives rise to diseases, such as the walnut and some others; but let them be sweet trees, with perfumed flowers and agreeable shade, like grapevines, pears, apples, pomegranates, sweet bay trees, cypresses and such like.
>
> Behind the lawn there may be great diversity of medicinal and scented herbs, not only to delight the sense of smell by their perfume but to refresh the sight with the variety of their flowers, and to cause admiration at their many forms in those who look at them. Let rue be set in many places among them, for the beauty of its green foliage and also that its biting quality may drive away noxious vermin from the garden. There should not be any trees in the middle of the lawn, but rather let its surface delight in the open air, for the air itself is then more health-giving. If the [midst of the] lawn were to have trees planted on it, spiders' webs stretched from branch to branch would interrupt and entangle the faces of the passers-by.
>
> If possible a clear fountain of water in a stone basin should be in the midst, for its purity gives much pleasure. Let the garden stand open to the North and East, since those winds bring health and cleanliness; to the opposite winds of the South and West it should be closed, on account of their turbulence bringing dirt and disease; for although the North wind may delay the fruit, yet it maintains the spirit and protects health. It is then delight rather than fruit that is looked for in the pleasure garden.

8 This French manuscript of Crescenzi (*c* 1485) depicts the planting of vines from baskets, a valuable proof of the care taken in transplantation. The training of vines on poles and the gathering of the grapes are also seen

9 The symbolic Castle of Roses of the *Roman de la Rose*, though imaginary, closely resembles real fortresses; the landscape beyond the moat also is like what the defenders could have seen in real life from their great tower. Magnificent specimen trees are planted at strategic points in the view. The roses planted along the wall-walks, double red and double white, are low bushes as was normal at the time (*c* 1485)

10 This Italian miniature of *c* 1400 shows a 'hermitage' in a garden, found elsewhere in the Middle Ages (as at Hesdin), and suggests deep roots for the mock-hermitages of Painshill and other gardens of the eighteenth century

11 A South Netherlands master illustrating St Augustine's 'City of God' (*c* 1475) gives a picture of a large seigneurial garden with specimen trees and shrubs, a splendid fountain with hexagonal basin, and separate fenced herbers: one of these contains beds and irregular paths. Through the garden, at the foot of a steep declivity, a river cascades, to escape beneath the walls

Crescenzi, nearly half-a-century later, took over this whole chapter without acknowledgment and with only the slightest alteration: for example, he added to the sweet-smelling herbs of the garden marjoram and mint, but omitted the columbine.

Albert was a member of the greater nobility of Germany, a highly educated and much travelled churchman, and by the time that he was writing was Provincial of the Dominicans at Worms. Bartholomew also came of a distinguished family, spent much time in Paris and in Germany, and was an outstanding Franciscan. Certainly they were both well aware of the types of garden cultivated in the middle of the thirteenth century over wide areas of the continent. That this tradition of horticulture was also rooted in England is proved by the descriptive and archival evidence going back to the time of the Norman Conquest. The high society of the time, royal, noble and ecclesiastical, was international rather than national, and to many personal links of blood and marriage were added the journeys to and from Rome of large numbers of clerics, and the constant coming and going of members of the greater religious orders from mother houses abroad to their colonies and cells in Britain, Scandinavia and elsewhere. It is highly significant that so many of the gardens described as beautiful or ornamental, or made for recreation and repose, should be those of bishops and archbishops, abbots or monastic houses.

Disregarding for the present the ultimate origins of the pleasure garden in the East, its introduction into England at the time of the Conquest is demonstrated by the exploits of Geoffrey I de Montbray, bishop of Coutances in Normandy from 1049 to 1093. After a journey to Apulia and Calabria to visit Robert Guiscard and other barons related to him, as well as his pupils and acquaintance there who were associated with Guiscard in the Norman Conquest of southern Italy and Sicily, he returned with much gold, silver, precious stones and rich stuffs. He

> bought for £300 from William the most victorious duke of the Normans, afterwards also the glorious king of the English, the better half of the city suburbs (of Coutances) ... Afterwards he built the bishop's hall and other offices and planted a considerable coppice [or garden: *virgultum*] and vineyard ... he also made two pools with mills; he won part of the site of the park from the Count of Mortain and surrounded the park with a double ditch and a palisade. Within he sowed acorns and took pains to grow oaks and beeches and other forest trees (*quercus et fagos caeterumque nemus studiose coluit*), filling the park with deer from England.

Somewhere about 1092 can be placed the famous visit of William Rufus to the garden of Romsey Abbey. Wishing to see Edith of Scotland, the heiress of the Saxon line, then aged twelve and boarding in the convent school, he with his courtiers demanded admission 'as if to look at the roses and other flowering herbs.' Gerard archbishop of York, died on 21 May 1108 'in a certain garden (*viridario*) near to his house' where, being somewhat ill, he had gone to lie down 'to enjoy the open air with a healthier breeze, to which the flowers of the plants, breathing sweetly, gave life.' 17,21. In this we have the reliable evidence of the contemporary historian, William of Malmesbury, and similarly it is to a contemporary of St Bernard that we owe the detailed account of the gardens at Clairvaux, the first abbey of the Cistercian Order, founded in 1115. A few years later it could be said:

> within the precinct there is a wide level area containing an orchard of many different fruit-trees, like a little wood. Close by the infirmary, it is a great solace to the monks, a spacious promenade for those wishing to walk and a pleasing spot for those preferring to rest. At the end of the orchard a garden begins, divided into a number of beds by little canals which, though of still water, do flow slowly ... the water thus serves a double purpose in sheltering the fish and irrigating the plants.

12 The Madonna of the Fountain, painted in 1439 by Jan van Eyck, includes recognizable flowers such as roses and flag iris behind the turf bench, and in the foreground lilies of the valley

The story of English royal gardens and parks begins under Henry I who, about 1110, bought from William FitzWalter the land outside Windsor Castle which became the King's Garden, and at Woodstock in Oxfordshire enclosed a large area with a stone wall and stocked the park with exotic wild animals. We know too that the same king had a garden of nine acres at his manorhouse of Kingsbury by Dunstable, and a resident gardener holding hereditary office at Havering in Essex. Although we do not have detailed descriptions of these royal pleasances, they cannot have differed greatly in kind from two in northern France dating from only a little later in the twelfth century. At Le Mans Bishop Guillaume de Passavant built a stone manorhouse of considerable size in 1145–58:

> next the chapel he laid out a hall, whose whole design (*compositio*) and particularly that of its windows, was of such beauty ... that there the architect might be thought to have outdone himself. Lower down ... he had a garden (*viridarium*) planted with many sorts of trees for grafting foreign fruits (*per insertionem fructus alienos*), equally lovely; for those leaning out of the hall windows to admire the beauty of the trees, and others in the garden looking at the fair show of the windows, could both delight in what they saw.

Between 1183 and 1206 the bishop of Auxerre, Hugh de Noyers, improved the grounds of his manor at Charbuy (Yonne), a town five miles west of Auxerre:

> he provided every pleasure and improvement that the industry of man could accomplish. The woods, beset with briars and undergrowth and thus of little value, he cleared and brought into cultivation. There he made gardens and planted trees of different sorts so that, apart from deriving pleasure from them, he also got great quantities of fruit. He surrounded a large part of the woods with a ring fence carried from the gate at the near end to the dam of the third pool, and enclosed within a pretty quantity of wild beasts. These might be seen grazing in their herds by those in the palace, a pleasing sight.

In these extracts we have all the elements of deliberately designed landscape, where the aesthetic motive is either primary or at least co-equal with the utilitarian **59**. Of particular significance is the conversion of the wild woods at Charbuy to cultivation: here is an actual instance to set against the argument that the mediaeval management of woodland consisted merely of enclosing it and leaving it to grow. The deer brought from England to Coutances soon after 1066, and those which were a pleasant sight for the bishop and his guests on the borders of Burgundy by 1200, provide an early ancestry for the English landscape and the *ferme ornée*.

Returning to Britain, we find Gerald the Welshman waxing lyrical over the lovely setting of Manorbier Castle where he was born *c* 1146. Writing in 1188 he describes

> a noble pool of deep waters and a very beautiful orchard by it, shut in by a wood of hazels on a rocky eminence.

A few years later Gerald was telling the story of a monk who visited Gloucester and chaffed Geoffrey, the prior of Lanthony (see plan, p. 83), for his ambition to become bishop of St Davids (which he afterwards did, in 1203), saying that it was strange to covet a miserable little cathedral in a savage land, among hostile people, when already prior

> of so noble a house, in a place so beautiful and peaceful, provided with fine buildings, fruitful vines, set about handsomely (*amoene*) with pleasure gardens (*viridariis*) and orchards (*pomeriis*).

There is, in fact, abundant evidence of expenditure on pleasure gardens in England. Much of this is naturally derived from the surviving accounts of works at royal palaces and estates, but herbers, *viridaria* and park layouts with pools were also made for the higher nobility, for archbishops and bishops, notably for some of the abbots of greater monasteries, and for wealthy priors. The glimpses we get are of many different kinds: in 1259 the gardens of the Palace of Westminster were being levelled with a roller, and turf laid and later mown 7; by 1307 we know that there were the gardens of the privy palace and of the Prince's palace, with vines, pear-trees and paved walks, as well as lawns, and a great Conduit with taps, evidently an ornamental feature **1,11,12,15,19,32,34,60,83**. At the Tower of London there was a small walled garden within the fortress, but also another outside on Tower Hill, for which plants were bought at a cost of £10 in 1263. At the Mews for the king's hawks at Charing Cross there was a turfed garden with a lead bath for the birds having a metal image of a falcon in the middle **34**. At Windsor Castle in 1195–6 the then immense sum of £30 (at least £15,000 in 1980) was spent on making the king's herber, which may have been the one in the Upper Ward surrounded by a cloister linking the royal apartments. In 1236 Henry III had a window with opening glass casements fitted in the Queen's suite, looking into a courtyard with covered alleys and a herber in the centre **13**.

At Windsor, as at the Tower, there was a larger garden outside the wards of the Castle, the site for which had been bought by Henry I. Henry III in 1246 had it developed by moving the gardener's houses to another position, making good the hedge, and having a beautiful pleasure-garden (*unum pulcrum virgultum*) laid out. In Winchester Castle there were several gardens: a herber made in 1178 for Henry II and planted with grafts five years later; a lawn (*pratellum*) between the new chapel and the chapel of St Thomas, mentioned in 1252; and by 1306 the Queen's Garden, a turfed enclosure with a channel of water running through it. When Arundel Castle came into the king's hands, Henry II had a herber made before his bedchamber in 1186–8; at Marlborough Castle too there was a great lawn (*pratello*) beneath the king's bedchamber, and the king's garden there was enclosed for John in 1202–3. Henry III had the herber in Gloucester Castle made up, and in 1238 had a wall built round the herber in Nottingham Castle between the Great Gate and the Queen's Chapel; the king's garden there had been made a feature by Henry II as far back as 1183.

There were obviously greater opportunities for the creation of gardens at the country estates of the Crown, less cramped for space than the castles. At Kempton in Middlesex the king had two lawns and a garden by 1243, and in 1254 orders were given to build a wall 330 feet long between the Queen's Herber and the garden of Thomas le Hare, with a pentice over the steps leading to the Queen's Herber. The dimensions imply that the queen's pleasure garden probably covered two or three acres. In the manor outside Guildford Henry III had a cloister with marble columns built in the King's Garden in 1256, and in 1268 he ordered work to be done in the separate Queen's Herber according to instructions which had been given to his court painter, William Florentyn. Florentyn was to receive 6d. a day while directing the work. Woodstock, where the great park had been enclosed for Henry I, included after 1165 the walled pleasance of Everswell, consisting of an orchard with a series of pools fed by the natural spring. This was famous as Rosamund's Bower, and gave its name to a whole class of enclosed pleasure gardens. Here again Henry III had works carried out, in 1250 building walls about the Queen's garden and forming a herber by the king's pond where she could walk for recreation; ten years later a hedge was to be made around the King's garden and preserve (*servatorium*), and the covered walk about the springs of Everswell (*appenticium circa fontes*) repaired. Lastly Clarendon may be mentioned, where the enclosure about the king's chamber was turfed in 1167–8, and in 1254 a length of paling comprising

660 feet moved from the top of the park to the bottom, towards the lawn. This lawn must have been of great size, since its side open towards the park was a full acre in length: the mediaeval measured acre was not only an area (4,840 square yards or 43,560 square feet), but was commonly thought of as a plot of ground 660 feet long by 66 feet in width.

That extensive pleasure grounds were reckoned as a normal part of the state kept up by earls we know from Matthew Paris, who wrote a mocking biographical note on the new rich Sir Paulin Peyvre or Pever, who rose to be steward to Henry III and died in 1251. Of relatively humble origin, Pever acquired more than 50 carucates of landed estate (say 6,000 acres)

> and could be seen to have risen to the wealth and luxury of earls. He was an insatiable buyer-up of estates and an unrivalled builder of manorhouses. To say nothing of the rest he so beset one, named Toddington (Bedfordshire) with a palisade, chapel, chambers and other houses of stone, roofed with lead, and with orchards and pools, that it became the wonder of beholders. For during many years the workmen on his buildings were said to be paid as much as £5 a week or frequently 10 marks (£6 13s. 4d.) for their wages.

Since a labourer then took about 3d. a day or 1s. 6d. a week, and a skilled craftsman 4d. to 6d. a day, this suggests that Pever was employing at least 50 men. We know that the famous Hubert de Burgh, created Earl of Kent in 1227, had walled gardens and lawns at Kempton before the estate passed to the Crown, and this may have been the main reason for Henry III's anxiety to obtain it. Hampstead Marshall in Berkshire, the seat of the Earl Marshal, had by the time of Roger Bigod, 5th Earl of Norfolk (1270–1306), a garden within a cloister, an East garden with a fishpond, and also a West garden.

The archbishop's garden at York has already been mentioned, but by the 1180s if not earlier he had a permanent gardener at his manor of Southwell (Notts.) also. At Canterbury the archbishop's garden lay to the south of the Palace hall, and from three versions of the story of Becket's murder, one in French and two in Latin, come three words to describe it: *vergier, pomerium, virgulto*. At Lambeth the archbishop had a new herber by 1236. The bishop of Durham at Bishop Auckland had both a park and a garden, whose hedges were repaired in 1241; there were fees paid to the regular chief gardeners of the bishop of Ely's manor at Somersham (Hunts.) in 1169–72, and of the bishop of Lincoln for his palace gardens in 1168. Before the end of the thirteenth century the palace of the bishop of Worcester at Alvechurch (Worcs.) had a garden of more than two acres with double moats on top of a declivity, below which an elaborate series of fishponds was arranged.

It was at some of the larger abbeys, and at the palatial manor-houses of their abbots, that the greatest horticultural display was made outside royal circles. At St Albans there was a little garden (*virgultum*) within a cloister, which Abbot William of Trumpington (1214–35) protected with a wattle fence (*pariete concraticulato*) and assigned to the Guest Master, implying that this was a recreational garden for those who used the abbey as an inn. Bury St Edmunds, at about the same time, enclosed a vineyard especially for the solace of sick monks and those who had been bled, and this seems to have been the type followed in many other houses. Malmesbury had an area of some 43 acres next to the abbey, with streams, pools, fishponds and fruit-trees, kept for the monks to walk in; and Abbot William of Colerne (1260–92) further planted a vineyard and a herber, and filled his own garden with vines and apple-trees. He also had gardens made at two of the Wiltshire manors belonging to the abbey, Crudwell and Purton, the latter with two pools and, close by, a mill with a millpond. During the abbacy of Godfrey of Crowland (1299–1321) there was great activity at Peterborough and on the abbey's estates, both in gardening and tree-planting (see plan, p. 85). In 1302 the abbot

> had made a beautiful herber next to the Derby Yard, (*gardinum Dereby*) and surrounded it with double moats (*stagnis*), with bridges and pear-trees and very lovely plants (*herbis delicatissimis*), costing £25 [say £12,000] ... In (1308) he made a new wall between the *herbarium* and Derby Yard.

The area of this herber, of which we shall have more to say, was about two acres, and with the associated Derby Yard on one side and large private fishponds of the abbot on the other, some six acres. Abbot Godfrey did a great deal else, and at the manor of Eye (Northants.) enlarged the existing garden, enclosed it with a new wall and within made four lovely pools (*stagna pulcherrima*), in 1310; and in the next year took in ground to make a new orchard (*pomoerium*) around the new wall, planted fruit trees of divers sorts and surrounded the whole with hedges and ditches. The cost of the works of these two years at Eye amounted to £20 6s. 9d. (something like £10,000 nowadays).

John, prior of Spalding (Lincs.) in 1253–74, made a garden there and planted vineyards and orchards. Even more important was the rural retreat of the priors of St Swithun's at Winchester, about four miles south-west of the city at Silkstead. By 1276 the estate had both a vineyard and a herber, the latter surrounded by a wall which was being capped with tiles; within the next few years there is mention of another garden containing apple trees, and there was also a kitchen garden. Outside the gardens was the wood of Beauforest, planted in 1276 with a bushel of nuts bought for 8d. Great improvements were made for Prior Richard of Enford (1309–26): in 1311 Gilot the gardener was looking after the vines and putting in order the walks in the vineyard, and men were hired to make another herber next to the chapel, walks in the garden and in a close next to the garden, and turf was dug for laying. A stone wall was built next the vineyard, over 100 feet long, 9 feet high and 2 feet thick; in the next year it was capped with 3,000 tiles and 80 ridge-tiles (*creste*). Gilot the gardener continued to spend part of each season at Silkstead, and in 1314 he was concerned both with the vines and with the walks in Beauforest, a valuable scrap of evidence linking the garden with the woodland and indicating the largely recreational intent of both.

Considerable emphasis must be placed upon facts of this kind, since they run counter to the orthodox view, that there was no such thing as woodland planting until after the Renaissance. It has been, of course, admitted that fruit trees were planted in orchards and that other trees were occasionally planted by themselves or in rows [14], as we shall see shortly. On the other hand, Miles Hadfield (1967) states that when Burleigh ordered the sowing of acorns on 13 acres of Windsor Park in 1580, it was 'the oldest authenticated regular plantation recorded'; and more recently Oliver Rackham (in *Arboricultural Journal*, 1977) has enunciated the general proposition that 'the planting of trees in woods appears to be a post-medieval development' and adds that 'the majority of hedgerow trees, except in new hedges, were not planted but promoted from existing saplings and suckers.' Matters are by no means so clear cut, and the direct proofs of planting must be set out in some detail. As to hedges, it has to be said that in some districts and on certain estates it became, by the end of the Middle Ages, a positive stipulation in leases that trees such as oak, ash or elm should be planted near the bounds and fences.

To deal first with explicit evidence for the planting of woodland, we begin with Alton Priors, a Wiltshire manor belonging to St Swithun's, Winchester. In 1260–1 an assart was made of 'Thesmede' (later Tawsmead), the land being ploughed up by boonwork of the

13A
13B

13A The most fully detailed picture of a royal herber of the late Middle Ages is in a French manuscript of the *Livre du Cuer d'Amours espris* of *c* 1465, now in Vienna. The garden, surrounded by turf benches, is of grass only and is marked off on three sides by low rails. A taller trellis, covered with double roses, shields it from the castle, and behind runs a tunnel-arbour of trellis covered by vines, and with a flower border seen beyond it against the foot of the wall. Specimen fruit-trees are planted in the herber

13B Against the low rails are planted border flowers: carnations and pinks, then just coming into fashion; columbines, mallow, stocks and what may be stickadove, with rosemary (bottom right)

14 This view of *c* 1470–80, by Jean Robertet of Bruges, well displays the rows of pollard trees and other landscape planting which had become usual in northern Europe and in Britain by the thirteenth century if not earlier still (see also **58, 59, 62**)

15 The background of a painting of *c* 1520 by Quentin Massys shows courtly gardens of high quality terraced above a distant landscape. On the right is a pinnacled Gothic fountain backed by a thick hedge of roses in bloom; to the left, finely wrought wooden railings support heraldic beasts. Chequered small beds include low border plants and sweet herbs, with trained and trimmed shrubs

16 The painting of the family of Sir Thomas More in 1528, attributed to Holbein, shows the important place in decoration given to three vases of garden flowers: Madonna lilies and carnations, with narcissus and possibly hollyhock, on the left; in the central vase, shown here, borage, columbines, flag iris and a double narcissus, as well as stocks (?); on the right, a third arrangement includes peony, pansies, perhaps a day lily (*Hemerocallis*), and again iris, columbine and stock

17 A French miniature (*c* 1502) of Petrarch dreaming on a turf bench shows a trellised fence bearing both red and white double roses (*R. gallica* and *R. alba*, contrasting with the improved roses of **71**). By the fence are herbaceous plants: single pink, marigold, flag iris and columbine. Artist's licence has also produced a climbing pansy and stock!

tenants and sown with 19 quarters of nuts bought for £1 5s. 4d. and 8½ quarters of acorns bought for 8s. 6d. A ditch of 323 perches in length was dug about the wood, and hedge plants gathered and planted, at a cost of £2 9s. 1d. The length of the local perch is in doubt, but the area of the wood must have been at least 12 acres and was probably about 20. In 1275 the annals of Dunstable Priory refer to the plantations of William, lord of Studham (Beds.), probably implying the deliberate planting of woodland. The sowing of nuts at Silkstead in the following year has been mentioned above. When the Prior of Dunstable visited the remote property of Bradbourne (Derbyshire) in 1287, he found that the little wood on the north side, which Canon Henry de Newton had formerly planted there of ashes and other kinds of trees, was then grown up and quite delightful to see (*tunc fuit altus et satis delectabilis ad videndum*). Once more we find that notice was taken of aesthetics. One foreign instance may here be given, of the planting of sweet chestnuts at Vernon in Normandy in 1290; a few were grown in England for timber, but the only instance found by Salzman was of a hundred chestnut trees being taken from Milton in Kent in 1278 for the works of Dover Castle.

Just after 1300 come two campaigns of planting by the reforming abbots of great monasteries. Godfrey of Crowland, abbot of Peterborough, already instanced as a gardener, in 1304 planted a wood called Childholm on the east of Cranmore (Lincs.), and in the next year one by the manor-house of Northolme (Northants.). In 1318, at Werrington (Northants.), he planted Nabwood 'where no wood was before' and surrounded it with a ditch and row of willows. This has been identified by Mr Donald F. Mackreth as a wood felled over a century ago but visible as crop-marks on air photographs taken before the building of the Werrington by-pass; it contained about 3 acres. Also in Northamptonshire lies Harlestone, where the local squire Henry de Bray in 1305–6 sowed with acorns his enclosed grove of 4 acres called Leycroft. In Surrey Abbot John Rutherwyk of Chertsey in 1307 had young oaks planted and acorns sown on the east side of Hardwick grange (in Chertsey); and in 1331 and 1339 made further sowings of acorns near Hardwick. From manorial account rolls of the Dean and Chapter of Norwich, Rackham quotes an interesting case of 1312–13, when two men were paid for six days spent pulling ashes at Hindolveston, to be planted at Hindringham (6 miles away) and Gateley (7 miles off in another direction). The Hindringham account also survives and shows that a man there was paid 1½d. a day for 13½ days for planting the ashes within the manor. In this case there is nothing to show whether the trees were planted as woodland, in hedges, or as ornament.

A much later example of sowing comes from Durham, where the Prior had acorns sown in the park of Beaurepair (now Bearpark) in 1429–30. This may well have been an instance of ornamental planting, of which there is evidence much earlier. In 1243 small elms had been planted (*hulmellos plantatos*) outside the west front of Wells Cathedral, then still unfinished. They were near the south side of the front and extended towards the west, presumably implying one or more rows of trees parallel to the axis of the cathedral church. About 1252 the London house of Franciscan Friars was endowed with land in the parish of St Nicholas Shambles, together with the trees planted on it (*cum arboribus inibi plantatis*). In 1304, in order to open out the way leading to the house of the Earl of Gloucester, a paling at the churchyard of St Mary Woolchurchhaw in London was to be removed as far as the elms growing nearby, which must have been planted trees. At York in 1309 the archbishop had a foss dug in his castle of the Old Baile and ordered plants to be procured to put in the foss.

Later in the fourteenth century extensive works of planting and gardening were done by three successive abbots of Evesham. William Chiriton (1317–1344) enclosed Shrawnell Park in Badsey and had oaks, ashes and other trees sown; he also in 1328–34 had buildings erected in the garden for the sick and blooded monks. At Evesham itself, in the lower orchard towards Hampton, he planted trees which later grew tall to the great benefit of the abbey. His successor, William Boys (1345–1367) granted a garden called Sturdy to the prior and convent for their rest and solace (*pro recreatione et solatio*); this lay by the lower garden and orchard next the Avon, and was planted with herbs and trees, as well as having fish-ponds. Abbot John Ombresley (1367–1379) obtained licence to enclose 300 acres of land and water at Ombersley (Worcs.) to make a park in 1376.

It is obvious that for such sowing and planting to be possible, there had to be a systematic background of methods by which seeds and plants could be obtained. As we shall see later (p. 82), there was in London by the time of Edward I a nursery trade able to supply trees, flowering plants and turf ready for laying. Even in the countryside the acorns and nuts sown at Alton Priors in 1260 were bought, not gathered. Thorold Rogers collected prices paid for plants of willow (from 1297, 240 for 2s.), elm (from 1334; in 1341 a dozen cost 8d.), and poplar ($7\frac{1}{2}$d. a hundred in 1337). The bishop of Worcester in 1246–7 obtained 300 willow plants to plant on his estate at Fladbury. In 1316–17 Merton College paid 1s. for 3 bushels of acorns to sow in the garden at their manor of Cuxham (Oxon.). This suggests a nursery bed, with later transplantation; and at Merriott in Somerset in 1369 the premises of the manor house included a nursery (*la noresirie*) adjoining the garden and the park, and there was also a wood called 'Egwode'. In the accounts kept by the Forester of the Bishop of Durham are references to plantations of young trees called 'spryng' in English and *virgultum* in Latin expressly for keeping of the new seedlings growing there (*pro saluacione noui germinis infra eiusdem spryng crescentis*). Work on the hedges about a *virgultum* called 'le Oldespryng' enclosed within the park of Wolsingham, Co. Durham, cost 13s. 4d. in 1528–9.

To sum up, it may be said that there is ample proof that ornamental gardening flourished, in England as well as in north-western Europe, from the late eleventh century if not earlier; that it was based on a keen delight in the appearance of plants and their perfumes, and also in the sight and sound of running water. Trees were planted, not only for timber or for fruit, but as decorative adjuncts to houses; the therapeutic value of their shade was recognized, and walking under trees, or where their beauty could be appreciated, was an accepted recreation and also a factor in convalescence. All this formed a living tradition, reflected in the accounts of gardening given by the encyclopaedists but not derived from the reading of their books: Bartholomew, Albert, and Pietro de' Crescenzi were not teachers in this respect, but careful observers of what was done by royal and noble patrons and by the skilled gardeners who worked for them. Nevertheless, what was written down helped to continue the existing tradition, and was studied by later generations of patrons of horticulture. For the Middle Ages, like all periods of high and refined culture, was a time when men and women loved gardens and trees.

CHAPTER ONE

The Legacy of Classical Gardening

THE STORY OF GARDENING begins in eastern countries: in Babylonia, Persia, Egypt, China; and directly or indirectly all European horticulture has been influenced by these oriental sources. The gardens of Europe in a strictly geographical sense, however, begin in classical Greece and the historical details are known to us mainly through the works of Roman writers. The Roman Empire was the medium by which antique knowledge was carried through Western Europe and as far as Britain, and for many centuries the only textbooks in use were in Latin. The Latin language and much of its literature dominated learning in Britain from the mission of St Augustine in AD 597 for some eight centuries until a period of translation into English began shortly before 1400. In so far as our methods of cultivation and design were influenced during the Middle Ages by book-learning, it was almost exclusively derived from Latin books. The books themselves had been based on experience in a southern climate; the plants whose culture was described were mainly southern, and much of the contents of the classical treatises was of little use in northern France or in England.

Although a small amount of information regarding the pleasure gardens of antiquity can be derived from Latin literature, hardly any of it is contained in the treatises on agriculture and rural affairs which alone preserve any serious or scientific information on the cultivation of plants. They were almost exclusively concerned with fruit and vegetables; neither the aesthetic aspects of garden design nor the specialized culture of flowers was thought worthy of notice. Once the military, political and economic links with Rome had been broken, in the first half of the fifth century AD, the tradition of gardening in Britain depended for survival upon personal contacts alone. How far such contacts prevailed against the impact of invasion and several centuries of warfare is still a matter for controversy. We have no real idea of the extent to which 'pockets' of Romano-British culture were able to maintain effective continuity or to hand on to their enemies and successors: Angles, Saxons and Jutes, any elements of their own partially Romanized way of life.

In this connection a single instance of possible survival may be given, in advance of a fuller discussion of the plants introduced by the Romans. Among the fruits not native to Britain, but cultivated here in or before the Roman occupation, were the species of domesticated plum. Now in the Dark Ages, almost the whole of eastern England was rapidly overrun by the

Map of Western Europe, to show the area dealt with and the chief places mentioned. For Britain, see p. 55.

Teutonic settlers from the Continent, but there was one notable exception, the kingdom of Elmet in south Yorkshire and touching York itself. Cerdic, the last British king of Elmet, was not conquered by the pagan Northumbrian Edwin until shortly before his conversion to Christianity in AD 627. Cerdic's capital and royal demesne were at and around the hill settlement now known as Sherburn-in-Elmet, and it may be significant that the neighbourhood of Sherburn has for centuries been famous for the 'Winesour' plum, of peculiarly fine flavour. It is a conspicuously hardy variety, raised from suckers (i.e. not grafted), and a heavy cropper. May we legitimately wonder whether it is a survival, through fifteen centuries of storm and stress, from the royal orchards of the Romano-British ancestors of King Cerdic?

We must continue with a short account of the Latin treatises and the historical background of the transmission of their manuscripts. There is no reason to doubt that copies of many important classical works existed in Britain, as well as in the continental provinces of the Empire, and some of them may have continued to be read as long as there were Britons who knew Latin. Whether so much as a single book, copied before 410, escaped deliberate and accidental destruction to be read again after 597 is very doubtful. The extent to which southern Britain has, since the fifth century, differed from the rest of the former territories of the Roman Empire seems to indicate that the cleavage went deep. That there was not an even deeper division is due to the partial renewal of the Empire in the form of the Catholic Church.

Even if Britain had never been occupied by the legions, a substantial degree of romanization would have been achieved in the association, from 597 to 1534, with the Papacy. The country was linked to all the other nations of the West in a common culture dominated by a common ecclesiastical government. Since the individual members of the clerical order: (secular priests, monks and friars), shared a single language – Latin – and a single obedience, art and science were throughout the period far more unified than they have since become. This applies to a varying extent in different fields, but certainly with considerable force in the case of gardening. It was not until about 1300 that there were any books on relevant subjects written in vernacular languages or even translated into them. The sources of information were similar in every country of western Europe, with the partial exception of the Iberian Peninsula, which had access to an extensive literature in Arabic.

It was indeed under the influence of Arabic civilization that the era of modern science began during the Middle Ages. Whereas western Christian learning remained under the dead hand of verbal authority, direct observation and experiment inspired learned men of Islam, from the frontiers of India to the Atlantic coast of Morocco. The Arabs had, by the ninth century AD, achieved political domination over Mesopotamia and Persia, but under Persian influence came to draw fresh inspiration from the ancient East as well as from the great scientists of Greece. Between 830 and 910 an immense literature of Arabic translations was produced by a research institute set up in Baghdad, and this was to influence both Spanish and Turkish horticulture, at opposite ends of Europe. Until this new body of information, based upon a truly scientific approach, gained a sound footing in the West, much of higher technology still depended on the Latin treatises which survived.

So far as the principles of agriculture and horticulture are concerned, the channel of effective survival was far narrower than used to be supposed. To understand the historic process we have first to recapitulate the books written in Latin which were relevant to the subject. What descended from antiquity consists of four complete works on agriculture and one encyclopaedic work including books on botany with agriculture, horticulture and *materia medica*. Each of the four specialized works was termed *De re rustica*: in chronological order they are those by Cato the Elder (Marcus Porcius Cato, 234–149 BC); Varro (Marcus

Terentius Varro, 116–27 BC); Columella (Lucius Junius Moderatus Columella, mid-1st century AD); and Palladius (Rutilius Taurus Aemilianus Palladius, fourth century AD), whose book dates from *c* 380–95. The encyclopaedia is that of Pliny the Elder (Gaius Plinius Secundus, *c* AD 23–79), termed *Naturalis Historia*. Pliny's immense compilation rested upon some 500 authorities, many of them Greek, and it had the good fortune to survive complete and in a substantial number of manuscripts. In the eighth century Bede possessed a copy, and Alcuin was able to get access to the book; but there is nothing to suggest that it was ever in general use as a source of information on gardening. Nor was the Agriculture of Cato well known, but the names of Varro, Columella and Palladius were recognized as authorities. Hudson Turner in 1848 went so far as to state that 'Manuscripts of Varro, Columella and Palladius were of frequent occurence in the monastic libraries of the middle ages', but this does not seem to have been true of the two first.

So far as surviving manuscripts which can be identified as having belonged to British religious houses are concerned, we now have the immense work of Neil Ker, *Medieval Libraries of Great Britain*. From this it is possible to count up four copies of Palladius at four different monasteries: Byland in Yorkshire; Canterbury St Augustine's; Waltham Abbey; and Worcester Cathedral. These copies were written in the late twelfth or early thirteenth century, at the same time that most of the surviving monastic copies of the works of Alexander Neckam were being made. The works of Neckam (see p. 66ff.), still surviving and identifiable with particular monasteries, number 20 in the libraries of 16 different houses. The three great encyclopaedias of the thirteenth century were less popular: of Bartholomew there are 6 MSS coming from 6 houses; Albertus Magnus was represented by 7 copies at 7 different houses; and Vincent of Beauvais by 8 copies at only six libraries. So far as this information from chance survival may be valid, it suggests that the student wishing to find an authority on plants would more easily get at the subject in Neckam's works than elsewhere. What does seem highly significant is that no copies of Varro or Columella are recorded.

That there was a demand for Palladius is shown by the fact that his book was translated into English early in the fifteenth century, and also by the existence of the compilation known as 'Godfrey upon Palladius' in many MSS. To that extent there was a literate transmission of late classical precepts on cultivation; but their value was lessened by the rather poor quality of Palladius' book. Though mainly derived from Columella, it frequently disagrees with the earlier author, and the advantage rarely lies with Palladius. His popularity was largely due to his method of arranging hints on what to do in each month of the year, in Gardener's Calendar form. For example, part of the work to be done in February concerns rose-beds, continuing with lilies, violets and saffron crocus. Modernizing the spelling of the Colchester Castle version of *c* 1420 we learn that:

>With craft eke roses early ripened are;
>Twain handbreadth off about their rootès do
>A delving make, and every day thereto
>Do water warm. Now lily bulbès sow
>Or set, and them that of rather [sooner, earlier] grow.
>In weeding them thou must be diligent
>For hurting of their bulb, or of their eye.
>But bulbès small up from their mother hent [taken]
>Let put in other land to multiply.
>The violet to plant is now to try,
>Now saffron bulbès be to set or sow,
>Or subtily to delve, if that they grow.

There evidently was a market, late in the Middle Ages, for written treatises of this kind, apparently aimed at the modest literacy in English of an increasing number of lay owners of gardens. Just how serviceable these antique hints were is another matter: we do not know how the skilled gardener, many years master of his craft, may have reacted to his employer telling him what to do out of a book. Doubtless many of the master gardeners could read, but it seems unlikely that more than a handful of them would be prepared to unlearn what they had received in the years of their pupillage or apprenticeship. There was also the basic difficulty that Palladius and the still earlier sources on which his work was based were written in the South of Europe for a Mediterranean flora. The lengthy sections on the treatment of olives, pomegranates and pistachios, as well as citrus fruits, are ridiculously inapplicable to a northern climate without benefit of greenhouses. The more general doctrines of sowing, transplanting and grafting, which emerge from a thorough reading, have real value and may to some extent have influenced practical method. What seems certain is that the treatises on agriculture and horticulture, along with herbals and lists of synonyms for the *materia medica*, did in many cases get printed at the end of our period and entered into the stream of *post-mediaeval* bibliography.

While it remains doubtful whether actual methods of cultivation were much influenced by direct study of the texts of classical treatises, it is unquestionable that the garden flora in Britain had been enriched by living descendants of certain kinds of plants introduced by the Romans from the South. There were also cultivated plants that had reached Britain before the Roman occupation, as is evidenced by remains found in archaeological excavation of sites dating from the Iron Age or even earlier. That the Romans played an important part is proved by the existence in Anglo-Saxon and in Old German of plant-names derived from Latin for a substantial group of naturalized sorts: fruits such as sweet chestnut, cherry, mulberry, peach and the grapevine; almonds and figs; beet, cabbages (kale, coleworts), lettuce and radish; and in the flower garden the rose, lily and violet. We have to accept these names as constituting a guarantee of the foreign origin of the plants, distinguishing them from cultivated members of the native northern flora which would have had their own names in each vernacular language. There may in a number of cases have been fresh introductions of kinds which had been introduced in Roman times but which became extinct in Britain during the Dark Ages.

Although there are rather vague and general descriptions of Roman gardens in some of the classical works, these could hardly have formed the basis of any theory of garden design. At the Renaissance in Italy the immense layouts which became fashionable in the fifteenth century and laid the foundations of French and later European style were certainly the result of antiquarian research into the villas of Roman times. They owed little or nothing to the model 'designs' of Crescenzi, based on Albertus and by him observed rather than invented. We may, therefore, feel certain that the forms taken by the gardens, orchards and parks of the earlier Middle Ages (down to say 1250) were neither dictated by the reading of classical works (which did not contain any precepts of design), nor by the new treatises of the encyclopaedists or the arm-chair compiler Crescenzi. Certainly there was not, during the Dark Ages, any direct survival of a Roman tradition in Britain, nor the slightest possibility of a local creation of garden style from within. We are left, by a process of elimination, with a single source of inspiration, the horticulture of the Near East. With this, either through intermediaries like Bishop de Montbray of Coutances, or by direct contacts of pilgrims, crusaders and merchants, the West was put in touch in the century following 1050. The recovery of the pleasure garden, as well as higher techniques in cultivation, went hand in hand with the general rediscovery of ancient science and technology through the scholars of Islam.

Surprising as this complete break between classical and mediaeval gardens may seem at first sight, it is after all precisely comparable to what happened in architecture. So far as there was a continuing tradition of aesthetic style in building through the Dark Ages and the next few centuries, it was a progressively debased version of the Roman orders, rightly described as Romanesque. Even this hardly existed in Britain until Norman buildings were deliberately copied under Edward the Confessor from about 1050 onwards. There was no continuous evolution of this style beyond the opening of the twelfth century: it was displaced in revolutionary fashion by Gothic, whose keynote of the pointed arch was derived from the East, contrasting sharply with the whole concept of the Romanesque and, in Britain, Norman canons of building. There is then no line of descent connecting our gardens of the Middle Ages with such layouts as may have existed at the palaces and villas of Roman times. The recent archaeological excavations of the palace at Fishbourne in Sussex, dateable to the late first century AD, revealing sophisticated pleasure gardens aesthetically designed, are an amazing triumph of modern research, but do not reveal any line of ancestry for the gardens of which we are now in search. The principal technique involved in the design, that of topiary hedges, was not revived until the reign of Henry VIII, when it was reintroduced from Italy.

The legacy which the Middle Ages derived from Roman gardening was thus non-existent in landscaping and design, probably slight in technique, but none the less substantial on the side of plants. As we have seen, plants can often be identified by the derivation of their names from Latin originals. In a few instances a plant genuinely native to Britain long before the Roman invasion may only have been recognized as having economic value after the arrival of the overlords from Italy. Such plants are probably Betony (*vettonica*), Box (*buxus*), Common Mallow (*malva*), and Sweet Violet (*viola*), of which Box is regarded as only doubtfully native, an argument which has lost much of its force since it was shown by C. D. Pigott and S. M. Walters in 1953 that the box-tree is after all native in northern France. Improved garden varieties of the violet may well have been introduced by the Romans along with the name. A second small group comprises Lily, Pine and Rose, whose names *lilium*, *pinus*, and *rosa* are certainly Latin, but which may stand for introduced species. In the case of the lily, the only possible native is *Lilium martagon* L., the Purple Turk's Cap, whereas the introduced lily was *L. candidum* L. The Mediterranean pine, producing edible pine-kernels in cones long known as 'pine-apples', is *Pinus pinea* L., probably brought by the Romans but not easy to establish. It certainly did not survive here into mediaeval times, but its name was transferred to the not unlike Scots Pine, *P. sylvestris* L. The introduced rose was unquestionably *Rosa gallica* L. in one or more of its forms, *the* cultivated rose contrasted with the native wild briars.

Setting aside some dubious species such as the Almond for future consideration among introductions of the Middle Ages, we are left with a substantial body of trees, herbs and vegetables which have in most cases been here continuously since Roman times. These are plants which are so hardy as to be unlikely to die out completely once fully established. Among trees they include the cultivated forms of both Sweet and Sour Cherry (*cerasus*), the Spanish Chestnut (*castanea*), the cultivated Pear (*pirus*), the Plums (*Prunus domestica* L., *P. insititia* L.), and the Vine (*vinea*). Other trees certainly introduced in Roman times, but which may have died out completely in the Dark Ages, are the Fig (*ficus*), Mulberry (*morus*), Peach (*persicum malum*), and as a rarity the Medlar (*mespilus*), to be included on archaeological grounds. These will need to be considered again as possible reintroductions, along with the Almond and the Walnut. The plums and just possibly the chestnut may have been here before the Romans.

Vegetables and herbs which go back to the Iron Age or even earlier, but are not true natives, are Alexanders (*olusatrum, petroselinum alexandrinum*), the Broad Bean, Beet (*beta*),

Coriander (*coriandrum*), which has been found in sites of the Bronze Age, and Opium Poppy (*papaver*). Probably of Roman introduction are Dill, Fennel (*foeniculum*), Hemp (*cannabis*), Kale and Colewort (*caulis*), Lettuce (*lactuca*), Mustard formerly called Senevey (*sinapi*), Pea (*pisum*), Radish (*radix*), Vervain (*verbenaca*), and Vetch (*vicia*). There are of course several native species of vetch, and vervain may be truly indigenous and have received its name from Roman physicians who recognized its properties. Opium poppy was presumably a deliberate introduction of an important medicinal plant. Hemp was not brought as a drug, but for the manufacture of rope and canvas, which became major industries in mediaeval England. There is a good deal of doubt as to the precise types of lettuce grown in Roman and in mediaeval times, but that they were edible and appreciated forms of the genus *Lactuca* appears to be certain. In addition to the plants discussed it is not unlikely that certain plants of the family *Chenopodiaceae*, besides those truly native, may have been introduced as foodstuff by the Romans and then became naturalized. There is archaeological evidence suggesting that a wide spectrum of this group was used, long before the appearance of the real Spinach (*Spinacia oleracea* L.)

In view of the unquestioned gap between the highly skilled gardening of the Romans in Britain and that which developed here after the Norman Conquest, the classical authorities are almost entirely irrelevant to the subject of this book. They do, however, provide a good deal of information on the history of species of utilitarian interest. For instance, we learn that the wild Strawberry was already being brought into cultivation in Italy by 200 BC, and Cato discussed the growing of asparagus. Columella describes the forcing of cucumbers in baskets of dung sheltered by plates of *lapis specularis*, thought to be mica. Martial in some of his epigrams, as well as Pliny and Columella, refer to the forcing of fruit in some form of hothouse. In the course of the two hundred years from Cato to Pliny the number of different varieties of apples grown had risen from four or more to 22, and of pears from five to 36. Cato already knew seven sorts of olive, and six each of vine and fig. He does not mention the cherry, which was a later introduction of Lucullus, after his defeat of the king of Pontus, Mithradates, in 68 BC. This was of course the sweet dessert cherry, but the sour cherry or Morello may have reached Rome at the same time, as both types seem always to have been grown on a large scale in northern Asia Minor. The cherry was taken to Britain before Pliny wrote in the middle of the first century AD. Since *Prunus avium* L. is regarded as the ancestor of the sweet cherry and is a native of Britain, we have here an outstanding instance of the distinction between botanical and horticultural evidence.

The grapevine may have been introduced to Britain fairly soon after the Roman occupation, but it cannot have become common until after *c* 280, when the Emperor Probus reversed the former policy of protection for Italian vineyards. Whereas previous emperors had strictly forbidden the planting of wine-grapes outside Italy, Probus ordered his troops to employ themselves in forming vineyards wherever they were stationed, to prevent their idleness. This decrease in the soldiers' leisure was more and more resented, and when Probus in 282 was in garrison at his birthplace Sirmium (now Mitrovica) on the River Save, and commanded his troops to set about draining the extensive marshes, they mutinied and murdered him. It is one of the strangest ironies of fate that the strict sense of discipline, directed to utilitarian ends, which brought Probus to his death, should have been responsible for stocking Britain with the vine 27. For here, as we know, the vine has not in the long run been of material importance as a crop-plant. Yet throughout the Middle Ages it remained the chief climber in general use, and as a covering for walls, pergolas, and arbours, one of the greatest glories of the English garden.

CHAPTER TWO

Before the Millennium: AD 500-1000

THE MIDDLE AGES is a term of convenience given to the whole period between the end of classical antiquity and the renaissance of classical knowledge and form. They cover roughly a thousand years from the fall of the last Western Emperor Romulus Augustulus in 476. In general usage, however, it is customary to speak of the Dark Ages as succeeding the fall of Rome, and to restrict the term Middle Ages to the second five centuries, those following the crucial year 1000. There are two main justifications for this: firstly, the age from 500 to 1000 really is dark; secondly, the passing of the millennial year was one of the psychological turning-points of history. Most Christians had come to accept the view that after one thousand years the world as they knew it would come to an end. Few long-term or large-scale undertakings would have seemed to be worth while, and men and women in large numbers retired into some form of religious life. There was besides a practical reason for this tendency to withdraw from the world, the appallingly dangerous nature of the times: invasion and wholesale destruction were the rule of life rather than the exception. Tending a garden may well have seemed good counsel, many centuries before Voltaire, but it could only have been a very small and primitive plot.

From the fifth to the tenth century our knowledge of the history and life of Northern Europe is indeed slight, and even with the help of recent excavational archaeology there is little to say of the horticulture practised during these years. It is only towards the end of the period that a few manuscripts survive, some of them with colourful but misleading pictures intended to aid identification for the medicinal use of herbs. None is a book on gardening, unless we count the surprising Latin poem of the monk Walafrid Strabo, written about 840. The information conveyed in this *Hortulus*, the 'Little Garden', in fact forms part of a much larger documentation of gardens and plants of the time of Charlemagne and his immediate successors. The sources for this one period, mainly concerned with one region of northern Europe, form a singular oasis in the wilderness constituted by the age as a whole. Disregarding copies of the illustrated herbals of antiquity, rendered virtually useless by the progressive degradation of draughtsmanship, the surviving documents consist of several lists of the names of plants grown in gardens, and a remarkable plan showing the layout of an ideal monastery which was to have a kitchen garden, a physic garden, and a burial ground treated as an orchard and shrubbery.

Before dealing in detail with this Carolingian group of sources, it is necessary to look at the scanty records which alone give a glimpse of the three preceding centuries. Hardly any of them relate to England, though the statement has been made that olive trees existed here in the eighth and ninth centuries. It is not clear what evidence there is for this, though it is perfectly true that the climate of the time was relatively favourable. By a strange paradox, the time of disaster and destruction was also one of unusually excellent climatic conditions. It is thought that the sixth century was probably the warmest of the whole Middle Ages, implying a growing season of possibly a month longer than that normal about 1900. With some fluctuation these improved temperatures lasted, as we have seen (p. 2), until after 1300. That there was a continuing interest in gardens among the Britons is shown by the story of St Teilo of Llandaff (c 512–563). About the middle of the sixth century he crossed over to Brittany to pay a visit to his former fellow-student, bishop Samson of Dol, with whom he spent several years. While there he planted an extensive forest of fruit-trees, said to have been three miles across, and to have survived 500 years later. We do not have to believe the details, but there may well be fundamental truth in Teilo's planting of an orchard near Dol.

What little has come down may be divided under three main heads: gardens and flowers in relation to the religious history of the Western Church; laws and legal records that relate to plants; and literary references in poetry. Of the first category the most important evidentially is the monastic rule of St Isidore, bishop of Seville (c 560–636), specifying the need for a garden in the cloister. There is also a large body of more generalized evidence for the growing of flowers in the gardens of Benedictine monasteries especially for decking the altars on feast days. It was, and indeed still is in the Catholic countries of Europe, the custom also to scatter roses in churches as symbols of the gift of the Holy Spirit. This naturally applies only when the rose is in blossom, applying to the feasts of St John Baptist (24 June) and St Peter (29 June), but more notably to the movable Whitsun and Corpus Christi. The date of Whitsun varies between 10 May and 13 June, that of Corpus from 21 May to 24 June as extremes, though the earliest and latest days are very rare. The availability of rose blossoms is affected by the change in the calendar, which everywhere fell later and later in the season as time went on, from AD 300 until the reform of Gregory XIII in 1582. To take an example, in AD 1001 Whitsun fell on 1 June and Corpus Christi on 12 June; but to these (from 1000 to 1099) six days have to be added to arrive at the true date in the natural (and New Style) calendar, that is to say the 7th and 18th June.

We need not take seriously the legend of the rose garden at Subiaco in Italy, the *Roseto* sometimes alleged to have been planted by St Benedict (c 480–544). The more sophisticated version takes the origin of the roses back only to 1216, when St Francis of Assisi visited Subiaco, miraculously transforming into roses a bed of thorns which Benedict had set to mortify his flesh. Of considerably greater interest is the story told by Gregory of Tours (c 538–594) of the priest Severus who gathered *flores liliorum* to decorate the walls of his church. In this case the problem is of identity: are we to understand 'fleurs de lis' in the sense of the yellow water-flag, or white Madonna lilies from a garden? There is no reason to doubt the story of St Fiacre, an Irish nobleman, who in the seventh century founded a monastery in France at Breuil, 35 miles east of Meaux and then deep in the forest. Fiacre and his companions, clearing the woods, made so fine a garden that he has ever since been regarded as the patron of gardeners in France. In Germany the patroness was St Gertrude, and St Dorothy also is associated with horticulture since her emblem is a coronet of roses, or a bunch of roses held in her hand.

The chief legal record, the Salic Law of the Franks, preserved in garbled form, dates between c 510 and 750. The laws are authentic and were undoubtedly in force before the time of Charlemagne. For us their importance is that they give legal definition to the concept of an orchard (*pomarium*): it is constituted by the planting of at least 12 trees in a garden. The relevance of this was that the penalties for damage, which in any case were heavy for trespass on crops, were five times heavier for breaking into a hedged garden than in the case of unenclosed ground. Similar laws were enacted later in Anglo-Saxon England, King Alfred laying down compensation for damage to vineyards or fields. Legal authenticity attaches also to the record of the endowments of the abbey of St-Denis outside Paris, which among a great extent of land and forests was given by King Pepin the Short in *c* 768 some hop-grounds (*humlonarias*); this is one of the first pieces of historical evidence for the cultivation of hops.

Poetry takes us back even further than law. The pleasure gardens of late Roman times survived under the barbarian Goths and Franks, whose royal and noble families rapidly gained some appreciation of the culture they had displaced. We know this largely from the verse of Venantius Fortunatus (530–609), an Italian from Ceneda in the mountains north of Venice. After study at Ravenna and Milan he went to France in 565 and was made welcome at the Gothic and Frankish courts. At Poitiers he found a generous patroness in Radegunda, the widowed queen of Clotaire I (d. 561). Radegunda (521–587) had founded a nunnery outside the walls of Poitiers and laid out a garden by it, in which Fortunatus was permitted to wander. His poems record the 'apple, and the tall pear, which now pour forth their fragrant scent', and a gift of violets which he sent to the queen: 'none of the sweet-smelling herbs I send can equal the nobility of the dark violet. Glowing in royal purple, their petals bring together perfume and loveliness.' Fortunatus, who spent the last ten years of his life as bishop of Poitiers, also wrote of the gardens of another queen, Ultrogotha the widow of Childebert I (d. 558). These were close to Paris, on the left bank of the Seine between the city and St Germain des Prés, noted for their fragrant roses:

Paradisiacas spargit odore rosas.

The Venerable Bede (673–735), writing towards the end of his life, states that Britain excels for grain and trees and produces vines in some places, showing that the grape can never have died out in the south 27. That he knew the Madonna lily is evident from his poetic description of the flower as the emblem of the Virgin Mary, the white petals signifying her bodily purity, the golden anthers the glowing light of her soul. From a little after his time we get a glimpse of conditions in England in a letter sent to St Boniface in Germany. Boniface (680–754) was born at Crediton in Devon, but spent the greater part of his career as a missionary to the heathens of northern Europe. He also had opportunities to visit the cities of the Merovingian Empire, and this was presumably why he was asked for help, specifically to obtain books of secular science and in particular of medicine, and also to get *segmenta ultra marina* mentioned in books which his correspondents already possessed. It is possible that the words quoted mean no more than 'drugs from overseas', *segmenta* being used for ingredients in prescriptions; but it seems possible that living cuttings of plants may have been intended, since the literal sense of *segmentum* is 'a piece cut off.' The letter goes on to say that the '*segmenta*', whatever they were, 'are unknown to us and difficult to get' (*ignota nobis sunt et difficila ad adipisandum*). Even though this can be taken as implying that England felt itself to be worse off than the continent, and that its physic gardens did not amount to much, it does at least show that we were not entirely cut off from civilization.

Boniface was the link, in English learning, between Bede and Alcuin (*c* 735–804), who was born at about the time of Bede's death. A York man by birth, Alcuin was educated at the cathedral school there and became master in 766. Later he travelled to Rome in search of manuscripts and then for ten years from 780 was at the court of Charlemagne where he was the real founder of the famous Palace School, the earliest effective university in north-western Europe. On a short visit to York in 790 Alcuin found that conditions in England were too bad for a longer stay to be possible: 'What should I do in Northumbria where no one is free from fear?' After his return to France he spent some years in academic work, and the last eight of his life as abbot of St Martin at Tours. To us he is of particular interest as a garden lover, writing of his cell at Tours being adorned by white lilies and little red roses: '*Lilia cum rosulis candida mixta rubris*, and he sent physical plants to the Abbot of Aniane in Languedoc, the famous Benedict who played a great part in monastic reform under Charlemagne.

Fischer suggests that it was Benedict of Aniane who was instrumental in producing the famous list of plants which formed a schedule to one of the laws of Charlemagne, the *Capitulare de Villis* or Decree concerning Towns, promulgated about 800, when the great king of the Franks was proclaimed Roman Emperor by Pope Leo III. Until his death in 814 he ruled over the whole of France, Belgium, Holland and Switzerland, with the areas now forming West Germany and Austria, more than half of Italy and the northern fringe of Spain already reconquered from the Moors. Charlemagne had friendly relations with Anglo-Saxon England, from which he drew not only Alcuin but a large number of other scholars. In the opposite direction he exchanged gifts with Harun al-Rashid, the Abbasid caliph of Baghdad, who sent him a live elephant which is said to have spent four years on the road, and made its entry into Aachen on 20 July 802. Once again the topic of royal menageries is touched upon, and the evidence shows that Charlemagne formed a park as well as gardens. We know too that his interest in wine-growing extended to the importation, for vineyards near his palace at Ingelheim, of stocks from Spain, Italy, Burgundy, Lorraine and Hungary. Furthermore, among the birds which were kept on his demesnes were peacocks (*pavones*), not for food alone Pl.**VIIa**,1,42,44,48,60,74.

There has been much discussion of Charlemagne's list of plants, particularly in regard to its precise significance. Much of this controversy is irrelevant to our purpose, and we can accept that it fits into the latter part of the long reign of the king and emperor, probably between 794 and 812. Since plants which do not occur in classical authors are included, there is no doubt that the compilation was a fresh one, or drawn from comparatively modern sources. Fischer-Benzon in 1894 suggested that it was based by a Benedictine monk on earlier glossaries, perhaps helped by memory and by experience of gardening. Fischer (1929) considered that the south of France was the most likely area for the plants listed to have been brought together, and that Aniane (16 miles west of Montpellier) is a strong candidate. He pointed out that Abbot Benedict of Aniane is known to have met Abbot Tatto of Reichenau at Inda (Kornelimünster) a short distance from Aachen. Tatto was the master of Walafrid Strabo the garden poet, and his island abbey of Reichenau near Constance is within a day's journey of St Gall. This series of personal contacts might indeed account for the remarkable phenomenon of linked documents on gardening within a period of well under fifty years.

Fischer-Benzon held that, at least in south-western Germany, there was evidence for great uniformity in the flora grown in peasant gardens for many centuries, and that this pointed to the hypothesis of centres of distribution, which could have been certain of the gardens stocked in accordance with the list in the *Capitulare*. He accepted that this could hardly be true over the whole area of Charlemagne's empire, and this brings up the central problem posed by the list. While a large number of the plants would grow more or less anywhere in western Europe, some are definitely southern. They might, like rosemary, be easily acclimatized; but in other cases such as colocynth and the Stone Pine they would be quite out of place in the greater part of Germany and in northern France and the Netherlands. There is one simple explanation which provides a way out of the difficulty, not only here but also with later lists such as Neckam's, namely that what was listed was a 'portmanteau' selection of the most desirable plants that could be grown within the total relevant area, in this case the Carolingian empire. Individual species that could not be grown at a given place would simply be omitted.

Whatever the explanation, it is hard to imagine that the list would have been officially promulgated unless it were regarded as widely acceptable. We now have to examine it in some detail, partly to consider the difficult cases, but chiefly to deduce as much as possible of the character of gardens around 800. The decree laid down that the crown lands in every city of the Empire should have a garden planted with 'all herbs' as well as certain trees and fruits. The herbs listed are 73 in number, the fruits and nuts 16, making a grand total of 89 species. There is also mention of varieties of fruits, though by no means as many as there had been in Pliny's day. There were among the Apples kinds called Gozmaringa, Geroldinga, Crevedella and Spirania, as well as categories of Sweetings, Sour Apples, Keepers, Earlies, and apples to be eaten as soon as ripe. Pears were divided into three or four kinds of Keepers, Sweet Pears, Earlies and Late pears. Plums, Peaches and Cherries were also said to be of several sorts.

It is not improbable that some of the entries stated in the plural may also have been intended to include more than one species or variety. For instance, we find that the first two entries are *lilium, rosas*: Lily in the singular, Roses in the plural. This must surely imply the inclusion of more than one kind of rose, at least the red and the white. If this principle applied throughout it would mean that there were then in cultivation several species or varieties under the headings of Cucumber, Melon, Gourd, Colocynth, Lettuce, Endive, Beet, Marshmallow, Mallow, Carrot, Parsnip, Orach, Blite, Kohl-Rabi, Kale, Onion, Leek, Radish, Shallot, Teasel, Broad Bean, Pea, Spurge. Chives (*britlas*) is omitted on the ground that the English name is in any case in a plural form, and the nature of the plant warrants a plural description. There is much to be said for this interpretation, which applies well to virtually every plant named. The entry *cardones*, generally taken to mean the Fuller's Teasel, might perhaps be intended for the Artichoke and the Cardoon.

There is another striking thing about the start of the list: the fact that what is primarily of utilitarian interest is headed by the two plants which, throughout the Middle Ages, were those of the highest decorative quality. This may be explained, by those who favour the symbolic, as merely a common-form expression of reverence for the Virgin Mary. On the other hand, it is difficult to accept that Charlemagne's interest in horticulture did not rise beyond the needs of diet and medicine. Both roses and lily-bulbs were used in mediaeval medicine, but not to so preponderant an extent as to warrant their names being placed at the top of the list. It seems altogether more reasonable, bearing in mind the mediaeval determination to find both beauty and utility in all the works of the Creator, to regard the lily and the cultivated roses as given pride of place precisely on account of their ornamental character. There are, of course, in the rest of the list a good many other plants worthy of the flower garden: Chicory, Clary, Fennel, Flag Iris, Mallows, Mints, Poppy, Rosemary, Rue, Sage, Savory, Southernwood, Tansy, and the Sweet Bay tree.

There are a few surprising omissions, notably the Violet, which was highly regarded for its medicinal virtues as well as for its beauty and its perfume. Two other plants which actually occur in the inventories of Charlemagne's gardens, but not in the *Capitulare*, are Agrimony and Betony, both noted for their physical virtues and almost universally grown in herb gardens for many centuries, even though fairly common as wild plants. One might have expected Lavender, seeing that it was well known in England before the introduction of Rosemary, but it was unknown to the ancients (apart from Stickadove, *Lavandula stoechas* L.)

and late in cultivation. Balm (*Melissa officinalis* L.) and Hyssop (*Hyssopus officinalis* L.) are also unexpected absentees. The Sweet Bay tree, or true Laurel, is on the contrary in Palladius and all the early mediaeval lists and undoubtedly had become naturalized throughout the milder areas of western Europe and in the south of England by late Roman times. In the list it is given in the plural, *lauros*, which may hint at the cultivation of other trees and shrubs with a similar evergreen leaf, such as Laurustinus (*Viburnum tinus* L.), in the southern parts of Charlemagne's realm.

Before going through the list as a whole we have to look at the problems of identification. Most identities are certain, but in a few cases there is real doubt, not just as to variety or species, but as to the family. Mediaeval Latin terminology was at best confused, and every attempt to obtain clear-cut synonyms is frustrated by conflicting evidence; at different periods or in different countries the names were positively not the same. Yet the compilers of explanatory glossaries might lump together completely different plants, herbs regarded as having the same medicinal property being given the same name. Sometimes there was a real botanical relationship, but more often there was not: a modern analogy would be to put Christmas Rose, Guelder Rose and Rock Rose in the Linnean genus *Rosa*.

For convenience consecutive numbers are here given to the plants in the list, 1–73 standing for herbs and 74–89 for trees. There are serious problems of nomenclature or of identity in about a dozen cases:

The translation 'pumpkins' has commonly been given to (10) *cucurbitas*, but the true pumpkins (*Cucurbita pepo* L.) are all American. This can only have been the Bottle Gourd (*Lagenaria vulgaris* Ser.)

The 'kidney-bean' of antiquity, not that of modern times, is meant by (11) *fasiolum*. In this case too an American genus of plants, *Phaseolus*, has usurped the name of a plant which would now be placed in the genera *Dolichos* or *Vigna*.

Either of two unrelated plants may be meant by (18) *dragantea*: *Artemisia dracunculus* L., Tarragon; or *Arum dracunculus* L., Dragons. For the latter, as a drug, other species of Arum might be substituted, in the South *A. italicum* Lam., in Britain *A. maculatum* L. There is little evidence for the cultivation of tarragon before the sixteenth century, so that dragons is the identification generally favoured. For (20) 'Colocynth', see the Appendix (p. 166).

Both Chicory and Pot Marigold (*Calendula*) could be intended by (21) *solsequiam*; here it is all but certain that it means chicory, *Cichorium intybus* L.

Many candidates, all of them umbellifers, have been proposed for (23) *silum*. Fischer-Benzon thought that it was Laserwort, *Laserpitium siler* L. (*Siler montanum* Crantz.), but more recently Hermann Fischer suggested that it stood for 'sium', the *sion* of Dioscorides or Skirret, *Sium sisarum* L., once a well known root vegetable.

There is general agreement that, though not otherwise recorded in this spelling, (28) *parduna* is likely to stand for *bardana* the Great Burdock, *Arctium lappa* L., a physical herb much in use in the Middle Ages.

The next problem, that of (38) *diptamnum*, is much more difficult. The confusion of three distinct plants was recognized by Turner in 1548. What he called 'righte Dittany', *Origanum dictamnus* L. (*Amaracus dictamnus* Benth.) or Dittany of Crete, is a somewhat tender marjoram. Climatically a more likely contender is *Dictamnus albus* L., Fraxinella, Burning Bush or Bastard Dittany; and another possibility is False Dittany, *Ballota pseudodictamnus* (*acetabulosa*) Benth. In mediaeval England, however, 'dittany' usually meant Dittander, the possibly native cress *Lepidium latifolium* L.

Confusion also occurs over (46) *febrefugiam*. Literally this might mean Feverfew, *Chrysanthemum parthenium* (L.) Bernh., but the unrelated Lesser Centaury, *Centaurium erythraea* Rafn. (*Erythraea centaurium* L.) has the better historical claim, though both plants were used in the treatment of fevers.

One main difficulty, perhaps rather hair-splitting, arises over the members of the onion tribe. Besides Chives, Garlic and Leeks, the manuscript names (58) *uniones*; (62) *ascalonicas*; and (63) *cepas*. The simplest solution is to equate (58) with its literal counterpart as Onions, and to read the other two together as 'Onions of Ascalon', what we call Shallots, *Allium ascalonicum* L. Some botanists are not convinced that shallots could have been in cultivation by AD 800, but it is hard to overthrow the evidence of the name and, in view of the easily portable bulb, there seems no obvious reason why shallots should not have been an early import from the Near East. Shallot might, however, be represented by *ascalonicas* alone, leaving *cepas* to stand for *Allium cepa* L. the true Onion; in that case *uniones* would have been used for *Allium fistulosum* L., the Welsh Onion, in French *ciboule* and the 'chibol' of mediaeval England.

The two distinct senses of *cardones* (66) have already been mentioned (p. 29). Fischer-Benzon, though accepting that in another section, Capitulare 43, the word certainly meant Teasel, was inclined here to identify it with the Artichoke and Cardoon. The position of the entry, however, immediately following (65) *warentiam*, Madder used as a dye-stuff, seems to confirm the industrial plant rather than the delicacy. Similarly the position of (68) *pisos Mauriscos*, following (67) *fabas maiores*, Broad Beans, implies that these were peas, very likely the Field Pea, *Pisum arvense* L., but the epithet 'Moorish' is not found elsewhere in this context. Does it mean that the Pea as a food crop had recently been brought into Christian Europe from Spain? Attractive as this suggestion may appear at first sight, it has to face two difficulties. The pea was a very ancient crop in Europe, having been found in Swiss lake dwellings of the Bronze Age as well as in the botany of Theophrastus; and there does not seem to be any clear indication that it was cultivated by the Moors in North Africa or the Peninsula.

We have seen that there are in the list as it stands certain natural groups brought together: three mints are Nos. (41)–(43); the onion tribe runs from (58) to (64), with the intrusion of (61) the Radish, conceivably because of its bulbous shape; cucumbers, melons and gourds were rightly seen as naturally related, (8)–(10). The natural grouping of the umbellifers (30)–(36), alexanders, parsley, celery, lovage, with dill and fennel, is broken mysteriously by (34) the medicinal shrub Savin. The compiler was either using earlier catalogues on a scissors-and-paste method, or was making jottings from memory, partially systematic and yet haphazard and unrevised. In fact it is possible to make rather better sense out of the contents as a whole if they are re-arranged in the categories used much later by the seedsmen's shops of the seventeenth century. No such division can be clear-cut, since many herbs were employed both for meat and medicine: Sage was a pot-herb and a physic; the same species (*Apium graveolens* L.) was regarded as the physical herb smallage in its wild form, but as celery was a salad plant; endive and chicory were mostly put in the pottage, as were the leaves of beet, the root not being in use for centuries.

In the list from the Capitulare as here set out, the numerical order has been preserved in each category, rather than an alphabetical re-arrangement concealing the original.

(I) *Flowers*: (1) Lily; (2) Rose; (17) Flag Iris

(II) *Physical Herbs*: (3) Fenugreek; (4) Costmary; (5) Sage; (6) Rue; (7) Southernwood; (10) Gourd; (12) Cumin; (13) Rosemary; (14) Caraway; (16) Squills; (18) Dragons; (19) Anise; (20) Colocynth (see Appendix, p.166); (22) Ammi; (25) Black Cumin (*Nigella sativa* L.); (28) Burdock; (33) Lovage; (34) Savin; (35) Dill; (36) Fennel; (46) Centaury ?; (47) Poppy; (49)

Asarabacca; (50) Marshmallow; (69) Coriander; (71) Caper Spurge; (72) Clary; (73) Houseleek

(III) *Salads*: (8) Cucumber; (9) Melon; (24) Lettuce; (26) Rocket; (27) Cress; (30) Alexanders; (31) Parsley; (32) Celery; (38) Dittander ?; (39) Mustard; (59) Chives; (61) Radish; (70) Chervil

(IV) *Pulse*: (11) 'Kidney Bean'; (15) Chickpea; (67) Broad Bean; (68) Pea

(V) *Pot-herbs*: (21) Chicory; (29) Pennyroyal; (37) Endive; (40) Savory; (41) Horse Mint (*Mentha aquatica* L.); (42) Mint (*M. spicata* L.); (43) Wild Mint (*M. rotundifolia* (L.) Huds.); (44) Tansy; (45) Catmint; (48) Beet; (51) Mallow; (54) Orach; (55) Blite (*Chenopodium* spp.); (56) Kohl-Rabi; (57) Colewort

(VI) *Roots*: (23) Skirret ?; (52) Carrot; (53) Parsnip; (58) Onion; (60) Leek; (62), (63) Shallot; (64) Garlic

(VII) *Industrial Plants*: (65) Madder; (66) Teasel

(VIII) *Fruit trees*: (74) Apple; (75) Pear; (76) Plum; (77) Service; (78) Medlar; (80) Peach; (81) Quince; (84) Mulberry; (87) Fig; (89) Cherry

(IX) *Nut trees*: (79) Chestnut; (82) Hazel; (83) Almond; (86) Pine (*Pinus pinea* L.); (88) Walnut

The (85) Sweet Bay (*Laurus nobilis* L.) is on its own, as a tree which is highly ornamental and in that respect belongs with the flowers in Class (I); bore berries that were famed for their medicinal virtue, putting it among the physical herbs (II); and whose leaves were a delicate flavouring among the pot-herbs (V). It will be noticed that, by adopting the solution of '*ascalonicas cepas*' as shallots, in class (VI), the total number of species has been reduced to 88. This can be increased to 90 with the two species which, curiously, are not in the Capitulare but do occur in the inventories of the imperial gardens at Annappes near Lille (Asnapium), and 'Treola' (possibly Trieux near Thionville). Out of a total of 20 herbs and 8 trees at the first, all occur in the Capitulare except *vittonicam*, Betony; of 26 herbs and 10 trees at Treola, all are already accounted for except *acrimonia*, Agrimony. Elsewhere in the Capitularies, and in other official documents of Charlemagne's administration, are mentions of *napos*, Turnip; *linum*, Flax; *canava*, Hemp; and of seven different cereals: Wheat, Spelt (*Triticum spelta* L.), Barley, Oats, Rye, and two sorts of Millet, *Panicum miliaceum* L. and *Setaria italica* Beauv. So the cultivated Carolingian flora rounds up to the even hundred, without counting varieties.

Charlemagne died in 814, and within the next few years was made the extraordinary plan **18** for an ideal monastery, a copy of which has been almost miraculously preserved at the great abbey of St Gall in Switzerland. The author of the plan may have been Abbot Haito of Reichenau, and as the plan is addressed to Gozbert, Abbot of St Gall from 816 to 836, there is no doubt as to its approximate date, within a generation after the compilation of the Capitulare list. For us the important aspect of the plan is that it shows two gardens and an orchard. At the north-east corner of the site, next to the physician's house, is a square infirmary garden, *herbularius*, containing 16 beds, each with a named herb: 'Kidney Bean', Savory, Rose, Horse Mint, Cumin, Lovage, Fennel, Tansy or Costmary (*costo*), Lily, Sage, Rue, Flag Iris, Pennyroyal, Fenugreek, Mint and Rosemary. Near the south-eastern angle and next to the poultry yards, is a much larger *hortus*, the kitchen garden. This was to have eighteen beds, each running north and south, with a central path running east-west and dividing them into two rows of nine beds each. In these the plants were Onions, Garlic, Leeks, Shallots, Celery, Parsley, Coriander, Chervil, Dill, Lettuce, Poppy, Savory, Radishes, Parsnip, Carrots? (*magones*), Coleworts, Beet and Black Cumin (*gitto*).

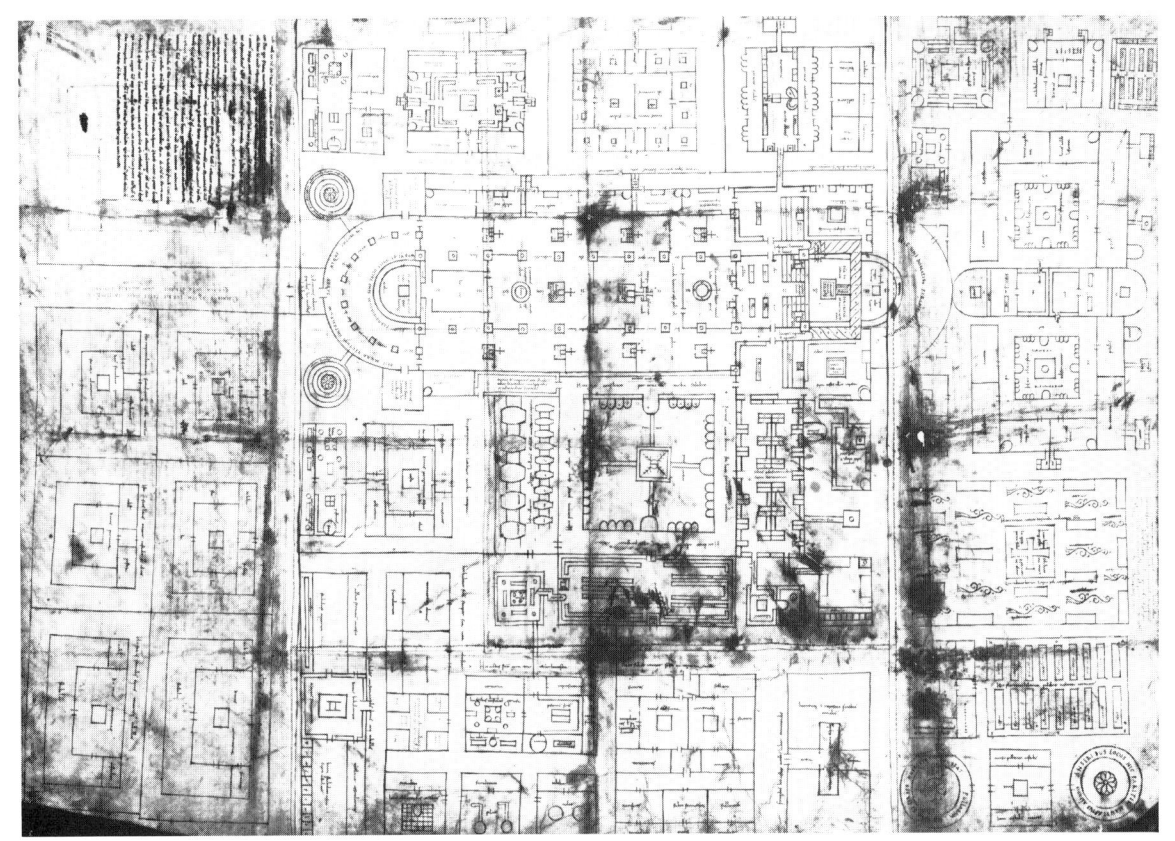

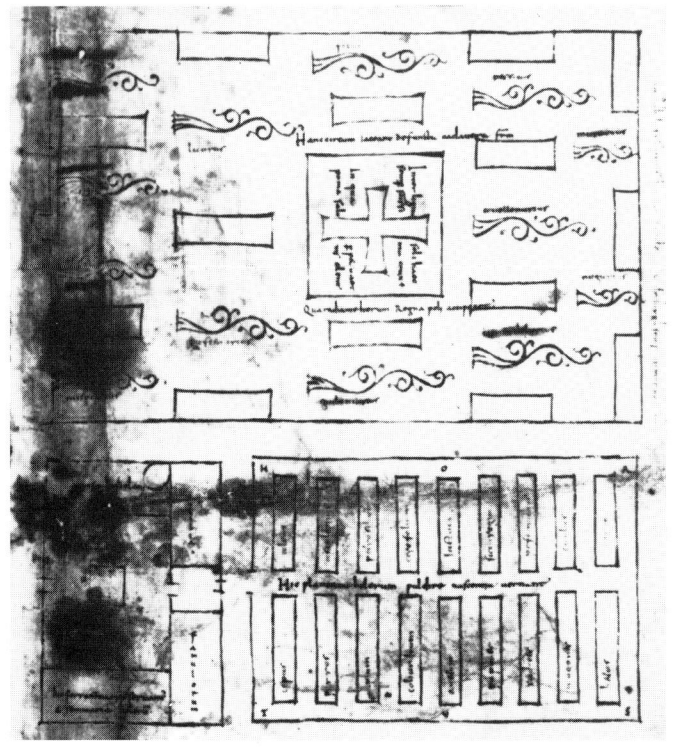

18A The St Gall plan (*c* 816–20) for a projected ideal monastery shows three gardens: one of medicinal herbs next the house of the resident physician (top right); a kitchen garden beside the poultry yards (bottom right); and next to it the monks' cemetery treated as an ornamental orchard with different sorts of trees

B Whereas the physic-garden and the vegetable plot contain merely utilitarian arrangements of beds, the cemetery (above) was already made the opportunity for aesthetic arrangements around a central cross

Savory occurs in both gardens, not improbably Winter Savory in the infirmary garden along with the other woody herbs sage, rue and rosemary, while the annual Summer Savory as a delicate flavouring could have been a crop with the pot-herbs and roots. Placed next to the north of the kitchen garden and the gardener's house with its tool sheds and quarters for the labourers, was the monks' cemetery, treated as an orchard and shrubbery planted with 15 sorts of trees. These are identical with the fruit and nut trees of the Capitulare except that either Pine or Cherry is omitted. The total of different species represented in the three gardens is 48, all of them included in the list: the only discrepancy is that carrots are termed *carvitas* there, but *magones* on the plan. It is obvious that the planting deliberately reflects the choice of the most important herbs and trees from the great list, roughly halving the number of kinds. It was still a comprehensive series of plantations, worthy of a great monastery of the period.

The last important document of the Carolingian group is the poem of Walafrid Strabo already mentioned, written about 840. As a work of literature it can now be adequately appreciated, the Latin original faced by an English translation, in the fine edition of Raef Payne and Wilfrid Blunt. What is particularly notable is Walafrid's appreciation of the beauty of ornamental plants, Sage, Flag Iris (*I. germanica* L.), Lily and Rose, both to sight and to smell. Walafrid again was a member of the Court circle, and from 829 when he was about 20 was tutor to Charles, son of the Emperor Louis, for nine years. Small wonder that most of the plants which he describes are in the Capitulare. Those to which individual stanzas are devoted number only 23, but there are incidental references to nine others, and bare mentions of three or four more. Of the 23 plants, 18 are in the Capitulare and two, Agrimony and Betony, appear in the Inventories. The three remaining are: *absinthium*, Wormwood; *ambrosia*, possibly a form of Tansy; and *marrubium*, White Horehound. Among the nine additional names there are Apple, Grapevine, Mugwort (*Artemisia vulgaris* L.), Peach, and Nettle as a weed. There is also *costus hortensis*, possibly Costmary, No. (4) in the Capitulare list, and the exotics Frankincense, Indian Pepper and Pomegranate. The passing mentions are to Alder, Hyacinth, Violet, and *auricula* in a context which may mean the common Primrose.

Roughly contemporary with Walafrid's poem is a verse gardener's calendar in Latin by Wandelbert, a monk of Prüm, between Aachen and Trier. Fischer criticizes this as making gross mistakes such as gathering Strawberries in May and collecting Violet and Hyacinth flowers in June, but these are explicable. The change in the calendar, already noted, means that May then extended to 4 June in our present calendar; secondly, 'Violet' may just as well have been used in the sense of *Hesperis*, or possibly *Cheiranthus*, as of *Viola*, and the mediaeval 'Hyacinth' was normally *Gladiolus communis* L., which is certainly in flower in June. It is clear that by the ninth century the tradition of monastic gardens of considerable size and distinction had been founded in western Germany, and a century later Reichenau in particular was praised for its walled garden, well looked after and watered, with the boughs of the trees swaying in the wind, lovely as an earthly paradise.

After depending for so long on continental evidence we return to England. In the ninth century, about the same time that Wandelbert and Walafrid were writing in Benedictine monasteries in Germany, there was a sacrist's garden close to the Saxon cathedral at Winchester, which may even have been on the site of the garden known for centuries as 'Paradise', beyond the north transept of the present cathedral. We know that the laws of Alfred (reigned 871–899) provided compensation for damage to vineyards, and the great king's choice of a title for his last book, *Blostman*, i.e. 'Blooms' implies an interest in flowers even though used in the sense of an anthology. Medical prescriptions were sent to him by the Patriarch of Jerusalem, so that he is likely to have been as well informed on herbs as he was on most of the subjects included in the science and art of his day. Alfred was not only a great military leader and a great king, he was a man of exceptional learning and accomplishment in his own person, and it must not be forgotten that as a child he had twice journeyed to Rome and back, the first time at the age of five, and returning from the second trip at eight. His interest in foreign countries was notorious, and proved by personal additions to his translation of the history of Orosius. We know nothing of his gardens, but he surely had some at his chief palaces and estates; his laws prove his interest in vineyards; finally, his knowledge of forestry is demonstrated by the unusual symbolism of his preface to *Blostman*, where he described his own efforts as a writer as those of someone finding suitable timber in a great wood, in which others too might get their materials for works of all kinds.

The last century before the millenium must have been an anxious time for many, in spite of the apocalyptic hopes of some. Notwithstanding the pacification wrought by Alfred, and the co-existence between Saxon and Dane in much of England, renewed attacks by the Northmen were not conducive to the development of gardens. It is held that this was a time when beans and peas became more widely grown food crops, and that this change in rotation helped to conserve the soil, but this was not horticulture. From the Viking kingdom of York recent archaeological research brings evidence of normal town diet and plants grown in and around a major urban settlement. Fruit and nuts were eaten on a substantial scale: sloes and the cultivated plum, and probably a damson, are represented by their stones, and flax, hops and coleworts were cultivated. Some of the 'weeds' found may have been grown as medicine: chickweed, groundsel, mugwort, nettle, poppy, devil's bit scabious, and sorrel; the tiny flax *Linum catharticum* for a yellow dye. Another physical herb, of which fossil remains have been found elsewhere in a tenth-century context, is the Masterwort, *Peucedanum ostruthium* (L.) Koch, also known as False Pellitory-of-Spain. References to this as a cultivated plant for several centuries mean masterwort rather than the true *Anacyclus pyrethrum* DC.

Gardens as adjuncts to a quiet and religious life emerge in the biography of Eadfrith, Abbot of St Albans (939–946), who spent a considerable time as a hermit, tending gardens, with herbs and vegetables, and water (*hortos coluit, herbis, et leguminibus, et aqua*). In charters of the middle of the century there are mentions of individual grapevines as landmarks, implying that they were big old stocks deserving their Saxon name of 'wine-tree' (*wintreow*). The old Welsh Laws collected and re-enacted by Howel Dda in *c* 945 reflect a considerable interest in orchards. The value of a grafted tree was set for damages at 4d., and rose by 2d. each year until it bore fruit, after which its price was 60d. This proves not only the survival of effective grafting but also the exceptionally high pecuniary rank of sound trees. Though English and Welsh systems of law were in many respects very different, it is striking that both gave protection to horticulture as a primary department of social life.

What we know of English gardens in the latter part of the tenth century is mostly connected with the great Bishop of Winchester, St Ethelwold (908?–984). The splendid manuscript Benedictional which he had illuminated at Winchester in *c* 975 contains one of the first illustrations of the Madonna Lily, seen in the hand of Queen Etheldreda the foundress of Ely minster. The Benedictional was apparently written for the newly refounded monastery of 970, where the first Abbot, Brithnoth (died 981) was famed for his laying out of gardens and orchards (*plantationes et semina fructuum diversorum*). Ethelwold also had built at Thorney in Cambridgeshire a little stone church enclosed on all sides with trees of various kinds (*undique . . . vallatum arboribus diversi generis*). The abbey at Thorney was later described by William of Malmesbury as being set in a Paradise, the surrounding marshes bearing a multitude of trees growing tall without a knot (*quae enodi proceritate luctantur ad sidera*); the level plain delights the eye with its green grass; the ground is filled with apple-bearing trees and the fields with vines which either creep on the earth or are supported on poles. There is a mutual struggle between nature and art that one may produce what the other overlooks (*mutuum certamen naturae et cultus ut quod obliviscitur illa producat iste*). Even in the tenth century it is clear that the principle of multiple use was already honoured, and one of the uses was beauty.

CHAPTER THREE

Gardens of Southern Europe

IN FOLLOWING WESTERN GARDENING from the downfall of Rome to AD 1000, we have hitherto been concerned with internal developments. The civilization of north-western Europe, including Britain, was largely that of the Roman Church, and even when the centre of the new 'Roman' Empire was placed at Aachen in 800 the tradition of the older administration based 700 miles to the South was not altogether forgotten. As we have seen, those plants which were not native had been introduced in imperial times, and so far as there was a literature of the subject it was a Latin one. Not only artistic style, but most aspects of higher culture, were still Romanesque. For five centuries or more Western Europe had been living on the 'hump' of antiquity but, to change the metaphor, it was a clock running down. What was needed was a new set of works.

Far older than the Roman Empire, older than the Greek states, were the ancient civilizations of the Middle East: Sumeria, Babylonia and Assyria; Persia; Egypt. Through the phenomenally rapid spread of Islam from Arabia in less than a hundred years from the death of Mohammed in AD 632, the whole area of all these early cultures came under a single government. Still more, that government of the first Caliphs was dedicated to the world-wide expansion of a new religion, Islam. Though the expansion was by military force, this was under very strict discipline and Abu Bakr the first Caliph (632–634), in setting the war machine in motion, gave the order that no palm-trees were to be destroyed, no cornfields burnt, no orchards cut down. Unlike the Greeks, who ravaged the fields of the fellow-Greeks with whom they were at war, cutting down their olive-groves, the Muslims were at pains to avoid destruction and, as soon as possible, restored peaceful government and prosperity to the countries they overran.

Notwithstanding these simple virtues, the Arabs were not themselves a highly civilized people, and the later cultural triumphs of Islam were largely due to the fact that, on taking over Persia, the conquerors were themselves taken over by its ancient heritage of art and science. Real power passed to the Persians behind the scenes with the setting up of the Abbasid caliphate in 750 and the founding of Baghdad 12 years later. Under Harun al-Rashid (reigned 786–809) and his Persian Barmecide advisers an academy of translators was formed to produce Arabic versions of all important philosophical and scientific works, mainly Greek but including also oriental sources. Among many other classics the *Materia Medica* of

Dioscorides was put into Arabic and became the fundamental book throughout the Islamic world for the study of plants and their properties. Fresh research in botany was undertaken by Abu Hanifah al-Dinawari (c 820–895), the 'Father of Arab Botany'. His new *Book of Plants* and the latest information were taken to Spain about 880 by Yunus ibn Ahmad al-Harrani, along with living plants and medicinal drugs. Al-Harrani, so named from his birthplace Harran (in modern Turkey, between Urfa and the Syrian frontier), an ancient seat of learning, settled in Cordova, then the greatest city in the whole of Europe, capital of Moorish Spain and of the Omayyad dynasty.

Not long afterwards a major compilation on agriculture was produced by Ibn al-Wahshiyya al-Kaldani, who claimed to reveal the secrets of the ancient Nabataeans. This claim was false and seems merely to have been an early publicity stunt. At any rate, copies of al-Kaldani's 'Nabataean Agriculture' reached every part of the Arabic-speaking world and spread the knowledge of up-to-date methods. In due course it became one of the most widely quoted of all source-books. This too reached Cordova, more or less coinciding with an embassy of 949 from the Byzantine Emperor, Constantine VII Porphyrogenitus (913–959). He sent as a gift to the Caliph of Cordova, Abdarrahman III (912–961), a copy of the Greek text of Dioscorides with coloured illustrations of plants. We can get an idea of its magnificence from the famous illustrated copies which still survive: the Codex Vindobonensis of AD 512 and the Codex Neapolitanus of the seventh century. At the time of its arrival in Spain, nobody in Cordova knew Greek, but so much public interest was aroused by the book that the Caliph negotiated with the Emperor for the services of a translator. In 951 an Arabic-speaking Greek monk named Nicholas came from Constantinople, and not only translated Dioscorides afresh but taught Greek in lectures thronged by the Cordovans and even attended by the prime minister. The plants known to Dioscorides in southern Asia Minor lacked many native to Spain, so that a supplement was required. It was compiled from personal botanizing by Ibn Juljul, physician to the Caliph Hisham II (976–1009), and was issued in 983.

At the same time, or more precisely in the 40 years 936–976, the Caliphs had been building, five miles from Cordova, the amazing palace-city of Medina Azahara. This contained immense pleasure-gardens and orchards on a terrace, below the palace but above the level of the great mosque and town. The garden city had its own system of aqueducts bringing plenteous supplies of water and ensuring the luxuriance of the vast plantations. From the Arab chroniclers we learn that for these and other palatial gardens of Andalusia the caliphs spared no expense, sending as far as India for rare plants and seeds and, according to one account, introducing the pomegranate from Damascus, though it seems to have been in North Africa much earlier. The pomegranate became the badge of Granada and so eventually passed into the royal coat-of-arms of United Spain, but it is not likely that there is any real etymological connection with the name of the city. What is certain is that all these magnificent gardens of the South were, as al-Maqqari wrote of Murcia: 'filled with scented flowers, singing birds, and water-wheels with rumorous sound.'

Not in southern Spain alone, but throughout the Peninsula, there was by the tenth century a fully developed tradition of ornamental gardening. This was adequately based upon a highly skilled technique of cultivation applied to many different kinds of plants and trees. Until well into the twelfth century the dominions of the Moors stretched almost as far as Barcelona, and Toledo was not reconquered by the Christians until 1085, nearly 20 years after the Norman Conquest of England. Saragossa was Moorish until 1118, and its Muslims remained an extremely powerful community even after 1500. Large numbers of the Spanish population, Muslim and Christian, spoke both Arabic and Castilian, or Catalan, and this remained true throughout the Middle Ages. There was not perpetual warfare between

19 This German miniature of David and Bathsheba from the *Liber Humane Salvationis* of *c* 1395 is one of the very earliest objective pictures of a garden. The king, seated in a splendid 'Gloriette', overlooks the fountain and basin in which Bathsheba is bathing. Beyond the battlements can be seen the trees of a large park

Christians and Muslims, and peaceful penetration of ideas went on through such channels as the medical school of Montpellier, founded by Arab physicians and incorporated by 1221. Montpellier was the northern outpost of Spanish science, for it belonged to the Crown of Aragon from 1202 to 1349. Its university, founded in 1289, formed a main international link, and appropriately came to possess the oldest botanical garden in France, opened by Henri IV in 1593. Our synonym of Petygrew (Provençal *petit greù*, little holly) for Butcher's Broom may reflect former contacts between Montpellier and England.

Post-Renaissance botanic gardens started in Italy, where those of Pisa (1543) and Padua (1545) are regarded as the earliest in the world. This overlooks the far older gardens of the Arab botanists under the patronage of Moorish rulers. In 1031 the western caliphate fell and Muslim Spain broke up into succession states, the most important centred on Toledo and Seville. At both were notable palace gardens of the sultans, maintained as scientific botanical gardens. That at Toledo was founded by Ibn Wafid (999–1075), and his colleague and successor Ibn Bassal carried on until the Christian conquest in 1085 forced him to seek sanctuary in Andalusia, where he improved the royal gardens at Seville for the sultan al-Mu'tamid (1069–1091). The most famous of these scientific collections of plants was set up a century later at Guadix by Muhammad Ibn 'Ali Ibn Farah for the Almohad sultan Muhammad al-Nasir (1199–1214). The comparative study of plants and the systematic introduction of exotic species with experiments in their cultivation all derive from these Moorish gardens on European soil.

The two successive superintendents of the gardens at Toledo, Ibn Wafid and Ibn Bassal, were among the most significant figures in the history of gardening. Their garden was very large, being outside the city on the opposite bank of the Tagus near the modern railway station, and still known as the Huerta del Rey, the king's garden. The sultan whom they served, al-Ma'mun, made use of the best hydraulic science to provide the gardens with irrigation and himself with a pavilion cooled by streams poured down upon it on each side. Both Ibn Wafid and Ibn Bassal wrote treatises which have survived to be rediscovered in recent years. Ibn Wafid was primarily a physician but also wrote a book on agriculture which included a chapter on flowering and aromatic plants. Ibn Bassal, however, was primarily a botanist and also a horticulturist of distinction whose personal experiments were remarked upon by his contemporaries, notably by Abu 'Abd Allah al-Tignari, of Albolote near Granada. From al-Tignari and other sources we get scraps of information which build up into a fairly detailed picture of the great man.

Thus: 'the eminent master Ibn Bassal, learned both in theoretical and experimental agriculture, an expert cultivator who had mastered the subject'; 'he told me that he had seen the blue lily (? *Iris germanica*) in Sicily and in Alexandria'; 'I saw this species of garden asparagus sown by Ibn Bassal in the Sultan's Garden'; 'all these sorts of jasmine are found in the neighbourhoods of Valencia, Sicily, Alexandria and Khorasan, as I have been told by Ibn Bassal among others.' Al-Tignari gives details of Ibn Bassal's method of dealing with a disease which affected the orange-trees, cutting down and burning those infected, and later making choice among the new shoots from the root. He also carried out experiments in planting the pomegranate, and discovered that the fig and the vine could be planted at any season. Ibn Bassal had travelled widely and collected plants in Sicily, Egypt, at Mecca, in Khorasan in north-eastern Persia, as well as in various parts of Spain. In his later career at Seville he experimented in the cultivation of imported seeds, but his great book seems to have been written before 1085, since it was dedicated to his royal master al-Ma'mun, the sovereign of Toledo.

The *Book of Agriculture* of Ibn Bassal, *c* 1080, is essentially on gardening, for it hardly touches upon field crops. It is methodically divided into 16 chapters, dealing with Waters, Soils, Manures, the choice of ground and its preparation, Trees, methods of planting, Pruning, Grafting and the seven Climates, Secrets of Grafting, Pulse and Industrial Crops, Condiments, Cucumbers etc., Roots, Vegetables and Salads, Aromatic and Ornamental plants, Miscellaneous. Most of the species mentioned are accorded a monographic treatment, though a few others are simply mentioned in passing. The fruits include, as might be expected, the Mediterranean and eastern sorts: Almond, Apricot, Citron, Date-palm, Fig, Olive, Orange, Peach, Pistachio, Pomegranate and Sebesten, as well as the Apple, Cherry, Grape, Pear, Plum, Quince and Service. Among forest and ornamental trees are the Arbutus, Ash, Azedarach, Bay, Cypress, Holm Oak, with 'Black and White Elms' – perhaps Poplars, Chestnuts, Hazels and Walnuts. The industrial crops are Cotton, Flax, Henbane, Henna, Madder, Poppy, Safflower (*Carthamus tinctorius* L.), Saffron, Sesame and Teasel; the spices and condiments are Cumin, Caraway, Black Cumin, Anise and Coriander, as well as Sudan Pepper put with the root crops.

The root vegetables were Carrot, Radish, Skirret and Turnip, Leek, Garlic and Spring Onion; the pot-herbs and salads were: Cabbage, Cauliflower, Roman Cabbage (or 'Cabbage of the Christians'), Egg-plant (Aubergine), Spinach, Purslane, Blite or Wild Amaranth, Spinach-beet, Chicory and Lettuce; as well as three plants perhaps grown for medicinal purposes, Bindweed of four kinds, Glaucous Celandine (? *Chelidonium* or *Glaucium*), and Leadwort (*Plumbago europaea* L.). The most interesting chapter deals with flowers: Rose, the Wallflower and Stock, Violet, Lily, a white bulbous flower, Narcissus, Basil, Marjoram, Balm, Rue, Marshmallow and Hollyhock, Camomile, and Wormwood. There are incidental mentions of the Oleander, and of Melilot as being grown in the same way as Camomile. From this relatively long list, as well as from the references to the 'blue lily' and various sorts of jasmine studied by Ibn Bassal on his travels, we can see that the purely ornamental garden was already highly developed.

Ibn Bassal knew the 'Nabataean Agriculture' of al-Kaldani, the one text-book in circulation during the main part of his career. In general, however, his work is original to an unusual degree and based upon his own practical experience. His book is fundamental, in that it is neither a plagiarism nor filled with quotations; the much larger treatise of Ibn al-'Awwam, written a century later, is avowedly a work of scholarship largely quoting from Ibn Bassal and many other authorities. Besides dealing with a much larger number of species, Ibn al-'Awwam breaks new ground by suggesting here and there principles of design. Thus cypresses might be used to mark the corners of beds and in rows alongside main walks, and other trees suitable for planting in rows were cedars and pines, with citrus fruits and sweet bay, while jasmines were presumably intended to be trained on trellis or pergolas. Pools of water should be shaded by the planting of trees nearby, such as the pomegranate, with the elm, poplar and willow. For hedges box and laurel could be used, as well as climbing plants such as ivy, jasmine, and the grapevine considered as an ornament.

Unlike the book of Ibn Bassal, that of Ibn al-'Awwam covered the whole of agricultural activity with cattle, horses, poultry, peacocks and the keeping of bees. It is a much longer work and contains far more detail on a greatly extended range of species of plants. The total number is about 160, but there are also many varieties mentioned which considerably increase the real coverage given, and this is more especially true of the flowers and ornamental plants. Even after making allowances for the greater length and more exhaustive treatment, it has to be concluded that during the century that separates the two books, *c* 1080–*c* 1180, there was a good deal of introduction of exotic plants into Spain, as well as the bringing into cultivation of wild natives, expressly advocated by Ibn al-'Awwam in connection with ivy and with a great bindweed known as poor man's rope bearing handsome bell-shaped flowers: these he suggests should be trained on a trellis for display. Violets should be sown in shady and sheltered beds, and also in new perforated flower-pots, in either case laying a bed of crumbled brick and builder's rubbish mixed with a like quantity of pigeon's dung. The author had himself seen them grown in this way at Seville and Cordova.

In general Ibn al-'Awwam gives the impression of borrowing much of his descriptions from earlier writers: the Nabataean Agriculture, Ibn Bassal, and his fellow Sevillian Abu -l-Jayr Ibn Hajjaj who had flourished a hundred years before him, a contemporary of Ibn Wafid and Ibn Bassal. Abu -l-Jayr is quoted on the sorts of 'Cheiry', that is the crucifers which we now term Stocks and Wallflowers. Of this group there were eight kinds in cultivation: the common purple, white, yellow, white-and-scarlet mingled, a 'turquoise', a very brilliant brown, a tawny, and a sky-blue; as well as a small wild sort, which Richard Gorer suggests may be *Moricandia moricandioides*; and a 'Water Wallflower', purple and flowering in summer, which sounds like Sweet Rocket (*Hesperis matronalis*). The purple, the white, and the red and white varieties were presumably Stocks (*Matthiola incana*); the yellow, brown, tawny, Wallflowers (*Cheiranthus cheiri*); the sky-blue and the turquoise seem beyond identification. It is worth mentioning in this context that Abu -l-Jayr's description of roses is quoted as including sorts with blue flowers, and with petals yellow outside and blue inside. If blue was a mistake for red, this last could be *Rosa foetida bicolor*.

Introductions to Andalusian gardens during the twelfth century seem to have included, among trees: Azarole (*Crataegus azarolus* L.), Banana (*Musa* sp.), Carob (*Ceratonia siliqua* L.), Jujube (*Zizyphus jujuba* Mill.), Lemon, Lotus (*Celtis australis* L.), Medlar (*Mespilus germanica* L.), all for their fruit; for ornament, several Jasmines, Judas Tree (*Cercis siliquastrum* L.), Plane (*Platanus orientalis* L.), and Willows. Important herbs were Dill, Dragons, Elecampane, Fennel, Lavender, several Mallows, Savory; and mainly for ornament: the Hollyhock (*Althaea rosea* Cav.), *Hibiscus rosa-sinensis* L., sorts of Iris and Water Lily. New food plants were the Artichoke, Celery, Fenugreek, Lupin and Sorrel, and in the industrial category Chufa (*Cyperus esculentus* L.), Cotton, Indigo, Lucerne (*Medicago sativa* L.), Sugar Cane, Sumach (*Rhus coriaria* L.), and Woad (*Isatis tinctoria* L.). Of these a good many were not hardy in northern Europe. There is therefore an obvious climatic reason, apart from others, why there was in many cases a long delay before the plants reached the British Isles. The blame should not be laid entirely on a supposed lack of interest in aesthetic plants for their own sakes.

Practical difficulties also stood in the way, and we have to consider the possible means of introduction of plants from Spain and other southern parts to Britain. Obviously many seeds could be brought by returning travellers, particularly if the merchant or pilgrim had any special knowledge: we know, for instance, that seeds were carefully collected in cloth bags by gardeners, and cuttings of such woody plants as rosemary specially wrapped. Living shrubs and trees would present much greater difficulties, though these were undoubtedly overcome in some instances when it was a question of gifts exchanged between sovereigns (see p. 45). Many bulbs and rhizomes, such as those of lily, iris and narcissus species, were certainly carried over very great distances and were probably a relative commonplace. Then there is the question of personnel: between Spain and England there was a considerable interchange of learned men throughout the Middle Ages. This was in part due to a mutual political interest as, very often, common enemies of France. On the one hand there were scholars like Daniel de Morley, who studied under Gerard of Cremona (1114–1187) at Toledo and is known to have returned to England about 1185 'with a precious multitude of books'. In another category were clerks belonging to royal households who moved to and fro on diplomatic missions. Some served both in England and in Spain, like Geoffrey of Eversley who was in the employ of

Edward I and also of Edward's brother-in-law Alfonso X of Castile (reigned 1252–1284) in 1276–82, at the very time when the learned king was producing the scientific treatises and the Alfonsine astronomical tables which have immortalized his name.

Much earlier there had been scholarly co-operation involving England and Spain. The English scientist Adelard of Bath, after studying in France at Tours and teaching at Laon, travelled for seven years in the Mediterranean and the Near East. He visited Salerno and Sicily before 1109, Tarsus and Antioch in 1114, and returned about 1115 with Arabic manuscripts including a version of Euclid's *Elements*. Whether he visited Spain is uncertain, but his translation of Euclid from Arabic into Latin, issued soon after 1120, depended on close collaboration with Petrus Alfonsi, a converted Jew. As Moshe Sephardi, Petrus was already a famous scholar before his conversion in 1106 at the age of 44, when he was baptized at Huesca in Aragon with the king, Alfonso I, as godfather. Soon after his conversion Petrus produced a reasoned polemic against Judaism, which aroused such violence of feeling among his former colleagues and co-religionists that he fled to England in 1110, to become Henry I's physician. He was still active in England after 1120 and moved in the most learned circles of his adopted land. Other Jewish scientists from Spain brought Arabic knowledge to the cities of southern France, and one of them, the astronomer Abraham ibn Ezra of Tudela, who had been in Narbonne in the 1130's later recorded that he was in a city of England in December 1158. Such contacts are of particular importance in that they show how plants could have been transmitted to the herb-gardens of the Jewish physicians who were among the best doctors in England in the period before 1290 (see p. 78). It is worth noting, too, that among the *Quaestiones naturales* considered by Adelard of Bath in the light of Arabic science (c 1116) was that of the graft: how did the graft draw its nourishment from the stock?

Horticulture and botany remained primary subjects of study in Muslim Spain, and knowledge of some 1,400 kinds of plants was included in the enormous Pharmacopoeia of Ibn al-Baitar of Malaga, the leading botanist of his time. After extended travels in North Africa, Palestine, Lebanon, Syria, Antioch, Edessa and Anatolia he became physician to the Ayyubid sultan al-Kamil (1218–38) and his successors, and died at Damascus in 1248. A great scholar, Ibn al-Baitar made full use of earlier authorities, quoting more than 60 times, and up to 400 times, from fifteen standard works. He added some 200 new plants to 1,200 for which the basic information was derived from Dioscorides. Arab botanists in Spain were by the thirteenth century starting to compile local floras for the first time, and it seems that in this and in other directions they were in advance of the Muslims of the East. Exception must be made of the botanist Ibn al-Suri (1177–1242), born at Tyre, who is known to have explored the Lebanon for plants in company with an artist who made coloured drawings of them at different stages of growth. His work has not survived and there is nothing to suggest that there were, for several centuries to come, any eastern treatises on gardening, botany or the pharmacopoeia of equivalent importance to the work of the Spaniards Ibn Juljul, Ibn Wafid, Ibn Bassal, al-Ghafiqi (died 1165), Ibn al-'Awwam, and Ibn al-Baitar, to say nothing of several others noted for their journeys or for major works now lost. Among these we must especially lament the study of the *Plants and Trees of Andalusia* by the geographer Ibn Amr (d. 1094).

The value of these Arabic treatises was recognized in Christian Spain, and translations of some of them into Castilian were made as part of the great programme of scientific works initiated by Alfonso X. Of these, a substantial part of the versions of the works of Ibn Wafid and Ibn Bassal has come down to our times. Another text which has come down in a Catalan translation is Ibn Wafid's *Book of Simples*. The significance of these translations, and of the original scientific works produced under Alfonso the Learned, lies largely in the fact that they were in vernacular languages, not Latin. There is a presumption that the users of these books were largely laymen with a direct interest in craft skills. For such readers the precepts of a practical gardener like Ibn Bassal, writing from his own experience, would be of real importance. At a later date we shall find comparable attempts to put practical advice into English, along with translations such as those made by John Trevisa, Henry Daniel and others at the end of the fourteenth century. On the other hand, Latin books by clerical and arm-chair authors like Pietro de Crescenzi, can have had relatively little influence until they were translated as Crescenzi was into French (see p. 76).

At this point we reach the earliest surviving gardens of Europe, those of Granada at the Alhambra and Generalife. These are now only reconstructions, in large measure mistaken, but the design of their architectural features and surroundings remains. Modern archaeological investigations would now make it possible to reproduce the original forms with greater accuracy, but in the upper gardens of the Generalife (c 1319) we still feel traces of what Dr James Dickie has described as 'the Muslim sensibility with its emphasis on the intimate and the within.' Mediaeval *Christian* sensibility was at one with Islam: the impression made by the Generalife and by the small patio gardens of Cordovan town houses is, *mutatis mutandis*, still essentially mediaeval. Dr Dickie has compared the Arabic literary evidence with the archaeological remains to provide a picture of Andalusian gardens between the tenth and fifteenth centuries. We need not go into detail, but two major points are striking: the Spanish love of sunk beds beside raised paths, giving the illusion of walking on a carpet formed by the tops of the plants – contrasting with northern raised beds. As Richard Gorer suggests to me, this may be due to the climatic need to collect or drain the rainfall. Secondly, and this resembles the greater gardens of mediaeval France and Britain, the plan with a central pavilion or gloriet, surrounded by flowers, by rows of trees, and by pergola-arbours covered with vines on trellis. The name gloriet comes from the Spanish *glorieta*, a translation of the Arabic *'azīz*, still surviving at the palace of La Zisa in the royal gardens at Palermo (p. 48), where an inscription reads: 'Here is the earthly paradise... this is called *al-'azīz* (the Glorious).' (See also pp. 103, 106.)

The Andalusian garden reached its highest peak in the Alhambra at Granada during the central years of the fourteenth century. The Court of Myrtles was built and its garden laid out for Yusuf I (reigned 1333–54), and the royal apartments including the Court of Lions for his son Muhammad V soon after 1354. It was at this time that the third of the great garden books of Moorish Spain was being written, by Abu 'Uthman ibn Luyun al-Tujibi of Almeria (1282–1349). Composed in 1348, within the last year of his life, this is a poem in simple verse which has been known to the outside world as the 'Andalusian Georgics.' It is in fact a masterpiece of compression, scientifically abbreviated from the best sources including Ibn Bassal and a number of the Greek and Latin classical authorities from Aristotle to Columella. Sections on soils, water and levelling, manures and labours such as ploughing are followed by a detailed treatise on propagation of all kinds and of the various categories of plants. In all more than 150 species are named, over 30 of them grown for the beauty of their flowers or for their scent. Somewhat unusually for a work in verse, this is fully referenced in over 350 notes directing to the sources.

In a final section Ibn Luyun lays down the basic rules for planning a pleasure garden, on a southern aspect with a well or watercourse shaded by evergreens, and a pavilion at the centre with views in all directions. Around would be flowers of different sorts, then trees including fruit trees, and climbing vines along the boundaries. There should be paths surrounding the garden under (arbours of) climbing vines; fruit trees should be planted in basins so that they give protection from the north wind without shading the plants from the sun. The overall shape of the garden should be oblong. In all this there are many striking points of fundamental likeness to the northern layout described a hundred years earlier by Albertus Magnus (p. 6). Both in the Christian North and the Muslim South there was to be a central place to sit in and observe the beauties of the garden; in Spain necessarily shaded by a pavilion. Trees and vines for shade were to surround both gardens, outside a diversity of flowers. The one curious contrast is that, whereas the cold garden in Germany was to lie open to the health-giving north wind, the warm pleasance of the south was to be protected from its violence. The other principal difference is that, in Andalusia, emphasis is laid upon water, whereas in northern Europe the main essential was the level expanse of grass lawn. The cool green lawns of northern gardens are indeed substitutes for pools of water.

So admired were these southern gardens, described by Ibn Luyun and constructed by the sultans of Granada, that they were closely imitated by the Christian king of Castile, Pedro I (1334–1369), at his palace in Seville, the Alcázar built in Moorish style by imported Moorish craftsmen in 1364–66. These gardens have disappeared beneath the Renaissance overlay of the time of the Emperor Charles V. So too have the later fourteenth-century royal gardens of the kings of Navarre at Olite and Tafalla, but in this case vestiges were seen and drawn by Pedro de Madrazo in 1865 just before their destruction. These were works done under Carlos III (1387–1425), the main layout at the castle of Olite dating from 1389–1408, while Tafalla was rather later, begun about 1405. Olite was famous for its 'hanging gardens', terraces at wall-walk level carried on arcades similar to those of the old Crucero garden in the Alcázar at Seville. The designer was apparently the master mason Semén Lezcano, and large quantities of bricks were bought from Moors of Valencia. In the gardens were a ball-court, an aviary with a basin and evergreen pine trees, a plantation of oranges, a small garden containing baths, a pavilion set in a garden with a fine cascade of water, and surrounding cloisters and galleries. These cloisters were planted with different trees: Cypress, Pomegranate, Grapevine. There was also a menagerie and swans and peacocks were kept.

At Tafalla **22** the royal gardens were extensive and surrounded by strong walls plastered over and originally painted, and with small pavilions at the centre of each side of the square plan. There was a look-out linked to the keep and by a staircase to the gardens below; and a dining pavilion of open Gothic arches with pinnacled buttresses said to have carried vanes which played organ-music as they revolved. Madrazo sketched what was left of this pavilion, and two stone seats **22C,D**. The historical importance of these gardens can hardly be exaggerated, since Navarre straddled the Pyrenees, and its king was also lord of great domains in France as far north as the county of Evreux and the port of Cherbourg. During the Hundred Years War Navarre became an ally of England; Cherbourg was even in English occupation under lease from 1378 to 1393. Henry IV of England married Joan, sister of Carlos III, in 1401. Frequent diplomatic missions between Pamplona and London provided ample opportunity for knowledge of Spanish gardens, and at least some seeds and plants, to pass northwards. That such horticultural transactions did take place we know from the remarkable account of the ancient orange tree at Versailles called the 'Grand Connétable'. This was sown by Leonora of Castile, queen of Carlos III of Navarre, about 1411, and was one of five trees sent in a box from Olite to France as a wedding present at the marriage of Louis XII to Anne of Brittany in January 1499. Plants of citrus fruits were already being overwintered in wooden sheds warmed by coal fires as early as 1490, and we hear of a garden near Llandaff with a furnace in the wall by 1537.

The orange trees at Olite were probably, like the brick for the building works, an overland import from Valencia. At about the same time the gardens of Valencia were described by Lorenzo Valla in his biography of Ferdinand I of Aragon (1412–1416) as being entirely of

20 In a manuscript of his poems (c 1360), Guillaume de Machaut sits writing inside a walled wood by a spring. The artist leaves no doubt that this embattled paradise is a highly artificial plantation of different kinds of trees

21 Manuscripts of the political tract *Somnium Viridarii*, the Dream of the Garden, open with the scene of the author asleep in a garden before the King and his Court. The likeness of the throne and chair to the garden furniture formerly at Tafalla (**22**) is striking in this French picture of c 1445

22A

22B

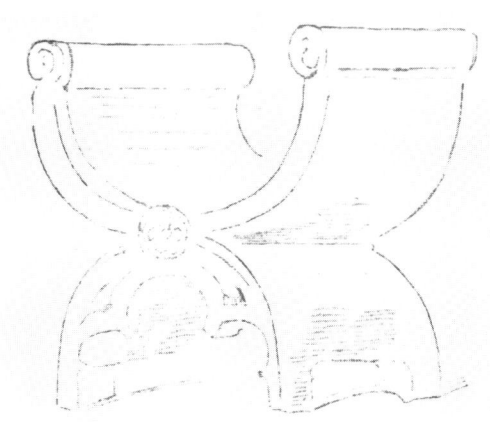

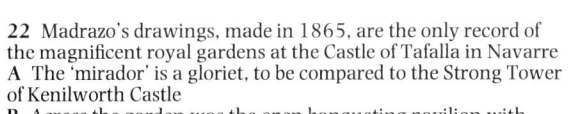

22C

22 Madrazo's drawings, made in 1865, are the only record of the magnificent royal gardens at the Castle of Tafalla in Navarre
A The 'mirador' is a gloriet, to be compared to the Strong Tower of Kenilworth Castle
B Across the garden was the open banqueting pavilion with pinnacled buttresses originally surmounted by musical vanes
C, D The stone chair and throne parallel those of **21**

22D

citrus trees, with walls of citrus trunks, and the soil covered with blue tiles. Thirty years later another account was given by Lorenzo Strozzi, who remarked that in Valencia orange trees were used for hedges, as jasmine was in Florence. The great city of the Levante is worthy of horticultural fame in another respect, in that in 1460 the Carnation as a garden flower first makes a distinct appearance in western Europe at Valencia, afterwards moving northwards and across France where it seems to have become fashionable about 1475 **Pl.VIIB,26**, and where the name *oeillet* first appears in 1493. This, of course, refers to the double clove carnation; various species of single *Dianthus* had been in occasional cultivation from the late fourteenth century. Although Valencia, as a great sea port, may have been a principal centre of horticultural activity by 1450, the whole of the Peninsula seems by that time to have contained outstanding gardens. On the extensive travels of the Bohemian noble, Leo von Rozmital, in 1465–67 (cf. p. 135), he noticed especially fine gardens (*horti elegantissimi*) at Coimbra in Portugal, and others near the east end of the Pyrenees at Figueras.

Setting aside the difference of climate and the inevitably distinct flora, there was probably much less to separate the Spanish garden from its northern counterparts than might be supposed. Yet there were at least two aspects of horticulture in the Peninsula where there was a substantial difference of emphasis. Firstly, it was only in the Iberian kingdoms that, before the Renaissance, *purely* ornamental gardens were acknowledged as an end in themselves, even though this aim was implicit in the *viridaria* of Albertus and, still earlier, the *virgulta* of Bartholomew. Secondly, it seems from the available evidence that among the Moors at least, quite small gardens of humble folk were a form of art. Soon after the Reconquest the Venetian Andrea Navagero (1483–1529) visited Granada and was struck by the multitude of ordinary houses that had gardens with pools of water and plantations of myrtles, roses and musk roses. The musk rose, famous throughout the Islamic world for its perfume and also as an autumn flowering shrub, was not generally known in the Christian West until later in the sixteenth century.

The early origins and continuity of tradition of the gardens of Spain contrast with the obscurity of Italian horticultural history before the Renaissance. To the presumed survivals of Roman tradition in central and northern Italy we shall return, but must first deal with the Saracenic intrusion into Sicily and the South. The story of Muslim penetration in this area is completely different from that of the conquest of Spain. The Arabs in Sicily were at odds among themselves and though they had effected a standing as invading freebooters in the middle of the ninth century it was not until 965 that they succeeded in capturing Palermo, which they held for only three generations. In 1072 it passed to the Normans, and most of the evidence for Saracenic culture in the island actually dates from the period of co-existence with the Norman overlords and settlers. There is no Arabic literature of Sicilian gardening, and what little can be deduced of the gardens themselves comes from the country palaces around Palermo built by the early Norman kings. In the royal park are 'La Favara' with an artificial lake, and 'Mimnermo', both built by Roger II who effectively became ruler in 1112, was crowned king in 1130, and died in 1154. His son William I (reigned 1154–1166) erected the famous 'La Zisa' (see above, p. 44); while William II (1166–1189) who near the end of his life married Joan the daughter of Henry II of England, built 'La Cuba' in a park with lakes and woods scattered with kiosks and pavilions, of which 'La Cubola' survives.

These parks and country palaces very likely represent the sites of earlier pleasances dating from before 1072, but surprisingly little is known, historically or archaeologically, of the cultural life of pre-Norman Sicily. There is not much to indicate that it shared in the glories of Baghdad, Damascus or Cairo on the one hand, or of Cordova, Seville or Toledo on the other. Influences from Sicily, as distinct from Southern Italy, on northern Europe are relatively late,

23 Though of far less botanical value than Jean Bourdichon's Hours of Anne of Brittany, the *Grimani Breviary* of *c* 1510, illustrated by artists of the school of Ghent and Bruges, is valuable for its realistic details of contemporary gardens. Raised rectangular beds, some containing trained trees, and plants in ornamental pots provided with saucers (therefore perforated) are prominent in this detail. At the centre of the garden a bottle gourd (? as a watering pot) lies on the path

24 Details from Stefan Lochner's 'Virgin and Child' of 1440 show the treatment of an exedra (recessed seat) as a flower-bed rather than a turf bench. Protected by a low rail at the back, it carries a rich variety of plants. The Virgin (in the centre of the painting) is seated on a cushion in the recess, not on the plants
A Angel with spray of semi-double roses
B Single carnations or pinks

25 A manuscript of *c* 1465 depicts a sports garden with archery butts, ornamental trees, and a summer-house buffet. Such places of entertainment were widely spread over the Continent by the fifteenth century and there were doubtless some in England, forerunners of Vauxhall and the tea-garden plant centres of the eighteenth century

from *c* 1150 onwards. By that time there was a double dynastic connection with Christian Spain: Roger II married Elvira the daughter of Alfonso VI of Castile, and their son William I was to wed Margaret daughter of García Ramírez, king of Navarre. On the whole it is probable that the role of Sicily in the transmission of Islamic garden design has been somewhat exaggerated. It is worth noting that Henry I's emparking of Woodstock *c* 1110, with the formation there of a menagerie, was earlier than the first accession to power of Roger II in 1112, as count at the age of 19; and that Henry II's work on the spring at Everswell in Woodstock Park in 1165–6 came over 20 years before his daughter's marriage to the king of Sicily. With the possible Sicilian influences at Hesdin in Artois we shall deal later (p. 106).

The main line of Arabic influence outside Spain lay rather through the mainland of Italy itself, where the port of Amalfi carried on a large-scale trade with the Saracens, and the medical school of Salerno was the only strictly scientific institution of the kind on Christian soil before the founding of the school at Montpellier. We have seen that Bishop Geoffrey of Coutances visited his Norman relatives in southern Italy before the Conquest of England in 1066, and therefore could not have carried back the idea of forming a park by deliberate sowing and planting of trees and making of pools from Sicily, which was not taken over by the Normans until 1072. Parks of the Islamic type must therefore have been established on the mainland before this period. To the same time belongs the career of the doctor, translator and herbalist Constantine the African (died 1087), who joined the school of Salerno bringing to the West for the first time Arabic treatises on medicine which he put into Latin. In his book *Duodecim graduum* he enumerated 200 medicines which employed 168 different plants. The more famous *Regimen Sanitatis Salerni*, a compilation of the school, was written for 'the king of England' and issued in 1101. It is thought that this dedication resulted from a misapprehension, since Robert duke of Normandy, on his way back from the Crusade in 1099–1100, was cured of a wound at Salerno at the time that his younger brother Henry seized the throne.

The name of Salerno long remained famous in medicine, and much more was attributed to the doctors of the school than they wrote in reality. By the thirteenth century the leadership in medical research had passed to Montpellier which, as we have seen, was in contact with Spain. Some individual Salernitans, however, continued to do impressive work in botany and the study of herbs: *Circa instans* by Platearius was written about 1150–75, and Matthaeus Silvaticus who was a member of the school by 1288 had a physic garden to which he brought seeds from Greece and plants of Arum colocasia (*Colocasia antiquorum* Schott.). His major work, the *Opus pandectarum medicinae*, was finished in 1317 and printed in 1480. Another great Italian compilation of the period was the *Clavis sanationis* of Simon Januensis, based on 30 years of botanical and pharmacological work, and completed between 1288 and 1304. At the end of this early botanical tradition based on southern Italy comes the Herbal of Rufinus, a Franciscan by 1264, completed about 1290. Rufinus had studied in Naples and Bologna and became penitentiary to the archbishop of Genoa.

How far any remains of Roman garden design survived the barbarian invasions of Italy is an unsolved problem, but early in the eleventh century Landulf described Milan as having gardens green as God's Paradise, beautiful with noble trees arranged in various ways, implying deliberately aesthetic design. In 1030 there was a Gardeners' Company in Rome, and in 1070 a 'Paradise' was laid out at the Benedictine monastery of Monte Cassino 'in the Roman fashion.' There seems to have been little to distinguish Italian gardens in general from those of France and Germany until the onset of the Renaissance, but municipal public gardens were a feature of the greater cities from the later thirteenth century. Florence in 1290 passed a statute setting up a common meadow (*pratum commune*) for public enjoyment

31, and a large artificial lake was added in 1297. There were also parklike layouts around private houses between the inner city and the walls and, as in Spain, the inner courtyards of town houses were often turned into small gardens. Another public garden, the Prato della Valle, was made at Padua about 1300, and another decreed at Siena in 1309 'to increase the beauty of the town as a pleasure resort for the inhabitants and for foreigners.' Such public gardens were, of course, not peculiar to Italy, and Gothein pointed to the famous names of these ancient open spaces: the Prado at Madrid, the Prater of Vienna, and in Paris Le Pré aux Clercs and St Germain des Prés. A later development in the North of France and Flanders was a garden with a club-house and shooting-stands 25, for example at Boulogne.

Following in the tradition of Moorish Spain, Venice in 1333 gave official support to the scheme of Gualtherus, a doctor, for laying out a physic garden with medicinal herbs. Such ideas were probably in the air, for within the next quarter-century an ambitious botanical garden was formed at Prague for the Emperor Charles IV (reigned 1349–1378) by Angelo of Florence. Another very remarkable garden was a few miles south of Prague, at the Cistercian abbey of Königssaal (Aula Regia), by the west bank of the Moldau, destroyed by the Hussites in 1420. Private gardens in Italy were, by the mid-fourteenth century, becoming sufficiently interesting to be described 32. Among the first to be noted was that by the palace of Azzo Visconti the lord of Milan (1328–39), with a fountain formed by a column surmounted by a statue, a fish-pond and a lake for waterfowl. At Parma the poet Petrarch 17 built a house and laid out his own garden in 1347, but before he could enjoy its first season came the calamity of Laura's death of the plague in the following April. It was to escape this terrible plague of 1348 that Boccacio's story-tellers of the *Decameron* left Florence, to stay in a country villa believed to be the Villa Palmieri some two miles to the north-east. Its garden, perhaps the most famous in mediaeval literature, had 'around the edges and through the middle long arbours covered with vines ... which joined the other flowers in bloom to give off an exquisite scent. Roses both white and red, and jasmine, clad the walks to keep off the sun. There is no need to mention the many kinds of plants and their elegant arrangement, since all that will grow in our climate was there ... In the midst ... was a meadow plot of green grass, powdered with a thousand flowers, set round with orange and cedar trees ... In the centre ... from a fountain of white marble, exquisitely carved, a jet of water gushed ... falling with a most delightful sound ...'

CHAPTER FOUR

Gardens under the Normans

WE HAVE NO REAL KNOWLEDGE of British gardens in the later Anglo-Saxon period. Certainly garden crops existed and there were orchards and, in the South, vineyards whose presence is betrayed by occasional place-names; but it is likely that everything was on a small scale, even compared with what was achieved on the Continent under Charlemagne. On the other hand, it is evident from the leech-books that many sorts of plants were recognized and used medicinally, and on common-sense grounds it has to be supposed that a proportion of them were cultivated so as to be ready to hand. Even in this obscure period there are rare glimpses of contact with the world outside, as when a Greek monk named Constantine joined the abbey at Malmesbury and worked in the vineyard which he formed on the hillside to the north. Something has already been said (p. 3) of the information derived from Aelfric's vocabulary of 995, but in addition to a large number of names of plants, and of words descriptive of parts of plants, there are gardening operations and parts of gardens and woods, which have evidential value for the next couple of generations also.

The daily conversation in Aelfric's school dealt among much else with the distinction between *silva*, 'wudu', a wood; *nemus* or *lucus*, 'bearu', a grove; and *saltus*, 'holt', a copse; adding for good measure *betulentum*, 'byrcholt', a birch copse. *Arbustum*, 'iung treow', was a young tree, but *frutex, spartus, spina* or *sentrix* were all interpreted as 'thyfel', a bush or shrub. Both *sirculus* and *virgultum* were 'sprauta', a sprout, very likely in the technical sense of a scion or sucker. *Plantaria* were 'gesowena plantan', seedlings or saplings. *Ablaqueatio*, 'niderwart treowes delfing, bedelfing', was the operation of digging round beneath a tree to loosen the soil; *putatio*, 'screadung', was pruning – the Saxon word survived in the form of shredding in this sense until the second half of the eighteenth century.

One continental development belongs here: the Latin poem of 'Macer Floridus', *De viribus herbarum*. From internal evidence this was written after 849 and before 1112, but in fact is believed to be the work of a French physician Odo Magdunensis of Meung-sur-Loire near Orleans, who lived in the first half of the eleventh century. It contains 2,269 lines of hexameter verse and discusses some 80 plants, of which 15 are imported drugs. Most of the rest are identifiable as hardy in northern Europe, but there is considerable uncertainty as to a few of the names, and in several cases a single name covers more than one species or even two

26 A large plant of single red carnation, grown in a basket and pushed on a wheelbarrow, forms a humourous marginal aside in this Flemish Book of Hours of *c* 1500. The heavy work is left to the gardener's wife

or more quite distinct plants. The importance of Macer is as a herbal very widely disseminated in many copies, both in Latin and in vernacular languages: an English version probably written at Oxford about 1395 has been published by Gösta Frisk. Macer also has the bibliographical distinction of being the first herbal ever to be printed, at Naples in 1477.

As in so many other fields, the Norman Conquest of England in 1066 had revolutionary significance for gardening. Duke Wiliam and his leading companions formed a closely knit military artistocracy able to impose strong government and the rule of law, but many of them were also close kin to those other Normans who had in recent years likewise conquered all southern Italy and, six years later, were to gain possession of Sicily. By the end of the century still other Normans would cross the eastern Mediterranean and rule in Antioch as a result of the 'First Crusade'. In fact there had been earlier crusades, and one of them had had outstanding significance only two years before the Conquest. In 1064 an army, largely composed of Normans and under the command of William VIII, duke of Aquitaine, had captured Barbastro in Aragon from the Moors, taking several thousands of prisoners of whom some were sent to Rome and to Constantinople but many held in France. It was shown by Menéndez Pidal that this influx of Moorish personnel, including singers and musicians, was directly responsible for the fact that the son and heir of Duke William of Aquitaine was the first of the troubadours, making use of Arabic forms of stanza which he must have learned from the artist prisoners at his father's court. Many prisoners were allotted to the Normans on their return, and there is nothing rash in the assumption that a sprinkling of them came on to England a year or so later, bearing with them unusual skills from the South.

This may well have an important bearing upon the increased emphasis on vineyards **29** which is revealed by the bare entries of Domesday Book, compiled in 1086. There are 38 vineyards mentioned, as major taxable assets, mostly in the southern counties from Essex and Kent to Gloucestershire and Dorset, but also in East Anglia. At Bisham in Berkshire one vineyard was of some 12–15 acres. The grapes of Gloucestershire were renowned for their sweetness and for producing a wine not inferior to that of France. As far north as Cheshire there is mention of a little timber church with vines climbing over it, at 'Lixtune' (? Leighton). Even in London itself, before the 1140s, the Earl of Essex, Geoffrey de Mandeville, had seized land at Smithfield to turn into a vineyard. Vinedressers in the king's service at Windsor appear in the accounts on the Pipe Rolls for the 1150s when the series begins.

The Norman Conquest brought Britain into much closer touch with continental events than it had been in Saxon times, and we can accept the evidence of what was happening in northern France and in Germany as generally applicable here. The end of the eleventh century saw considerable activity in the north of Germany, where Archbishop Adalbert of Bremen (1043–1072) and Bishop Benno of Meissen in Saxony were busy laying out gardens and vineyards. Most of the evidence for orchards is rather later, but Delisle brought together many instances of fruit produced in Normandy in the twelfth century. Walnuts were grown at Angreville near Gaillon, Peaches at Caen, and at Avranches Richard Coeur-de-Lion had Sweet Chestnuts *c* 1190. Between 1180 and 1200 there were rents paid in pears both at Caen and Rouen, where there was also a rent of pearmains in 1211. In 1195 apples were sold from the Hexham estate of the Archbishop of York, and before 1204 Runham in Norfolk, four miles from Great Yarmouth, was held by petty serjeanty, the service being the yearly payment of 200 pearmains and 4 firkins (*modios*) of 'wine made from pearmains' at Michaelmas. This rent was still being paid in kind in 1315.

There is ample evidence from Germany for the part played by monastic houses in the transmission of fine fruit and other plants, though the mother houses from which the sendings originated were generally in France or Burgundy. The Cistercian Order played an

Map of England with Wales and southern Scotland, marking the principal gardens and estates dealt with in the text

27 Pruning and training vines, from an English copy of the Utrecht Psalter, *c* 1000
28 An illustration to the *Chronicle* of Florence and John of Worcester (*c* 1130–40) represents King Henry I asleep with his dream of armed countrymen presenting demands. On the left a gardener carries his spade, iron-shod, at the slope

29 This French illumination of *c* 1325 shows the detailed construction of the normal supports for grapevines, frequently renewed at great expense. Such props are distinct from the tunnel-arbours and pergolas built in pleasure gardens for ornamental vines

30 A French miniature of the late fifteenth century shows St Elizabeth, teaching the Baptist to read, in a tunnel-arbour covered with red and white climbing roses. These are double blossoms of cultivated type and evidence that there were already climbers with double flowers before the end of the Middle Ages. See also Pl. VI and p. 164

31 An address of *c* 1335 to Robert of Anjou, King of Naples, from the town of Prato in Tuscany, alludes to the name of the town in this symbolic representation of a flowery mead (*prato*). The upper panel (A) shows fruit-trees (orange, citron, date-palm and pomegranate) underplanted with shrubs; in the lower (B) is a herbaceous border (both white and orange lilies, dwarf and purple iris) backed by white and red roses

outstanding part, and the abbey of Morimond, north-east of Langres (northern Burgundy), one of the four daughter houses of Cîteaux, was particularly famous for its orchards with many sorts of trees and shrubs, each kind being grown by itself. In Upper Bavaria the Benedictine abbey of Tegernsee supplied Benediktbeuren with seeds and cuttings of useful and physical plants. In its turn Benediktbeuren in 1185 was sending seeds and plants to Jachenau. The Cistercians sent apples of certain kinds from Burgundy to northern and eastern Germany, as far as Silesia. William, a monk of St Geneviève in Paris, went to Denmark in 1165 and eventually became Abbot of Eskilsø, whence *c* 1193 he wrote back to Paris asking for seeds, slips and grafts to be sent (*caeterorum olerum semina et herbarum diversarum atque radicum et arborum surculos*). Not all the expert work in this field was done by monks, for about 1200 the secular clergy of Cologne Cathedral were busying themselves with the improvement of apples and cherries.

Although the information in England is less explicit, the impression of considerable horticultural and arboricultural activity is much the same. We hear of the great fire at Crowland Abbey in Lincolnshire in 1091 which caught the green trees, ashes, oaks and willows growing about the buildings. These had undoubtedly been deliberately planted. Gloucester Abbey had an important garden (*hortus*) outside its precincts before 1100, when it was commandeered by the king as the emplacement for the Castle keep; other land was eventually given in exchange in 1109. Close by were 12 acres of royal orchards which in 1199 were granted to Lanthony Priory by King John. Not only fruit-trees but flowering plants were cultivated by the monasteries, as we know from the garden of the nuns of Romsey in being before 1092; at Barnwell Priory, Cambridge, founded in 1112, the refectorer had to provide flowers, mint and fennel. On a much grander scale there must have been splendid gardens attached to the immense Benedictine house of Bury St Edmunds where, about 1120, one of the monks painted from nature a number of the illustrations for the Herbal of Apuleius, now MS. Bodley 130 **38**. The work in such gardens was largely done by lay labourers such as the two *famuli* in the garden of Ramsey Abbey who, *c* 1170, were granted two acres of land each to work for themselves, and a weekly allowance of 14 loaves of bread **28**.

The technique of horticulture was advancing. From the reign of Henry I (1100–1135) onwards we find the field names 'impgarth', 'impyard' etc. used in the sense of a nursery-plot for grafts in the first instance, and then for transplanted seedlings generally, usually of trees. At Pontefract in Yorkshire, so famous five centuries later for its trade nurseries and its liquorice beds, there was an 'Impecroft' by 1215. The earliest mentions of wheel-barrows in England date from *c* 1170 and 1209, and mark one of the most significant of technological revolutions in a craft with very few fundamental changes. This was, of course, the period of the 'Twelfth-century Renaissance', and behind the fragmentary scraps of practical evidence there lie hidden the personalities of artists and scholars whose works are lost. For instance Henry, Archdeacon of Huntingdon (died 1155), one of the soundest of historians for nearly 50 years of the contemporary scene, also wrote a work in eight books on plants, perfumes and gems (*De Herbis, de Aromatibus, et de Gemmis*). Robert, Abbot of Malmesbury in 1171–1177, had previously been one of the royal physicians to Henry II and was surnamed 'de Venys' (of the Vines), very likely because of his skill in viticulture.

There are signs of quickening interest in aesthetic gardening both at home and abroad. This is rooted in appreciation of landscape, already notable about 1110 in the journal of a visit to Fécamp in Normandy made by Baudri, Archbishop of Dol in Brittany (1107–1130):

> At length I saw Fécamp, of which I had heard much from pilgrims ... Not to pass over the site,
> I shall acquit myself in a few words on the place. It is like a garden of Paradise, set in a lovely

32 A page from the Cocharelli manuscript of the late fourteenth century, illuminated in North Italy. Members of the nobility stand beside a marble fountain in a garden planted with trees: fig, orange, pomegranate, grapevine etc.

enclosed valley, between two hills, surrounded by farmland on one side and a charming little wood on the other. This seems to be of such even growth that it might be thought to have grown on a single day or to have been cropped back in height. The summits of its boughs and leaves and twigs are so thick that by their shade and strength they favour both the earth and the view: they keep off the heat of the sun and repel the onset of the rains. The trees stand up somewhat from their stocks, not very tall, but pleasant to stroll under. The sea is close to Fécamp, for it lies not a mile off, abounding in fish, with daily tides; there is a sheltered harbour where the pleasant clean water laps the quayside. There are springs of fresh water and it is a place fit for orchards, growing good apple trees.

Once more from Germany comes this epitome of a good garden, out of the Life of St Liutgart of Wittigen:

A delightful garden should have violets and white roses, lilies, fruit trees, green grass and a running stream **20**.

Again, the Low German *Glossarium Helmstadtiense* of the twelfth century names among garden plants the Columbine, the Heartsease (*Viola tricolor* L.) and the Wallflower (*Cheiranthus cheiri* L.), probably the earliest reference to this last as in cultivation north of the Alps.

Aesthetic appreciation and interest in exotic plants are topics which emerge from accounts of the Emperor Frederick I Barbarossa (*c* 1123–1190), whose reign began in 1152. His shooting-box of red stone is described as having a tank with fish and birds, beautiful to look at and good to eat, adjoining his park. In 1167 he sent an embassy to Baghdad which brought back reports of gardens with fountains in crystal basins; and in 1175 Gerhard of Strassburg was sent as the Emperor's ambassador to Cairo, where he saw and described a Balsam Garden **33**. Barbarossa, like Alfred and Howel Dda long before him, laid strict penalties against the destruction of vineyards, orchards or gardens. Returning to England we get an unusually vivid picture of an enclosed garden in the *Life and Miracles of St Godric*, the hermit of Finchale, written by Reginald a monk of Durham. Godric, a historical personage, died in 1170. In the *Life* is recounted the vision of a young man who found himself led by St John Baptist from Durham to Finchale, some three or four miles, and then to the west side of the church where Godric's buildings had been erected:

He took him into his garden, laid out on a quadrangular plan (*horto quadrangulo schemate facto*), fenced about on all of its four sides by the protection of surrounding hedges. In the midst of this garden he found a man of tall and handsome figure standing at a reading-desk, well designed and enriched (*analogium satis decenti ornatu compositum*). On this he had open a very large book in a red cover, and with it spread open before him, he frequently turned its pages and ... read in it.

This is a description of the *herbarium* (though called simply *hortus*) on a square or rectangular plan, hedged about and with a central feature, in this case a lectern of some kind, where there might normally be a fountain or a pool **34**. The quadrangular plan probably implies division into four quarters by paths or channels meeting at the central feature, the classical *chahar bagh* ('four gardens') of the East. We shall meet gardens of this kind on until the sixteenth century, but it must be emphasized that these small 'close gardens' were far from being the only mediaeval gardens, though they provided, as it were, the horticultural chamber music of the time. Notwithstanding their small scale they gave scope for great variation: in the type of enclosure, by hedges of different sorts of shrubs and trees, or by vines and honeysuckle on trellis, with climbing roses (probably at first only wild briars and dog roses with single blossoms); in the arrangement of turf benches, with or without small flowering plants in the turf; in the layout of the central lawn with or without paths of sand and gravel, and with or without separate beds for flowers, sometimes accompanied by small flowering shrubs or trimmed evergreens as seen in many of the later paintings **34,35,42–62**.

Though monastic and ecclesiastical gardens and orchards were for various reasons the most significant in early Norman times, the royal gardens became predominant from the reign of Henry I, at any rate so far as ornamental gardening is concerned. Not that the Crown was behindhand in the production of kitchen and orchard crops, which at times were even sold to the public. The impression that mediaeval diet consisted mainly of bread, with meat, fish, poultry and game according to the economic standing of the consumer, is false. It is based on the lack of evidence in account rolls for the *purchase* of fruit and vegetables. These were grown in the gardens of the individual, from king to cottager, and figure only to a very limited extent in the financial records, to which we shall come at a later stage. One document may be quoted here since it refers to ancient custom, the well known petition to the Mayor of London in 1345 from:

> the Gardeners of the Earls, Barons and Bishops and of the citizens ... that the said gardeners may stand in peace in the same place where they have been wont in times of old, in front of the church of St Austin at the side of the gate of St Paul's Churchyard ... there to sell the garden produce of their said masters and make their profit, as heretofore ...

Because of the nuisance to the priests singing Matins and Mass in the church (St Augustine, Watling Street),

> as also to other persons passing there both on foot and horseback ... who by the scurrility, clamour and nuisance of the gardeners and their servants there selling pulse, cherries, vegetables, and other wares to their trade pertaining, are daily disturbed ... the gardeners of the City, as well aliens as freemen ... should have the space between the churchyard of the said church and the garden wall of the Friars Preachers at Baynard's Castle ...

From this it is evident that there was a gigantic trade in the produce of market gardens in the Middle Ages, largely in the hands of the professional gardeners to magnates, who sold on behalf of their masters the earls, barons and bishops (who all had important London houses). The royal gardeners may not have sold here, but they probably bought in case of necessity, and this must have been one of the ways in which they could obtain plants and sundries such as turf ready for laying, expressly recorded as bought in some instances. As a general rule, however, it cannot have been necessary for the royal gardeners to go outside the large 'pool' of what was available in the grounds of Westminster, the Tower, and the other royal houses near the capital. Such an area as the nine acres of the Kingsbury garden at Dunstable, where Henry I was accustomed to stay, would have yielded a great deal of fruit and vegetables even after providing an ample pleasance which would to some extent 'double' with the orchard.

Most of the detailed information on the English royal gardens in the twelfth century comes from entries on the Pipe Rolls, which survive for 1130 and from 1155 onwards. In Henry I's time one Salomon was the keeper of the king's garden at Havering in Essex, being paid $1\frac{1}{2}$d. a day, and the same fee was paid to his son Ralf by Henry II and to his grandson Geoffrey by Richard I and John. It is probably significant that the keepership specified the garden and the

33 A real interest in landscape is reflected in this imaginary 'City of Babylon' with its Balsam Garden across the river, splendidly depicted in the book of French romances given to Queen Margaret of Anjou by the Earl of Shrewsbury in 1445. Note the entirely European character of the buildings: palace, Gloriette on left, and timbered watermills. The scene well exemplifies the greater garden of the managed park, in contrast to the small enclosed herber (34, opposite)

34 The pattern for the small herber appears in the *Grimani Breviary* of *c* 1510. The Garden Enclosed, with its fountain surmounted by a falcon (compare that at the King's Mews at Charing Cross *c* 1275, p. 11) contains small lawns intersected by paths. There is a clump of Madonna lilies, and a large rose-bush in one corner. Outside is the well-head of living waters, with an olive-tree. Picturesque park-like grounds intervene between the garden and a distant city of Flemish character

paling of the park, an association implying that this garden was primarily of recreational significance. We cannot insist upon a Saracen or Jewish origin for Salomon, since the name was also used by Christians, but the possibility that this important royal gardener was of oriental origin must be kept in mind. The garden at Havering in the sixteenth century seems to have consisted mainly of an area to the east of the old house of about 250 feet by 180 feet, or roughly one acre. In 1130 the rent for the king's garden of Carlisle was duly paid by William FitzBaldwin, but he still owed the same amount, 30s., for the year 1129. The gardens at Carlisle seem mainly to have been apple orchards, since bitterness at the Scottish invasion of 1173–74 centred around the barbarous barking of the trees. Several of the works on Henry II's gardens have been mentioned already. Others were the enclosing of the king's hunting-lodge and garden in Cannock Forest at Radmore in 1158, at a cost of £6, and the spending of £30 (say £15,000 in 1980) on the wall of Woodstock Park in 1165.

The gardens and orchards of the greater magnates, even if limited in size by the defences of castles, were possessions of importance, as is demonstrated by the appointment of a keeper *c* 1190 by Ranulph III, 6th Earl of Chester. In a charter bearing the earl's great seal, enrolled on 3 February 1191, Ranulph confirmed to William the Mounter (*munitor*; that is, cavalryman):

> the keeping of my garden and my orchard at Chester with the houses and their appurtenances, To have to him and his heirs in fee and inheritance from me and my heirs and his livery in my house of Chester for one man, whoever he may be, in my household at Chester. I grant also to the foresaid William and his heirs his 'restingtree' and the residue of my apples after the shaking down (*excucionem*) of the trees of my garden 36, and a garden to be made in the ditch of my Castle of Chester. And the foresaid William and his heirs in my house of Chester shall find for me and my heirs sufficient kale (or coleworts, *caules*) from the feast of St Michael each year until Lent and leeks through the whole of Lent in respect of all services and demands.

The '*restingtre*' may possibly be read as '*reftingtre*', but neither form is a word found elsewhere. From the context this means the stock tree from which grafts would be taken. The same arrangements continued in force for centuries, and in 1353 it was said that Philip Raby was the gardener of Chester Castle and entitled to the tree and to the residue of the apples, by ancient custom. A new stock tree was presumably substituted from time to time. There was certainly horticultural continuity from the time of Richard Coeur-de-Lion down to the sixteenth century, and the garden survived until new fortifications were made in 1745.

Where no plans have survived, and in the whole of the Middle Ages they are excessively rare, it is seldom possible to avoid confusion over the positions and areas of different gardens, orchards, vineyards and herb-gardens recorded at the same place, be it palace, castle, or monastery. In one instance the lucky survival of a large plan has illuminated this particular problem in the case of Christ Church cathedral priory at Canterbury **Pl.I,37**. Although produced to elucidate the water-supply of the institution, the plan shows intelligibly enough the whole layout of the buildings. Taken together with written rentals and deeds it has enabled William Urry in his brilliant study *Canterbury under the Angevin Kings* to reconstruct the whole area as it was in the 1160s.

Within the monastic buildings, to the east of the great cloister, was another galleried courtyard, part of which is marked on the plan as *Herbarium*, enclosed between wattled fences. Rows of plants are shown, so that there can be no doubt that the correct translation in this case is 'herb-garden', especially as it lies on the way to the Infirmary. There were other

35 The making of a new garden at a stately home (*c* 1485): wooden fence-posts are being driven in to carry a railing round borders and edged square beds already formed. A wheelbarrow of quite modern type is seen in the foreground

36 The orchard (*c* 1485): on the right is a nursery of young trees behind a wattled fence; on the left, harvesting the apple crop. In one tree a man beats down the fruit with a stick (see p. 64), perhaps for making verjuice. Another tree, presumably of a choice desert variety, is being carefully picked from a tall ladder

gardens at the same period, outside the city wall to the north, beyond Northgate Street, first the old garden, then an added area described as the new garden. These gardens lay outside the precincts, as did others marked on the ancient plan, to the north-east alongside the aqueduct, where there was a large garden and beyond it the vineyards. Returning to the precincts, trees are shown on the south side of the Monk's Cemetery at the place known as The Oaks. To north-west of the cathedral was the Archbishop's Palace, with its hall lying between a great open yard on the north and the palace garden of about one acre to the south. The tree under which Becket's murderers took off their cloaks was in the yard on the north, not in the palace garden or orchard which we have already found mentioned under the three names *vergier, pomerium* and *virgultum*.

Within ten or fifteen years after the revealing plan of Canterbury Cathedral comes the famous *Description of London* by William FitzStephen, written as a prologue to his life of Becket, who in the interim had become a martyr. Beyond the houses of the suburbs of the city, that is outside the walls, were gardens on all sides adjoining one another, planted with trees and both spacious and lovely. FitzStephen goes on to describe the wells to the north of London, notably Holywell, Clerkenwell and Clement's Well which were the most famous. Around the wells there were public gardens of some kind, with walks shaded by trees, frequented by students and youths who went out from the City on summer evenings, walking to take the air; the *paseo* was in the twelfth century as normal in London as it now is in Madrid. The trees planted for shade and recreation were usually elms, oaks or ashes, and willows near watercourses.

In the second half of the twelfth century two long lists of plants were compiled, the earlier in Germany, the second in England. The first is that by, or attributed to, Abbess Hildegard of Bingen (1098–1179). The abbess, undoubtedly a deeply learned woman, may well have written the botany ascribed to her, and Fischer defended her claims. On the other hand, Charles Singer regarded the botanical works as insertions made soon after her death. In point of date this is hardly material, and the internal evidence of direct knowledge of plants and their popular names does guarantee the authenticity of the information. The listing is not necessarily of cultivated plants but rather of plants actually known, plus a group of foreign drugs. The special value of Hildegard's work (accepting the attribution to her) is that she established categories, notably that of ornamental plants: the White Lily, Rose, Violet, Purple Flag Iris and Sweet Bay tree. Among wild plants with vernacular names were Columbine, Colchicum (*hermodactylus, heylheubt*), Germander, and the trees Hornbeam and Cornelian Cherry (*Cornus mas* L.) in addition to the Dogwood (*Cornus sanguinea* L.). Other trees worth noting are the Almond, Linden, Black Mulberry and Walnut; among the garden herbs and vegetables: Chives, Dittany (? *Dictamnus albus*) as well as Dittander (*Lepidium latifolium*), Lavender, Pot Marigold (*Calendula*), Purslane and Waterlily. Among the vegetables are also Red, White and Turnip-rooted Cabbages as well as Colewort. Perhaps the most surprising entry is *boberella*, Winter Cherry (*Physalis alkekengi* L.), even though it occurs in early herbals.

The English list compiled by Alexander Neckam takes two forms. The first, very well known, is in his prose book *De Naturis Rerum*, where chapter 166 is devoted to the herbs, trees and flowers growing in the garden (*horto*); the other can be deduced from his long poem *De Laudibus Divinae Sapientiae*, where the seventh division is devoted to plants, and the eighth to trees and crops. Put together these include about 140 species, rather more than Hildegard's work a generation earlier. Neckam, born in 1157, had completed his great scientific compilation while still a young man. It was in circulation well before 1200, and as we have seen (p. 21) existed in many libraries as the most used encyclopaedia for the remainder of the Middle Ages. The late Edward Hyams rightly protested against the sweeping condemnation of

Neckam's list of garden plants on the ground that it included exotics. He pointed out the evidence for an exceptionally warm period in Britain throughout Neckam's life, and the serious deterioration which set in only a century later. Out of 77 plants in Neckam's prose list for the garden, only ten at most need cause surprise: Acanthus, Date-palm, Dragons, Lemon, Mandrake, Myrtle, Orange, Pellitory, White Pepper, and Pomegranate. Several of these have undoubtedly been wrongly identified: Dragons (*colubrina*) probably stands for Bistort (*Polygonum bistorta* L.); Myrtle (*myrtus*) in northern contexts always means Sweet Gale (*Myrica gale* L.); Pellitory can be either Pellitory-of-the-wall (*Parietaria officinalis* L.) or the False Pellitory-of-Spain (*Peucedanum ostruthium* Koch), both hardy in Britain. 'White Pepper' (*piper album*) was Dittander or Pepperwort (*Lepidium latifolium*), or else Rocket (*Eruca sativa* Mill.). The true Acanthus (*A. mollis* L.) and Mandrake (*Mandragora officinarum* L.) can both be grown in the open air in England, and mandrake actually was in the fourteenth century. In the case of acanthus it is possible that the plant meant was the 'False' Acanthus, now called Hogweed (*Heracleum sphondylium* L.). The Pomegranate, though not likely to ripen fruit, was grown outdoors by Henry Daniel (see p. 160), and its fruits were imported in considerable quantity by royalty and nobility.

Of the ten dubious plants we are left with only three: Date-palm, Lemon and Orange. All of them can very easily be got up from seed as pot plants, set out in the garden in summer and brought into protection in winter. With the decidedly warmer climate of the twelfth century they could all have been marginally hardy in the South. Besides, it has to be stressed that Neckam states that the garden should be adorned (*hortus ornari debet*) rather than that everything in it should be profitable or produce fruit. Furthermore, he expressly excluded the exotic spices such as ginger, cloves, cinnamon and several others, whose names he merely introduces with the phrase: 'I say nothing of . . .' (*taceo de*). In any case there is a general common-sense provision which should be applied to all ideal lists: 'See if you can get them to grow'. We are dealing with gardens at the highest level of society: Neckam was, after all, foster-brother to King Richard Coeur-de-Lion.

Two plants in the prose list call for comment because they now first appear in a catalogue of things that really were grown in the noblest gardens in England: Borage, and Narcissus. Of the identity of borage there is no doubt: it is the annual Common Borage (*Borago officinalis* L.), unique in appearance and later in evidence as the canting badge (French *bourracher*) of the Bourchier family. What was meant by narcissus is less certain, but the choice seems to be limited to the native *N. pseudonarcissus* L. or the dubious *Lilium martagon* L., which could have been introduced if not native and which was termed 'narcissus' in some continental sources. Neckam's poem gives a much larger number of plants, 130 or so, but these do include some exotics: Cedar, Chickpea, Cork Oak, Cypress, Ebony, Nutmeg, Olive, Plane and Terebinth (*Pistacia terebinthus* L.) among others. Of these the Cypress certainly, and the Oriental Plane probably, reached England before the end of the fourteenth century, and a few specimens might have come sooner. Incidentally, Neckam adds to his prose list a short but important section distinguishing certain plants often confused, notably *solsequium* from *solsequium nostrum quod calendula dicitur*, i.e. the Blue Chicory from the Orange Pot Marigold; and between *artemisiam* and *artemisiam nostram quae febrifugium dicitur*, presumably Mugwort and Feverfew. *Jovis barba*, Houseleek, is to be distinguished from *Barba Jovis*; the latter is identified in a thirteenth-century manuscript as *sticados* (*Lavandula stoechas* L.), French Lavender or Stickadove.

Dynastically, we have already left the Normans behind, but it is convenient to bring together the whole period from the Conquest to the majority of Henry III, which nearly coincided with the appearance of Bartholomew's encyclopaedia and with the sudden

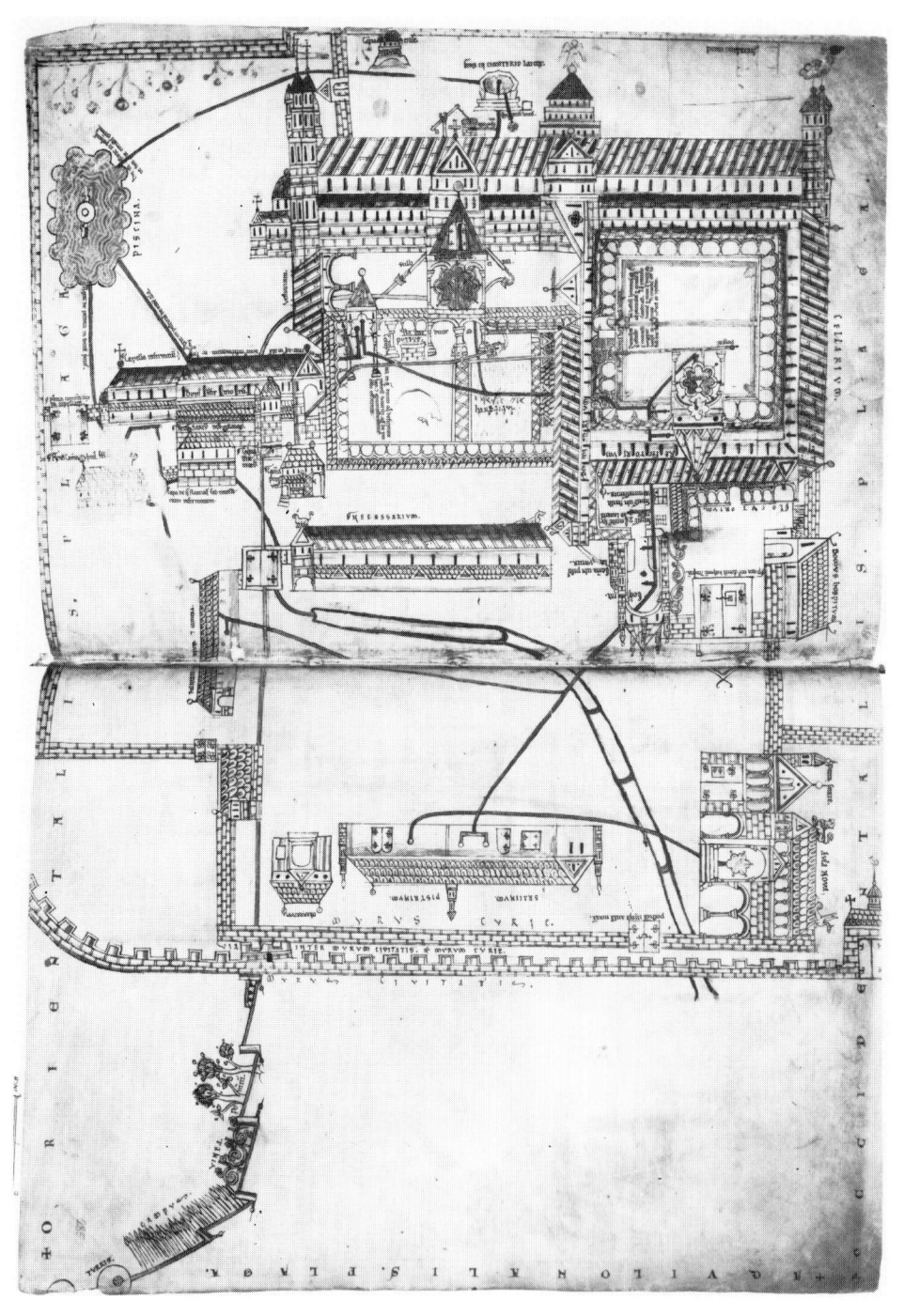

37A The plan (*c* 1160) shows the system of water-supply to the great Benedictine monastery of Christ Church, Canterbury. North of the church and east of the great cloister is the herb-garden ('Herbarium'), with rows of plants and a trellis fence (see B). Outside the precinct are the Vineyard ('Vinea') and the Orchard ('Pomerium'), between the city wall and the open fields

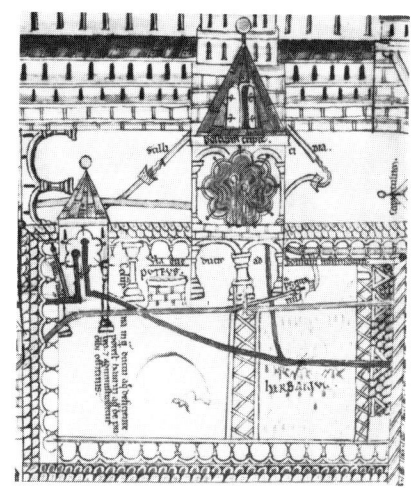

37B Detail of the herb-garden

38 The great herbal from the abbey of Bury St Edmunds (*c* 1120) was illustrated by an artist who in many cases, but by no means all, rejected the traditional distortions and drew direct from nature. This page includes both methods: the unrecognizable 'Foxglove' above, an exquisite study of Chamomile below

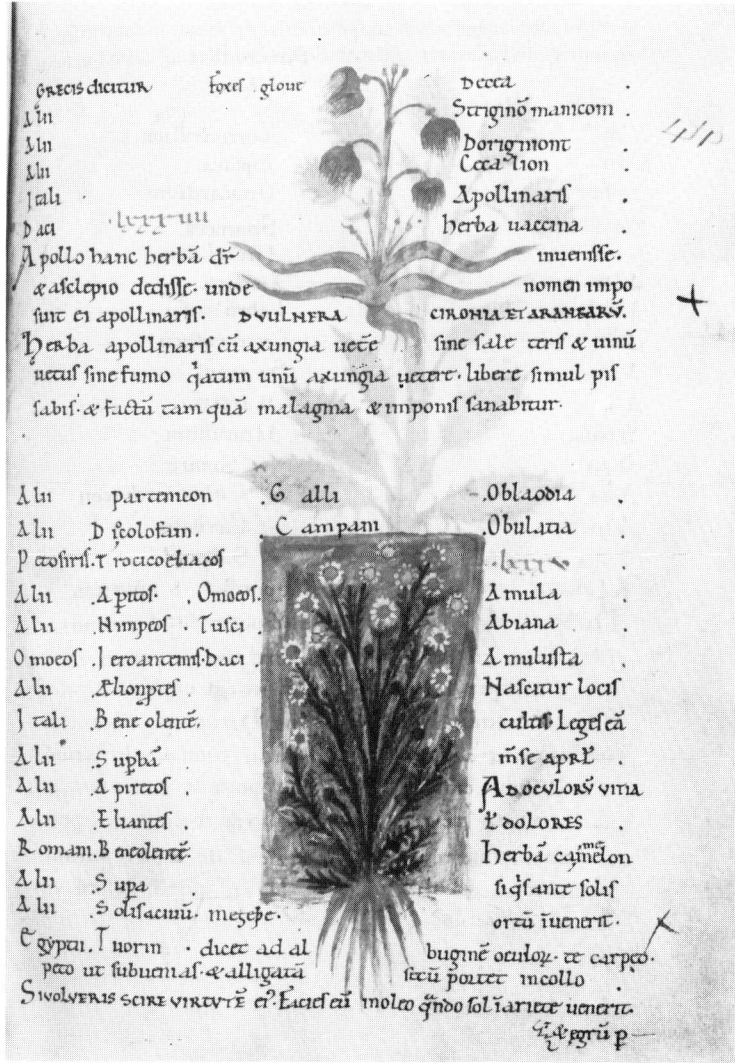

proliferation of written records. More than any other single event, it was the marriage of Henry III to Eleanor of Provence in 1236, that ushered in the High Middle Ages in England. After that, a more highly sophisticated and luxurious culture replaced the heroic virtues of the troubadours and trouvères and, in real life, of Henry II and Richard Coeur-de-Lion. We get, from some of the early poems and romances, the feeling of fresh delight in gardens which was already present before the age of greater sophistication and development. A woodland park beside a lake, walled around for the king, is described in *Erec* by Hartman von Ouwe who was writing his poems about the last decade of the twelfth century. Ganzenmüller quotes a fragment on 'the wood's edge, with a single Linden tree and on it the bird,' and Wright long ago collected several verses in Old French on the habit of dining and sitting with friends in gardens **59,70,76**. The same theme recurs in German poems, as in *Mai und Beaflor* with its garden of trees 'full of white-rose bowers to sit in, where poor and rich ate together'; and in *Die Nachtigall*, with an arbour made in the garden by the house, to sit and eat in summertime. The garden had both flowers and grass, with noble trees, lovely and clad with leafage. Hyams found mention of an arbour covered with a single climbing rose – presumably a wild dog-rose – so big that it could give shade to twelve knights together **Pl.VI;39**. This suggests the enormous ancient dog-rose at Hildesheim Cathedral, popularly believed to be a thousand years old at the beginning of this century, trained against the crypt. Its branches in 1910 spread 30 feet wide and 24 feet high.

Some of the poems and legends appear to be fundamentally based on fact, while others are not. For instance, we may note that the universal reference to the linden tree in early German verse is paralleled by strictly factual mentions of the lime-tree in the lists of plants and in historical records. The chronicler Lambert of Ardres, writing *c* 1195, refers to a wayside cross where an Abele (White Poplar, *Populus alba* L.) and a Linden were planted 'for the rest and solace of pilgrims.' The Dutch poem *Walewein* speaks of a Linden standing in a churchyard, ringed about with a wall. On the other hand, the historical minnesinger Tannhäuser, writing about 1240, lists summer flowers poetically but unconvincingly:

>There stood violet and clover,
>Summer sprouts, germander,
>There were crocus (?)
>Flag iris (?) found I there, lilies and roses.

The experts cannot agree on the identification of *zitelosen*, theoretically Colchicums but here supposed by some to be spring Crocus, by others Anemones; *ostergloien* has been interpreted as a German equivalent of 'Easter Gladdon', therefore a flag iris, which others deny; and the mysterious 'summer sprouts' or 'sprigs', *sumerlaten*, may not stand for any particular plant. The germander (*Teucrium chamaedrys* L.) was popular in the Germanic lands and appears again about 1300 in a poem by the Swiss Johans Hadloub, along with violet, mints and clover. As we shall see, it had reached England before 1400, but never found a niche in our literature. Another contrast is concerned with the lime-tree which, enormously popular in Germany both in real life and in verse, is rarely mentioned at all in England. Although both parent species are native with us, the hybrid Common Lime (*Tilia* x *europaea* L.) seems to have been an introduction from the Continent after the end of the Middle Ages.

In some instances there is a very close parallel between fact and fiction. In the second quarter of the thirteenth century the Emperor Frederick II had hanging gardens built on the buttresses of his palace at Nuremberg, and laid out a park; among his advisers were

39 In this painting by the Meister des Marienlebens (*c* 1470) a turf bench of recessed exedra form is sheltered by a pergola covered with vines. The front posts support climbing roses bearing white double flowers (see Pl. VI. 17, 30, and p. 164). Among the plants growing on the bench are Madonna lilies; the lawn is a flowery mead of many different species including daisy, dandelion and strawberry

superintendents of the gardens who had to see to the proper cultivation of foreign plants acquired through his alliances with the Saracens and the Spaniards. Thus far fact: at the very same time Guillaume de Lorris was writing in the *Roman de la Rose*:

> C'est cil cui est cil biax jardins
> Qui de la terre as Sarrasins
> Fist ça ces arbres aporter.

which Chaucer was to English as:

> With Mirthe, lord of this gardyn,
> That fro the lande Alexandryn
> Made the trees be hider fet,
> That in this gardin been y-set.

Some of the poets no doubt had special knowledge, and it may be that Wernher the Gardener, author of the poem *Meier Helmbrecht*, was monk-gardener of some abbey. One such it may have been who wrote a treatise on the proper way to gather herbs (*tractatus de colleccione herbarum*):

> The flowers of herbs and their seeds [should be saved] in little bags or in wooden boxes in a chest, or in leaves [? pressed between wooden leaves] is very good (*Flores vero herbarum et herbarum semina earum in saccellis uel in loculis ligneis in archa aut in foliis vero bonus*).

Herbs were to be gathered when neither too green nor too dry; those found in the mountains had greater virtue than those of meadows and watery places.

With the exception of the royal Pipe Rolls, the first continuous series of English accounts are those for the bishopric of Winchester, starting in 1208 and going on with hardly a break until well past the end of the Middle Ages, for 250 years in rolls and thereafter in book form. Taking the second surviving year, 1210–11, of which there is a good modern edition, we get several glimpses of gardening and other relevant work at the bishop's manors. At Southwark, the London palace, there was a payment of £2 5s. to the gardener, apparently for purchases and expenses, besides his fee (*stipendio*) of 5s. Willows were cut for 4s.; onions and shallots (or scallions: *scalonibus*) were bought for planting to the amount of 16d.; 2lb. of onion seed cost 6d.; *vinutis* (? small vine plants) were bought for 15d.; leeks for 2½d.; (broad) beans for planting were 8d.; a gallon of colewort or kale seed (*cholet*) was 3d. At the bishop's country seat at Highclere (Hants.) the enclosure of 111 perches around the park cost £1 0s. 1d., with 14s. 3½d. wages paid to the men who brought timber for planks to the park, and 14s. 8d. for preparing and setting up the planks (evidently as a fence). At West Meon, also in Hampshire, ditching and planting 80 perches came to 13s. 4d., and 3s. 4d. for hedging about (*circumsepiendo*) the ditch. Grafts (*insitis*) to the number of 180 were bought and planted for 24s. At Taunton Castle in Somerset 30 apple trees were bought for 5s. to restore the garden, and 2s. was spent on wages for 12 weeks of planting brook willows (*sileris*) in the park.

Another source of information consists of early legal records concerned with actions for damages. At Talworth in Long Ditton (Surrey) in 1220 there was a prosecution of £5 worth of damage said to be due to cutting down 140 apple, pear, oak and other trees in a garden. At Clere (Hants.) in 1229 two gardens of beans and peas were stolen. Since pulse were usually field crops, the growing of these in a garden probably means that they were to be eaten green.

In 1233 one malefactor not only cut down and carried off 20 ash trees, but rooted out saplings as well, presumably to plant. In a curious case at Bodmin in Cornwall in 1221, pieces of tin were discovered hidden under 'worts' (colewort or kale plants) newly planted in the ground. These records seldom refer to anything but common plants and trees, but it is worth remembering that contemporary chroniclers recorded that King John brought on the dysentery which caused his death by swilling down peaches with copious draughts of new cider, in October 1216. Baker's *Chronicle* states that the peaches were green, which might well be the case with home-grown fruit obtained in South Lincolnshire.

In 1222 there was a tempest in the neighbourhood of Worcester that brought down great trees in gardens as well as in woods: this mention of 'great' trees in gardens implies ornamental gardens rather than fruit orchards and may refer to the recreational grounds of the monks of the cathedral priory. We hear of such grounds at Evesham Abbey in 1206, when the Prior's share of Bengeworth included crofts of land, a garden, fish-ponds and a meadow within the precinct of the manor. There is also mention of the Keeper of the Vineyard and Garden. In the Close at Ely in 1229 there were 16 acres of vineyard within the Close, as well as a garden of 6 acres. The Keeper of the Ely vineyard had $10\frac{1}{2}$d. a week and a yearly robe (or suit of clothes) costing 10s. Walter of St Edmunds, abbot of Peterborough (1233–1245) built a mansion at Eye in Northamptonshire and surrounded the whole wood there with a wide ditch provided with a drawbridge; this sounds like an ornamental layout. Gardening was a main duty of some of the tenants of Glastonbury Abbey at Damerham, Wiltshire, *c* 1235; the customary shows that each *gardinarius* should receive the apples of an orchard (*poma unius pomerii*) and every day two gallons (*lagenas*) of cider when they make cider. A more distinguished gardener was William, who held the office of Gardener to the Castle of Lancaster for at least the quarter-century 1226–50. He held 7 acres of land by serjeanty, his services being to find the Castle kitchen in worts and leeks; the serjeanty of gardening was reckoned as worth 2s.; the value of the plants produced, 2s. 4d.; matters had been simplified by 1246 when William held the 7 acres and a garden by payment of 5s. rent.

The period fitly closes with the enumeration of plants grown by the English scholar John de Garlande in Paris about 1220. In Garlande's *Dictionarius* we read:

> In the garden of Master de Garlande are various herbs: Sage, Parsley, Dittany, Hyssop, Celandine, Fennel, Pellitory (*peretrum*), Columbine, Rose, Lily and Violet; by the sides grow Nettle, Thistle and Gorse (*saliunca*). The following are medicinal herbs: Mercury, Mallow, Agrimony, Nightshade and Chicory (*solsequio*). Master John's gardener (*ortolanus*) grows in his garden worts (*olus*) called Kale (*caulis*), and there grow Borage, Beet (*bleta uel beta*), Leek, Garlic, Mustard of which table mustard (*sinapium*) is made, Spinach-Beet (? *porreta*), and Chibols (*siuolli siue cepule*), Scallions (*innule*), and in the groves (*nemor'*) grow Burnet (*pimpinella*), Hawkweed (*pilocella*), Sanicle, Bugloss, Ribwort (*lance*) and other herbs good for man's body. In Master John's orchard (*virgulto*) the Cherry-tree bears cherries, the Pear-tree pears, the Apple-tree apples, the Plum, Quince (*coctanus*) and *esculus* (? Service), Medlar, Peach, Chestnut, Walnut (*nux*), Hazelnut (*auellana*), Fig, the Vine bearing grapes. Here are the names of the wild trees in the wood (*luco*): Oak, Beech, Pine, Bay, Mulberry (*celsus*), Blackberry (*morus*), Cornel, Hawthorn (*cinus*), Box, Buckthorn (*ramnus*), Briar (*bedagar*), Bramble, Poplar, Willow, Aspen, Linden, and the Bullace bearing bullaces which the common folk eat ... The dyers of cloths dye with Madder (*maior'*), Woad (*gaudone*) and Weld (*sandice*).

Gorse makes better sense than the doubtful 'Foxglove' for *saliunca*; Chicory might be Marigold; the *esculus*, a fruit-tree in various lists, may well be Service. On the whole Garlande gives us a convincing picture of the plants and trees that he knew and grew.

CHAPTER FIVE

Gardens of the High Middle Ages

THE HIGH MIDDLE AGES in England lasted for about 150 years, from the early manhood of Henry III, with his vitally important marriage to Eleanor of Provence, until the fall of Richard II in 1399. It is this period above all, some five human generations ruled by five sovereigns, that we regard as the kernel of the whole epoch. Within these years, as yet untouched by the faintest breath of the Italian Renaissance of classical style in literature or art, we may expect to find the most notably horticultural manifestations of the age. As we already know, this was a period of international learning when encyclopaedias were produced and studied in monasteries, cathedral libraries and universities. But the whole truth does not lie in these treatises and compilations. As has been abundantly demonstrated in the arts of music and architecture within recent years, the actual practitioners did not follow the precepts of the theorists but were far in advance of the written word. Hence we are to take such statements as retrospective accounts of what the scholars saw before their eyes, possibly representing the innovations of a generation, or even a century, before their time.

What Bartholomew de Glanville and Albert the Great said on pleasure gardens has been quoted, but we have here to consider what they can tell us of cultivation. What a primed canvas is to an oil painting, so is a lawn to a garden, and Bartholomew gives fundamental information on 'meads' and on grass (Trevisa 1399, spelling modernized):

> *De prato*, a mead. Meads be y-hight with herbs and grass and flowers of divers kind. And therefore (for) fairness and green springing that is therein, it is y-said that meads laugheth. Also meads, for (that) they be green, be liking to the sight, and for sweet odour they be liking to the smell, and feed the taste with savour of their herbs and of their grass.

In his chapter on Grass he stresses the importance of compressing the turf and treading it down (*si compressa fuerit aut mediocriter conculcata*), to avoid luxuriance and bursting forth into seed **5**. This point was later elaborated by Albert (above, p. 6) and by Crescenzi, and we have seen the lawns at Westminster being rolled in 1259. The production of a hard even surface, tightly clad with short grass, was essential in the days before the lawn-mower.

Hedges are described as a protection made of brambles, thorns and wood (*ex sentibus, spinis atque lignis*). This may refer to woody shrubs and trees rather than to posts and stakes, for later in the century *Fleta* tells landowners that hedges ought not to be made of apples, pears, cherries or plums, but of willows and hawthorn. Charles Joret, in his great monograph on the Rose, stresses the originality of Bartholomew's own additions to the basic facts of gardening which he took from Pliny. In this respect he shares with Albert the Great high credit as a true scientist, whereas Vincent of Beauvais and Pietro de Crescenzi were simply compilers. Bartholomew says of the garden rose that it is to be cultivated like the grapevine, 'for if it remain uncultivated and be not rid of suckers, it degenerates into the wild form (*si remanserit inculta et a superfluis non purgata, degenerat in syluestrem*).' The species of plants listed by Bartholomew, without counting obvious exotics, amount to 115.

Albert the Great lists some 270 species, of which 170 were well known in Europe. He knew at least five sorts of rose, commenting on the large number of petals of the garden rose as compared with the wild kind, counting up to 50 or 60 in the White Rose. He repeats the ancient doctrine of transplanting in the first quarter of the moon, found in the Nabataean Agriculture. Albert was one of the few advanced theoretical scientists of the Middle Ages, but seems also to have had considerable practical understanding of plants. The famous story that in January 1249 he displayed a flowering winter garden to William of Holland, the young King of the Romans (1227–1256) in the Dominican Friary at Cologne is by no means improbable. It is not clear why so many authorities have ridiculed the idea that Albert could have followed classical precepts and recreated a form of glasshouse; the fact that his example was not generally followed proves nothing beyond his eminence.

Albert's most brilliant pupil, Thomas de Cantimpré (1201–1270 ?), himself wrote a large compilation *De Naturis Rerum* in the years 1241–56, never printed. It had considerable circulation in manuscript and was often attributed to Albert. Its sections on trees and herbs formed the basis on which the Flemish poet Jacob van Maerlant (*c* 1230– *c* 1300) wrote *Der naturen bloeme* about 1260. Work on related subjects, literary or scientific, was in progress all over Europe: in Denmark in the middle of the century appeared a pharmacopoeia by Henry Harpestreng. At about the same time the Cistercian monks of Hovedø in Norway (a colony from Kirkstead, Lincs.) introduced exotic medicinal herbs which survived down to modern times. From *c* 1258 the archbishop of Cologne, Engelbert II, was forming magnificent gardens at Bonn, whither he had retired after a quarrel with the citizens. The fame of the rare and extraordinary plants which he collected there was such that he induced a party of prominent burghers of Cologne, his adversaries, to visit the gardens from curiosity, whereupon he promptly imprisoned them. That gardens could play an important part in German affairs is also shown by the state wedding of Hermann of Brandenburg and the daughter of duke Albrecht of Austria in a garden in 1295.

In France too, more attention was being paid to the royal gardens, and at the Louvre in Paris the great garden of the palace was connected to the Petit Jardin on the other side of the street by a private arched bridge. Delisle's researches brought to light valuable material on Norman gardens of the thirteenth century. At the abbey of Jumièges in 1234 a great garden (*magnus gardignus*) was mentioned; twenty years later the abbey of St Ouen in Rouen leased part of an island at Léry in the River Eure to Nicolas, son of Jourdain le Balistaire, for a yearly rent of 4*l*. 12*s*. 6*d*. tournois. The land, probably about three English acres, was to be cultivated as a garden of grafted pears and apples, with willows and osiers on the rest of the island. The Chapter of Evreux Cathedral undertook great clearing of land in the Forest of Neubourg and sowed it with Wheat, Barley, Oats, Peas, Beans, Vetches, Flax, Hemp, Leeks, Onions and Garlic, precisely the crops that were then (1281) usual in England. A less common crop was harvested at Le Houlme near Rouen, where many roses were grown and in 1291 are recorded as paying tithe. Presumably they were for medicinal use and for making rose-water.

That there was nothing new on the Rose in the book of Crescenzi was the verdict of Charles Joret, and it has to be admitted that the *Liber ruralium commodorum* is mainly an arm-chair compilation. Pietro de' Crescenzi, or Petrus de Crescentiis, was born at Bologna in 1230. He became a lawyer and after an eminent career involving much travel returned to his native city at the age of 69, to write his book in the next six years. Dedicated to Charles II of Anjou, king of Naples and Sicily, the work was issued in 1305 and had a wide circulation in manuscript. Translated into French by order of Charles V in 1373, then into the Italian vernacular before the end of the fourteenth century, it was a very early printed book: the first edition in Latin came in 1471, in Italian in 1478, in French in 1486; and a German version, omitting some plants, was published in 1493. It has never been put into English, but a surprising number of manuscripts of the Latin text were copied in England in the fifteenth century, and King Edward IV had a copy of the French version written and illuminated for him at Bruges after 1473 **68**. Crescenzi died at the age of 90 late in 1320.

Crescenzi was able to use Cato, Varro, Columella and Palladius among the ancients, and also took material from Avicenna; but his principal debt, completely unacknowledged, was to Albertus Magnus. He did, however, add two further chapters to the earlier account of the pleasure garden, which he applied to small gardens of around an acre. Next he added a chapter on the gardens of the middle class (*mediocrium personarum*), of 2, 3, 4 or more *iugera* (in theory about five-eighths of an English acre); thus these might have been between about an acre-and-a-half and three acres. Finally, for kings and other illustrious and rich lords, he suggested layouts of 20 *iugera* or more, roughly $12\frac{1}{2}$ acres. Since Crescenzi, like most earlier writers, was in effect describing existing gardens, we may assume that the major royal and ducal gardens of Europe measured something like 10 to 15 acres. This is strikingly confirmed by what is known, from Norden's plans, of the King's Garden outside Windsor Castle **40**. This measured $5\frac{1}{2}$ acres, but including the adjacent Orchard some 13 acres in all. The main original contribution of Crescenzi was his list of trees which did not bear fruit, and which he evidently considered purely ornamental. Many of these were from the mountainous parts of northern Italy, which he knew from personal observation **Pl.II.**

The importance of Crescenzi's book is that it gives a complete picture by a cultured observer, of the mediaeval garden at its most expansive, before the onset of the Renaissance. It was primarily concerned with Italy, but Luigi Dami in his classic on the Italian garden admits that it was not until after 1300 that there is any trace of variation in Italian horticulture from the mediaeval Gothic norm of the rest of the Continent. Crescenzi was, besides, concerned largely with the flora of the North and the Alps and most of his plants would have grown in England; very many of them did. Italian influences affected horticulture as well as other arts elsewhere. For instance Humbert II, the dauphin of the Viennois, in 1336 brought to Nice 20 orange trees for planting in his garden, paying 10 tareni, the tarin weighing 20 grains of silver, almost the same as the English silver penny of the same period. Humbert also had a 'Glorietta' or pavilion built in the garden by Master Raymund his carpenter. A little further off, in the Palace of the Popes at Avignon, an Italian painter who was probably Matteo di Giovanetto from Viterbo was in 1343 executing the frescoes of the Tour de la Garde-Robe, the earliest to give us an observational impression of the noble pleasure grounds of the epoch.

We left England at the mid-century when Bartholomew was producing his account of botany. Soon afterwards records become much more numerous and a new age was well under way. It was a time of agricultural prosperity for lay magnates and religious houses, who from around 1200 for well over a century made a profit by farming their own demesne lands. Part of this profit provided the surplus investment in finer buildings, works of art, and

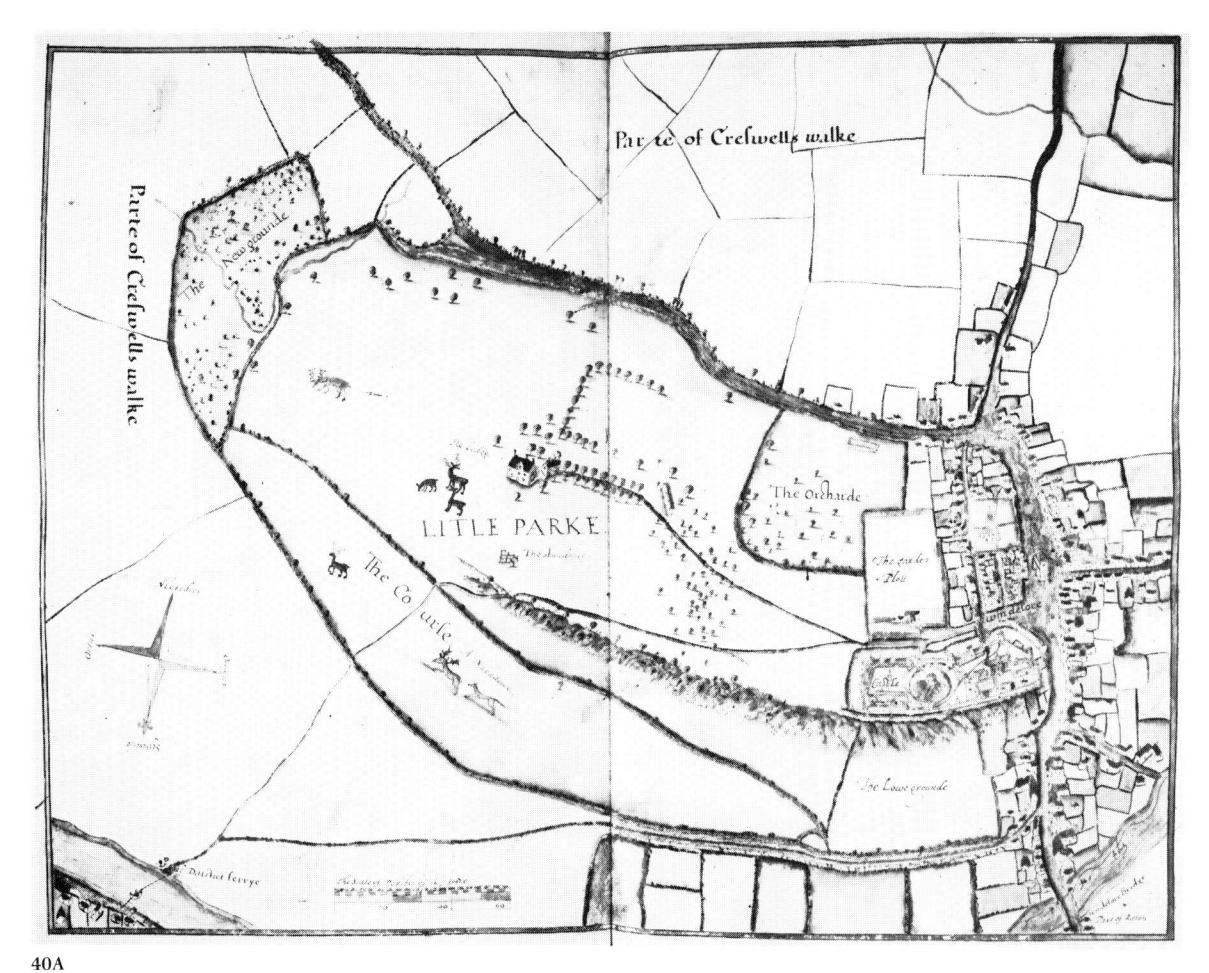

40A John Norden's survey of 1607, made only a lifetime after the end of the Middle Ages, preserves the layout of the Garden, Orchard and Little Park outside Windsor Castle, and shows the contrast between this major horticulture and the small-scale herbers within the Castle

B Detail from Norden's survey, including Windsor Castle and the 'Garden Plott' opposite to the Earl Marshal's Tower where James I of Scotland was a prisoner of war. The King's Garden, or 'Plott', was the main pleasure garden at Windsor from the twelfth to the seventeenth century; it contained about $5\frac{1}{2}$ acres, but with the adjacent Orchard and pool, some 13 acres (p. 76)

larger and finer gardens. It was also a time of scientific enquiry and, in Britain, renewed scepticism. This spirit, found much earlier in the *Questions* of Adelard of Bath, inspired Roger Bacon (*c* 1214–1293) and, in a more practical way, the Buckinghamshire knight Sir Walter of Henley who entered the Dominican Order about 1280 and a few years later wrote his treatise of *Husbandry*. This is especially noteworthy for the dictum that one should not sow one's own saved seed but obtain it from outside. This experimental discovery was being put into practice by the bishop of Winchester, John of Pontoise, who asked his bailiffs to get 'outside' seed by purchase or exchange. For, as Henley put it:

> Seed grown on other ground will bring more profit than that which is grown on your own. Will you see this? Plough two selions at the same time, and sow the one with seed which is bought and the other with corn which you have grown: in August you will see that I speak truly.

The scientific approach was also exemplified in the Norwich herb-garden maintained by Solomon, a Jewish physician and son of Rabbi Isaac, also a physician, about 1266. This was the earliest private herb-garden known to the late Dr Charles Singer in his researches in the history of English medicine. The Jewish community was in a good position to obtain seeds and plants of physical herbs from practitioners on the Continent and particularly the Peninsula, where Jewish physicians were highly regarded. On the other hand, this was by no means the only channel by which new plants and new skills might enter the country. Henry III's master gardener at Windsor from 1268 was Fulk le Provincial, evidently one of the queen's countrymen; he survived Henry and continued in his job until 1277 taking $2\frac{1}{2}$d. a day and allowances. Edward I's first queen, Eleanor of Castile, was a keen gardener and on getting the lease of King's Langley in Hertfordshire from the Earl of Cornwall in 1279 spent two years on having a new garden made and planting it with vines and fruit-trees. By 1280 she was buying grafts of the 'Blandurel' apple, and shortly before her death in 1290 made a handsome gift of £2 to her gardeners who had come from Aragon to work at Langley and were returning by her licence to their own country (*Gardinariis Regine qui venerunt de Arragon & morabantur apud Langelee reuerten' ad partes suas de Licencia Regine*). The fact that the gardeners came from Aragon, virtually a foreign country to Castile, is of considerable significance. Aragon was still an integrated country of Muslims, Christians and Jews, and had at its disposal the accumulated knowledge both of East and West, as well as a tradition of advanced horticulture centred on Valencia.

In spite of the less scientific basis of English gardening, the period was one of effective practical development, and an increasing number of sorts of food plants was grown. The Westminster Abbey Customary, compiled about 1270, laid upon the monk-gardener the duty of finding the monastery in beans, apples, cherries, plums, pears, nuts, medlars and all kinds of herbs that they might require. Summarizing the evidence as to what such herbs were, Beriah Botfield was able to instance as pot-herbs boiled with meat: 'cabbage, lettuce, spinach, beetroot, trefoil, bugloss, borage, celery, purslane, fennel, smallage (wild celery), thyme, hyssop, parsley, mint, a species of turnip, small white onions'. Some of them, he added, were eaten as salad raw, with oil and spices. For 'cabbage' we should substitute 'colewort', botanically the same species but not a heading variety; the plant then called 'spinach' is not clearly identifiable; beet was eaten for its leaves but apparently not for its root. Recent archaeological evidence would be able to add several more species, at any rate to the pottage of the urban poor.

This wide spectrum of different sorts cultivated for food rested upon a rapidly expanding seedsman's trade. Thorold Rogers published tables showing large-scale purchases of various seeds: from the early reign of Edward I there is evidence for trade in seeds of onion, mustard and hemp, and manorial accounts add seed of leek and of colewort, onion sets as well as seed, and little plants of 'worts' as articles of commerce. By 1296–97 we get proof of such business in a suit brought before the Fair Court of St Ives (Hunts.) held in 1300. John Spicer of Godmanchester and Peter Chapman of St Ives were in Huntingdon in January 1296 and entered into partnership to do business in various parts of Scotland. Spicer loaded horses with leek seed (*oneratis seminis porettorum*) bought with £3 put up by Chapman and took it to Scotland. In April he returned from a second journey, and in February 1297 undertook a third trip with three horses loaded with leek seed. A profit was made, but the partners could not agree on its division.

Prices of seeds fluctuated greatly: onion from $1\frac{1}{2}$d. up to 1s. the lb.; mustard between 1s. 8d. and 6s. 8d. the peck (quarter bushel); hemp from 2s. 8d. to 6s. 8d. a peck. Colewort seed bought in country districts might cost as little as 1d. a lb. There was also a flourishing business in grafted fruit-trees. At Rimpton in Somerset in 1265, 119 grafts for planting cost 6s. $6\frac{1}{2}$d.; next year 129 more grafts, of apples and pears, came to 11s. 6d.; at Southwark in 1267 43 roots of apples were charged at 2d. each, while 100 roots of pears cost 12s. Apple plants were only $\frac{3}{4}$d. each at Cuxham (Oxon.) in 1288, were up to 2d. in 1295, and in 1299 had dropped to $1\frac{1}{4}$d. By 1302 they had risen again to $1\frac{1}{2}$d. From many areas there are entries for making new orchards and re-planting old ones. In 1267 a ditch was filled in, thorns cleared and grafts (*ente*) planted at Chilbolton (Hants.) for 2s. At Wellingborough (Northants.) in 1284 grafts were bought and planted in a garden for $10\frac{1}{2}$d.; 5s. 8d. was spent in 1294 on plants of apples bought at Oxford to take to Cuxham, fodder was allowed for the horses carting them, 8d. wages paid to the man who planted them, and 1s. 9d. spent on the expenses of a gardener coming from Oxford for three weeks. We shall see other evidence of the role of the gardener as a visiting expert.

At an earlier period we learned (p. 52) the word *ablaqueatio*, and in 1283 at Silkstead (Hants.) find that 2s. $6\frac{1}{2}$d. was paid for the process: digging and removing earth round apple trees in the garden of the Prior of Winchester there, to manure them. William Sapt and Geoffrey Sattifer, gardeners, came to prune and tie up the vines. Cutting the vines accounted for 1d. at Cuxham in 1291–92, and Paul Harvey tells us of apples, pears, cherries and nuts being grown there. Not only fruit trees were grown: besides the evidence already mentioned for the sowing and planting of woodland trees, there is the likelihood that a plantation of ashes was involved in a forest plea of 1269, where the defence was put in that a load of ashes had been cut down in the defendant's own curtilage outside the forest bounds. Oak timber, whether or not it was deliberately planted, was managed as a crop. The manorial records of South Malling, Sussex, about 1273, included references to control by thinning and by selective and rotation felling. The Statute of 1306 against the felling of churchyard trees states that they 'oftentimes are planted to keep away the force of the wind for hurting of the churches.' The same year, in a church council held at Ripon, it was decreed that no layman was to fell trees or to mow grass in churchyards. These prohibitions stem from a decree of 1280 in which Archbishop Pecham declared that the planting of trees in churchyards was a notable adornment.

Soon after Henry III's marriage much was done in the royal gardens, of which at least nine were important. There was continuous work at Windsor Castle for the fifty years from 1222 to the king's death in 1272; at Woodstock from 1239 to 1268; at Clarendon from 1247 to 1270; at the Tower of London and Westminster from 1239 to 1268; in the Manor of Guildford from 1251 to 1268; in Winchester Castle from 1247 to 1269; in Nottingham

Castle from 1230 to 1269; in Gloucester Castle between 1252 and 1265; and at the Manor of Kempton (Middlesex) from 1237 to 1254. It would be impossible to deal with the development of all these gardens, but some salient points may be mentioned. At Windsor in 1253 thorns and large pieces of alder were carried in from the forest to enclose the King's Garden and to support his vine therein 29. The bridge on the way to the Garden was repaired in 1260, and next year a new house was built for the gardener and the hedge replaced by a wall. In 1262 a pool of water was to be made and the king's herber turfed.

Woodstock was the scene of great activity: building went on at Everswell in 1239 upon a larger pool surrounded by a great cloister, and a small pool **Pl.IIIB** had a bench set about it; in 1240 iron trellis was placed in the garden. Five years later a herber was to be made near the Queen's Chapel, and in 1248 two herbers, one on each side of the King's Chamber. In 1250, as we know, the Queen's garden was walled to give her a private place for walking. That herbers normally included an expanse of lawn is shown by the order of 1252 'to cause our great herber (at Woodstock) to be turfed' (*magnum herbarium nostrum ibidem turbari*). In 1264 the king ordered 100 pear saplings to be planted in the Everswell garden, and they had been bought and set by 1268. Two things are significant: the number of trees shows that Everswell had a large area devoted primarily to the spectacular effect of pear-trees in bloom and later in fruit; and that there was, probably at Oxford, a local nurseryman able to fill such an order for bought trees.

Various herbers were made and repaired at Clarendon, one for the queen in 1247 and two years later one under the king's chamber. In the king's great herber a bench was made in 1250, and the wall above it whitened; another herber was to be made under the north side of the king's chamber. Again and again this motive of gardens beneath bedroom windows comes up, and raises the question of an early origin for ornamental plans giving rise to the later 'knot' of the fifteenth and sixteenth centuries. Grafts of fruit-trees were bought and planted in the king's garden at Westminster in 1239, and in 1262 six 'Cailhou' pears were to be planted in the little herber enclosed next to the leaded pentice between the king's chamber and Westminster Abbey church. At the Tower also the same variety of pears was to be planted among other trees in the garden on Tower Hill, and William the Gardener was being paid a regular 3d. a day. In 1250 Roger the son of William le Gardener occurs at Westminster, and this may well be the Roger Herberur of whom a good deal is heard.

Guildford had the important cloister garden, made in 1256, and another herber was created in the king's courtyard there in 1260. At Winchester Castle both the king's herber by the chapel and a herber between the queen's chamber and the chapel are mentioned; the paling about the garden of Nottingham Castle was repaired in 1240 and a dovecote was to be built and a garden made in 1269. The considerable sum of 5 marks (£3 6s. 8d.; now over £1,500) was spent on the herbers and vineyards in Gloucester Castle in 1252, and five years afterwards a bridge was built over the ditch to give access to Lanthony Priory, a feature which was to take on particular significance twenty years later (see p. 84). Other royal residences were not totally neglected. A new herber was made at Havering between the king's and Edward's chambers in 1251, and in 1256 the king's herber at Hereford Castle was to be enclosed. Altogether the long reign of Henry III was one of very substantial expenditure on pleasure gardens, some of which were large by the standards of the time. Besides the small enclosed herbers of perhaps a quarter-acre or less there were much larger gardens and great lawns, and expanses planted with orchard trees as well as vineyards. The marble cloister at Guildford and the iron trellis at Woodstock give a glimpse of garden architecture too.

As in other fields of art, the reign of Henry III saw the beginnings of a system of regular appointment of master gardeners. Whereas responsibility for upkeep had earlier been placed

41 Martin Schongauer's Madonna of 1473 gives a detailed view of roses grown on rails, with peonies (left) and wallflowers (right) planted in the turf of a bench. A plant of strawberries grows in the turf at the Virgin's feet

on the shoulders of administrative officials, there was soon after the middle of the thirteenth century a tendency to rely on technical experts. At Windsor by 1266 robes were being issued to Emo the Gardener, who may be the same as the Edmund found there in the next few years, alongside Master Fulk from Provence. Both received robes from time to time, and were paid 2½d. a day each. At the Tower of London, William the Gardener was getting 3d. a day in 1262 and was continuously employed there until 1278, when he was also supplying plants for Westminster. Roger the Gardener or 'le Herberur', probably his son, was getting 2¼d. a day at Westminster Palace from 1268 until 1286; he may be the same as the Roger who worked there and for the king at York Place in 1301–1307. The description of 'Herberur', also found at York in 1351, probably implies a specialist in pleasure gardens. (For the royal gardeners see Appendix, p. 155).

With the return of Edward I from his years of Crusade, followed by a slow journey across Italy and France, there was a change of policy. Much less was done outside London, but the royal gardens within and outside the Tower, and those in the Palace of Westminster, received special attention. From a letter of Robert Burnel to Walter of Merton, from whom he was taking over the chancellorship in 1274, we know that the king took great pleasure in the garden at the Tower (*gardinum . . . in quo dominus meus plurimum delectatur*), and it already had vines planted in it. A good deal of work was done immediately and substantial sums were paid for turf and for plants. Near the mills to the west of the Tower 9,000 turves were laid in 1277–78; these were dug, but other turf was bought for £2 12s. 0d. ready to lay to cover an earthen wall made round the garden. For the Tower and for Westminster Palace plants were bought: grafts of pear-trees called 'Kaylewell' (probably the same as Cailhou) cost as much as 3s. 6d. each, others were bought at 1s.; 2s. 6d. was spent on rose-trees and 1s. on a quart of lily bulbs. A great herber was made between the Chapel and the Receipt of the Exchequer at Westminster, costing £3; supporting the vines in the garden cost £4 5s. 7d. This new herber must have taken up about half-an-acre of the Palace precinct.

There are further records of plants bought which give direct information on some aspects of ornamental gardening. William le Gardener supplied 3 quinces and 2 peach-trees for 3s., gooseberry bushes (*greseiller*) for 3d., another quart of lily bulbs for 1s., another peach for 6d.. John of the Tower (de Turri) was paid 6s. for 600 vine stocks, and 2s. for peony roots in the spring of 1277 **41**. William again was the supplier of 100 cherry-trees costing 1s. 6d., 500 willows (4s. 6d.), white roses (2s.), and one palm (*palma*) for 3d. The last item was most probably a yew-tree since yew was used to supply palm-branches for church use; the price, half that of a peach-tree, is vastly too high for any kind of willow, but not enough for a rarity. John le Fruter, probably the same man as John of the Tower, was paid 2s. 1d. for a single graft of the 'Kayl.' pear. In 1278 both William and Roger were supplying grafts, and William also provided plants of sage for 4s., probably a floral display bed rather than for the kitchen garden. Another gardener, Peter, paid 4½d. a day, worked on the herber and a pool next the king's chamber, and elsewhere. As Master William was still being paid only 3d. a day the implication is that Peter was an expert adviser, perhaps from his name a Spaniard sent for by the queen. In the 'new garden' in Westminster Palace was the Queen's Pool, lined with lead, and the Queen's 'Oriol' overlooked the pool. In 1279 come more prices: one Nicholas le Cuvreur was paid 2s. for two grafts of 'Kaylew', and 16s. was paid for another order of 12 grafts of 'kayl, rewl and gilefr.' Rose-trees cost only 2s. 6d. for 500 plants, and again a quart of lily bulbs was 1s.

The relative value of fruits is set out in the fruiterer's bills for 1292 published long ago by Hudson Turner. Ordinary apples were 3d. a hundred, but costards 1s.; ordinary pears of several named varieties, 2d. or 3d., but Martins 8d., St Regle and Pesse-pucelle 10d. and

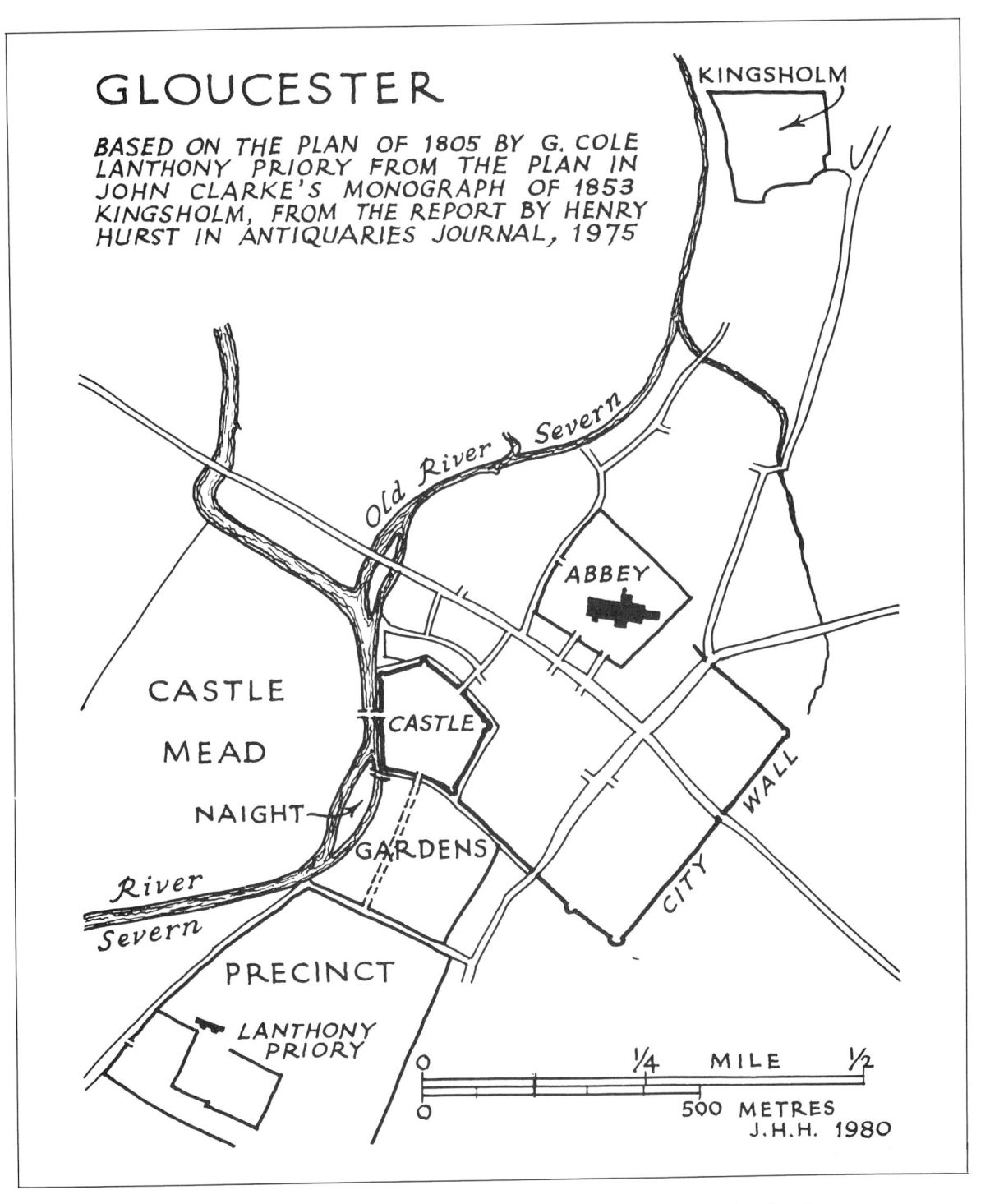

Plan of the town of Gloucester, showing its relation to the ancient palace and garden of Kingsholm to the north, and Lanthony Priory on the south. The gardens between the Castle and Lanthony, with the island or 'Naight' in the river Severn, had been given to the priory but were later used as a royal pleasance

more, Caillou as much as 1s. the hundred, quinces 4s., evidently a scarcity price, but Queen Eleanor may have wished for the quince-cheese, 'mermelada', of her native country. Spanish chestnuts cost only 2d. the hundred. Another clue to royal tastes is given by the $8\frac{1}{2}$ lb. of fennel seed bought for the king's wardrobe as one month's supply. The queen took an interest in a manor not far from London, Langley Marish (Bucks.), where there was a garden next her chamber and vines grew by the door of the hall. We already know of her keen interest in the gardens at King's Langley right up to her death in 1290. The queen had a herber at Conway in 1284, when 3d. was paid for watering it for one night, and 16s. was paid for two carts bringing green turves for this herber and for the queen's garden at Conway. At Chester, the base for Edward I's thrust into North Wales, 200 plants of apples and pears were bought in 1287, and the gardener's obligation in 1290 was to find worts (*caules*) from Michaelmas to Lent and leeks throughout Lent. In 1302 the gardener, 'T.', and his mate (*socio*) were digging and carrying green turves and making three herbers in Chester Castle with them. There was already a King's Garden, ditched and hedged, at Caernarvon Castle by 1295, and a man made a herber by contract for 3s. 6d. in Northampton Castle in 1305–06.

The evidence for extensive gardening of a utilitarian kind is immense and repetitive and need not be detailed. The account of the Earl of Lincoln's Holborn garden, printed in Alicia Amherst's classic, shows the large and commercial scale of operations reached by 1295. Apart from the usual fruits and vegetables, and unspecified herbs, the account is interesting for the mention of 'great nuts' being sold, as this certainly stands for walnuts which otherwise are little evidenced as being grown in England until after 1400. There were also roses sold, and little plants (*plantettis*) of vines. This indicates what was probably the normal way of stocking a garden or vineyard: all over the country, at houses of great lords and at monasteries, there were gardeners in a position to sell seeds or plants of the commoner kinds. Only at a few centres outside London, notably Oxford, York and Norwich, was there likely to be much of an organized nursery trade in addition. That there were itinerant seedsmen selling common vegetable seeds off the packhorse we already know.

By the end of the thirteenth century the fashion in laying out gardens and vineyards seems to have made great strides. At the Prior of Winchester's manor at Silkstead (Hants.) the vineyard is first mentioned in 1276, and by 1311 it required 800 stakes for the vines. The Bishop of Worcester had a garden and a vineyard, with herbage and fruit worth 10s. a year by 1282; at White Ladies Aston (Worcs.) the great garden of nearly $7\frac{1}{2}$ acres was worth 6s. 6d. for its herbage in 1288, and by 1299 there were two gardens with an average improved value of £1 6s. 8d. In 1294 there was a garden with vines at Burstwick (Yorks.) in the flat windswept plain of Holderness. At Meaux Abbey, not far away, the Prior had a garden and there was also a garden of the Abbot's chamber. At Haughmond Abbey (Shropshire) the Prior was allotted a garden called Longenores with a dovecote. Out of many other references to monastic gardens one is of special importance: the new making of the Infirmarer's herbgarden at Westminster Abbey, with two benches (*scaunis*) outside the door of the hall above the pool (*stagnum*) in 1305–06.

In 1277 there had been a surprising development at Gloucester Castle, where Eleanor of Provence, the queen dowager, was living. She approached the Priory of Lanthony, whose land came up to the south-western ditch of the Castle, to obtain their permission to have a bridge thrown across so that she and the members of her household might walk in the priory garden (*ad dictum Gardinum spaciandi causa possimus transire*). The gardens were very large and spread over much of the half-mile that separated the Castle from the Priory. A century later, when Richard II was holding Parliament at Gloucester, he in turn made special arrangements to cross the priory gardens to and from the Castle for his convenience

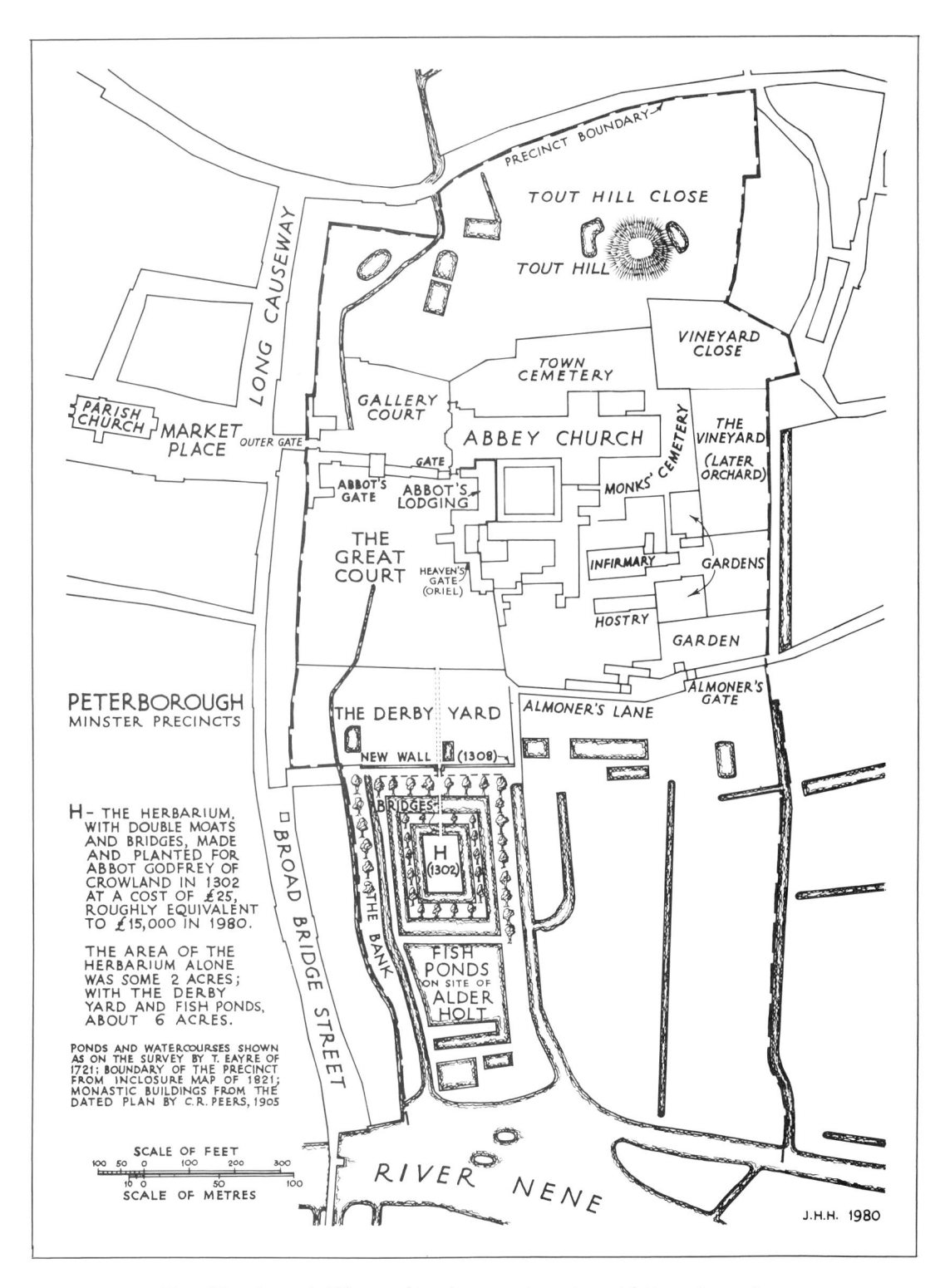

Plan of Peterborough Abbey marking the monastic precinct with its gardens and vineyards, and the Abbot's Gardens, including the new 'Herbarium' formed in 1302, between the Derby Yard and the Fish Ponds towards the river Nene

(*aisiamento*) giving an undertaking that his private path should not become a public highway. Where the Castle ditch entered the Severn, at the south-west angle of the defences, there was an island in the river called Naight, and it may well have been this that gave Richard II the idea for his own island-pleasance in the Thames by Sheen.

After the death of Edward I in 1307 another phase set in: the arts of peace became more obviously luxurious and even extravagant. This was to lay up seeds of trouble for, as we know, the climate was taking a disastrous plunge into lower temperatures and extremes of weather. At first there was little sign of what was happening, and it took the combination of several other adverse factors: the Famine of 1315, the outbreak of the Hundred Years War in 1340, recurrent outbreaks of bubonic plague from 1348 onwards, political strife and economic exhaustion, to bring the country to its knees in 1400 after the usurpation of the throne. In the meantime English gardening reached a high peak, only now beginning to be revealed as scraps of evidence emerge from historical records or archaeological investigation.

Whatever may have been the case in Norman times, there was from the reign of Edward I no question of England being a backward country. From 1274 the English king was the arbiter of western Europe; and even if his son was no equivalent match for the Scots or for his own dangerous wife Isabella, his grandson Edward III was to restore in full measure the great reputation of England. The Edwards were sovereigns of high international standing, and it is ridiculous to suppose that any of them would have yielded in dignity or artistic quality to any other western court. Edward III became Vicar-General of the Emperor for the lands west of the Rhine in 1338 and in 1347 would have been Emperor himself had he not declined the honour. His grandson Richard II, brother-in-law of the German king Wenceslaus, was himself a candidate for the Empire in 1397. Moving on such a level, the kings of England certainly maintained a state – for instance in architecture – not inferior to any other in western Christendom. That their gardens matched their buildings should never have been doubted. The royal accounts show the great outlay on horticulture year after year, and it was at this time that a genuinely scientific approach to botany can be discerned in the king's servants, men such as the forester and poet Geoffrey Chaucer, the physician John Bray and surgeon John Arderne, and the Dominican confessor Friar Henry Daniel.

There is even more specific evidence for the high esteem in which horticulture and arboriculture were held. Writing his famous *Philobiblon* in 1344, Richard of Bury the bishop of Durham and former tutor of Edward III placed them at the head of the arts surpassed only by the writing of books: 'destined to benefit endless generations . . . with which no planting of groves, no sowing of seeds . . . may be compared (*cui nulla virgultorum plantatio, nulla seminum satio comparatur*)'. Joret quotes the report of Guillebert de Metz that the taxes laid by the king of France on the supply of roses and other flowers used for chaplets and bouquets brought in 10,000 francs a year. Thorold Rogers found 2,000 hazelnut plants bought for 4s. 1d. in 1335, and in the next year 30,000 madder roots bought at 5d. the thousand, both transactions in Oxford. That there was a commercial outlet for transplanted hazel shows an advanced concept of woodland management which would not otherwise be suspected.

The gardener to the archbishop of Canterbury at Lambeth Palace, Roger, was able to buy seed of a wide selection of vegetables and herbs in 1321–22. He sowed 2 gallons (or pints ? – *lagen'*) of leek seed costing 2s. 8d., a gallon of worts (*olerum*) at 4d., 2 gallons of parsley seed for 1s. 6d., pennyworths of skirret (*Sium sisarum* L.), clary, and cress (*touncressis*); then cabbage (*caboche*) for 2d.; cucumber and gourd together (*concombr' & gourde*) for 2d.; hyssop for 6d.; spinach (*spynhach*) for 4d.; borage for 2d.; lettuce (*lutuse*) for 3d. and 'centurages' (? centaury) for 6d. Saffron, first mentioned at Saffron Walden in 1359, could soon be bought in quantity and its cultivation spread over a large area. In Abingdon in 1383–4 the monastic

Treasurer bought 12 elms from the gardener for 3s. Vine stocks for the vineyard at Windsor Castle were imported from La Rochelle in 1361–2, showing that the international carriage of living plants was already effective in the North, as we know that it was, long before, in the Islamic South **8**. Plant exchanges between friends are implied by a metaphorical allusion in Eustache Deschamps' ballad to Chaucer, where in complementing him on his English translation of the *Roman de la Rose*, Deschamps adds that Chaucer 'had long ago laid out a garden (*vergier*) for which he asked for plants.'

A good deal of attention was paid to the gardens in Windsor Castle, and we hear of other gardens such as the King's Garden near London Wall, a garden in the park at Odiham, and one at the manor of Henley in Ash (Surrey). Of these the one at Odiham was certainly a pleasure garden, surrounded with 124 perches (2,046 feet) of new hedge costing ¾d. the perch. The cost of making a herber in the park in 1332 was £3 17s. 7d., and four men were paid £1 12s. 0d. working for 24 days at 4d. each, on felling six oaks and getting 742 boards for the paling, others sawing timber and making the carpentry of the herber, with five doors, benches, and turf dug to cover them. This herber was especially made for Queen Philippa, a keen gardener like Eleanor of Provence and Eleanor of Castile. At Henley in 1343 the garden was dug and sown against the coming of the king and queen, which suggests adequate notice being given to get such annuals as borage into flower. There was a drawbridge between the hall and the garden, a watchtower, possibly a gazebo (*garetta*), and a fishpond. At Woodstock the princess Isabel's chamber had a balcony made to overlook the park (*ad respiciendum versus parcum*) in 1354. There are many references to turfing walks and supporting vines: at the Black Prince's manor of Kennington (Surrey) in 1362 timber and poles for the vines and mending the alleys of the garden cost £4 19s. 0d., showing that the vines were grown over tunnel-arbours or pergolas.

At Eltham the principal garden had a rampart walk, and a second walled garden was made in 1388–9 for the king and queen to have dinner there in summer time **70**. Rather earlier a garden pavilion or kiosk had been built at Sheen, on an island ('La Nayght') in the Thames, similarly a private retreat for the king and queen. Of the garden at Eltham we have a personal glimpse through the eyes of the Flemish chronicler Froissart. On his return to England in July 1395 he met his old friend Sir Richard Stury and they talked together walking up and down the gallery before the king's chamber at Eltham, and in the garden 'where it was very pleasant and shady, for those alleys were then covered with vines'. Richard II also kept up the vines in his father's old 'great garden' at Kennington, and at Windsor gave the Vineyard to Queen Anne; it produced 30 tuns of wine yearly.

Outside the royal gardens were others at the homes of the greater nobility and the manor houses of bishops and abbots. We hear of the garden of the Earl of Warenne at Sandal Castle in Yorkshire in 1309, some two acres in size with herbage worth 10s. yearly; of another garden of two acres in Golden Lane, London, belonging to the Earl of Suffolk in 1382; and a great garden of Sir James Audley in Shoe Lane off Fleet Street in 1382. From surviving accounts we know most about the gardens of the Lady of Clare, Elizabeth de Burgh, at Clare Castle (Suffolk) and at her manor of Bardfield in Essex ten miles away. On the utilitarian side the gardens of Clare produced green beans, leeks, apples, pears, onions and garlic, fuller's teasels, madder and hemp, and in normal years there was a surplus which was sold, as in 1336–37. That year a bushel of beans was bought for sowing and a quart of teasel seed, with garlic and onion sets as well as onion seed. Both at Clare and at Bardfield there was a master gardener, William, receiving 6 ells of stuff for a yearly robe each in 1343. William, the Castle gardener, was paid 2s. in 1341 for going to various places to get vine scions to plant. In 1342 a certain house in the herber was roofed for the Lady's deer (*pro ceruis domine*); and there is mention of the pool about the garden, part of the moat. Robert the carpenter made a 'tomb' above a 'sepulchre' in the lady's herber, taking 5 days at 3d. a day, with William his mate at 2½d. a day. Two men were repairing the glass chamber in the house of pheasants (*pro camera vitrea in domo feysants*); and in the following year two sawyers were sawing boards for the 'tomb' in the lady's herber, viz. rails, groundsill, lintels, pillars, studs etc. (*rales groundcell linteles pilers stothes*) for 'the said screen' (*pro dicta parclos*'), taking 13 days on the job and being paid 6s. 6d. William the carpenter covering (*tegent*') the same tomb (*tumb* written over *sepultur* deleted) for 3 days was paid 7½d **10**.

Four cartloads of rods were brought to support the vines by the Great Gate of the Castle, and quickthorns were obtained for planting. In 1345–46 Michael the carpenter was working on the Lady's herber for three weeks, which presumably means setting up rails and pergolas; and iron casements were supplied for two glass windows in the Lady's Upper Chamber, from which she might look down on the garden. In 1347 sand was taken from the mount next the Lady's Chamber to the garden and two men spent two days sanding, strewing and gathering stones in the garden and walks. The herber was cleaned and railed with rods round the walks (*aluras*), and turf was dug near Clarethall (another estate in Essex) and brought to repair the surface of the Great Herber. In 1348–49 one penny was paid for measuring the herber. Miscellaneous gifts presented by the Lady in 1351 included 1s. to a boy of Madame La Zousche, 4d. to John the Harper of Queen Philippa, 1s. 4d. to the wife of the Gardener of Bardfield for a cock and six hens, and 4d. to two little children 'who fished in front of my Lady (*qui pescherunt deuaunt ma dame*)' on the 23rd of May. Five pomegranates (*pommes garnetz*), bought for my lady from Bartholomew Thomas, cost 10s. In the next year 93½ perches (1,542¾ feet) of new hedge was made in the garden, about the woodyard, behind the garderobe, and against the gate of the Manor at Bardfield, and a man mended a bridge leading to the garden there. At Clare a 'fonteyne' was made in the Castle, costing £2. 16s. 11½d. In 1352 there is again mention of railing the Lady's herber. Expert forestry is suggested by William Harrison's statement, 200 years later, that the oak 'growing in Bardfield Park is the finest for Joiner's craft.'

What we are to make of some of this is not obvious. The glass chamber for pheasants (a boy was paid 2d. for taking three 'fesan' to Bardfield in 1356) and the wooden structure described as a tomb above a sepulchre are mysteries, but one may suggest that the first was an aviary and perhaps also an early glasshouse; the second was more probably a model of the Holy Sepulchre at Jerusalem than a real tomb or a mere piece of garden architecture. Some of the more humdrum details, however, are important evidence tending to dispel hoary superstitions on the subject of mediaeval gardens: that they had no paths, and that the fashion of railed beds came in only at the very end of the period. In fact there is a great deal more buttressing evidence on both these points in the accounts for the gardens at Westminster Abbey and at Winchester College. Lambeth Palace in the fourteenth century had a great garden and a flower garden as well as some nine acres of ground that eventually became Archbishop's Park. William of Wykeham at his manor of Highclere (Hants.) had a 'trapdoor' between his own private garden and the main garden, and in 1379 the bridge between the garden and the park was rebuilt. When the bishop was getting on in years, in fact about 74, in 1398, he had a new shelter and pentice made by which he might go down into the garden; 23,000 plain tiles and 250 ridges were used to cover this, which at standard sizes implies a structure about 280 feet long and 8 feet 6 inches wide. At Wykeham's principal country seat at Esher his gardener in 1393 was one J. Bury.

We already know of Abbot Godfrey's large herber of 1302 at Peterborough, identified by its double moat having survived to be planned in 1721 and altogether constituting a major

42 Simon Bening's miniature in the *Hennessy Book of Hours* (*c* 1510), showing Saints Cosmas and Damian, includes the grounds of a large mansion, with specimen trees, a pinnacled Gothic fountain, peacock, trellised herber and tunnel-arbour; the saints sit on a turf bench in a lawn of daisies and perhaps chamomile

43 The Virgin and Child, attended by angels, are in a summer-house from which the whole prospect of garden and landscape can be appreciated. Painted by a follower of Hans Memling for Queen Isabella of Spain (reigned 1474–1504), the contents of the picture are entirely Netherlandish (for detail see Pl. **VII A**)

44 Contrasting with **43** with its open raised beds is the roughly contemporary (*c* 1490) 'Mystical Marriage of St Catherine', where the garden proper consists of three parts. In front of a palace with open portico is a herber of square plots of lawn divided by paths; in the foreground, separated by a low embattled wall on which peacocks perch, is a flowery mead, with a shelter-arbour near its gate. To the left, beyond another dwarf wall, is a Gothic fountain in a hedged enclosed garden. To the right beyond sloping lawns a river flows between specimen trees into a skilfully designed landscape. Notwithstanding the contrast between these inner gardens and that of **43**, it is noteworthy that the treatment of lawns, river and trees is strikingly similar

complex of perhaps six acres (see plan, p. 85). Before 1335 there were large pleasure grounds of about three acres belonging to Winchester Cathedral Priory, described as *viridaria et deambulatoria* and approached through a *garite*, watch-tower or gazebo. In 1336 the monks, through the Archbishop of Canterbury, obtained a licence from the king to build an archway carrying a gallery (like the later Chain Gate at Wells) over the city wall and what is now College Street to reach these gardens without having to use the public road. Outside Winchester, at Manydown and Wootton St Laurence they had other pleasances for rest and exercise. Their Prior, as we know, had his country seat at Silkstead; and in the Close itself there were in 1335 the Convent Garden, the Almoner's Garden, and 'Le Joye' Garden kept by the Keeper of the Works. From the Convent Garden Robert Basing, the monk-gardener, had to provide flowers to deck the altars at high feasts, apples for Lent and Advent, and vegetables for the daily pottage. At Abingdon Abbey too there were separate gardens of the Sacrist, Treasurer, Precentor and Keeper of the Works. Bicester Priory (Oxon.) had the Prior's, Canons', Infirmarian's and Sacrist's gardens as well as the Great Garden, Kitchen Garden, and Orchard. The gardens at Durham belonging to the Cathedral Priory seem to have been mostly utilitarian, but besides the country rest-house of Finchale Priory there were parks around the city and we know, for instance, that payments were made in 1331 for cutting and pruning branches in Shincliff Park: possibly woodland management, possibly landscaping, perhaps both at once. The Master of the Infirmary in 1355–56 bought turf to mend his garden, and there is ample evidence that Durham was technically advanced in its horticulture. It had nursery plots called impgarth and impyard, and on the Priory estates there were strict conditions in leases as early as 1365, when the tenant of an orchard at Billingham had to manure the roots of the trees; while another lease there of 1374 stipulated for the clearance of the roots of old trees and the planting of new apples and pears (cf. p. 140). This compares with a German instance of 1350 at Fahrnau, where the tenants of St Blasien in the Black Forest were bound to plant seven young fruit trees each year. By 1383 a Durham Priory lease at Billingham insisted on the yearly planting of pears and other trees.

For details of fourteenth-century gardens of the highest rank we return to continental records which fill gaps in our own. As early as 1314 there was a wood of some 31 hectares (say 76 acres) at Helmond in the Netherlands, being the park attached to the Castle; but it was open for the public to wander there. It is likely that this case was not unique. Then we have the remarkable letter of about 1385 stating that in 'the Bois de Duc in France they grow flowers in glass pavilions turned to the South', which tends to confirm a wider interpretation of the glass aviary of 1343 at Clare. In Paris, though the largest garden actually in the old Louvre was only 6 toises in width, less than 40 feet, Charles V (1364–1380) formed at the Hôtel St Pol in the upper Rue St Antoine a pleasure garden of over 20 arpents, roughly 20 acres. Under Philippart Persant his chief gardener this was provided with trellised pavilions, a labyrinth, tunnel arbours, plantations of cherry-trees and many kinds of ornamental plant of which rose, rosemary, lavender, wallflower, marjoram and sage are recorded. In the 1390s the Archbishop of Rouen bought peacocks Pl.VIIA;42,44,48 for his manor of Déville, two miles west of the city, and the vines, seats and lawns of his gardens are mentioned. At his country gardens of Alihermont near Dieppe in 1397–98 grafts of fruit-trees, hazelnuts and roses were planted, alleys (*aleurs*) made and covered with vines.

The most complete inventory of purchases for an ornamental garden is that for Charles VI's replanting of the gardens of the Hôtel St Pol in 1398. There the Jardin du Champ-au-Plâtre was planted with a wide selection of trees and flowers which are recorded with their prices in *sous Parisis*. At the time the *sol parisis* was worth between 2d. and 3d. of contemporary English money. The *quarteron* was 25 (or 26) items sold by a price per hundred. There were 3 quarterons of Bordeaux grapevines and 375 '*gouais de morets*', apparently a type of vine not used for wine-making, but probably to train over the arbours; 115 grafts of pears at 21 *sous Parisis* the hundred; 100 common apple trees at 12*s.P.*; 12 Paradise apples at 4*s.P.* each; 1,000 cherry trees at 6*s.P.* the 100; 150 plum trees at 8*s.P.*; and 8 green bay trees, bought on the Pont-au-Change for 2*s.P.* each. The flowering plants were 300 bundles of white and red roses at 20*s.P.* the bundle (*gerbe*); 300 bulbs of lilies at 6*s.P.* the 100; and 300 flag iris (*flambes*) at 9*s.P.* We must bear in mind that Charles VI was an art-loving king of exquisite refinement, for whom some of the noblest works of art of the whole Middle Ages were commissioned: we cannot doubt that the design of the garden reached the same standard. The materials look so simple, only a dozen species and varieties of plant, it would seem – and of course grass. Yet, satiated with Versailles, what would we not give to see again the Jardin du Champ-au-Plâtre in spring and early summer?

CHAPTER SIX

The Garden and its Plants

WITH THE FOURTEENTH CENTURY we can take stock of the garden as a whole. In contrast to earlier periods there is now sufficient evidence to give a detailed account of the works that went to the making of the garden and of the plants both native and introduced. It was indeed a time when deliberate introduction of exotics is evidenced, as well as purely aesthetic interest in plants, and the formation of gardens of botanical importance. For the first time there are illustrations which bear out literary descriptions and the evidence of records, and even pictures of actual gardens in and near Paris and within 250 miles of London.

The literary information on gardens is of the highest authority, coming from the Court poet Chaucer and his immediate followers, pupils and imitators. Chaucer himself had a considerable knowledge of trees and other plants, and it is evident that he was particularly fond of flowers. Some of his own portraits were even adorned with the daisy, which he so praised:

> Now have I than swich a condicioun,
> That, of alle the floures in the mede,
> Than love I most these floures whyte and rede,
> Swiche as men callen daysies in our toun.
>
> ———
>
> And I love hit, and ever y-lyke newe,
> And ever shal, til that myn herte dye.
>
> ———
>
> Hoom to myn hous ful swiftly I me spedde
> To goon to reste, and erly for to ryse,
> To seen this flour to sprede, as I devyse.
> And, in a litel herber that I have,
> That benched was on turves fresshe y-grave,
> I bad men sholde me my couche make . . .

Again, in *The Marchantes Tale* he described the pleasance of the old knight Januarie, who

>   Shoop him to live ful deliciously.
>   His housinge, his array, as honestly
>   To his degree was maked as a kinges.
>   Amonges othere of his honest thinges,
>   He made a gardin, walled al with stoon;
>   So fair a gardin woot I nowher noon.
>   For out of doute, I verraily suppose,
>   That he that wroot the Romance of the Rose
>   Ne coude of it the beautee wel devyse;
>   Ne Priapus ne mighte nat suffyse,
>   Though he be god of gardins, for to telle
>   The beautee of the gardin and the welle,
>   That stood under a laurer alwey grene.

while in *The Frankeleyns Tale* we hear that

>   ... on the sixte morwe of May,
>   Which May had peynted with his softe shoures
>   This gardin ful of leves and of floures;
>   And craft of mannes hand so curiously
>   Arrayed hadde this gardin, trewely,
>   That never was ther gardin of swich prys,
>   But-if it were the verray paradys.
>   Th'odour of floures and the fresshe sighte
>   Wolde han maad any herte for to lighte
>   That ever was born ...

The fact that gardens were large and complex is brought out by *Pierce the Ploughman's Crede* of c 1394:

>   And all was walled that wone though it wid were
>   With posterns in pryvitie to pasen when hem list,
>   Orcheyardes and erberes eused well clene.

Still more detail comes from the supplementary *Tale of Beryn* (spelling modernized):

>   The wife of Bath was so weary, she had no will to walk.
>   She took the Prioress by the hand: 'Madam! will ye stalk
>   Privily into the garden, to see the herbès grow?'
>   ———
>   The Prioress, as woman taught of gentle blood, and hend [polite]
>   Assented to her counsel; and forth then go they wend,
>   Passing forth full softly into the herbery;
>   For many a herbè grew, for sew [pottage] and surgery;
>   And all the alleys fair y-pared [trimmed], y-railed and y-maked;
>   The sage and the hyssop y-fretted and y-staked;
>   And other beds by and by full fresh y-dight:
>   For comers to the host, right a sportful sight.

In Lydgate's *Troy Book*, written between 1412 and 1420, but still reflecting the type of planting and gardening of his youth in Richard II's time, we even see a complete prototype of the English landscape of a distant future:

> And all about this mighty chief city,
> Whereas Cethes held his royal see,
> Were fresh rivers of which the water clean
> Like crystal shone against the sun's sheen;
> Fair plains, as Guido beareth witness,
> And wholesome hills full of lustiness
> And many a lea and many a lusty well....
> Full many a park, full fair and fresh to seen
> And many woods and many meadows green,
> With sundry flowers among the herbès meynt [mixed],
> Which on their stalks nature hath depeynt [painted]
> With sundry hues...
>
> And Aurora, of heart and whole intent,
> With the sweetness of her silver showers
> Bedewed had the fresh summer flowers
> And made the rose with new balm fleet [overflow],
> The sweet lily and the marguerite.
> For to unclose their tender leaves white,
> Oppressed hearts with gladness to delight
> That dreary were afore of night's tene [trouble];
> And honeysuckles among the bushes green
> Embalmed had environ all the air.

This mention of the honeysuckle certainly refers to the climbing woodbine, where earlier usage generally signified species of clover.

Finally the noblest imitator of Chaucer, King James I of Scotland, imprisoned in the Earl Marshal's Tower of Windsor Castle **40** from 1413 to 1424, gives us a thumb-nail sketch of the great King's Garden across the ditch and opposite his barred window, where he first caught sight of his future queen Jane Beaufort, granddaughter of John of Gaunt:

> Now there was made fast by the tower wall
> A garden fair, and in the corners set
> A herber green, with wands so long and small
> Railed all about: and so with trees close set
> Was all the place, and hawthorn hedges knit
> That no one though he were near walking by
> Might there within scarce any one espy.
>
> So thick the branches and the leafage green
> Beshaded all the alleys that there were,
> And midst of ev'ry herber might be seen
> The sharp and green sweet-scented juniper,
> Growing so fair with branches here and there,
> That, as it seemed to any one without,
> The branches spread the herber all about.

Further on he alludes to 'this garden full of flowers', and among them the fairest was the Lady

45 The calendar for April, from the destroyed part of the *Turin Book of Hours* (*c* 1400), was one of the earliest detailed views of the small garden with its fences and trellis. (From the collotype plate of the edition of the manuscript by Paul Durrieu, 1902)

46 This miniature (*c* 1415) from a French manuscript of the poems of Christine de Pisan, depicts lovers in a garden forming an imaginary counterpart to that at Windsor where, in real life, James I of Scotland courted the Lady Jane Beaufort. In the background, on a lawn with raised turf benches set with flowers, stand ornamental trees. The loving couple stand on a flowery mead hedged in by a low trellis to which are tied roses, apparently the white *Rosa alba* on the left, and a striped red-and-white rose of the type of 'Rosa Mundi' (*R. gallica versicolor*) on the right

Jane; but there is no reason to doubt that this was indeed a herber richly set with ornamental plants.

In a contemporary French miniature of two lovers in a garden **46** we can see almost exactly the setting of the real-life romance of James and Jane. On a lawn of close turf, sprinkled with pink daisies and taller white camomile or marguerites, stands a low trellis covered with white and red roses. In the background are trees and turf benches against the battlements of a castle wall. There is even an English picture, painted about 1400 by the illuminator John, showing a king and queen seated on such turf benches in a castle garden, playing chess **Pl.IIIA**. Here the benches are set against a close paling fence within the outer ward; and on the far side of the way between the outer and inner gates is another paled garden with trees, a gardener trimming shrubs with a billhook **47C**, and a flower-border against the wall beyond. Other French, German and Italian miniatures, though less actual and more symbolic, agree in their impression of ornamental gardens with trees, shrubs, fountains, wells and springs, and flowers growing in the turf of extensive lawns. Although many elements constantly re-appear, there was great variety in the design of gardens and of garden architecture **45–62**.

Within a few years all these indirect portrayals of the garden fade before the Flemish realism of Hubert Van Eyck and Pol de Limbourg. Van Eyck, in the calendars for April and June of the destroyed *Hours of Turin* shows precise details of a trellised garden and of fruit-picking in an orchard **45**. The *Très Riches Heures du Duc de Berry* goes a step further and provides what are virtually colour-photographs of the landscape and garden at the Château de Dourdan and at the Palais in Paris. Dourdan **Pl.IVB** may stand for the type of horticulture practised in England at Kenilworth Castle (see plan, p. 107). In the background is the castle, with the houses of the town clustered beyond its barbican, overlooking a large lake in which men are fishing from boats with nets: this could be observed, as at Kenilworth, from ranges of windows high in the castle walls. On the hither side of the lake is a wide expanse of grassy parkland, planted with trees in rows or clumps: pollard willows near the water's edge, tall timber trees on the left, and a grove to the right. In front of this is the garden of a lodge or 'standing' in the park, protected by high stone walls against which shrubs are planted on the outer side. Inside, a tunnel-arbour is built against the walls, formed of the long and slender wands described by King James, and grape-vines are planted to cover these arbours. The garden within the arbours is divided by a trellis and on one side of it are chequered beds and plots of turf. In the beds are fruit-trees in flower. The view of the Parisian palace **Pl.IVA** is less revealing, being taken from a lower angle, but above the embattled wall we can see trees, a tunnel-arbour running parallel to the Seine, and behind it a covered staircase of masonry and timber framing descending from the upper apartments to the level of the garden courtyard. At the south end of the arbour, no doubt at the intersection of another alley leading eastwards towards the west front of the Sainte Chapelle, is a lofty dome of rods, covered like the arbours with vines.

Within the general framework of these descriptions and pictures we can easily interpret the records of work at actual gardens. At Ely Place in Holborn in 1372–73 new hedges were made around the great garden, to a total length of 121 perches (1,996½ feet), which implies an area of nearly six acres. Four cartloads of thorns cost 6s. 8d. and two men made the hedge at 3½d. the perch, amounting to £1 15s. 8½d. and with the quicksets £2 1s. 11½d. At Lambeth Palace was an even larger Great Garden of the Archbishop of Canterbury, provided with a new hedge of 156 perches (2,574 feet) at 3d. a perch in 1410–11. Two cartloads of 'raylys' were felled in Norwood and taken to Lambeth for 3s. and three men spent 13 days on railing the vines in the Little Garden and on pruning. On the west side of the walled garden in 1428–29 elms were felled in 'le Rowe Garden', which suggests that Lambeth had elms

47 Jean Bourdichon's calendars in the *Hours of Queen Anne of Brittany* (1501–07) for the months March, April and May show details of horticultural activity

A In May, revellers with green branches disport themselves in a park with artificial planting that includes a tall trained 'estrade' tree surrounded by a triple-tiered wickerwork bench

B April depicts a small enclosed herber with turf benches and roses on trellis. In spite of the earliness of the seaon, roses are being picked to make coronets and garlands

C March gives a realistic view of a gardener active with his bill-hook

48 Jan van Eyck's famous Madonna (*c* 1425) includes a detailed view of a terrace garden overlooking a Gothic city. A wall-walk behind the battlements, enlivened by peacocks, is reached by stone steps from a sunken garden in which a narrow path separates thickly planted beds: identifiable flowers are limited to flag iris (left) and Madonna lilies (centre). Low-growing herbaceous plants are set along the wall-walk at the foot of the parapet

49 The garden in Rogier van der Weyden's 'Virgin, Child and St Luke' (*c* 1440) is a prototype of the harbour scene (see **51**), but is horticulturally distinct. The wall-walk here is paved, and the garden a flowery mead of plants growing in turf, without paths or beds

50 The garden seen through the window of van der Weyden's 'Annunciation' (*c* 1460) displays another variant of the courtyard herber enclosed within turf benches which are planted with flowers. Trained trees in tubs, probably tender evergreens, are placed inside the castle wall, and the inner space is divided by a path. In the foreground is a 'flowery mead' lawn; beyond the path is a large raised bed divided into sections. On the left the first division has a low rail, while in the centre is a horizontal framework, probably to give support to pinks or carnations

51 In the Master of St Gudule's painting of *c* 1470, the terrace-garden of a castle overlooks a harbour (see **49**). Within the brick battlements is a raised bench of turf with a few clumps of flag iris and other border plants including columbine (right). The terrace is a sheet of gravel with regularly placed beds, slightly raised and edged with bricks laid flat. Some beds contain a single species, ? rosemary or hyssop, lavender, ? rue, pinks; another is planted with trained shrubs

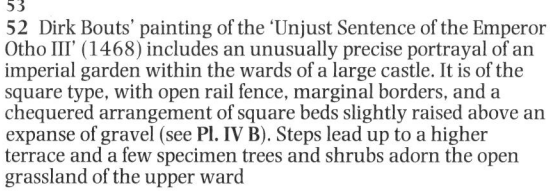

52 Dirk Bouts' painting of the 'Unjust Sentence of the Emperor Otho III' (1468) includes an unusually precise portrayal of an imperial garden within the wards of a large castle. It is of the square type, with open rail fence, marginal borders, and a chequered arrangement of square beds slightly raised above an expanse of gravel (see **Pl. IV B**). Steps lead up to a higher terrace and a few specimen trees and shrubs adorn the open grassland of the upper ward

53 Jan Mostaert's 'Portrait of a Man' (c 1510) includes a roof garden with a trained 'estrade' tree and a pergola, and also a balcony garden with a canopy of vines

54 Jacopo de' Barbari's map of 1500 marks suburban villas on the Giudecca at Venice. The ornamental gardens of the two largest houses, one with a loggia, show the mediaeval system of small beds combined with the simplest form of open knot

55A

55A One of the illustrations in the French version of Crescenzi (*c* 1485) presents the intimate walled herber, beyond which stretches the distant landscape of the park. Note the stream of water in the foreground, the small beds surrounded by brick edging, and the elaborately trained shrubs as centrepieces.
B The detail shows one method of supporting fine plants of carnations. Within the first generation from its effective introduction into northern gardens, the care of the carnation had become a highly developed cult.

55B

planted in lines like the earlier ones at Wells Cathedral (p. 16). In 1413 that good but irritatingly sanctified 'creature', Margery Kempe, had an interview with Archbishop Arundel in the garden at Lambeth and boldly reprehended the cursing and swearing of the clerks, squires and yeomen of his household. The archbishop was astonishingly patient and talked with her 'till stars appeared in the firmament.'

Another important garden on the South Side belonged to the London Bridge House. Near St Olave's church, it contained an arbour, a fountain and ponds; in it official entertainments were held after the audits of the Bridgemasters' accounts **Pl.VIII**. The feast of 1423 cost £4 19s. 6d. (say £2,500 in 1980). A London ironmonger, Robert Parish of St Michael's, Queenhithe, in 1406 left £1 (say £450 – £500 now) to Eleanour 'the woman who looks after my garden across the Thames (*custodienti gardinum meum deultra Thamisiam*).' This was perhaps a commercial market garden like one in Tower Ward near London Wall which in 1375 had been leased for 30 years at 10s. (about £250) a year. The six-acre Holborn garden of the Bishop of Ely was leased for £1 yearly from 1379, and the vineyard for £2 (say £1,000).

The leasing of land was again becoming general, and the terms of leases reveal the value set on gardens. In 1390 the lord of Glynde in Sussex, Sir William Waleys, granted a lease of Glynde Place for 20 years to John Russel and his wife Joan: the Russels were to be free to cultivate the gardens but Waleys reserved the fruit to himself. In about 1350 a croft of land near Bristol was granted along with an adjoining herber and a strip of land a foot wide all round its benches (*cum uno pede terre in latitudine circumquoque extra banchos herbarij*) **50**. When dower was assigned at the manor of Teynham at Sharsted in Doddington (Kent) in 1374, the premises included a 'kechengardyn' running from the new chamber east to the ditch of the great garden, these gardens amounting to 2 acres, with another garden of 3 acres called Bournes. We already know (p. 17) of the garden and nursery at Merriott in Somerset delivered in 1369 to the widow of Sir John de Meriet. In 1390 Joan, widow of Sir Ralph Basset of Drayton, had dower in his manor of Sheringham (Norfolk), including a granary and an enclosed garden west of it, with the pools inside the garden. The widow of a Norwich mason who died in 1469 was assured 'her plesur in the gardeyne at all tymes.'

From such records we get an impression of the different categories of gardens: the kitchen garden distinct from the great garden; the herber as a close garden surrounded by benches; the manorial garden with pools – surely a pleasure garden – which Lady Basset could enjoy in her widowhood. In some cases, and Merriott was one, the gardens are associated with parks and woods as in Lydgate's description. It is here that we reach the explanation of the fallacy regarding the supposed small scale and lack of importance of mediaeval gardens. The pleasure grounds of palaces and mansions included not only small herbers but orchards with fish-ponds and other pools, and at times aviaries and menageries. The creation of such luxuries was a recognized activity: as far back as 1176 Peter of Blois, archdeacon of Bath, writing to the archbishop of Canterbury, Richard Dover, asked mockingly what glory it was to construct ponds (*vivaria*) and to shut up wild beasts in a park (*indagine*)?.

Factual records bring garden and park together, as at the Bishop of Worcester's manor of Alvechurch in 1299, when the pasture of the garden was not valued because the animals from the park browsed on it. The Almoner of Durham Priory in 1373 accounted for £1 12s. 10d. spent on enclosing the Park of Codesley by Durham and making a garden there. We have seen the substantial evidence for sowing and planting trees, but must here recapitulate what concerns the tradition of the 'greater garden' as a precursor of post-mediaeval developments. Beginning with Henry I's Woodstock a chain of royal works runs parallel to the paradises of Spain, Italy and Avignon. A key concept is the 'Gloriette' **1, 56–59**, a word of Spanish origin for a pavilion placed at the centre of a garden of four quarters of

56 This Flemish miniature, in *L'instruction d'un jeune Prince* (c 1470), showing the book's presentation to Charles the Bold, Duke of Burgundy, places the function in a large garden in front of a 'Gloriette' built of brick and stone, with open loggia. There are low rectangular beds and high turfed benches, a trained plant in an ornamental vase, and an octagonal picnic table. In the right foreground is a large plant of columbine.

57 A garden from the *Roman de Renaud de Montauban* (1468–70) shows a 'Gloriette' or summer-house fitted up for open-air meals. Behind are large rectangular beds of turf between paths; one bears a trained 'estrade' tree. In the foreground is a flower border with violets and strawberries.

1 Canterbury Cathedral: stained glass in the west window includes a figure of Adam of *c* 1178. Delving with an iron-shod spade outside the Garden of Eden, he stands as the prototype of English gardeners

II Florence: Medici Palace, Chapel. Wall-painting by Benozzo Gozzoli, 1459-63.
The landscape, though notionally representing oriental lands traversed by the Magi, is evidently based on North Italy and shows planted and managed woodlands, with rows of trees and individual shrubs. The treatment of road, river, bridge and embankments indicates a highly artificial rather than a natural landscape

III A *(top)* An English illuminator who signed his name as 'Johannes' shows a king and queen at chess on their castle lawn, which is studded with flowering plants. The fences are of close upright boards; in another garden in the background a gardener is trimming shrubs with a billhook; behind him is a herbaceous border against the castle wall (*c* 1400)

III B A French minature from the *Roman de la Rose* of *c* 1400, showing Narcissus at the spring, within a garden of the 'wilderness' type. Beasts and birds amid the trees show that the walled paradise is in fact a game park

IV The *Très Riches Heures* illuminated for Jean, duc de Berry, by Pol de Limbourg and his brothers in 1409-16, provides the earliest precise information on the appearance of European buildings and landscapes now lost. Two of its views are the first representations of actual mediaeval gardens to survive

IV A *(top)* Pol de Limbourg's calendar for June gives us almost a colour photograph of the royal palace at Paris, alongside the Seine. Great tunnel-arbours covered with vines surround the privy garden, connected at the angles by domes of 'birdcage' framing. Out of sight were beds of brilliant flowers and roses on low trellis (see also **46**)

IV B The calendar for April, another superb miniature by Pol de Limbourg, shows the landscape setting of the Château de Dourdan, with trees deliberately placed, a lake with fishing from a boat, and in the foreground a lodge or gloriet with its own walled garden. This has one of the normal arrangements of vine-clad arbours along the walls, trellis, and a chequerwork of small beds and patches of lawn (see also **52**). On the beds standard fruit trees are coming into flower

V   One of two famous paintings (*c* 1410-20) by a master from the Upper Rhine, this provides the best evidence for mediaeval plantsmanship. The use, in combination, of trees, border flowers, and smaller plants, displays a tradition quite distinct from that of small beds set between paths or grass lawns. For a discussion of the plants see p. 126; and for another picture by the same master, see **72**

VI Stefan Lochner's famous painting of the Madonna in the Rose Arbour (*c* 1440) is one of the first to show climbing roses trained over a pergola (see also **39**), an open construction quite unlike the shady walk provided by a tunnel-arbour. For the problem of such double-flowered climbing roses, see **30** and p. 164. In the turf, a flowery mead, daisies, violets, red clover and strawberries can be identified

VII A *(top)* A follower of Hans Memling painted (*c* 1490) for Queen Isabella of Spain a religious subject set in a summer-house with a complete view of a northern garden. In front of a Netherlands mansion are formal rectangular beds and sanded walks, with trimmed 'estrade' shrubs, carnations supported on trellis, and a railed bed of lavender. Peacocks have the freedom of wide lawns stretching down to the river with swans, backed by a landscaped park. For the whole picture, see **43**

VII B This miniature, in the *Roman de Renaud de Montauban* of *c* 1475, shows Maugis and La Belle Oriande seated in a garden of rather formal design based on expanses of open gravel. The pot of trained red carnations exhibits this flower in the first flush of its introduction to Northern Europe, but the turf is still beset with plants in the old manner of the flowery mead

VIII Festival of the Guild of Archers, 1493. The 'Master of Frankfort' has here pictured a garden feast typical of those held by civic bodies and the greater companies and guilds of the western world, including Britain. The turf plots are largely composed of flowers, mainly daisies and buttercups; in the apple tree above the canopied Master's bench hangs a song-bird in its cage

58 The *Tractie de Conseil* (*c* 1500) contains views of a pavilion and park. Two gardeners are here at work, one digging and the other trimming a tree with a bill-hook. The impression of open landscape, with trees and plantings of shrubs, is noteworthy (see also **14, 59, 62**).

59 Jean Miélot's miniatures in Christine de Pisan's *Epistle of Othéa to Hector*, dated 1461, depict scenes in the park of the Duke of Burgundy at Hesdin. Note the artificial character of the tree planting (see **14, 58, 62**)

Moorish type: hence *glorieta* still signifies a 'circus' at the intersection of avenues, or a summer-house placed there. Later the word was used for a 'lodge' of seigneurial apartments in a park or grounds. Everswell at Woodstock was in fact if not in name a gloriet, but the name too was given to the works at Leeds in Kent carried out for Edward I's queen, Eleanor of Castile, between 1278 and her death in 1290. A large lake was formed around the earlier castle, with an 'inner' island supporting the Gloriette, approached by a two-storied bridge.

This layout, for a Spanish queen who was sister of Alfonso the Learned, and given a Spanish name, is of outstanding importance for its date, a few years before the analogous developments at the castle of Hesdin. Count Robert II of Artois there enclosed a great park in 1295 and began a 'House in the Marsh' with a Gloriette in a great pool, approached by a bridge, an aviary and a 'chapel of glass', still unfinished at his death in 1302. Count Robert's works included a fantastic series of water-engines based on the Arabic *Book of Mechanical Devices* (AD 1206) of Ibn al-Razzaz al-Jazari of Diyarbakir. These produced surprise jets and showers, a talking owl, gadgets which dropped the unwary into a mass of feathers, blew soot and flour in their faces before confronting them with mirrors, and played many other practical jokes. However we view the taste of such entertainment, it is of the highest significance that the tradition of *burladores* in Spanish gardens, to drench the visitor, is not a device of the Renaissance but has a far older Islamic origin. The engines at Hesdin were kept in repair through the Hundred Years War but, along with the town, castle and park, were destroyed by Charles V after the siege of 1553. Some idea of the landscape and pavilions at Hesdin can be obtained, as Mlle. Marguerite Charageat has pointed out, from Jean Miélot's miniatures of 1455–61 **59**.

Another English gloriet was at Corfe Castle, where it was rebuilt for Richard II in 1377–78, and the 'spyhouse' of 1440–41 in the Mews at Charing Cross, with four windows, plastered, pargetted and painted green, was probably a small gloriet. The royal gallery for watching tournaments in Cheapside, London, built for Edward III about 1332, can be associated with the gloriets in that all were observation posts for the contemplation of scenery and gardens, or for spectatorship of fishing, hunting or jousting. The building of gloriets, belvederes, galleries and grandstands was not limited to royalty, but spread to nobles and prelates. At Dartington Hall (Devon), built for Richard II's half-brother John Holand, earl of Huntingdon, in 1389–99, is a garden gallery of two storeys overlooking a sunken terrace apparently formed for Holand's favourite sport of jousting. At Kenilworth, John of Gaunt the king's uncle (titular king of Castile) was building the Strong Tower in the state apartments, overlooking both lake and park. Henry V in 1414–17 added to Kenilworth a Pleasance in the Marsh (as at Hesdin) beyond the lake, a double-moated enclosure of nine or ten acres with a central area of some $2\frac{1}{2}$ acres around a banquet-house (see plan). In 1463 seven labourers were working in the Pleasance and six others on '*le Aleyes*' there, showing that it was maintained as a garden. Another garden in the Castle is implied in the same account by payments to 12 men digging foundations in the midst of the Garden for jousting (*in medio Gardini pro le Justyngplace*).

There was a big distinction between the magnates and the rest of the nobility, and we must only expect great pleasure grounds at the homes of earls or of the bishops and abbots who were peers of the realm. A few priors of monastic cathedrals shared this exalted position, notably at Durham and Winchester. The Prior's Lodging at Canterbury, too, finished at the north end in '*Le Gloriet*' overlooking the great gardens. At Broughton Castle (Oxon.), among works done for William of Wykeham *c* 1380 was an unusual belvedere above a tall loggia of two arches, looking over the battlements of the outer walls at the moat and at 'The Warren' on the opposite hillside. This lookout may have served also as a 'standing' from which game

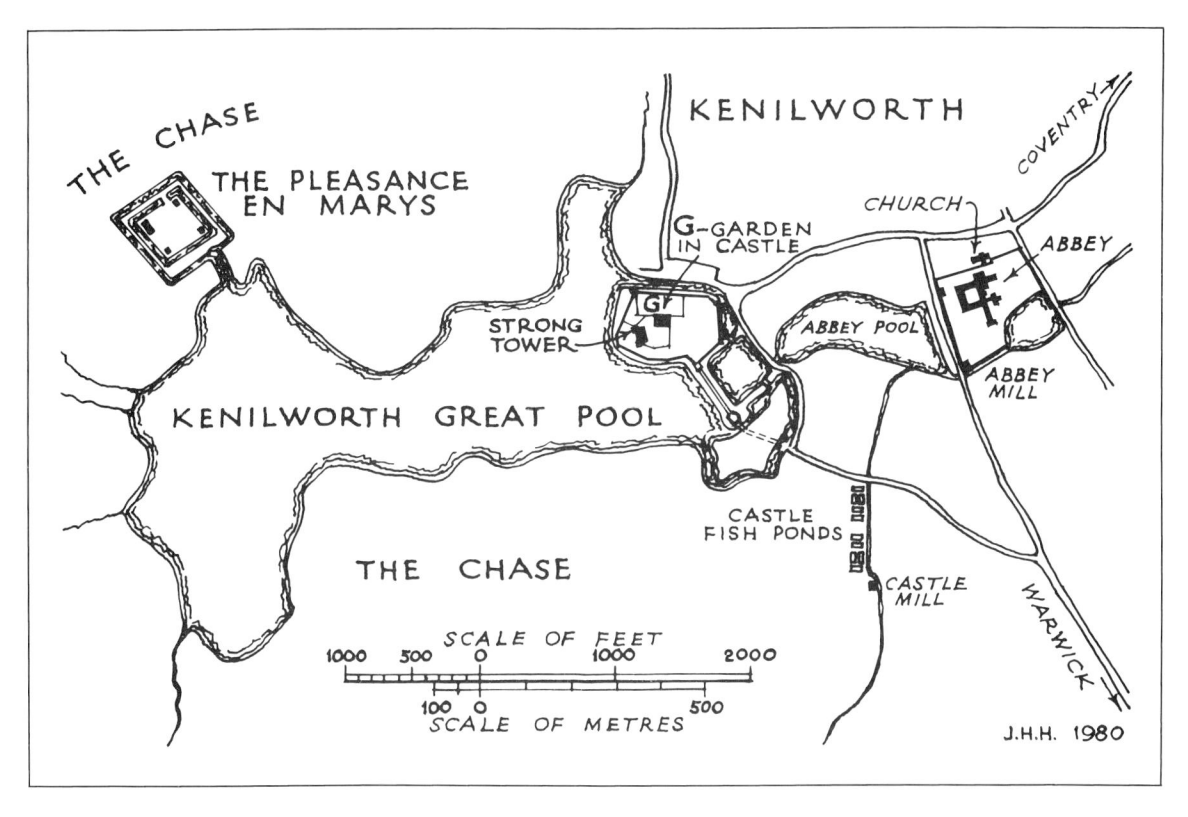

Plan of Kenilworth Castle and its outworks, with the Great Pool and the Pleasance in the Marsh, double-moated like the abbot's herber at Peterborough, and accessible only by water.

in the warren might be shot. Later such appurtenances of country estates became more common, and Charles Coulson has recently pointed out the permission granted to Richard Beauchamp, esquire, in 1460 to make a castellated pavilion in his new park of 1,300 acres at Bronsil near Ledbury.

Another category of gardens deserving mention is that of the grounds of university colleges. The element of recreation and pleasure could be developed in relative freedom from strictly utilitarian considerations such as tended to rule the layout of monastic precincts. Heads of houses and Fellows were as well placed as abbots, and the interest of academics in gardening goes far back. Konrad von Megenberg (1309–1374), the German scientist, noted that professors at Paris grew basil in the little gardens by their bedrooms (*in irn gärtlein vor ir slâfkamern*). In England there were at least small college gardens by the fourteenth century, both at Oxford and at Cambridge. At King's Hall, Cambridge, there was a 'serjeant of the garden' (*serviens in gardino*) who was paid for nailing up and pruning the vine in 1339. In 1362–63 the ground towards the river was laid out and a labourer paid 3d. a day to make herbers (*herbaria*). More material interests dictated the payment for saffron to grow in the garden in 1383. Corpus Christi College had a vineyard by 1348; Pembroke College in 1363 acquired an existing garden; Peterhouse in 1375 concentrated on growing its own food, buying seeds of vetches, colewort, cress, garlic, leek, parsley and saffron. At Wykeham's New College in Oxford vines were planted in 1390 and were tended as late as 1576; the garden there seems always to have been held in regard. So it was at Wykeham's junior school at

60 The Flemish illustrations to the *Roman de la Rose* (c 1485) show the noblest pleasure gardens of the fifteenth century. Trellised fences divide sections of herber from one another, designed in various ways, one with raised beds, turfed benches and roses grown on rails; another of turf pied with daisies about an ornamental fountain which feeds a channeled stream

61 On another leaf of the same manuscript a courtly company performs a stately dance to the music of harp, oboe and fife-and-drum. Within the walls of the garden, trees regularly spaced in ones and twos border a broad lawn, pied with daisies as before

Winchester, where the dozen adult fellows had not only a large kitchen garden but a pleasance termed 'Rosemoundes Bowre'. A succession of gardeners received a yearly fee from the beginning in 1394, as well as a livery of ray cloth and coloured cloth. Another sort of cloth called 'westmale' was also bought, for collecting and keeping the garden seeds. The garden, which lay at a low level in wet ground, was raised with many loads of 'robuse', and the walks laid out with hempen cords and measuring lines bought for the purpose. Seeds and young plants were bought regularly, as well as rods for the bower and to form railings, also called 'lez traylyngez', possibly trellis. Weeding, mowing the lawn, making hedges, laying turf and spreading manure were the order of the year, then as now.

Most of the processes of gardening are indeed age-old, and are mentioned again and again in surviving accounts. We cannot tell, in most cases, whether the costs incurred were for utility or pleasure, but generally it is safe to assume that the doctrine of multiple purposes held good. Here a number of extracts will be given in methodical order, to show the techniques involved and to provide some index to mediaeval expenditure. When a garden was to be formed, the first essential was enclosure. This normally involved the formation of an external ditch with a fence or hedge on the bank made by casting up the soil inwards. We saw this operation carred out at Alton Priors in 1261; at Silkstead in 1332, 68 perches of such a ditch around Beauforest were cleaned for 1d. the perch; at Eltham in 1355 a length of 660 feet of ditch was dug about the king's garden; in 1400 at Clare Castle 396 feet of a ditch 12 feet wide by 8 feet deep were dug, cleared and cleaned, between the garden and the east side of the outer bailey, with another small ditch leading from the bridge called 'Pysenbrugg' to the same ditch. This work amounted to $45\frac{1}{2}$ days' works at 4d. a day. In the same year the roof of the gardener's house at 'le Dernegate' was covered with 6,000 tiles costing 3s. 4d. a thousand plus carriage.

Inside the bounding ditch might be a paling fence **Pl.IIIA**, like one made round the herber at Clarendon in 1251; or a live hedge, or a stone wall **62**. The Prior of Winchester at Chilbolton (Hants.) had a hedge made round the garden opposite the church in 1280, but in 1308 this was replaced by walls. At Silkstead in the latter year 38 perches of new ditch were dug at 5d. a perch to enclose the herbs and vines of the manor, and quickset was gathered for 1s. 7d. The hedge was made for 1d. a perch with the plants collected, and 5d. was spent on roofing the garden gate. Bought quicksets cost 1s. 6d. a thousand at Malden (Surrey) in 1316, but only 1s. 3d. at Weedon (Bucks.) in 1382. At Silkstead in 1321 they were bought at only $7\frac{1}{2}$d. the thousand. Live hedges had to be kept in condition, and in 1324 and 1336 those at Silkstead were pleached (*plessare, plasschare*): cutting and pleaching 61 perches of live hedge next Beauforest in 1324 and 43 perches next Tarent were charged at 1d. for every two perches. At Bardfield (Essex) two men were cutting thorns to make hedges for 3 days at $1\frac{1}{2}$d. each; a boy carried the thorns for a day at 1d.; and two men made a hedge around the 'Wodezerd' in 3 days, each being paid $1\frac{1}{2}$d. a day, in 1341; but at Clare in 1388 the daily rate of 4d. each was paid to John Bishop and John Priour working for 12 days on stopping hedges within the Castle and about the pool or moat (*stagnum*) in 'le Closgardyn' for keeping fish there, and digging out noxious weeds. A more ambitious type of hedge with trees deliberately planted in it was to be made by the abbot and convent of St John's, Colchester, in 1327, when it was agreed that they should have the boughs from the trees growing in the hedge for its support.

Walls were often built around gardens; though more costly in outlay they were generally economical in maintenance. To keep the weather out many walls were roofed with tiles, as at Silkstead in 1276 when pegs were bought for roofing the wall round the herber; but at Westminster Abbey in 1365 a wall in the garden was crested with reed thatch for 10s. Four high stone walls enclosed the green herber next to the great hall of Bristol where Crown pleas

62 The *Book of Hours of Isabella of Portugal* (c 1480) shows King René d'Anjou writing his treatise of the 'Mortification of Vain Pleasure' seated in his garden house. Details of the garden, with raised beds and walks of chequered paving, are well seen on the left. The whole complex constitutes a moated pleasance approached by a wooden bridge from the road, which is bordered by rows of trees

were heard in 1285; and in 1294 winter storms brought down walls about the garden and the priory herber at Dunstable, making repair difficult. Westminster Abbey had a stone wall **78** built next the vineyard in the garden of the Infirmary in 1311, and in 1319 Abbot Godfrey of Peterborough had a stone wall built round the abbey's new orchard at Kettering. At the Black Prince's manor of Kennington the great mason Henry Yeveley built a stone wall along the garden at £4 a perch of 16½ feet, and a wall along the highroad, 11 feet high, at £4 6s. 8d. a perch. A stone wall of ashlar was built round the Infirmarer's garden at Westminster Abbey in 1374–76 for £16 13s. 4d.

Buildings in gardens are frequently mentioned, sometimes the gardeners' houses, as at King's Langley in the vineyard in 1297. In 1391–92 at Westminster Abbey the Infirmarer had work done on the old chamber in his garden, and also spent £24 1s. 9½d. on building a new house there. Mentions of a timber-framed chamber in the garden around the Jewel House in Westminster Palace in the 1450s must imply a royal summerhouse **78**. We have seen that there were cloisters in some gardens, as at the royal manor of Guildford, and at Sheen in 1366–67 a cloister was paved and a herber made within it. Turf for the herbers and lawns has often been mentioned: at Westminster in 1307–08 it was dug locally at 'Hasardesmersh' and Tothill for 1s. per hundred turves. In 1457 the Westminster cloister garth was scythed three times. The ravages of moles in lawns are often brought to mind by payments to mole-catchers such as Thomas 'Mollere' who was paid 4s. in 1344 for catching moles in the meadows and lands at Bardfield. In 1422–23 the Master of the Infirmary at Durham paid 3s. 4d. for catching mice about the herber.

Turf was also provided for the benches, as in 1311 at Windsor Castle, when 1,300 turves were dug for the benches of the herber between the hall and the royal lodging to the east of it on the north side of the Lower Ward. In 1312–13 at Westminster some 10,000 turves were dug and brought to the palace from Fulham and elsewhere, when benches were being made. In the 1380s the benches of the palace gardens were again repaired with turf. A special type of bench, often seen in garden pictures of the fifteenth century, was made round a tree with a wattled circular wall holding the soil, on top of which turf was laid **47,59**. In 1484 the Westminster Abbey Almoner had such a bench (*Le Bank*) made round a tree in the Cloister for 2s. 4d., and in 1498 stakes and rails were provided for the tree in the Cloister. Miss Verena Smith has discovered that a woodcut border depicting the picking of fruit from an apple-tree planted within a bench of this kind, printed in Paris in 1503, was used as a cartoon by the carver of the De La Warr Chantry of 1532 in Boxgrove Priory, Sussex **63**.

A labourer made paths in the Westminster Abbey gardens for ten weeks in 1359, and 5s. was paid for sand to strew on them, agreeing with Lydgate's reference in *The Churle and the Bird*, that 'all the alleys were made playne with sand.' At Kenilworth in 1440 three cartloads of gravel were brought to lay in the Castle entrance. Some walks were beneath tunnel-arbours, which were presumably what William Worcestre meant when he wrote in 1478 that the 'Wethwynde' or bindweed (*Calystegia sepium* (L.) R. Br.) twined about *herbores*, bearing its white flowers like the little church bells called 'sacryingbell.' As has been mentioned, rails and railings often occur: some of them were relatively tall open fences of trellis type, others formed a low edging **Pl.VIIA;13,50**. 'Lez railes' for the Bishop of Ely's garden in London were mentioned in 1312, and in 1395 three cartloads of 'Rayles' for the Westminster Infirmarer's garden cost 6s. Concerning garden beds we have not much information before detailed pictures of gardens begin about 1400, but we do know that as early as 1494 'a knot in a garden, called a mase' (maze) was an understood commonplace. The date when artificial mounts were first made in gardens is quite uncertain, but in 1366 the Chamberlain of Durham Priory accounted for 3s. 4d. received for the herbage of the mount

63A

63B 63C

63 Miss Verena Smith has discovered that the carved north-east pillar of the De la Warr Chantry in Boxgrove Priory, Sussex (1532) is based on a woodcut (A) by Theilman Kerver in a Paris Book of Hours dated 1503. The theme is gathering apples from a tall standard tree encased in a circular bench supported by wickerwork. *Photographs by the kindness of Miss V. Smith*

(*montis*) of the garden at Dalton, and in 1483 Caxton wrote of brambles and bramble berries being 'founden ofte in gardyns on the mottes', *motte* being the French for a mound **79**. It may be that the general adoption of mounts in gardens was due to Burgundian influence *c* 1475, as Sedding suggested, but they could have come about naturally: Oliver Rackham points out that whenever a moat turns a sharp corner, there is 'a mound formed by the earth cast up from both sides of the ditch.'

Water in gardens is frequently mentioned: at Windsor Castle in 1256 a well in the king's garden was to be walled in freestone; a leaden trough for keeping pike was remade for 2s. 6d. in the vineyard at King's Langley in 1292, and the gardens there included two little islands in the river. A fishpond was to be constructed in the king's garden at Woodstock in 1252, and four years later a hedge set about it. The Almoner of Durham had a garden made about an existing pool (*stagnum*) in 1369; and at Wykeham's manor of Highclere in 1372 the pool in the park was stocked with fish brought from Harewell in seven horse-drawn carts, the cartage taking three days. The garden of Queen Margaret of Anjou at Sheen was enclosed with a brick wall in 1445, and at Byfleet-by-Sheen a cloister was made with a lead cistern fed by a conduit and having eight devices made from moulds on its sides. Sixty small 'carpes' were put into the 'mote' in the close garden of Tendring Hall at Stoke-by-Nayland (Suffolk) in 1465. Most references to vines concern wine grapes grown in vineyards or are ambiguous, but in some instances they were used as ornamental climbers, as at Michelmarsh (Hants.) in 1325, when the vine near the door of the hall was pruned and trained. Whether for use or ornament, the supports for vines entailed a great deal of labour and materials: at Rotherhithe Manor in the late 1350s 100 'standards' and 3,500 rods were used to hold up the king's vines **8,29**, and 24 men worked for 5 days at $3\frac{1}{2}$d. a day each on making 'coumbles' for the vines – possibly tunnel-arbours, since the French *comble* means roof. Bundles of withies for binding the vines occur at Sheen and at Eltham in the 1380s.

As has been said, there are many references to nurseries for young plants, under such names as impgarth, impyard, impton, and even nursery itself at Merriott in 1369. In most cases it is probable that these were for trees and especially for grafted fruit-trees; but in 1413 at Methley (Yorks.) it was young oaks that were stolen from the 'impeyards'. We have seen (p. 17) that the English word 'spring' and its Latin equivalent *virgultum* were used for plantations or nurseries of young trees. The series of 'impyard' words has a general distribution over most of the country, and as far as can be ascertained, with uniform sense. 'Spring' often means the new growth of a coppice or, by extension, the coppice itself. As with all questions of mediaeval vocabulary, it is necessary to beware of any hard-and-fast rules of interpretation. Words meant what the clerks intended them to mean, and over technicalities such as plant-names there was no standardization.

The tools and utensils used in mediaeval gardens did not differ greatly from those of the early years of the present century **28,64–69**. The fundamental techniques of horticulture do not, after all, change much. The complete inventory of the monk-gardener of Abingdon Abbey for 1389 is in print and includes a good deal that we might not now expect to find, such as a 'hauk' for the masons, but the basic needs of the gardener are served. There are four ladders, an axe, a saw and three augers, two sieves, a rope, two iron forks for autumn (presumably pitch-forks), a seed-basket, a bushel measure, a mallet and a trowel, two pairs of shears, a scythe and two sickles, three spades and three shovels, and two rakes for gathering moss (*pro musco colligendo*). There are also implements for fishing and for making wine and cider, as well as furniture and household goods, pots, ladles, and cups and dishes. From the accounts for Chilbolton (Hants.) for 1326 we can add two water-pots (*urceol'*) repaired for 6d.; from Winchester College an ell of linen cloth to make the gardener an apron in 1407–08, costing 5d., and an iron for extracting weeds bought for the Infirmary garden at Durham in 1422–23. The Norwich accounts of 1484 show that moss was extracted from the cloister garth, which was mown twice, and the garden three times in the year.

What has changed enormously is the cost of labour 65, which in the Middle Ages ranged from cheap to extremely cheap. Whereas in 1359 at Windsor Castle the master of the King's vines, John Roche, was paid 1s. a day like other master craftsmen of high rank, the chief gardeners to the Black Prince at Kennington at the same period, John Aleyn and Nicholas le Gardyner, took only 2d. Gardeners in country districts might get only 1½d. a day, though they probably had commons as well and other perquisites. Royal head gardeners were pensioned off at monastic houses, and John Gardyner from Westminster Palace who retired in 1365 to St German's in Cornwall, was still alive in 1400 when he accepted a cash payment in lieu; he was recently dead in 1405, when it appears that his real name was John Pennalowe. Gardeners of some standing in royal manors were graded with substantial differentials: at Rotherhithe in 1358 Alan Gardiner took 5d. a day, William Devenyssh 4d., and Robert Coventre 3d. Women, who commonly did the weeding, might get only 2½d., and boys were hired at very low rates to do such jobs as planting leeks at Westminster Abbey in 1321.

So much for the gardens: it is time to have a look at the plants which they contained. In all departments there was considerable change in the course of our period, but it was not a simple story of continuous progress. We have the explicit statement of William Harrison, in his *Description of England* written in 1576, that 'such herbs, fruits and roots as grow yearly out of the ground, of seed, have been very plentiful in this land in the time of the first Edward and after his days; but ... grew also to be neglected, so that from Henry the fourth till the latter end of Henry the seventh ... there was little or no use of them in England.' There is some evidence to set against this, and Harrison probably gave an exaggerated picture of falling off in vegetable growing, but the garden as a whole suffered from the sad decline in the English polity and economy after 1400. This was the more tragic in that fourteenth-century England had enjoyed a period of noteworthy progress in science and craftsmanship. For two or three generations there was consistent advance in knowledge and in the systematic development of technique, accompanied by the resurgence of English as a literary language under the impetus of Chaucer, himself a notable scientist.

More or less contemporary with King Edward III were two great medical men, the physician John Bray (died 1381) and the surgeon John Arderne (1307–fl. 1378), both of whom were distinguished botanists. Arderne laid the earliest foundations of British topographical botany, while Bray in his list of synonyms makes a number of comments which show him to have been a sound observer and classifier. It is the outstanding drawings of plants in the splendid English manuscript of Arderne's works (Add. 29301 of the British Library) that put an end to the ages of debasement and began the upward climb towards accurate botanical draughtsmanship. Rather later in the century an Englishman writing in England, but in Latin, produced the original herbal known as 'Agnus Castus' and very widely used after its translation into English about 1440. The English poem by Master Jon Gardener (see Appendix, p. 155) on the actual operations of horticulture, existing in two versions both partly defective, though not likely to go back to a Latin original, was probably composed before 1350 since it makes no mention of rosemary, the outstanding introduction of the century.

The relationships of the two surviving versions to one another and to a hypothetical Latin original in prose have been explored by A. G. Rigg from a linguistic and literary viewpoint. His conclusions are not entirely satisfactory, however, since they imply that the work itself is not original but merely a scissors-and-paste job based on arbitrary lists taken from a herbal or a vocabulary. This fails altogether to account for the practical hints on cultivation which are

64 The Flemish miniature in a copy of Crescenzi (*c* 1460) shows gardening in progress on a large courtyard herber of many rectangular raised beds. Each is planted in a different way, some with central shrubs or dwarf trees. Note the form of the spade, and the wooden rake in the foreground

65 This Flemish miniature of about 1490, a calendar for March, shows gardeners at work 'bedding out' potted specimen plants in a small garden. Note the boarded edgings of the beds and the wattled fence

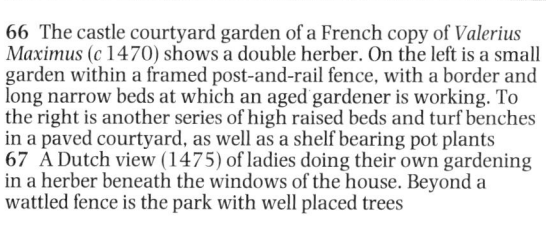

66 The castle courtyard garden of a French copy of *Valerius Maximus* (*c* 1470) shows a double herber. On the left is a small garden within a framed post-and-rail fence, with a border and long narrow beds at which an aged gardener is working. To the right is another series of high raised beds and turf benches in a paved courtyard, as well as a shelf bearing pot plants

67 A Dutch view (1475) of ladies doing their own gardening in a herber beneath the windows of the house. Beyond a wattled fence is the park with well placed trees

68 A man digging with a long-handled spade in the large raised bed of a cloistered garden, from the copy of the French version of Crescenzi's *Book of Rural Profits* produced in Bruges for King Edward IV about 1480

69 This French miniature in a Book of Hours (*c* 1500) depicts the incident of Mary Magdalene with Christ as the Gardener in the Garden of Gethsemane. This appears as a trellised herber of grass-plots intersected by paths, with specimen trees and a covered gallery or pentice

the vital new element paralleled only by the treatise on growing Rosemary, also of the late fourteenth century. Rigg's objections to the natural assumption that the original work was based on experience are not well founded: he considers that the 'moss liverwort' *Marchantia* is meant by 'lyuerworte' for April sowing, and that 'wurtys' are cabbage, which indeed are not ready in six weeks from seed. What 'Master Jon' actually says is that worts, really colewort, not heading cabbage, may be pulled for eating two weeks after transplanting of four-week seedlings. This is true: the pottage of the Middle Ages, and of much later times, included pullings of young colewort, which thus becomes evidence for the veracity of Master Jon. The liverwort of the herb list was not *Marchantia*, which is well described in 'Agnus Castus', but apparently a species of sage, as we shall see in considering the work of Friar Henry Daniel (p. 130).

Before leaving Master Jon there are several points which arise from Rigg's recent re-editing of the text. Most of the plants were identified and discussed by Alicia Amherst in her classic paper of 1893, but a few have remained puzzling, notably 'carsyndyllys'. Rigg's new reading, certainly correct, separates this into two words: 'carsyn' and 'dyllys', of which the former occurs in the second version of the poem from the 'Loscombe' MS. Since 'tuncarse' has already appeared for Cress (*Lepidium sativum*), the plural 'carsyn' must stand for Watercresses (*Rorippa nasturtium-aquaticum*), and 'dyllys' is Dill, a plant to be expected but not otherwise represented. The dialect is now shown to be not Kentish but extremely Southern, and it survives in the commonplace book of a monk of Glastonbury which has overwhelming Glastonbury associations. The second version, in the Loscombe MS., is Anglo-Irish, and this explains the odd reference to 'all the herbs of Ireland' ('yrlonde', 'Ierlonde'); Glastonbury had Irish property, so presumably the versification was made in Ireland. The original work, all the same, must have been written for English use, since Saffron, a new crop, had certainly not yet been taken to Ireland. The Loscombe copy actually preserves more than the other of the account of saffron.

The significance of Master Jon's work has been much discussed and it is unique in Britain, though closely paralleled by the garden chapter of the Parisian bourgeois's manual of 1393 for his young wife. The French treatise is valuable for its details of cultivation and its proof of the trouble taken to pack plants and cuttings for transport; but it mentions only 60 species, and beyond figs from Provence there is little to distinguish the list from an English one. Probably the root vegetables carrot, parsnip and turnip were more commonly grown in France. The full text is available in English and has been considered elsewhere.

On the other hand, little has been said of Henry Daniel, a Dominican friar living in 1379 but then probably aged. As a physician he translated medical treatises into English, and included one on the virtues of Rosemary, a text given to Queen Philippa by her mother in 1338 along with living plants of rosemary, brought back to England by the queen from Antwerp by 1340–42. In some manuscripts of Daniel's translation there is added a substantial and detailed account of the culture of the plant, obviously the result of personal experience in acclimatizing a hitherto unknown and rather tender evergreen. It is now evident that this gardening handbook, as we must term it, was also due to Daniel and fits neatly into place with other aspects of his work on plants as the most advanced herbalist of his time. His main botanical work, known as 'Aaron Danielis' (British Library Add. MS. 27329) is arranged in two parts: (i) *De re Herbaria*, (ii) *De Arboribus*, each in alphabetical order of well known Latin names, but the entries in English. The manuscript is of the fifteenth century, and seems to be a rearrangement of the contents of the earlier and far more personal MS. Arundel 42, from which a fair amount of Daniel's biography can be deduced.

This too consists of two parts, of which the first is an English herbal arranged under Latin names, and the second an *Alphabetum Herbarum* which, like other lists of synonyms of the period, includes medicinal substances in the pharmacopoeia other than plants. What is unusual about the herbal is that every plant is described under the Latin name (among its synonyms) which stands first, so that only a part of the alphabet, A–G, is represented and the herbal has, wrongly, been supposed to be imperfect. It has many other idiosyncrasies, narrating personal anecdotes, giving find-spots for uncommon plants, and frequently noting the beauty of particular flowers as well as commenting on the ease or difficulty of cultivation (see Appendix, p. 159). In several places Daniel refers to a garden which he formerly had at Stepney (Stebenhythe by syde London) in which he grew 252 sorts of herbs ('my xij. score & xij. erbis') and which contained at least one flowering plant brought from Queen Philippa's herber. Since most other sources would suggest that the total of plants in cultivation in c 1400 did not greatly exceed 100, and was only about 200 in the reign of Henry VIII, this is proof of an unexpectedly high development of horticulture in Edward III's time, as well as of the part played by the royal gardens four centuries before the founding of Kew.

The personalia of Arundel MS. 42 suggest an old man writing at a date probably not far from 1385. Not only is it evident that the date was after the death of Queen Philippa in 1369; it seems clear from a reference to a Lady Zouche that it was also later than the death in 1380–81 of Elizabeth, wife of William, 2nd Lord Zouche of Harringworth, who had succeeded to the title on 12 March 1351/2. In his 'young years' Daniel had worked seven years to learn medicine and botany; he was well acquainted with wild plants growing in the Forest of Rockingham, between Stamford and King's Cliffe and also between Stamford and Lincoln. In his later life he was living in the east of Britain (which he calls 'Brightlond'), though formerly in the London area, and had also visited Bristol, whence he had brought boughs of cypress to set in East Britain. He knew Eye (possibly the town in Suffolk, or the place near Peterborough); Chatham in Kent, where he found Juniper; and the borders of Dorset and Wiltshire near Shaftesbury with a heath on which 'Pety Juniper', evidently Whortleberry (*Vaccinium myrtillus* L.) from his description, and common heather ('lynk') grew in plenty close to the main road ('fasteby an heyh wey'). Sea Holly he saw on the shores of the eastern half of Britain ('in est half of Britlond on the see sandys').

Friar Daniel's anecdotes are of unusual human content, but what is most to our purpose in his book is his frequent aesthetic assessment of ornamental plants. The Purple Flag which of the sorts of Gladdon ('Gladene') is 'the principal of all, beareth purpure flowers wonder fair to sight'; a Cranesbill, presumably *Geranium sanguineum*, had 'flowers inch broad wonder fair and delightable to look on, to sight seeming from far fine sinoper, and near, sinoper and azure; and it is called of some Tronus Salomonis, Solomon's Throne.' What we call Wallflower was his Great Violet, with 'flowers fair and yellow wonder like flowers of Woodwax [Dyer's Greenweed, *Genista tinctoria* L.] . . . The Saracens call it "Keyrus"; we call it Violaria and Viola major. It groweth commonly on old stone walls by his own and gladly where it be set or sown.' Unlike the true Violet, it was still a plant that 'well few know'; – Merry England in the days of discovery, when the Common Wallflower was a rare exotic.

CHAPTER SEVEN

Introductions – the Planter's Palette

THE WORK OF THE FOURTEENTH-CENTURY HERBALISTS, and especially the writings of Henry Daniel, bring us into the era of scientific certainties rather than guesswork. Six hundred years after the *Capitulare* of Charlemagne it is possible to take stock effectively and see what had happened to the cultivated flora of western Europe. About AD 800 there were roughly 100 kinds of plants officially regarded as worthy of cultivation; and by 1400 an exceptional physic garden near London could grow just over 250. Many of these were undoubtedly native plants used medicinally and therefore brought into the garden from the wild: from Daniel we know that these included Agrimony, Betony, Chicory, Crosswort (*Cruciata laevipes* Opiz.), Fennel, various Mallows and Marshmallow, and species of Spurge and Vetch, among others. Whereas the earlier Middle Ages, with their subsistence economy, had been unable to afford the luxury of pleasure gardens, there had been several centuries of increased prosperity in which new sorts of plants could be introduced. In most cases the precise dates and means of introduction are uncertain, but the arrival of rosemary *c* 1340 as a royal gift to the queen is probably not altogether untypical.

Comparison of the principal lists of plants, from Palladius late in the fourth century to Turner's *Libellus* of 1538, defines the hard core of European cultivated plants, distinguishes the British from the continental garden flora, and gives indications of the approximate dates of introduction of particular species (see Appendix). It seems clear, for instance, that it was not until after the end of the mediaeval period that Britain got Asparagus, the Kidney Bean in any form, Gith (*Nigella sativa* L.); and that the true Endive and Hops did not arrive until very late. On the other hand, Elecampane was in England in Saxon times, Borage had come by 1200, and the Almond tree and Lavender by the mid-thirteenth century at latest. Balm, Clary, Liquorice, Mandrake, the Cypress and the true Service were probably introductions of the fourteenth century; Caraway and the annual Lupin (*Lupinus albus* L.) as a crop a little later. The dock Patience or Monk's Rhubarb, Basil, Costmary, Fenugreek and true Spinach may not have reached the British Isles until the Middle Ages had barely a century or less to run.

Some at least of the late arrivals came from Italy and were symptoms of the Renaissance. It is known that by 1424 the garden of the Villa Paradiso at Florence had many trees and shrubs brought from afar, and by *c* 1460 Filippo Strozzi (1426–1491) had (globe) artichokes there. They first appear in England after 1500, in the 'Fromond' list, and probably came via the French court, since the plant was figured by Jean Bourdichon in the Hours of Anne of Brittany painted in 1501–07. Broad Beans were an ancient field crop, but the development of eating them green can only be traced back to the fourteenth century. Green beans were sold from the castle garden at Clare in 1341, and Daniel remarks that *Faba*, 'Beene' ... 'may be eaten green, but it giveth by little nourishing to the body.' On the continent there had been Kidney Beans from classical times, belonging to the modern genera *Dolichos* or *Vigna*: all forms of French Beans and Scarlet Runners belong to the genus *Phaseolus* and are of American origin. England does not seem to have grown any of the Old World beans of this group.

We have seen that seed of cabbage, as well as of colewort, was bought for the Lambeth Palace garden in 1322, but it is rarely mentioned until the fifteenth century; the Cauliflower, though well known to Ibn Bassal in Spain by 1080, does not seem to have reached the North for some four centuries, when it is said to have been brought to Italy from the Near East by the Genoese. Botanists have argued that the carrots known in the Middle Ages were purple, violet or almost black, but before 1400 in Paris carrots were 'red roots' sold in the market and *c* 1450 it was stated that 'carrot roots growing in gardens are red', and by that time they shared with skirrets a degree of popularity; the Parsnip, included by an Anglo-Flemish doctor in a list of synonyms, was said to belong 'more to meat than to medicine', but is not much in evidence before the sixteenth century. Celery, as distinct from the semi-wild March or Smallage, was probably a late arrival, though Delisle found that it was grown by the Hôtel-Dieu at Evreux in 1419. Chives, though not in the earlier English lists, was described by Daniel who wrote: 'We eat it as cress or porret; many say it destroyeth weak blood.' He also mentions both tame and wild Cucumber, grown from seed at Lambeth in 1322.

Daniel states that Endive is a herb well enough known, of two kinds, with a ragged leaf or a whole leaf; but it is not certain that either was the real *Cichorium endivia*, as the name was apparently applied to several plants of the lettuce tribe. The Gourd (*Lagenaria vulgaris* Ser.), however, was undoubtedly grown in England from a relatively early date, at Lambeth in 1322, and described at great length by Daniel (see Appendix, p. 160). Lettuce, like Endive, is a somewhat ambiguous name, and the first evidence of head lettuce is said to date from 1543. Peas, like Beans, started as a field crop, but green peas (*pisa virida*) are named as early as 1325, and there were 'white' peas as well as common peas in Normandy by 1318. A bushel of large early peas, '*gros poys hastiz*', were planted in the gardens of the Archbishop of Rouen in 1486, and peas called 'hastyngez' were among the products of the garden of St Augustine's, Bristol, in 1491 and onwards. It was very likely about this time that the gardener of the Hospital of St Mary of Roncesvalles at Charing Cross produced the improved Rounceval Pea that was to remain famous for several centuries.

Purslane is not much heard of in England, though it occurs in Neckam's list, but it found favour with Daniel who called it 'noble to eat with vinegar in great heat.' He also solves the mystery of 'White Pepper' frequently occurring as an English garden plant; this was one of the names of *Eruca*, 'mickle like the herb that is called *Synapis* mustard', i.e. Rocket. The identification of 'Spinach' is far more difficult (see Appendix, p. 166). As we have seen, Saffron was being grown at Cambridge and elsewhere soon after the middle of the fourteenth century, and this was certainly one of two or three species of *Crocus*: the autumn-flowering *C. sativus* L. and *C. nudiflorus* Sm., or the spring-flowering *C. purpureus* Weston. But before the end of the fourteenth century Daniel was describing not only the true saffron as *Crocus orientalis*, but also *Cartamus* as 'Crocus ortolanus, Safron of the gardyn or Safron of the west', that is Safflower (*Carthamus tinctorius* L.).

The problems concerning English arboriculture in the Middle Ages are of several kinds. That trees were planted, in rows or groups for shade and ornament, and in woods for timber and coppicing, has been seen already. Although this lies partly beyond the history of the garden, the cult of trees can never be separated from horticulture. As with flowers and vegetables, detailed and systematic information on the kinds of tree grown begins only in the fourteenth century. What Chaucer, himself a forester, regarded as 'homely', native or well known, trees comprised among fruits and nuts: Apple, Bullace, Cherry, Hazel, Medlar, Peach, Pear, Plum, Quince, and Service. He knew the Sweet Chestnut as a timber tree, since ripe nuts were obtainable only as an import. His other forest trees were: Alder, Ash, Aspen, Beech, Birch, Box, Dogwood or Cornel ('Whippeltree'), Elm, Fir, Holly, Laurel (i.e. the Sweet Bay), Linden, Maple, Oak, Pine, Plane, Poplar, Thorn (Hawthorn), Willow and Yew. Noteworthy omissions are the Hornbeam, Sycamore and Walnut, to which we shall return. On the other hand his mentions of the Sweet Bay, the Linden (presumably the small-leaved native *Tilia cordata*) and the Plane are of considerable interest.

Another independent list may be compared with Chaucer's, the compilation of a monk of St Albans writing about 1382. Of Chaucer's fruits he omits only the peach, and of other trees the bay, pine and plane. In compensation the St Albans catalogue adds Mulberry and Walnut, the wild fruit trees Crab and Sloe, the small fruit (Black)berry ('Berie', French *murs de rounce*), Gooseberry ('Theuthorne', *grosiler*), and Strawberry ('Streberie', *frese rouge*). To the forest trees the monk added Elder and Wych (Elm), with the ornamental woody plants Briar ('Hepetre', *eglenter*), Broom ('Brome', *genette*), Ivy (*ere du boys*), Rose-tree ('Rosetre', *roser*) and Honeysuckle ('Wodebynde', *cheuer'foil*). In a separate list of fruits are Fig and Raisin, no doubt as well known imports only. The inclusion of 'Pekede', French *cornaile*, in the list of fruits suggests that Chaucer's Whippeltree was *Cornus mas* bearing Cornelian Cherries, rather than the native *C. sanguinea*, and 'Cirue' (i.e. Serve), *alie*, confirms his 'aleys' for the service-tree. The omission of the Peach is not altogether surprising, since it is likely to have been only in a few exceptional gardens. What is highly significant is the appearance of several woody species of purely or mainly ornamental character.

The absence of the Apricot from these, and from all English plant lists confirms the accepted date of introduction in Henry VIII's time though, as pointed out in *Early Nurserymen*, the old year '1524' must be taken as a mistake for 1542, within the period of John Wolf's activity in finding fruit-trees for the king. We must, however, add the Almond as a known though uncommon tree, since it not only appears consistently in the lists of Aelfric, Neckam and Bartholomew, but is mentioned by Daniel, who says that

> It is ever more green leaved but if east wind or north wind or 'pirnale' wind in cold winter time make it, and yet within the 9 day after such weather it hath more leaves again.

Daniel's reference to the Fig is not explicit, but it is not impossible that there were a few fig-trees in sheltered places in the South of England and there could even be truth in the old tradition that Becket planted the first at Tarring in Sussex on his return from Rome in the middle of the twelfth century. In 1390 the fig-tree of Orcher, near Harfleur in Normandy, was given as a boundary mark.

The bilingual St Albans list is valuable for its confirmation of the identity of 'Theuthorne' with the gooseberry, which is clearly illustrated by Bourdichon as *Rhamnus, Grouselliers*. As we know, *greseiller* bushes were bought for Edward I in 1275, but the equation with *rhamnus* (which normally means Buckthorn, *Rhamnus catharticus* L., a British native used in medicine) has made it hard to accept that thewberry or dewberry meant *Ribes uva-crispa* L. rather than

Rubus caesius L. Gooseberries were picked in the gardens of the Archbishop of Rouen in 1489; it is worth noting that the French *groseille* by itself originally meant the gooseberry, not the red currant as nowadays. The strawberry, like the blackberry, was no doubt for the most part picked wild, since as late as 1548 Turner could write: 'Every man knoweth well enough where strawberries grow'.

The Medlar has been grown as a fruit since early times, yet has never been particularly common. Its beauty as a highly ornamental tree was recognized in 1326 when a medlar was reserved for the bishop in a partition of the palace orchard at Wells (Somerset), and again by the author of *The Flower and the Leaf* (c 1450):

> I was ware of the fairest medlar tree
> That ever yet in all my life I see,
> As full of blossoms as it might be.

It used to be said that the Mulberry at Syon was the oldest in England, brought from Persia in 1548, but mulberries had grown here earlier. Besides the St Albans formulary, Daniel is evidence at the same period that *Celsus maior*, 'the great mulberry tree' is a tree well enough known, and he gives it the synonym of 'Sycomor', which occurs again in the fifteenth-century Sloane MS. 3548: '*Sicomorus, fructus celsi, vel mori*', with a reference to their acid flavour. The 'large sycamore' by the Archbishop's Palace at Canterbury, under which Becket's murderers left their gowns, was undoubtedly a mulberry; at York the prebendal house and garden of 'Mulberiahalle', 'Mulberihawe', was so named in 1276 and 1361.

We have seen that the Earl of Lincoln was selling walnuts from his garden in Holborn by 1295, and 'walnote ympes' were destroyed at High Easter in Essex in 1403, evidence of deliberate cultivation in an organized way. Both 'great nuts' and 'filberdis' were cropped at Kingston (Dorset) in 1375. The 'notebem' sold from the garden of Abingdon Abbey in 1413 was pretty certainly a walnut, and its price of 5s. proves it to have been a large timber tree, for two elms with faggots and brushwood were sold for 6s. 1d. the same year. This is of some importance as it bears out the testimony of the lists, which almost all include the walnut as well as the hazelnut. Its relative unpopularity seems to have been due to the notion that its name of *nux* indicated its 'noxious' nature, a belief incorporated by Albert the Great in his scheme for a garden and copied word for word by Crescenzi. Whether or not the walnut was introduced by the Romans, it can be accepted that since before 995 when Aelfric equated *juglantis vel nux* with 'hnutu', it has been a naturalized tree in England.

Turning to the forest trees named by the lists, by Chaucer and by the St Albans monk, we need mention the Birch only to point out that it usurped the Latin name *lentiscus*, so that the record of 24 'mastich' trees worth 4d. each at Bamburgh Castle in 1373 is capable of a simpler explanation than the early introduction of the tender *Pistacia lentiscus* L. from the Mediterranean to the coast of Northumberland. The Chestnut has already been mentioned as an uncommon tree, occasionally used for its timber; the very ancient specimen near Tortworth Church in Gloucestershire may well have begun life in the fourteenth century, and one by the house of Keir near Stirling is believed to date from near 1500. The Linden or Lime, though a known tree, is rarely named in England, but was a favourite garden specimen in mediaeval Germany. With the Plane and the Sycamore we reach a far more complex problem, which involves not only confusion between two unrelated trees but also in their nomenclature.

Neither the American Plane nor the allegedly hybrid London Plane is concerned here, but only the Oriental Plane (*Platanus orientalis* L.), the Persian *chenar*, one of the most famous of all trees in folklore and with a history of cultivation stretching back to antiquity in the Near and Middle East. It is absolutely hardy in Britain and extremely long-lived. Because of its ancient fame it is not surprising that it should be known to Chaucer, though it is only the reference in *The Knightes Tale* (line 2922) that is evidence for its occurrence in England. It is mentioned first by Neckam in the relevant lists, then by Bartholomew, then in the English *Promptorium Parvulorum* of *c* 1440 and slightly later in the Mayer MS. In general it is not found in the continental lists of the Middle Ages. One of the singular (indeed impossible) precepts for grafting put forward in the English treatise of *c* 1400 of Godfrey upon Palladius is that 'the peach apple will wax red if he be grafted on a plane tree', which at least sets up a *prima facie* supposition that the plane was already here. There is also the long standing tradition that the splendid Oriental Plane at Ribston in Yorkshire, formerly a preceptory of the Templars and then of the Hospitallers, was brought back from the Crusades by the knights, along with the very ancient Mulberry there. If the tradition ascribing the introduction to the Templars were correct, it would put the planting before their suppression in 1312. The tree in 1870 had a circumference of 18 feet and its branches covered a diameter of nearly 100 feet. The clinching proof, however, comes from the description of the Nonsuch estate in Surrey made by the Revd. Anthony Watson *c* 1582: 'To the north is a wide-spreading circular plane tree, its branches supported on posts, so that many people can sit beneath it.' In the view of Miles Hadfield, for a plane to have reached this state it would have to be over 150 years old, and the Nonsuch specimen would therefore go back at latest to the reign of Henry IV.

Besides being proof of great age, the description of the Nonsuch tree as having its branches supported on posts effectively excludes any possibility of its having been a Sycamore (*Acer pseudoplatanus* L.). This is crucial, since the two trees have been confused ever since the period, in the later sixteenth century, when they were both fairly common in this country. The name of 'Plane' has certainly been applied to the Sycamore in Scotland and parts of northern England for over two centuries; while 'Sycamore' has been for nearly as long an American usage for the Western Plane (*Platanus occidentalis* L.). What do we really know of the cultivated habitat of the Sycamore? It was studied in great detail by E. W. Jones, who points out that Turner in the second volume of his *New Herball* of 1562 stated that he knew the sycamore on the Continent but had not seen it in England. The earliest positively recognizable illustration is that by Bourdichon in the Hours of Anne of Brittany (1501–07), explicitly named 'Siccamor, *sicamour*', implying that the tree then grew near Tours or Paris. Jones regarded carved leaves on the shrine of St Frideswide in Christ Church, Oxford (*c* 1289) as representing 'unmistakably' both sycamore and maple; but apart from the notorious conflicts of expert evidence over such botanical identifications, this would only be proof that the carver either knew the tree, or had a pattern-book showing its leaves. The evidence for sycamores planted in Scotland (but not in England) in the fifteenth century is incredibly flimsy and rests on little more than a surmise recorded in 1842 that a very large tree near Dunblane was then 440 years old. Godwin remarks on the 'very comprehensive evidence of its rarity or absence in the British Isles in the mid-sixteenth century.'

There were very few evergreens available, though it was regarded as a dispensation of the Creator that he had ordained certain trees 'to be green winter and summer, as laurel, box, holly ('holme')'. The Laurel has now lost its name to the poisonous Cherry-Laurel, and is known as the Sweet Bay. Soon after 1300 the 'Outlaw's Song of Trailbaston' was composed 'in the wood beneath a laurel tree' (*cest rym fust fet al bois desuz un lorer*), and Daniel later in the century remarks that *Anachota*, 'the grete Lorer', is 'evermore green and well couth', that is, that it was too common to need description. In this case a Roman introduction is probable, and the tree is hardy enough to have survived throughout the southern counties. Turner in

1548 wrote that 'Bay trees are common in gardens in the South part of England', and does not suggest recent introduction. It occurs in most of the plant lists, continental as well as insular, and there is an item of 2d. spent on 'ropes to bind the Lorell tree' at St Stephen's Walbrook in London in 1483. By 1538 it was being grown on a commercial scale in the garden of the London Charterhouse, for after the dissolution three loads of bay trees were delivered to the King's Gardener, as well as others to the gardeners of Mr Richard Cromwell.

Box appears to be a native tree in southern England, but is decidedly local. Though not absent from the neighbouring parts of Europe, it is better attested in British lists of plants, like holly. It was sometimes used as 'palm' and was so called in Dutch. As a favoured live edging to garden beds it was probably first used in the Netherlands towards the end of the Middle Ages, but has only been recorded elsewhere after 1500. In 1487 the Archbishop of Rouen had 400 rooted plants of box taken from his estate at Houlme and sent to Grammont, but there is nothing to say that this was for dwarf edging rather than for an evergreen hedge of larger scale. Another evergreen, well known in Daniel's time and appearing more in English than in continental lists, was Savin (*Juniperus sabina* L.), used medicinally and noted by Turner in 1538 and 1548, when 'it groweth in many gardens in England.' Common Juniper (*Juniperus communis* L.) is a native, also used as a physical herb and as an evergreen shrub in the royal garden at Windsor soon after 1400.

Juniper and Savin are shrubs rather than trees, but the larger conifers aroused interest on the part of mediaeval observers because of their relative rarity. The fir-tree, by which Norway Spruce (*Picea abies* (L.) Karst.) was meant, was familiar as the timber of ships' masts. William Worcestre was informed in 1478 that fir trees for masts of ships grew on an island – probably Islay, not far from the mainland of the west part of Scotland. Pollen of the Pine (*Pinus sylvestris* L.) has been found in archaeological excavation on the site of Norton Priory near Runcorn in Cheshire, in soil of the period when the priory was founded in 1134. The Scots Pine is certainly the 'Pyne Appull' recommended as a plant for the herber in the 'Fromond' list of *c* 1525. Together with Chaucer's references to both fir and pine, it is safe to assume that these trees did exist in Britain and that a few specimens got into gardens here and there. The pine in particular, an extremely easy tree to grow from seed, was probably fairly well known by the end of the Middle Ages, though it was obviously confused by writers with the Stone Pine (*Pinus pinea* L.) which many must have attempted to grow from imported pine kernels, perhaps with limited success.

Of the Cypress (*Cupressus sempervirens* L.) Daniel had a good deal to say:

> *Cipressus*, Cipres. It is tree fair and large and high, leaves most like leaves of fir or of savin in colour and shape and in quantity (size) in so mickle that but it were laid together I knew not asunder, and evermore green as fir or savin. His fruit mickle like galls and hard as galls. I carried of his boughs and apples all fresh from Bristol into East Brightland (?Anglia) in the month of September and therefore I might not do them grow, and wit well for certain that it taketh in the ground as well as Rosemary or other manner boughs if it be duly cut and set in duly time.

In other words, cuttings set in September would not grow, but from general experience Daniel knew that it could be grown like rosemary, on which he was an expert. Oddly enough he has nothing much to say of the native Yew in his treatise *De Arboribus*:

> *Taxus* ye Yf tree; bows are made thereof. The seed maketh hens with 'eye' (eggs) as some say.

Although grown in so many churchyards the yew is rarely mentioned in records, and it is not until 1555–56 that we find a mention of 5d. being paid for 'you' to set in the churchyard of St Mary at Hill in London.

Daniel gives a valuable explanation of the different names attached to the Oak, in part based on a quotation from *Alphita*. His own version of the facts is this:

> *Quercus, Ornus, Ilex, Robur major*, Oak ... *Ornus* is while it is young ere it bear his fruit; *Quercus* when he beareth his fruit and *Ilex* when he beareth no more, but seareth in his crop and in his branches [i.e. becomes stag-headed] ... *Robur* when it is in his best liking ['it is in best might' in the *Aaron Danielis* version].

From *Alphita* is taken the definition of a fifth kind of oak, 'that beareth the grains that scarlets are litted (dyed) with.' This is the Kermes Oak (*Quercus coccifera* L.) of the Mediterranean, host to the cochineal insect or 'grains'; it was not introduced until much later. The significance of the various names of the oak eliminates the possibility that they were related to botanical recognition of such distinctions as that between the pedunculate and durmast species. Daniel does add one further valuable definition, that '*robur minor*', in contradistinction to the oak, was applied to *buxus*, the well known Box tree.

Proceeding to the flower garden, it has to be admitted that precise information is scanty, and that much of what there is relates to the early sixteenth century. From the accounts of 1275 we know that roses, lilies and peonies were bought for the royal gardens, and from Daniel that in the next century Queen Philippa had an important herber containing unusual flowering plants. From his references both to the beauty of certain species and to the setting and sowing of various native plants with ornamental as well as medicinal qualities we may further conclude that pleasure gardens made use of a valuable 'palette' largely borrowed from the physic garden. While the exact inventory of what was cultivated may never be known, much may be deduced from the lists, from literary references, and from the study of a few exceptional paintings made in Germany, France and Flanders. It is encouraging to find that deductions made in this way at least receive retrospective confirmation from the 'Fromond' list and other horticultural sources of the early sixteenth century.

For the portrayal of individual species two paintings are of outstanding importance, both by an unknown master of the Rhenish School and both painted *c* 1410–20, in the very first generation of accurate botanical observation. The Frankfurt picture of the Garden of Paradise **Pl.V** shows a Cherry tree and at least eighteen species of garden flowers: Borage, Rose Campion, Cowslip, Daisy, Purple Flag Iris, Hollyhocks of two colour varieties, Madonna Lily, Lily of the Valley, ? Scarlet Lychnis (*L. chalcedonica* L.), Peony, Periwinkle (*Vinca minor* L.), Sweet Rocket (*Hesperis matronalis* L.), Rose, Sage, Snowflake, Strawberry in flower and fruit, Violet and Yellow Wallflower. All of these were included by Bourdichon in the Hours of Anne of Brittany except for Lily of the Valley and Sweet Rocket: but both of these are confirmed by other paintings and by the literature. The second painting, the Virgin and the Strawberries at Solothurn 72, has red and white roses in a raised bed of strawberries, and growing in the lawn lilies of the valley, violets and snowflakes.

Other paintings of the fifteenth century vouch for Buttercup, Camomile, wild Campions, Columbine, Forget-me-not (*Myosotis* sp.), Mallow, Marguerite (probably *Chrysanthemum leucanthemum* L.), Pansy (*Viola tricolor* L.), Speedwell (*Veronica* spp.), and Stock (*Matthiola incana* (L.) R.Br.). Various species of *Dianthus*, at first single wild pinks, late in the century the true double Carnation, also occur. The cultivation of a perfumed single pink in Queen Philippa's garden in the middle of the fourteenth century is recorded by Daniel:

> *Garofilus* or *Garofila* or *Garofilata* ... *Gaya* or *Herba Gaij* is a herb most like Cockle if cockle and

> that be asunder, but together not so. This was one of my 12 score and 12 herbs, and at Stepney beside London had I it, and thither it was brought from the Queen Philippa's herber. It is a wonder sweet and it spiceth every liquor that it be laid in, and principally red.

Daniel continues with quotations attributed to Henricus Anglicus to the effect that kings love to have (spice) cloves in their wine, while other men carry cloves in their purses; and then states that 'many understand these things now said of Plat(earius) of that herb' namely the common *Gariofila*, *Gariofilata* or Avens (*Geum urbanum* L.), noted for the clove-like scent of its rhizomatous root. Daniel, or his authority Henricus Anglicus – whom he refers to in *Aaron Danielis* as Henry Englisch, leech and noble poet – may thus have started the tradition of 'sops in wine' as referring to species of pink. Bourdichon, however, applied the name '*souppes en vin*' to the clover (*Trifolium pratense* L.), a 'honeysuckle.'

Nearly a century ago Alicia Amherst listed some 30 sorts of handsome native plants which either have been or still are grown in the flower garden and which would have been available in the Middle Ages (see also Appendix, p. 164). In a few cases there is actual evidence that natives were then in cultivation, e.g. the Dog Rose, Campion, Cowslip, Daisy, Honeysuckle, Mallow, Peony, mentioned in records or seen in paintings. From Daniel's writings, specifying the setting of plants in gardens, several more can be added: Betony, Chicory, at least two sorts of Cranesbill (apparently *Geranium pratense* L. and *G. sanguineum* L.), Crosswort, Fennel, several Mallows, Marshmallow, and Mulleins. By implication he includes also the Daffodil (*Narcissus pseudonarcissus* L.) and what is probably the Bluebell (*Endymion non-scriptus* (L.) Garcke.):

> *Ligustra* Wild Lily. This is the second manner of wild lily that is called Lily of the wood for it groweth but in woods, but if it be set, ... many call it Daffodil of the wood, for it groweth like Daffodil, save he beareth flowers blue purple ('blo purpure'), and tame Daffodil yellow.

The cultivation of several more exotics is also described by Daniel in terms implying that they were grown for ornament rather than for use: Germander, Hollyhock, Sweet Rocket and Wallflower. Germander (*Teucrium chamaedrys* L.) we met much earlier as a garden plant in German poems, but Daniel goes into horticultural detail:

> *Camedreos* Gamandrea. It is nowhere but of setting or sowing, and of sowing but elvish [uncertain]. It hath many small white roots and growth up in many small stalks as a bush with leaves of penny broad or little more and gently indented, and come August and September shining as polished, and flowers skilful small and reddish. In warm place it keepeth itself above ground all year green.

The Hollyhock is described in a section on the Mallows: Daniel knew seven kinds, of which five seem to be native species: Tree Mallow (*Lavatera arborea* L.), Common Mallow, Marsh Mallow, Musk Mallow and Dwarf Mallow; and two others which answer to Red and White Hollyhocks. Daniel states that 'lewd [unlearned] folk call' the Tree Mallow 'Holyoc'; but the red hollyhock was known as *rosa hispanica*, Rose of Spain. 'In none author read I of properties of these seven foresaid species of mallow. All gladly they grow if it be set. All be good pottagers. . . .' His entry for the Wallflower, as the Great Violet, has already been quoted; the third kind of violet had 'the leaves end spearpoint and in his crops small white flowers', known as *Viola alba*, White Violet, undoubtedly Sweet Rocket.

That the hollyhock was called Rose of Spain almost certainly indicates the source of this oriental flower. We can only guess that it had reached England with Queen Eleanor of Castile

70A A series of North Italian wall-paintings of *c* 1415–20 in the Castello at Trent depict scenes from the zodiacal calendar: here 'Sol in Gemini' (May–June) shows a courtly picnic in progress in a landscape garden heavily planted with roses (see detail, **70 B**)

70B The roses at Trent show some progress in improvement from the flat mediaeval shape towards the 'cabbage' rose seen after 1500 in **71**

71 Bernardino Luini's Madonna (*c* 1510) sits in front of a trellis with fine roses of the 'Hundred-leaved' type. These are among the earliest truly double roses, probably infertile, clearly depicted. The Child grasps the stem of a fine columbine grown in a pot

72 The Upper Rhenish master of the Paradise Garden (**Pl. V**) also painted the Virgin of the Strawberries, where the Madonna is seated on a bench of strawberry plants. The painting also shows lily of the valley, violets and snowflakes growing in the lawn, and standard red and white roses on rails. Though double, the roses are not yet of the improved 'cabbage' sort (see **71**), but closely resemble the golden model (**73**) of the early fourteenth century. Historical verisimilitude is sought after in the Hebrew characters of the Virgin's book of devotion

73 The model rose, of gold and enamel, conferred by Pope Clement V (June 1305–April 1314) on the Prince-Bishop of Basel is the best surviving evidence for the type of the finest roses at the opening of the fourteenth century. Petals were numerous, but the flower retained the flat shape of *Rosa gallica*. The contrasting 'cabbage' forms developed later (see **71**)

in 1255 after her marriage to the Lord Edward, later Edward I, and that it was brought because of its then most unusual flowering season. As Daniel says, it has

> flowers fair and large as rose and like rose from far ... it is called also *rosa hyemalys*, winter rose, and *malva hyemal.*, winter mallow, for ... he beareth his roses till winter.

Another valuable plant for midwinter flowering was the true Black Hellebore (*Helleborus niger* L.), which Daniel confusingly calls 'white' in contrast to the 'black' hellebore which was green all over (*H. viridis* L.):

> *Adarasca* Hellebore the white and the black for leaf, crop and flower are nearhand like. The white hath his flowers in the top. The black, leaf, crop and flower are all nearhand of one colour, that is deep swart green ... Hellebore with the white top flowereth in cold winter, that other when the sun is in Aquarius [January–February]. Either of them beareth after his flower 3 cods and therein black seeds as Peony.

In the Arundel manuscript Daniel says mysteriously of a fourth kind of hellebore (men said that the third was Pellitory of Spain):

> Found I never yet body that me could tell name or property of this herb, but one only that was my disciple and now is my master; nor right none that me could tell the species of hellebore.

In attempting to classify the species and varieties of native and garden plants Friar Henry Daniel was far in advance of his time, but struggled manfully against a great cloud of unknowing, seeking out living authorities as well as old books. He describes three sorts of Mullein and then adds:

> And as I learned of a master wisest of all the east quarter of Brightland [Britain] in this science and in all seven Sciences that these three foresaid manner mulleins and that herb that is called *Cirotecaria* and *cauda equina*, Glovewort and Horsetail [i.e. Foxglove, *Digitalis purpurea* L.] – all four are called and are so: '*pulmonya*, pulmonye, lungewort.'

Whether any of these herbs was of real use in treating diseases of the lungs may be doubtful, but Daniel's master at any rate perceived the natural relationship of the genera *Verbascum* and *Digitalis* in spite of the marked dissimilarity of their flowers.

Another of Daniel's scraps of autobiography leads to a possible solution of the identity of the 'noble' Liverwort (as distinct from *Marchantia*). Besides the Garden Sage, *elifagus* or *lilifagus*, synonymous with *Salgia* or *Salvia ortensis* in mediaeval terminology (*Salvia officinalis* L.) there were various species of *Ambrosia* or Wild Sage, the commonest being White Ambrose, now Wood Sage (*Teucrium scorodonia* L.). Another kind also grew in woods and under bushes

> and else not but it be set or of his seed; stalk as a good wheat straw even upright height to man's knee at most, from a little above the ground unto the top in every navel a fair flower azure, shape like the flowers of *Campana silvatica major*, great Woodbell ... but nought red nor nowhere so great flowers nor none so rough leaf nor so great stalk nor so high as the great woodbell. I knew a lady, the Lady Sowche [Zouche], the best God's leech of Brightland in women, that in making of Nerval [a compound medicine] when she might not have white Ambrose she took this other of stead of that; the leaves of him both in grain and in shape and in colour there him liked best.

Under *Epatica*, Liverwort, Daniel states that this great Ambrose is well known and is a sage also called *epatica*,

> but the great hepatic ('epatyk') or else the great liverwort, for it is mickle greater.

Unfortunately we are left wondering whether the plant in question was really a bellflower or a labiate like sage, though other references make the latter a certainty.

What we regard as the typical aromatic herbs are mostly labiates, almost all of them introduced to Britain, but at different dates. Balm (*Melissa officinalis* L.) occurs in few early lists but is mentioned by Bray in the mid-fourteenth century and onwards. Clary or Oculus Christi was in Charlemagne's *Capitulare* and was apparently another late comer in spite of being well known to Walafrid, the Abbess Hildegard, and Crescenzi. This was the true Clary (*Salvia sclarea* L.), but we substituted the native *S. horminoides* and *S. pratensis*. Hyssop (*Hyssopus officinalis* L.) was one of the commoner herbs, appearing in all the lists from the eleventh century, and its seed being an article of commerce in London in the fourteenth. We hear of Lavender *c* 1265 and it was already well known before the arrival of rosemary. It was grown on a substantial scale as an aromatic and there was a large plot of it in the garden of the Archbishop of Rouen at Gaillon in 1410. Marjoram, that is Sweet Marjoram (*Origanum majorana* L.), is rather tender and Daniel found that it would only grow among us 'with great travail', though it was sweet and aromatic 'for thing strike withal taketh thereof a sweet smell.' To the culture of Rosemary he devoted a separate treatise, and it seems safe to conclude that he had been entrusted with the precious roots or cuttings by Queen Philippa after she had brought it to England in 1340. His experiments succeeded so well that by 1364 Alice Causton, a London alewife, found herself in court for having given short measure by spreading a coat of pitch one-and-a-quarter inches thick on the bottom of a quart pot and sticking sprigs of rosemary over it to look like a herbal spray. It was the badge of Richard II's first queen, Anne of Bohemia, and as such appears under the White Hart couched on the back of the Wilton Diptych. By about 1530 Sir Thomas More could write that he 'let it run all over my garden walls', and when Henry VIII had acquired the manor of Chelsea in 1543 he paid Henry Russell of Westminster, gardener, 13s. 4d. for two banks of Rosemary to set in the garden, and £1 6s. 8d. for six borders of lavender.

One of our most exquisite native plants is the blue columbine (*Aquilegia vulgaris* L.), planted by Garlande in his Paris garden about 1225 and later a heraldic charge and a badge of the House of Lancaster. As '*anquelie*' it is listed by Froissart in his *Paradis d'amour* of *c* 1375, along with the rose, fleur-de-lys, lily, lily of the valley, marigold, peony, violet and '*perselle*' (? cornflower), and his own favourite (like Chaucer's) the daisy 83. The columbine appears in several paintings 71, and in three varieties – purple, white, and double – in the Hours of Anne of Brittany. Another very beautiful native is the Jacob's Ladder (*Polemonium caeruleum* L.), formerly best known as Greek Valerian and described by Turner in 1548 as 'our common Valerian that we use against cuts, with a blue flower.' Nevertheless, Sir Harry Godwin tells us that the wild plant is morphologically distinct from the forms nowadays grown in gardens. The Lesser Periwinkle (*Vinca minor* L.) was well known in mediaeval gardens and noted as one of the few flowering evergreens available, as well as for ground cover. It is worth remarking that the romantic name 'Joy of the Ground', repeated from one writer to another, is no more than a misreading of the Stockholm manuscript's 'Ivy of the Ground', the word 'ivy' being written as 'juy'. It is a sad commentary on the prevalence of error that most of this literary chain of nonsense has been forged since R. C. A. Prior in 1863 published the correct reading in his standard work *On the Popular Names of British Plants*.

Prior also pointed out that in *The Flower and the Leaf* the reference to a green herber set with 'sicamour' and 'eglatere' (sweetbriar) must mean honeysuckle or some twining shrub; we can regard honeysuckle as in fact certain, marking up yet another meaning for the deceptive word 'sycamore' and still further reducing the potential evidence for *Acer pseudoplatanus* in mediaeval Britain. One other most extraordinary instance of the changing meaning of names is 'Palma Christi.' During most of the Middle Ages this meant the Spotted Orchis (*Orchis maculata* L. agg.), whose roots were described as having five fingers. From the middle of the sixteenth century the name has invariably stood for the Castor-oil Plant (*Ricinus communis* L.), an exotic certainly in English gardens before 1548. George Henslow in 1899 demonstrated the transition of meaning in the fifteenth century.

What then were the plants which were available to the typical mediaeval 'herberur' working for a royal or noble patron? What sort of a show could be made during the winter half of the year? Even if pine or fir was not to be had, the holly, juniper and yew could always be depended upon to provide some green background, along with periwinkle which has a happy habit of flowering at odd times through the year. In the South of England the bay too would form a noble tree of 20 feet or more in height. Juniper and savin, as well as box, were evergreen shrubs and at times small trees. From time to time, until cut down by a severe winter, even the cypress might serve to remind the returned traveller of his pilgrimage to warmer lands. Within the shelter of such perpetual greenery, and rows of deciduous trees from the woods or fruit trees destined to provide sheets of flower in spring – consider Henry III's hundred pears in blossom – there would be immense lawns of green grass, mown with the scythe, and rejoicing in invasion by daisies and blue speedwell at almost any season.

It is true that in autumn the main interest would be provided only by trees in fruit or berry, apart from the coloured leaves before the fall. Yet, besides the ubiquitous daisy, the periwinkle or the forget-me-not might show flower, along with the wild heartsease brought into the garden to start its career as the cultivated pansy. By midwinter in a lucky season the Christmas Rose, doing duty as 'White Hellebore' would be opening, to last for many weeks, and to be followed by its green kinsman in February and March. Primroses would be coming out and later cowslips, both of them providing long-lasting waves of flower. From their introduction in the fourteenth and fifteenth centuries the early flowers of rosemary and the snowdrops, its own Fair Maids, would enliven February. In March the daffodils, the blue speedwell and periwinkle once more, the first plum blossom, and above all the violets, purple, dark blue, pure white. Merging into April the high spring fills the orchards with blossom, apple and pear contrasting; the wild strawberry displaying its pure white flowers with their golden centres above the carpet of leafy tufts; the heartease and the buttercup.

As May follows, Hawthorn and Quince are the trees in flower, followed by the glory of the golden broom. In the beds and by the pools and streams are wallflowers and columbines, red peony, purple iris, the elegant Solomon's Seal or Ladder of Heaven, the yellow water-flag and brilliant brooklime. Midsummer fills the garden with roses: red and white double roses, heavily perfumed; the climbing field and dog roses, the burnet, the delicate sweetbriar sharing the arbours with the vines and woodbine. In beds or among the grass spring camomile, the glowing pot marigold, the jewelled sapphire of the hairy borage, the blue fragrant hyssop, perhaps the gay bluebottle for garlands and coronets; and all is lorded over by the strong spires of the pure white lilies and the sculptured strength of the medlar tree in leaf and flower. Later still come the tall border flowers: foxgloves purple and white, rose campion, gold-starred steeples of agrimony, the vervain with its mystic secret, the spiked speedwell of lapis lazuli.

When the roses on the trellises and arbours fade, the white bindweed and the everlasting pea will take over, with the long-lived honeysuckle. Lavender will fill the air with the perfume of its spikes, the tall hollyhocks will come like giants into their stride, to last for months into the short days of winter: red, white, blushing palely, darkest maroon in mourning. Along with them will be the yellow mulleins, likewise continuing for many weeks as floret after floret opens up their tall woollen spires. And so the declining year, punctuated by the return visits of plants which indulge in second flowering, sinks down once more, but still with daisies in the grass, and heps and haws and holly berries, and the orchard's fruit. We have forgotten the cranesbills, fennel, the wild bluebell brought in to set beneath the trees, sweet rocket white and mauve, the sweet marjoram brought up with difficulty, the wood bells, and Coventry bells and Canterbury bells; the loosestrife, and waterlilies white and yellow; the carp in the pool; the swans swimming on the moat; and the peacocks in proud display.

EPILOGUE

The End and a New Beginning

IN A SENSE, ENGLAND DIED at the abdication of Richard II in 1399; but the country would not lie down. The political chaos which was to ensue for some three generations was closely linked to underlying economic distress and that in turn was partly due to deterioration in the climate. So the fifteenth century was a period of recession, brightened by fitful glimpses: the few years of military success in which Henry V seemed to have conquered France for good and all; the cultural interests of his brothers and of his son the saintly Henry VI; the retrenchment and renewed prosperity of the Yorkist settlement after 1471 and at last the Tudor peace. Through all this gardens continued to be made, though we know all too little of them. There were notable contacts between the first English humanists and the Renaissance scholars of Italy, yet we cannot trace any Italian influences on horticulture beyond the indirect pressures of the book of Crescenzi upon literate opinion. Stylistically, and in regard to plant introductions, this appears to have had no effect whatever for a hundred years.

Far more effective were England's links with central Europe by way of the Low Countries and the Rhine, and it was not the colossal planned layouts of Italy but the imperial and patrician pleasure gardens of the Empire, instinct with the love of trees and flowers and running water, that were to be the dominant factor during the transition to Renaissance gardening. In the first age of printing, when the bulk of serious publications in botany came from Germany and the Netherlands, this influence was to be still more decisive, as it was again when the Reformation attracted Englishmen like William Turner to spend their exile in the Germanic countries. German horticulture had indeed reached a high peak early in the fifteenth century, as is vouched for by the reports of many travellers.

In 1434 the Russian Metropolitan Isidore, on his way to the Council of Florence, was particularly impressed by the noble gardens of Erfurt including market gardens famous throughout Europe. Other great centres of garden activity included Mainz, Würzburg and Bamberg, noted for seed-growing, and Frankfurt, Nuremberg and Augsburg, all provided with splendid flower gardens. The Italians themselves were impressed: Aeneas Silvius (Pope Pius II) praised the fine flower and fruit gardens of Germany in 1458, and in 1490 Antonio Bonfini found the whole district of Vienna an enormous garden filled with vineyards and orchards, adorned with beautiful country villas. So many birds could be heard from the saloons and summer pavilions that one might imagine oneself in the green forest while walking through the streets. By the end of the century the taste for roses and many sorts of flowers was noted among the citizens of Augsburg, Basel, Cologne, Nuremberg and Ulm. A new emphasis on both ornamental garden plants and on the native flora is seen in the illustrated *Herbarius* of Vitus Auslasser, a monk of Ebersberg in Bavaria but born in the northern Tyrol. He included not only the white lily, German iris, and peony, but also Canterbury Bells.

Leo von Rozmital, whom we have already met on his travels in the Peninsula (p. 48), also visited Brussels on his tour of 1465–67, seeing many fine fountains and pools; while in London he noticed various beautiful gardens with unusual trees and plants. It is not clear whether the flora was merely strange to him because English, or whether it included newly introduced exotics. There had been, through the middle of the century, another foreign influence upon English gardening, coming from Henry VI's queen, Margaret of Anjou. Her father, the art-loving King René (1409–1480), was the most famous horticulturist of his time. Although only titular king of Naples, he was in fact duke of Anjou and count of Provence, and at his many castles and estates across France created a series of great gardens between 1447 and his death. He is credited with the first introduction of the Carnation from Provence into northern France and at Aix-en-Provence in 1447–49 certainly laid out a great garden with a circular mound bordered with wickerwork. Much of his life was spent in a garden pavilion with its own halls, chambers and courtyards **62**. Other gardens with pavilions were laid out for him in his northern estates near Saumur, where he is supposed to have followed Crescenzi's plan for a royal pleasance; at Les Ponts-de-Cé on an island in the Loire in 1454, and at the castle of Baugé in the following year. At his great castle of Angers, between 1453 and 1460, he built a two-storied pavilion overlooking the fishponds and formed an aviary. All this is likely to have had repercussions in the England of his son-in-law.

During the temporary ascendancy of the English dynasty the Duke of Bedford as Regent of France had made great changes in the royal gardens at Paris, planting many kinds of fruit trees and great numbers of white roses and bushes of rosemary. He also introduced the English Elm to France on a large scale in 1431 at the Palais de Tournelles, having trenches dug two feet wide and deep to a total length of 1,069 *toises* (equal to 6,836 English feet), in which were planted 5,913 elms costing 4 *livres Parisis* the hundred. Back in England a gallery was made at Greenwich overlooking a hedged garden with an arbour for the Queen to sit in, in 1447. After the Yorkist victory the greater royal gardens took on a new lease of life, and Edward IV at Windsor in 1472 personally conducted the Burgundian ambassador round his garden and 'Vineyard of Pleasour'. Ten years later the great garden had a new brick wall built round it at a cost of £13 10s. 0d., and 'lez Railez' were made within it. Under Henry VII the palace of Richmond was fitted up for the arrival of Catherine of Aragon in 1501 and had

> under the King's windows, Queen's, and other estates, most fair and pleasant gardens, with royal knots alleyed and herbed; many marvellous beasts, as lions, dragons, and such other of divers kind, properly fashioned and carved in the ground, right well sanded, and compassed in with lead; with many vines, seeds and strange fruit, right goodly beset, kept and nourished with much labour and diligence. In the longer end of this garden beth pleasant galleries and houses of pleasure to disport in, at chess, tables, dice, cards, bills, bowling alleys, butts for archers and goodly tennis plays, as well to use the said plays and disports as to behold them so disporting.

In 1505 the carpenter Thomas Binks was paid £8 6s. 8d. for his work on the gallery in the orchard at Richmond.

We cannot here follow the complex history of the royal gardens under Henry VIII, or the prominent place in Tudor gardening taken by his servants Cardinal Wolsey and Sir Thomas More **16**. It is, however, necessary to stress the fresh development of great gardens at the castles and houses of the nobility. Henry Algernon Percy, 5th Earl of Northumberland (died 1527), was one of the introducers of topiary work at his castle of Wressle in Yorkshire. John Leland saw the place soon after his death and noted

> the (exceedingly fair) gardens within the moat, and the orchards without. And in the orchards were mounts *opere topiario* writhen about with degrees like turnings of cockleshells, to come to the top without pain.

Leland commented on other topiary work at Little Haseley (Oxon.), where Sir William Barantyne 'hath a right fair mansion place, and marvellous fair walks *topiarii operis*, and orchards, and pools'; and at Ulleskelf (Yorks.) at the prebendal manor which had 'a goodly orchard with walks *opere topiario*'. The De la Pole mansion in Hull, opposite the west end of St Mary's church, had a 'goodly orchard and garden at large, enclosed with brick.' The great garden of seigneurial rank was the one being laid out with 'knotts' for the Duke of Buckingham at his new castle of Thornbury (Glos.) by his gardener John Wynde in 1520. On the south side of the living apartments is an enclosed garden nearly 150 feet long by 100 in width; east of this another garden of 200 feet by 105 in width; and beyond this again the orchard. The two gardens amount to three-quarters of an acre, and the orchard to several acres **77**.

Bishops and abbots emulated the Crown and the lay nobles. By the middle of the fifteenth century Thomas Bekynton, bishop of Bath and Wells, was spending over £4,000 on works at places belonging to the see and at Banwell laid out a most beautiful orchard with divers wonderful fruits. Not far away, at East Brent, John Selwood the abbot of Glastonbury *c* 1475 planted an orchard of over three acres with apples and pears of the finest fruit as well as elms and oaks. His successor Abbot Richard Beere about 1500 formed moats, pools and orchards within the precinct of his manor at Meare (Somerset), surrounding more than three acres with high thick walls, as well as another outer garden and orchard of $2\frac{1}{2}$ acres to the east and other plantations (*virgulta*); and probably formed the walled garden at Mells **79–82**. Near Glastonbury he enclosed the 382 acres of Sharpham Park with sawn oak palings, formed an orchard, and stocked the ponds with fish. The bishop of Durham made regular appointments to the office of gardener at his palace of Bishop Auckland, while at the abbey of Bury St Edmunds the courtyards and gardens of the precinct covered 40 acres. Of the last abbot of Glastonbury, Richard Whiting, we learn that at midsummer 1539, a short time before the dissolution, he was transacting business with Lord Stourton in an arbour of Bay in his garden. Alone of the greater abbeys, Westminster was revived under Queen Mary and survived for a short time into the reign of Elizabeth. John Feckenham the last abbot (1556–59), the last mitred abbot ever to sit in the House of Lords, was sent for by Queen Elizabeth soon after her accession, when he was planting elm trees in his garden: which may be considered the last act of mediaeval gardening in England.

A contributory cause of the Dissolution was the decrease in the number of monks and the consequent application of their revenues to individual comfort and the provision of luxuries. Among these luxuries good gardens ranked high, and we must suspect that the last two or three generations of English monasticism made a notable contribution to garden design and the improvement of plants and fruit-trees in particular. Certainly later monks in France and

74 The *Histoire de Charles Martel*, painted in 1470 by Loyset Liédet, really displays contemporary garden scenes at the Court of Burgundy. Here is a courtyard garden with a potted carnation given 'basket' support and placed on a turf bench. On the right a peacock in pride perches on the trellised railing of an enclosed herber

75 Another miniature by Liédet includes part of a courtyard garden and heraldic beasts bearing shields or banners at the head of ornamental steps

76 Liédet lovingly recorded the details of a palace garden in the episode of Pepin killing a lion. King and Court flee in dismay from the ruins of an open-air meal. A turfed bench is backed by a canopy or shelter-arbour formed of climbing roses with white double flowers (see **Pl. V. 17, 30, 70–73**)

77 When Thornbury Castle was built for the Duke of Buckingham in 1511–21, the 'Proper Garden' was laid out on the south side of the state apartments, and was in turn flanked on the south and west by a two-storied gallery of which the outer wall remains. The garden was filled with knots – probably heraldic – by the Duke's gardener John Wynde in 1520

78 Edward III expanded his privy garden in Westminster Palace at the expense of the Abbey, forming a re-entrant angle at the north-east corner of the Infirmary Garden, which extended to the precinct wall (left). The king's Jewel Tower (right) with its moat, was built by the royal architect Henry Yeveley in 1365

79 The square garden of the Abbot of Glastonbury at Mells Manor in Somerset formerly had mounts at each end of its northern terrace, giving views over the rising ground of the park to the North. The raised section of parapet at the north-west angle protected those standing on the mount. See also **80, 81**

80 The high wall of the great herber at Mells has regular bays marked by semicircular buttresses, agreeing in style with the probable formation of the garden by Abbot Richard Beere about 1500. See also 79, 81

81 The four-centred arch of the doorway in the west wall of the Abbot's Garden at Mells can be associated with other local works of the generation following 1490 and carried out under the last three abbots of Glastonbury. See also 79, 80

82 The background to a miniature of the Virgin and Child with St Anne (c 1500) shows a garden wall with buttresses, roughly contemporary with the surviving buttressed wall of the Abbot of Glastonbury's garden at Mells Manor in Somerset. (See 80)

Flanders were prominent improvers. To a lesser extent colleges and hospitals had a share in the work, as did such bodies as the greater City Companies of London, which often had large gardens by their halls. The London Grocers in 1431 had the garden made new with a fair 'Erber' and vines on rails producing in the season enough bunches for the 55 members of the Livery to take home two or three clusters daily. In 1486–87 the Pewterers paid £1 19s. 3d. for carpenter's work on a frame for their vine, and had sitting places made in their garden. The Corporation of Leicester in 1433 diked the Cowhay pasture in the town's South Field and planted willows and other trees there, with a double row along the south side, apparently for public recreation. At Cambridge in 1444 Canon John Whaddum of the Austin Canons of Barnwell, as vicar of Waterbeach, planted green trees (probably meaning evergreens) in the churchyard of St Giles; while at Wells in 1487 the Cathedral Treasurer was involved in a dispute concerning the pollarding and lopping of the trees in the churchyard. The Cellarer of Westminster in 1500 bought 20 little elms and had them planted between the Elms on the site of what is now Dean's Yard.

Several of the Cambridge colleges were involved in the making and enlarging of their gardens in the last century of the Middle Ages. King's College in 1450 had a new large garden on the west side of the river comprising nearly three acres including a lake with an island. The lake was surrounded by a grove of elms and there was a house or pavilion on the island. The walks in this garden, called 'le crouches', were probably tunnel-arbours. In 1468–69 a gallery was built of timber in the inner garden on the east bank, behind the college buildings. Further work was done on it ten years later, and in 1518–19 the gallery was repaired from a boat. Queens' College too had a garden and ponds on the west side of the river, with large groves on an island site surrounding some one-and-a-half acres of inner garden and orchard. A great hedge of thorns was made around them in 1511–12, and in 1539 the willows were trimmed, walks (*ambulacris*) were dug, and ten loads of sand were strewn on the walks in the orchard. Summerhouses and gazebos were in fashion, and Peterhouse in 1544–45 had the lookout (*spectaculi vocati ly neuwarke*) rebuilt in stone.

We saw that the royal gardens at Richmond in 1501 had ample provision for sports, and this was general at other Crown estates. The archery butts by the king's privy garden at Eltham were shaded by a row of plum and cherry trees planted in 1528–29, one of the first pieces of evidence for the ornamental planting of flowering trees outside orchards. There were butts elsewhere, and rather surprisingly in the Infirmary Garden at Westminster, where in 1468 there were purchases of herbs and 'turfes pro lez buttes.' This garden was also especially noted for its Damson trees. Westminster Abbey had several other gardens, and long before the Dissolution they were being leased out to lay tenants. The same thing happened at Norwich, where the great garden of the monastery was leased from 1466 for long terms of years. The planting of trees on other monastic lands was also made a condition of lease (p. 92), evidenced in Scotland and also in the South. In granting a lease at Radley (Berks.) in 1537 the Abbot of Abingdon stipulated that the tenant should each year plant four trees, two apples or pears, and two oaks, ashes or elms. Such stipulations became the practice of lay landowners after the Dissolution, and a considerable number of monastic precincts were converted to important nursery gardens. In both respects it seems probable that horticulture and arboriculture have benefited greatly by continuity of mediaeval practice.

Just how much of mediaeval gardening has survived the ravages of time and the heavy imprint of Renaissance and later layouts? Probably a great deal more than is generally supposed. None of the great gardens survive, except as areas subjected to repeated re-planning in subsequent periods. On the other hand, the walled plots of the Thornbury Castle garden are still there, and the great buttressed walls at Mells Manor in Somerset which

83 Henri d'Albret, titular King of Navarre, plucks a daisy ('*marguerite*') in the garden of the castle at Alençon in 1526, in honour of his approaching marriage to Marguerite d'Angoulême, the sister of François I. The trellised herber consists of paths and lawns, with a turfed flower border; in the background are a vine-covered gallery (right) and planted woodland, with a 'temple' enclosing an ornamental fountain

remain, probably from the days of Abbot Beere (1493–1524). The King's Knot and the associated parterre beneath Stirling Castle, though repeatedly reformed, do occupy the site of a great garden which was probably laid out by James I soon after 1424, in imitation of the King's Garden below Windsor Castle where he had first seen his queen. We cannot reconstruct the original design of these gardens, though future archaeological work may render such projects possible. It may well be that perseverance will eventually be joined by good luck at some site where both the plan of a mediaeval garden may be recovered, and the list of its plants, from stratified fossils and pollen.

In the case of smaller gardens, and especially those of little houses in the country whose owners or lessees have never been able to afford to keep up with fashion, it is likely that a great deal survives in principle. The planting of orchards near such houses often continues the mediaeval combination of the useful with the beautiful: the hedges and the trees in them sometimes perpetuate the ancient lines. What seems to have gone for ever is the tunnel-arbour covered with grapevines, though a few such arbours of other plants continue the tradition. In the forgotten cottage gardens of the few genuinely remote villages there are traces of the simple planting of the Middle Ages: little but a patch of lawn with daisies, a few roses and a clump of Madonna lilies, with some herbs for borders, and probably the purple flag iris, perpetually renewed by vegetative reproduction. Roses may come and roses go, but the old German flag has so far remained unchanged.

We owe to the Middle Ages our profound love of associating a garden, however small, with our home; our appreciation of trees, and notably fruit trees; our devotion to the Rose. Notwithstanding all that could be done to drown the garden with mechanized waterworks, to slice it apart with avenues and topiary, much of the older English tradition has survived. It is second nature to us and, though driven out time and again, it will none the less return. It is an integral part of our sense of human scale: gardens ought not to be too large, they should never trample down the landscape. It has been customary to decry the work of Capability Brown in the middle of the eighteenth century, and to deplore his destruction of the great avenues and layouts of the school of Le Nôtre. It is not necessary to take Brown's side on every issue; but his work can be seen as an instinctive return to a much older tradition, where nature had been almost imperceptibly improved by the hand of art to leave green launds between the clumps and copses of the park, that the deer might be seen or even shot. It is no mere chance that, in those mediaeval layouts which we know, the herber lay below the rooms of the house; the great garden beyond; further off still the orchard, with walks and pools; and then, beyond a ditch, or a paling, or a wall, the park. Each part, by a succession of proportionate scale, leads on to the next. Nowhere is there a violent transition; nor does the hand of man usurp the functions of the Creator.

For we are here on sufferance; we must not confuse earthly delights with those of a better world, the lesson taught by Bishop Hildebert de Laverdin (c 1056–1133), for a little space court poet at Westminster to that unlikely monarch William Rufus. In his exquisite *De Ornatu Mundi*, possibly the finest of all garden poems, alas! in most untranslatable Latin, he points this moral. Heaven is to be preferred to all this world's delights, yet to give some faint idea of ultimate perfection he is forced to describe the apotheosis of a garden: nature improved by art, the brook, the trees, the song of birds, sweet perfumed flowers, the apples yielded by the tree, wine from the grape: 'There every tree a double honour shares, Its boughs bear fruit, its shadow cloaks the soil. Both are enjoyed by men, its fruit and grateful shade.' Bird song, sweet scents and flowers in glowing hues are there to satisfy the senses; 'there spring not winter reigns.' We are transported in spirit by the details lovingly piled up, a poignant sermon which only mediaeval man could have written. And yet – not all may enjoy the future delights so sincerely enjoined by Hildebert; implicit in his call is the alternative, to make a garden here and now:

    O Paradise! thy rival is this place ...

Bibliography and Abbreviations

Works are cited by the date of first publication, but references given in the Notes are from the edition specified in the entry below.

AMHERST 1895 Alicia Amherst, *A History of Gardening in England* (2nd ed., 1896)
ARMSTRONG 1977 P. Armstrong, *Excavations in Sewer Lane, Hull, 1974* (East Riding Archaeologist, III)
ARMSTRONG 1979 J. R. Armstrong, *Traditional Buildings accessible to the Public* (Wakefield, EP)
J. A. Banqueri, *Libro de Agricultura . . . (de) ebn el Awam* (Madrid, 1802, 2 vols.)
BATES 1894 C. J. Bates, *Bamburgh Castle* (3rd ed.)
BENTHAM 1812 J. Bentham, *History . . . of the Cathedral Church of Ely* (2nd ed.)
BENTLEY 1831 S. Bentley, *Excerpta Historica*
Anna G. Bienfait & M. Kossmann, *Oude Hollandsche Tuinen* (The Hague, 1943, 2 vols.)
BL British Library
BLUNT 1950 W. Blunt, *The Art of Botanical Illustration* (3rd ed., 1955)
W. Blunt & S. Raphael, *The Illustrated Herbal* (1979)
BMQ *British Museum Quarterly*
BOTFIELD 1841 B. Botfield, *Manners and Household Expenses of England . . .* (Roxburghe Club)
BPR *The Black Prince's Register* (4 vols.)
BRAUNFELS 1972 W. Braunfels, *Monasteries of Western Europe*
BRODIN 1950 G. Brodin, *Agnus Castus: a Middle English Herbal* (Uppsala, English Institute of the University)
BURY 1903 R. de Bury, *The Love of Books* (King's Classics)
CCHR *Calendar of Charter Rolls*
CCLR *Calendar of Close Rolls*
CHEW & KELLAWAY 1973 H. M. Chew & W. Kellaway, *London Assize of Nuisance 1301–1431* (London Record Society, X)
CIPM *Calendar of Inquisitions post mortem*
CLIBR *Calendar of Liberate Rolls*
Cockayne, (T.) O., *Leechdoms, Wortcunning and Starcraft* (RS, XXXV, 3 Vols., 1864–6)
COULSON 1979 C. Coulson, 'Structural Symbolism in Medieval Castle Architecture', *Journal of the British Archaeological Association*, CXXXII, 73–90
COX 1935 E. H. M. Cox, *A History of Gardening in Scotland*
CPATR *Calendar of Patent Rolls*
CRISP 1924 Sir F. Crisp, *Mediaeval Gardens* (reprint 1966/1979, New York: Hacker)
CUL Cambridge University Library
DAMI 1924 L. Dami, *Il Giardino Italiano* (Milan)
DAVIES 1921 G. S. Davies, *Charterhouse in London*
DELISLE 1903 L. Delisle, *Etudes sur la condition de la classe agricole et l'etat de l'agriculture en Normandie au Moyen Age* (Paris); 1st ed., Evreux 1851
DIXON & RAINE 1863 W. H. Dixon & J. Raine, *Fasti Eboracenses*

DREW IHR J. S. Drew, Account Rolls of Manors of Winchester Cathedral Priory (Chilbolton, Michelmersh, Silkstead, Thurmond) – typescripts at Institute of Historical Research, London
EARLE 1880 J. Earle, *English Plant Names*
EETS Early English Text Society
EHR *English Historical Review*
FARR 1959 M. W. Farr, *Accounts and Surveys of the Wiltshire Lands of Adam de Stratton* (Wiltshire Record Society, XIV for 1958)
FISCHER 1929 H. Fischer, *Mittelalterliche Pflanzenkunde* (Munich)
FISCHER-BENZON 1894 R. von Fischer-Benzon, *Altdeutsche Gartenflora* (Kiel & Leipzig)
GANZENMÜLLER 1914 W. Ganzenmüller, *Das Naturgefühl im Mittelalter* (Leipzig & Berlin)
GARDINER 1930 Dorothy Gardiner, *The Story of Lambeth Palace*
GASQUET 1895 F. A. Gasquet, *Henry VIII and the English Monasteries*
GILES 1845 J. A. Giles, *Chronicon Angliae Petriburgense*
GODWIN 1956 Sir H. Godwin, *The History of the British Flora* (2nd ed., 1975)
GOODMAN 1927 A. W. Goodman, *Chartulary of Winchester Cathedral* (Winchester: Warren)
GOTHEIN 1928 Marie Luise Gothein, *A History of Garden Art* (translated from *Geschichte der Gartenkunst*, 1914/1925)
GRISEBACH 1910 A. Grisebach, *Der Garten: eine Geschichte seiner künstlerischen Gestaltung* (Leipzig)
GROSE 1808 F. Grose, *Antiquarian Repertory* (2nd ed.)
GROSS 1908 C. Gross, *Select Cases concerning the Law Merchant* (Selden Society, XXIII)
HADFIELD 1967 M. Hadfield, *Landscape with Trees*
HADFIELD 1969 M. Hadfield, *A History of British Gardening* (reprint, enlarged, 1979)
HARVEY 1946 J. H. Harvey, 'Side-lights on Kenilworth Castle', *Archaeological Journal*, CI, 91–107
HARVEY 1950 J. H. Harvey, *The Gothic World 1100–1600*
HARVEY 1961 J. H. Harvey, 'The Wilton Diptych', *Archaeologia*, XCVIII
HARVEY 1968 J. H. Harvey, 'The Origins of Gothic Architecture...', *Antiquaries Journal*, XLVIII, 87–99
HARVEY 1969 J. H. Harvey, ed., *William Worcestre: Itineraries* (Oxford Medieval Texts)
HARVEY 1972 J. H. Harvey, *The Mediaeval Architect*
HARVEY 1972.B   J. H. Harvey, *Early Gardening Catalogues*
HARVEY 1972.C   J. H. Harvey, 'Mediaeval Plantsmanship in England: the Culture of Rosemary', *Garden History*, I No. 1, 14–21
HARVEY 1974 J. H. Harvey, 'Spanish Gardens in their historical background', *Garden History*, III No. 1, 7–14
HARVEY 1974.B   J. H. Harvey, *Early Nurserymen*
HARVEY 1975 J. H. Harvey, *York*
HARVEY 1975.B   J. H. Harvey, *Mediaeval Craftsmen*
HARVEY 1975.C   J. H. Harvey, 'Gardening Books and Plant lists of Moorish Spain', *Garden History*, III No. 2, 10–21
HARVEY 1976 J. H. Harvey, *The Black Prince and his Age*
HARVEY 1976.B   J. H. Harvey, 'Turkey as a source of Garden Plants', *Garden History*, IV No. 3, 21–42
HARVEY 1978 J. H. Harvey, 'Gilliflower and Carnation', *Garden History*, VI No. 1 (1978), 46–57
HARVEY 1965 P. D. A. Harvey, *A Medieval Oxfordshire Village: Cuxham 1240–1400*
HARWOOD 1929 T. E. Harwood, *Windsor Old and New*
HEARNE 1726 T. Hearne, *Johannis Glastoniensis Chronica*
HENSLOW 1899 G. Henslow, *Medical Works of the Fourteenth Century... with a List of Plants...*
HKW *History of the King's Works*, ed. H. M. Colvin, vols. I, II (1963)
HMC Historical Manuscripts Commission
HOLMES 1957 G. A. Holmes, *The Estates of the Higher Nobility in Fourteenth-century England*
HOLT 1964 N. R. Holt, *The Pipe Roll of the Bishopric of Winchester 1210–11* (Manchester: University Press)
HOPE 1913 W. H. St.J. Hope, *Windsor Castle*, 2 vols.
P. Hulton & L. Smith, *Flowers in Art from East and West* (1979)

HUNT & KEIL 1960 T. J. Hunt & I. Keil, 'Two Medieval Gardens', *Somersetshire Archaeological and Natural History Society, Proceedings*, CIV, 91–101
HUNTER 1844 J. Hunter, *The Great Roll of the Pipe for the First Year of the Reign of King Richard the First*
HUXLEY 1978 A. J. Huxley, *An Illustrated History of Gardening* (1978)
HYAMS 1964 E. Hyams, *The English Garden*
HYAMS 1971 E. Hyams, *A History of Gardens and Gardening*
JOHNSON 1829 G. W. Johnson, *A History of English Gardening*
JOHNSTONE 1946 H. Johnstone, *Edward of Carnarvon*
JONES 1944 E. W. Jones, 'Biological Flora of the British Isles', *Journal of Ecology*, XXXII No. 1, 215–52
JORET 1892 C. Joret, *La Rose dans l'Antiquité et au Moyen Age* (Paris)
KAUFMANN 1892 A. Kaufmann, *Der Gartenbau im Mittelalter* (Berlin)
A. Kemp-Welch, *Of Six Mediaeval Women* (with) *A Note on Mediaeval Gardens* (1913)
KEMPE 1936 Margery Kempe, *The Book of Margery Kempe*, ed. W. Butler-Bowdon (re-issue 1940)
KIRK 1892 R. E. G. Kirk ed., *Accounts of the Obedientiars of Abingdon Abbey* (Camden Society, New Series, LI)
KITCHIN 1892 G. W. Kitchin, *Compotus Rolls of the Obedientiaries of St Swithun's Priory, Winchester* (Hampshire Record Society, VII)
KITCHIN 1895 G. W. Kitchin, *The Manor of Manydown, Hampshire* (Hampshire Record Society, X)
LEHMANN-BROCKHAUS 1955 O. Lehmann-Brockhaus, *Lateinische Schriftquellen zur Kunst in England, Wales und Schottland... 901–1307* (Munich, 1955–60)
LEMMON 1962 K. Lemmon, *The Covered Garden*
LOBEL 1969 M. D. Lobel, ed., *Historic Towns*, vol. I
LPL Lambeth Palace Library
P. de Madrazo, *Navarra y Logroño* (España, sus monumentos etc., Barcelona, 3 vols., 1886)
MANGIN 1887 A. Mangin, *Histoire des jardins anciens et modernes* (Tours)
METLITZKI 1977 Dorothee Metlitzki, *The Matter of Araby in Medieval England* (Yale University Press)
MIGNE *Patrologiae cursus completus*
MOORE 1897 S. A. Moore, *Cartularium monasterii... de Colecestria*
MORTET 1911 V. Mortet, ed., *Recueil de Textes relatifs à l'Histoire de l'Architecture... XIe – XIIe siècles* (Paris)
NEW COLLEGE J. Buxton & P. Williams, edd., *New College, Oxford, 1379–1979* (1979)
NICHOLS 1902 Rose S. Nichols, *English Pleasure Gardens* (New York)
NICHOLS 1925 Rose S. Nichols, *Spanish and Portuguese Gardens*
OSCHINSKY 1971 Dorothea Oschinsky, *Walter of Henley and other treatises on Estate Management and Accounting*
PAYNE & BLUNT 1966 R. Payne & W. Blunt, *Hortulus* (Pittsburgh, Hunt Botanical Library)
D. Pearsall & E. Salter, *Landscapes and Seasons of the Medieval World* (1973)
POWER 1928 Eileen Power, *The Goodman of Paris, c. 1393*
PRIOR 1863 R. C. A. Prior, *On the Popular Names of British Plants* (2nd ed., 1870)
PRO Public Record Office
PRS Pipe Roll Society
R. Pulteney, *Historical and Biographical Sketches of the Progress of Botany in England* (1790)
RACKHAM 1976 O. Rackham, *Trees and Woodland in the British Landscape*
RAVEN 1947 C. E. Raven, *English Naturalists from Neckam to Ray* (Cambridge University Press)
Rep. für K. 1919 E. Kuster, 'Belgische Gärten des fünfzehnten Jahrhunderts', *Repertorium für Kunstwissenschaft*, XLI, 148–58 (Berlin)
RIAT 1900 G. Riat, *L'Art des Jardins* (Paris)
RIGG 1966 A. G. Rigg, 'Some Notes on Trinity College, Cambridge, MS. 0.9.38', *Notes and Queries*, CCXI, 324–30
RIGG 1968 A. G. Rigg, *A Glastonbury Miscellany of the Fifteenth Century* (Oxford)
ROGERS 1866 J. E. Thorold Rogers, *A History of Agriculture and Prices in England*
ROHDE 1927 Eleanour S. Rohde, *Garden-Craft in the Bible and other Essays*

ROHDE 1932 Eleanour S. Rohde, *The Story of the Garden*
ROHDE 1932.B Eleanour S. Rohde, *Oxford's College Gardens*
ROSEN 1903 F. Rosen, *Die Natur in der Kunst* (Leipzig)
RS Rolls Series (Chronicles and Memorials of Great Britain and Ireland)
RUSSELL 1969 J. C. Russell, *Population in Europe 500–1500* (Fontana Economic History, vol. I.i)
Sir E. Salisbury, *Weeds and Aliens* (2nd ed., 1964)
SALZMAN 1952 L. F. Salzman, *Building in England down to 1540* (enlarged ed., 1967)
SAUVAL 1724 H. Sauval, *Histoire et recherches des antiquités de la Ville de Paris*, 3 vols. (Paris)
SEDDING 1891 J. D. Sedding, *Garden-Craft Old and New*
SIMMONDS 1976 N. W. Simmonds, ed., *Evolution of Crop Plants*
SPARKE 1723 J. Sparke, *Historiae Coenobii Burgensis Scriptores* (Historiae anglicanae scriptores, II)
SS Surtees Society
STEIN 1913 H. Stein, *Les Jardins de France des origines à la fin du XVIIIe siècle* (Paris)
SYPESTEYN 1910 C. H. C. A. van Sypesteyn, *Oud-Nederlandsche Tuinkunst* (The Hague)
TALBOT & HAMMOND 1965 C. H. Talbot & E. A. Hammond, *The Medical Practitioners in Medieval England* (Wellcome Historical Medical Library)
TAYLOR 1953 Gladys Taylor, *Old London Gardens*
THACKER 1979 C. Thacker, *The History of Gardens*
TOLKOWSKY 1938 S. Tolkowsky, *A History of the Culture and Use of Citrus Fruits*
TURNER 1848 T. Hudson Turner, 'Observations on the State of Horticulture in England in early times . . .', *Archaeological Journal*, V, 295–311
TURNER 1901 G. J. Turner, ed., *Select Pleas of the Forest* (Selden Society, XIII)
TWYSDEN 1652 R. Twysden, *Historiae Anglicanae Scriptores Antiqui*
URRY 1967 W. Urry, *Canterbury under the Angevin Kings*
WAM Westminster Abbey Muniments
WARNER 1826 R. Warner, *An History of the Abbey of Glaston* (Bath)
WCM Winchester College Muniments
H. Wegener, 'Die Lehrjahre der deutschen Blumenzucht', *Gartenflora*, LXXXV, 47–50 (Berlin)
WELCH 1900 C. Welch, *History of the Worshipful Company of Gardeners* (2nd edition)
WILLIS 1848 R. Willis, 'Description of the ancient plan of the Monastery of St. Gall . . .', *Archaeological Journal*, V, 85–117
WILLIS 1869 R. Willis, *The Architectural History . . . of the Monastery of Christ Church in Canterbury* (Kent Archaeological Society)
WILLIS 1916 Dorothy Willis, ed., *The Estate Book of Henry de Bray* (Royal Historical Society, Camden 3rd Series, XXVII)
WILLIS & CLARK 1886 R. Willis & J. W. Clark, *The Architectural History of the University of Cambridge*, 3 vols. (Cambridge)
D. Gay Wilson, 'Plant foods and poisons from mediaeval Chester', *Chester Archaeological Society, Journal*, LVIII 55–67
WINCHESTER COLLEGE 1926 *Winchester College: its History, Buildings and Customs* (Winchester College Archaeological Society)
X. de Winthuysen y Losada, *Jardines Clásicos de España* (Madrid)
WRIGHT 1871 T. Wright, *The Homes of other Days*
WRIGHT & WÜLCKER 1884 T. Wright & R. P. Wülcker, *Anglo Saxon and Old English Vocabularies*, 2 vols.

Notes to the Text

Abbreviations used, for works cited more than once, are those in the first column of the Bibliography.

Page
Introduction
2   Amherst 1895, 46; Rackham 1976, 145
    Climate – Godwin 1956/75, 481; Russell 1969, 24
3   Inferiority – Crisp 1924, I, 7; Hyams 1971, 105; Hadfield 1969, 28
    Aelfric – Wright & Wülcker 1884, I, 133–49
4   Sypesteyn 1910, 52–3
    Notker – Gothein 1928, 185
    St Victor – Migne, CLXXVII, 154 (*De bestiis et aliis rebus*, lib. iv, cap. 13)
    Neckam – RS, XXXIV (1863), *De laudibus divinae sapientiae*, vv. 295–302
    Bartholomew – *Bartholomaei Anglici de ... Proprietatibus* (Frankfurt 1601, reprint Minerva 1964), 947, cap. clxxvi; *On the Properties of Things* (John Trevisa's translation, Oxford U.P., 1975), 1068
6   Albert – *De vegetabilibus et plantis*, Lib. VII, Tractatus I, cap. xiv. The earliest detailed description of the design of a Muslim *chahār-bāgh* seems to be the literary account of the Garden of the Assassins by Albert's contemporary Ibn Khallikan (died 1282) – Metlitzki 1977, 226–7
    Crescenzi – *Ruralium Commodorum Liber*, Lib. VIII
    Coutances – *Recueil des Historiens de France*, t.xiv (1877), 76–80; cf. J. LePatourel, EHR, LIX (1944), 129–61
    Romsey – Amherst 1895, 7, quoting Migne, t. 159–60, sec. xii, Eadmer, 427
    York – *De Gestis Pontificum Anglorum*, RS, LII (1870), 259
    Clairvaux – Gothein 1928, 178; Hyams 1971, 91; cf. Rohde 1932, 32–3
10 Windsor – Harwood 1929, 111
    Le Mans – *Archives historiques du Maine*, II (1901), 462 ff.
    Auxerre – Mortet 1911, I, 96–8
    Manorbier, Lanthony – RS XXI, vi (1868), 92; iii (1863), 342–3
11 Westminster etc. – Devon 1837, 51, 53, 55, 65; HKW, 547; 507; 551; CLibR 1267–72, 2303
    Windsor – Hope 1913, 24, 62, 70
    Winchester – PRS, XXVII, 106; XXXII, 147; CLibR 1251–60, 47; HKW, 863
    Arundel – PRS, XXXVII, 107; XXXVIII, 185
    Marlborough – PRS, NS XVI, 161; CLibR 1251–60, 280
    Gloucester – CLibR 1260–67, 174
    Nottingham – PRS XXXIII, 99; HKW, 758
    Kempton – CLibR 1240–5, 172; 1251–60, 159
    Guildford – CLibR 1251–60, 289; 1267–72, 91; cf. HKW, 952
    Woodstock – Twysden 1652, I, col. 1151, 43; RS, XC (1887–9), ii, 485; RS, LXXIV (1879), 244; CLibR 1245–51, 292; 1260–7, 12
    Clarendon – PRS, XXX, 157; CLibR 1251–60, 180
12 Pever – RS, LVII, v, 242–3; VCH *Beds.*, III (1912), 439–40
    Kempton – HKW, 965
    Hampstead Marshall – HKW, 955
    Southwell – PRS, XXXIII, 39; Hunter 1844, 9
    Canterbury – Urry 1967. 214 and n. 4
    Lambeth – Gardiner 1930, 19–20; for information on the correct date of this roll (1236–7) and its condition in 1956 I am indebted to Professor C. H. Lawrence
    Auckland – CLibR 1240–5, 58
    Somersham – PRS, XV, 95–6; XVIII, 115–16, references for which I am indebted to Professor P. D. A. Harvey
    Lincoln – PRS, XII, 76–7
    Alvechurch – VCH *Worcs.*, III (1913), 253; IV (1924), 432
    St Albans – Salzman 1952, 380
    Bury – RS XCVI, ii (1892), 293
    Malmesbury – RS LXXII, ii (1880), 365–6
    Peterborough etc. – Sparke 1723, 155, 163, 164
13 Spalding – Giles 1845, 150
    Silkstead – Drew IHR (Silkstead), 125–6; 37; 201; 219
    Windsor – Hadfield 1967, 80
    Rackham – *Arboricultural Journal*, III No. 3, 176
    Alton Priors – Winchester Cathedral Library, Manorial Rolls, Box 59
16 Studham – RS XXXVI, iii (1866), 268
    Bradbourne – Ibid, 388
    Chestnut – Delisle 1903, 508; Salzman 1952, 252
    Cranmore etc. – Sparke 1723, 156, 162, 165; BL. Add. MS. 39758, f. 110v; Northants.

Record Society, XII (1947), 7
Harlestone – Willis 1916, 9, 50
Chertsey – Surrey Record Society, XIII part (1933), pp. xxv–xxix, nos. 477, 563, 575
Norwich – see p 13 above, Rackham quoting Account Rolls 4755, 4899
Durham – SS, CIII (1901), 710
Wells – HMC *Wells*, I (1907), 73–4; Cathedral Muniments, *Liber Albus*, f. 64v
London – RS IV, i (1858), 497; Chew & Kellaway 1973, 64
York – Dixon & Raine 1863, 390
Evesham – RS XXIX (1863), 292, 298, 301; VCH *Worcs.*, II (1906), 354, 356; cf. D. Cox, *Chronicle of Evesham Abbey* (Vale of Evesham Historical Society, 1964); C. J. Bond, Ibid, *Research Papers*, IV (1973)

17 Prices – Rogers 1866, II, 594; III, 564
Fladbury – Bodleian Library, Worcs. Rolls 4, kindly communicated by Professor P. D. A. Harvey
Cuxham – Harvey 1965, 39
Merriott – CClR 1374–7, 263–5
Wolsingham – Durham University, Box 83, rolls 190034 (CC), 190040; Box 32, 220224, f. 215v

Chapter One
20 Elmet – Harvey 1975, 15–18
21 Varro etc. – Turner 1848, 299
Palladius – *On Husbondrie*, ed. B. Lodge (EETS, 52 & 72, 1873–9)
22 Names – Earle 1880
Italy – Thacker 1979, 95–111
23 Gothic – Harvey 1950; Harvey 1972; Harvey 1968, 87–99
Box – Godwin 1956/75, 176
Introductions – Godwin 1956/75
24 Hemp – H. Godwin, *Antiquity*, XLI (1967), 42–9; Simmonds 1976, 203
Strawberry – Simmonds 1976, 239
Asparagus etc. – Johnson 1829, 13–19
Cherry etc. – Amherst 1895, 2

Chapter Two
26 Olive etc. – Russell 1969, 37–8; Fischer 1929, 5
St Teilo – Hyams 1964, 12–15
Isidore – Gothein 1928, 174
Roses – Joret 1892, 393
Subiaco – Nicholas 1902, 46
Gregory of Tours – Joret 1892, 391
St Fiacre – Rohde 1932, 60
Saints – Kaufmann 1892, 23; Fischer 1929, 150
Salic Law – Fischer 1929, 128–9
27 Hops – Ibid, 142
Venantius – Joret 1892, 155; Riat 1900, 55–6; Gothein 1928, 176; Rohde 1932, 27
Bede – *Historia ecclesiastica*, Book I, cap. i
St Boniface – Rohde 1932, 31 and note
Alcuin – Joret 1892, 156–7; Riat 1900, 58; Fischer 1929, 129–30
28 Capitulare – *Monumenta Germaniae historica, Leges*, sect. II, vol. i (Hannover 1883)
Elephant – Kaufmann 1892, 64
Viticulture – Fischer 1929, 154
Charlemagne – Delisle 1903, 489; Riat 1900, 57; Fischer 1929, 131–4; Fischer-Benzon 1894, 2 ff
32 St Gall plan – Willis 1848; Fischer 1929, 135 ff; Braunfels 1972, 37–46; Thacker 1979, 81
34 Walafrid – Payne & Blunt 1966; Thacker 1979, 81
Wandalbert – Fischer 1929, 140
Reichenau – Gothein 1928, 174
Winchester – Amherst 1895, 17; Rohde 1927, 99; Gothein 1928, 176
35 Laws – Amherst 1895, 21; Hyams 1964, 12 ff; cf. Rohde 1932, 32
Beans and peas – Russell 1969, 56
York – Harvey 1975, 112, and sources quoted at 180
Masterwort – Godwin 1956/75, 227
Eadfrith – RS XXVIII, iv (vol. 1, 1867), 20 ff
Vines – Amherst 1895, 21
Welsh laws – Hyams 1964, 12
St Ethelwold – Rohde 1932, 34; *Liber Eliensis* ed. D. J. Stewart (Anglia Christiana Society), I (1848), 167
Thorney – RS II, i (1858), 290; LII (1870), 326; Gothein 1928, 178

Chapter Three
37 Abu Bakr – Kaufmann 1892, 18
Arab horticulture – Harvey 1975.C; cf. Fischer 1929, 47; Rohde 1932, 26; Harvey 1976.B
40 Ibn Bassal – J. M. Millás Vallicrosa & M. Aziman, *Libro de Agricultura* (Tetuan, Instituto Muley el-Hasan, 1955); J. M. Millás Vallicrosa, *Al-Andalus*, XIII (1948), 347–430
41 Ibn al-'Awwam – J. J. Clément-Mullet, *Le Livre de l'Agriculture* (2 t., Paris, 1864–7); cf. Nichols 1925, 278
43 Adelard – Harvey 1968; Metlitzki 1977, 19–29; *Beiträge zur Geschichte der Philosophie des Mittelalers*, XXX (1934), 10–11
Ibn al-Baitar – L. Leclerc, *Notices et Extraits des manuscrits …*, XXIII, XXV, XXVI (Paris, 1877–83); Fischer 1929, 46, 48–9, 50
Ibn al-Suri – Blunt 1950, 17 note
Translations – *Al-Andalus*, VIII (1943), 281 ff; XIII (1948), 347 ff; L. Faraudo de Saint-Germain, *El "Libre de les Medecines Particulars" … de Ibn Wafid* (Barcelona, 1943)
44 Crescenzi – Stein 1913, 5
Granada – J. Dickie, 'The Islamic Garden in Spain', *The Islamic Garden* (4th Dumbarton Oaks Colloquium, Washington, 1976), 89
Ibn Luyun – J. Eguaras Ibáñez, *Ibn Luyun: Tratado de Agricultura* (Granada, 1975); review, *Garden History*, V No. 2 (1977), 6–8
45 Olite etc. – Madrazo 1886, 236–65
Orange tree Ibid, 236–7
Warm houses etc. – Jovianus Pontanus, *De Hortis Hesperidum* (1490); *Calendar of Ancient*

Deeds, VI, C. 7590
Valencia – Tolkowsky 1938, 192; Fischer 1929, 151
48 Carnation – Harvey 1978, 47
Rozmital – Kaufmann 1892, 33
Navagero – Harvey 1974, 7
50 Salerno – Kaufmann 1892, 36; Fischer 1929, 17, 22, 152
Clavis sanationis – Fischer 1929, 70–1
Rufinus – Lynn Thorndike ed., *The Herbal of Rufinus* (Chicago University Press, 1946/49)
Milan etc. – Gothein 1928, 197–8
Monte Cassino – Ibid, 173
Italy – Dami 1924, 7; Gothein 1928, 198–200; Rosen 1903, 39
51 Venice, Prague – Kaufmann 1892, 36; cf. Gothein 1928, 202
Milan – Dami 1924, 7
Parma – Hyams 1971, 95
Florence – Rosen 1903, 81–2

Chapter Four
52 Leech-books – O. Cockayne, *Leechdoms, Wort-cunning and Starcraft*, 3 vols., RS, XXXV (1864–6)
Malmesbury – Dom Aelred Watkin, VCH *Wilts.*, III (1956), 214
Macer – Earle 1880, lvi–lix; G. Frisk ed., *A Middle English translation of Macer Floridus de Viribus Herbarum* (Upsala, 1949)
54 Crusades – R. Menéndez Pidal, *Poesía árabe y poesía europea* (Buenos Aires, Espasa-Calpe, 1941)
Vineyards – Amherst 1895, 22–4, 34; cf. VCH *Berks.*, II (1907), 168; RS LII (1870), 291–2; PRS, X (1888), no. 28
Germany – Kaufmann 1892, 25
Normandy – Delisle 1903, 495, 500–4
Hexham – PRS, XLIV (1929), 29–30
Runham – Turner 1848, 302, quoting Blomefield, *Norfolk*, XI (1810), 242
58 Morimond – Kaufmann 1892, 25
Tegernsee etc. – Fischer 1929, 140–2
Denmark – Joret 1892, 191
Cologne – Kaufmann 1892, 26
Crowland – Lehmann-Brockhaus 1955, I, no. 1173
Gloucester – RS XXXIII, i (1863), 39; PRO, C 115/A.4, f. 213; cf. Amherst 1895, 20
Barnwell – J. Willis Clark ed., *The observances in use at the Augustinian priory ... at Barnwell* (1897), 68ff, 154
Bury – Bodleian Library, MS. Bodley 130; Raven 1947, 26
Ramsey – Amherst 1895, 10–11
Impgarth etc. – Harvey 1974.B, 22–3, notes at 213
Wheelbarrows – Huxley 1978, 111; cf. D. Sherlock, *Building*, 22/29 Dec. 1978, 22–3
Fécamp – Harvey 1972, 62–3
60 St Liutgart – Kaufmann 1892, 20
Helmstadt – Fischer 1929, 145
Barbarossa – Kaufmann 1892, 18, 26; Gothein 1928, 189–91, 197

Godric – SS, XX (1847), sec. 322
61 London – Welch 1900, 18
Dunstable – HKW, 925; *Monasticon*, VI, i (1849), 240; *Chronicon sive Annales Prioratus de Dunstaple*, ed. T. Hearne (1733), I, 49
Havering – PRS, NS XVII, no. 242; cf. HKW, 956
64 Carlisle – Amherst 1895, 34
Radmore etc. – HKW, 989, 1016
Chester – Chester City Records CR 63/2 (Earwaker MSS); Grosvenor MSS 1353–4; cf. Harvey 1974.B, 16
Canterbury – Willis 1869; Urry 1967, 229, 237–8, maps
66 London – H. E. Butler in F. M. Stenton, *Norman London* (Historical Association, 1934), 27
Hildegard – Fischer 1929, 25–31
Neckam – RS XXXIV (1863); Hyams 1964, 14
67 Sticados – BL, Royal MS. 12 E.VIII, f. 122v
70 *Erec* etc. – Gothein 1928, 189; cf. Ganzenmüller 1914, 268–70; Wright 1871, 296–302; Kaufmann 1892, 21
Rose arbour – Hyams 1971, 93
Hildesheim – *Encyclopaedia Britannica*, 11th ed. (1910), XIII, 462; Fischer 1929, 128. For the identification of the plant as *Rosa canina* I am indebted to Graham S. Thomas and Dr W. T. Stearn
Linden – Prior 1863, 1; Sypesteyn 1910, 55
Tannhäuser – Kaufmann 1892, 22; cf. Karl Bartsch, *Deutsche Liederdichter* (1864; 4th ed. 1900/28), 245
Hadloub – Bartsch, op. cit., 339
Nuremberg – Gothein 1928, 191
72 Wernher – Ibid, 178
Herbs – BL, Arundel MS. 369, f. 48
Winchester rolls – Holt 1964, 154; 95; 123; 171
Talworth etc. – *Curia Regis Rolls*, VIII, 358; XIII, no. 1617; X, 105
73 Worcester – RS XXXVI, iv (1869), 415
Evesham – RS XXIX (1863), 208
Ely – Bentham 1812, II, 53
Eye – Sparke 1723, 120
Damerham – Somerset Record Society, V (1891), 114
Lancaster – *Liber Feodorum ... Testa de Nevill* (1921–31), I, 349, 370; II, 1191, 1391
Garlande – BL, Harleian MS 1002, ff. 179, 181; cf. Delisle 1903, 490

Chapter Five
74 Practice and theory – Harvey 1972.B, 2
75 *Fleta* – ed. J. Selden (1685), 171 (Lib. ii, cap. 82)
Bartholomew – Joret 1892, 175
Albertus – Ibid, 164–70; Fischer 1929, 5, 34–41
Winter garden – Riat 1900, 76; cf. Fischer 1929, 141
Maerlant – Fischer 1929, 43
Harpestreng etc. – Joret 1892, 192

Bonn – Gothein 1928, 196
Wedding – Kaufmann 1892, 23
Louvre – Grisebach 1910, 7
Jumièges etc. – Delisle 1903, 485; 497; 279; 494; 491

76 Crescenzi – Joret 1892, 175–6; *Enciclopedia Italiana*, XI, 841; Fischer 1929, 153, 176–84
Humbert II – J. P. Moret de Bourchenu, Marquis de Valbonnais, *Histoire du Dauphiné*, t. II (Geneva, 1722), 274, 279
Demesne farming – P. D. A. Harvey, *Economic History Review*, 2 Ser., XXVII No. 3 (1974), 345–59

78 Henley – Dorothea Oschinsky ed., *Walter of Henley* ... (Oxford, 1971), 144–5, 175, 324–5
Norwich – Talbot & Hammond 1965, 3265; 95
Fulk – CClR 1268–72, 183; 1272–9, 156, 394; CLibR 1267–72, 1953, 2015
Blandurel apple – PRO, C. 62/57, m.9
King's Langley – VCH *Herts.*, II (1908), 235; HKW, 971; BL, Add. MS. 35294, f. 9v
Westminster Abbey – Henry Bradshaw Society, XXVIII (1904), 89–91
Herbs – Botfield 1841, xlvii
Archaeology – Dorian Williams in Armstrong 1977, 18–32, a reference which I owe to Miss F. E. Crackles

79 Seeds – Rogers 1866, II, 173–7, 594; III, 564; Farr 1959, 191, 203, 213, 222
St Ives – Gross 1908, 77
Rimpton – Hunt & Keil 1960, 95
Southwark – Hampshire Record Office, Winchester, Pipe Roll 159308, rot. 33
Cuxham – Rogers 1866, II, 594
Chilbolton – Drew IHR (Chilbolton), 177
Wellingborough – Northants. Record Society, VIII (1936)
Cuxham – P. D. A. Harvey, *Cuxham Manorial Records* (1976), 62
Silkstead – Drew IHR
Ashes – Turner 1901, 52
South Malling – Armstrong 1979, 20; and personal communication
Churchyards – *Statutes of the Realm* (1810–28), I, 221; *Memorials of ... Ripon* (SS, LXXIV, 1882), 76–7 and note
Windsor – CLibR 1251–60, 155, 501, 532; 1260–7, 14, 82, 128
Woodstock – Ibid, 1226–40, 412; 1240–5, 3, 307; 1245–51, 186, 245, 292; 1251–60, 67; 1260–7, 154; Pipe Roll 52, rot. 1d; I owe this last reference to the kindness of Mr R. E. Latham
Clarendon – CLibR 1245–51, 109, 239, 297
Westminster – CLibR 1226–40, 376; CClR 1261–4, 29
Tower – CLibR 1260–7, 103; CClR 1261–4, 29; W. J. Hardy & W. Page, *Feet of Fines for London and Middlesex*. I (1892), 34, 57
Guildford, Winchester, Nottingham – CLibR, passim

80 Gloucester, Havering, Hereford – CLibR, passim
Windsor – CClR 1264–8, 279
Roger le Herberur – PRO, C 47/3/31; cf. Harvey 1974.B, xii–xiii, 40
Tower – HKW, 723; PRO, E 101/467/6 (2, 5, 6); C 47/3/47; E 101/467/9, m.7; 467/7(3)

82 Plants – PRO, E 101/467/6(2), m.9
Peter etc. – E 101/467/7(2); (7)
Fruit – Turner 1848, 300, 302–3; cf. Amherst 1895, 40, 47

84 Langley Marish – HKW, 979
Conway – PRO, E 101/351/9, m.8
Chester – PRO, Chester Plea Roll 3, rott. 6, 2d, by the kindness of Mr R. E. Latham; SC 6/771/1, m.5, which I owe to Dr D. R. Howlett
Caernarvon – HKW, 381 note 3
Northampton – PRO, E 101/369/11
Bishop's Cleeve etc. – *The Red Book of Worcester* ed. Marjory Hollings (Worcs. Historical Society, 1934–50), 349; 90; 87
Burstwick – HKW, 905
Meaux – RS XLIII, iii (1868), 242
Haughmond – *Monasticon*, VI, 112
Westminster – WAM 19319
Gloucester – PRO, C 115/A.4, f. 215, 215v; CPatR 1377–81, 285; Lobel 1969 (Gloucester)

86 *Philobiblon* – Bury 1903, 35
Metz – Joret 1892, 417
Hazelnuts etc. – Rogers 1866, II, 594
Lambeth – LPL, roll ED 545, Forinsece
Saffron – Mrs D. Cromarty, *Essex Journal*, II (1967) No. 2, 109; No. 4, 182
Abingdon – Kirk 1892, 40, 48

87 Windsor – HKW, 881 note 4
Royal gardens – Welch 1900, 12; PRO, E 101/478/26; HKW, 961
Woodstock – HKW, 1016
Kennington – BPR, IV (1933), 441
Eltham – E. J. Priestley, 'The Manor and Palace of Eltham, Kent 1086–1663', London M.Phil. Thesis 1973, 300–02; PRO, E 101/473/2, m.12; I am much indebted to Mr Priestley for this material
Sheen – HKW, 997–8; cf. Harvey 1976, 144
Windsor – Harwood 1929, 111
Sandal – Dominic Bruynseels, 'The Eastern Section of the Manor of Wakefield', Durham BA Dissertation 1980, 78; I am much indebted to Mr Bruynseels and also to Professor P. D. A. Harvey for this reference
London – CIpm, XV, nos. 600–1; XVI, no. 193
Clare and Bardfield – PRO, SC 6/992/25; E 101/459/24; SC 6/1110/10, 12, 18, 20; E 101/458/4; 459/25, 26; E 101/93/12; SC 6/1110/25; E 101/93/19; and Gladys A. Thornton, *A History of Clare, Suffolk* (1930), as well as the London MA Thesis (1927) on which this was based, for permission to consult which I am greatly indebted to Mrs G. A. Ward; Harrison in Holinshed – see note to p. 115

88 Lambeth – Taylor 1953, 54–6

Highclere – Hampshire Record Office, Church Commissioners' rolls 159387; 159405
Esher – WCM 1, dorse, Stipendia familie
92 Winchester – Goodman 1927, no. 275; Winchester College 1926, 50
Manydown etc. – Kitchin 1895, 3–5
Winchester etc. – Kitchin 1892, 79; Amherst 1895, 16
Durham etc. – SS, XCIX, 115, 261; LXXXII, 46, 124, 179–80
Fahrnau – Kaufmann 1892, 45
Helmond – Sypesteyn 1910, 276
Lemmon 1962, 15
Paris – Mangin 1887, 70, 72
Deville etc. – Delisle 1903, 487, 489, 504
Hôtel St Pol – Sauval 1724, II, 283–4

Chapter Six
94 Chaucer – *Legend of Good Women*, 11, 40–211
Marchantes Tale, 11, 784 ff
95 *Frankeleyns Tale*, 11, 908 ff
Pierce – Amherst 1895, 65
Tale of Beryn – Chaucer Society, 2nd Series, XVII, 10
Troy Book – ed. H. Bergen (EETS, Extra Series, XCVII, 1906), 11. 1265–76, 1202–11
96 *The Kingis Quair*, vv 31 ff. I am indebted to Sir Robert Mackworth-Young for much information on the King's Garden at Windsor and for confirming that the Earl Marshal's Tower (where James I was a prisoner) commanded a good view of the garden
98 Ely Place – Amherst 1895, 27
Lambeth – LPL, ED 547.A; Gardiner 1930, 47; Kempe 1936, 64
London gardens – Welch 1900, 13–14;
103 London Corporation Record Office, Hustings Roll 168 (27); Welch 1900, 12–13; Amherst 1895, 26
Glynde – *Catalogue of Glynde Place Archives*, 113, no. 1190
Bristol – Bristol Archives Office, 5139/138; I am indebted to Mrs Frances Neale for this reference
Teynham – CClR 1374–7, 206; CIpm, XIV, no. 44
Sheringham – CIpm, XVI, no. 975
Norwich – Harvey 1975.B, 75–6
Peter of Blois – Migne, CCVII, 14–15
Alvechurch – *The Red Book of Worcester*, 210
Codesley – SS, XCIX, 210
106 Leeds – Nicholas 1902, 75; HKW, II, 697
Hesdin – M. Charageat, 'Le Parc de Hesdin', *Bulletin de la Société de l'Histoire de l'Art Français* 1950 (1951), 94–106; Comte de Laborde, *Les Ducs de Bourgogne*, 2 partie, I (1849), esp. 944; Mgr. Dehaisnes, *Histoire de l'Art dans la Flandre, l'Artois et le Hainaut* (Lille, 1886), 416–30; J-M. Richard, *Mahaut, Comtesse d'Artois* (Paris, 1887); Al-Jazari, *The Book of Knowledge of Ingenious Mechanical Devices*, ed. D. R. Hill (1974)
Mews – HKW, 551
Cheapside etc. – Harvey 1972, 65–6

Kenilworth – PRO, DL 29/463/7551
Nobility – Holmes 1957
Broughton – I here record my thanks to Lord and Lady Saye and Sele for showing me this unusual feature and for telling me the name of 'The Warren'
107 Bronsil – Coulson 1979, 75 and note 8; CChR 1427–1516, 137; cf. Harvey 1946, 91, as to the symbolic aspects of Kenilworth
Megenberg – Fischer 1929, 51–2, 151
Cambridge – Willis & Clark 1886, III, 578–9, 582; I, 122
New College – G. Jackson-Stops in *New College*, 202
110 Winchester – Harvey 1974.B, 25–6
Clare – PRO, SC 6/1112/11
Clarendon – CLibR 1245–51, 362
Quickset – Rogers 1866, II, 594
Colchester – Moore 1897, 509; I am obliged to Dr Oliver Rackham for this reference
Bristol – *State Trials of Edward I* (Camden 3rd Series IX, 1906), 7
112 Dunstable – RS XXXVI, iii (1866), 388
Westminster – WAM 19321
Kettering – Sparke 1723, 166
Kennington – BPR, IV, 247
Westminster – WAM 19344–5; 19351–2; 19366, 19376
Jewel Tower, Guildford, Sheen – HKW, 536–7, 953, 996 note 9
Westminster – PRO, E 101/468/21, f. 110v
Westminster Palace – BL, Add. MS. 17361, f. 7v; PRO, E 101/473/2
Abbey – WAM 19092, 19108, 19338
Lydgate – Amherst 1895, 55
Kenilworth – PRO, DL 29/463/7541
Worcestre – Harvey 1969, 125–6 note
Westminster – WAM 19383–4
Durham – SS, XCIX, 271
114 Caxton – *Dialogues* (EETS, Extra Series 1900), 13, 25; cf. Sedding 1891, 47; Rackham 1976, 117
Windsor – CLibR 1251–60, 289
King's Langley – PRO, E 101/466/1; Johnstone 1946, 30
Woodstock – CLibR 1251–60, 24–5, 272
Durham – SS, XCIX, 209
Highclere – Hampshire Record Office, Church Commissioners' rolls, 159382
Sheen – PRO, E 364/83, rot. E
Tendring – Botfield 1841, 563
Rotherhithe – PRO, E 101/545/36, m.3
Sheen, Eltham – PRO, E 101/473/2
Methley – Harvey 1974.B, 22–3
Abingdon – Kirk 1892, 57
Durham – SS, XCIX, 271
115 Norwich – Amherst 1895, 14
Windsor – Hope 1913, 218–19
Kennington – BPR, IV, 36, 91
Westminster Palace – CClR 1364–8, 167; 1399–1402, 130; 1402–5, 502
Abbey – WAM 19322
Harrison – Holinshed, *Chronicles* (ed. 1587), 208–10

NOTES TO THE TEXT

Arderne, Bray – Talbot & Hammond 1965, 111–12, 125; cf. Harvey 1974.B, 18–19; Harvey 1976, 123–4
'Agnus Castus' – Brodin 1950
Jon Gardener – Rigg 1966; Rigg 1968; cf. Harvey 1974.B, 18–22, 138–40

118 Bourgeois – Power 1928; Harvey 1974.B, 19–22
Daniel – Harvey 1974.B, 17, 34; Harvey 1976, 61–2

Chapter Seven

120 Introductions – Fischer 1929, 236–53
Florence – Kaufmann 1892, 36

121 Bourdichon – J. Delaunay, *Le Livre d'Heures de la reine Anne de Bretagne* (Paris, Curmer, 1859–61); Jules Camus, *Journal de Botanique*, VIII (1894), 325, 345, 366, 396 ff
Beans – Simmonds 1976, 168–71
Cauliflower, Carrot – Ibid, 50, 292; cf. Power 1928, 296; BL, Royal MS. 17 B.XLVII, f. 143v
Celery – Delisle 1903, 496
Lettuce – Simmonds 1976, 40
Peas – Delisle 1903, 327, 495–6; Bristol Record Society, IX (1938), 220–1
Spinach – Harvey 1974.B, 140

122 Trees – CUL, MS. Ee.4.20, ff. 163v–164
Apricot – Harvey 1974.B, 28
Fig, Gooseberry – Rohde 1932, 26; Delisle 1903, 504

123 Medlar – HMC, *Wells*, I (1907), 214–15; Rohde 1932, 35–6
Mulberry – Taylor 1953, 50; BL, Sloane MS. 3548, f.124; Harleian MS. 978, f.24v; York Minster, *Magnum Registrum Album*, pt. iv, f. 44, kindly communicated by Dr D. M. Palliser; Chapter Wills, Reg. 1, f. 33v
Walnut – Harvey 1974.B, 23; PRO, DL 29/682/11040, a reference which I owe to the kindness of Professor Paul Harvey; Kirk 1892, 75; cf. Simmonds 1976, 310
Birch – Bates 1894, 25, 84 note 137
Chestnut – Godwin 1956, 277; J. G. Strutt, *Sylva Britannica* (1826), engraving
Lime – Selden Society, XIII (1901), 63
Plane – BL, Harleian MS. 116, f. 156; Amherst 1895, 30, 161; Harvey 1974.B, 18

124 Sycamore – Jones 1944, 235; Godwin 1956, 170
Evergreens – *Dives et Pauper* (Camden Society VI, 1839); cf. R. B. Dobson & J. Taylor, *Rymes of Robin Hood* (1976); *Transactions of the London & Middlesex Archaeological Society*, V (1885), 350; Davies 1921, 330–1. I am grateful to Professor R. B. Dobson and to Professor R. B. Pugh in connection with the mediaeval occurrence of the Bay

125 Box – Sypesteyn 1910, 239–40; Delisle 1903, 487
Fir – Harvey 1969, 135
Pine – R. Macphail & H. C. M. Keeley, 'The Soils and Pollen of Norton Priory, Runcorn, Cheshire', kindly communicated by Mr Rob Scaife

126 Yew – EETS, OS 128, 403
Flowers – H. N. Ellacombe, 'The Flowers of Gower and Chaucer', *Gardener's Chronicle* (1911), 401–2, 24–5, 43, 84, 107, 126, 147, 165

131 Hyssop – WAM 19326; PRO, E 101/545/34, m.4; Amherst 1895, 27
Lavender – Delisle 1903, 491
Rosemary – Harvey 1961, 10; Harvey 1972.C; Harvey 1974.B, 27, 135–7; Harvey 1976, 62; Taylor 1953, 106
Columbine – Joret 1892, 296
Jacob's Ladder – Godwin 1956/75, 315

132 Palma Christi – Henslow 1899, 233
Marigold – Armstrong 1977, 18–19 etc.
Garlands – Wright 1871, 301; Amherst 1895, 18–19

Epilogue

134 Erfurt – Kaufmann 1892, 39; Fischer 1929, 150
Vienna – Kaufmann 1892, 53

135 Germany – Joret 1892, 186
Auslasser – Fischer 1929, 59
Brussels, London – Kaufmann 1892, 34
King René – Joret 1892, 183; Riat 1900, 65; Fischer 1929, 151; G. Arnaud d'Agnel, *Les Comptes du Roi René* (Paris, 1908–9), I, nos. 65, 358; II, nos. 1712, 1720; J. de Bourdigné, *Chroniques d'Anjou et du Maine* (Angers, 1842), II, 229; A. Lecoy de la Marche, *Le Roi René* (Paris, 1875), II, 9, 33, 35, 50
Paris – Sauval 1724, II, 283–4
Greenwich – HKW, 949
Windsor – *Archaeologia*, XXVI (1836), 278; Hope 1913, 239
Richmond – Grose 1808, II, *316; Bentley 1831, 133

136 Thornbury – PRO, E 36/220, p. 8
Banwell – Somerset Record Society, XLIX (1934), xl; Harvey 1969, 296–7
East Brent – BMQ, X (1935), 70
Glastonbury, Meare – Hearne 1726, 310, 316; Warner 1826, lxxiii–lxxv; Gasquet 1895, II, 338; R. W. Dunning in *Studies in Church History*, XIV (1977), 215
Bishop Auckland – Durham University, Church Commissioners' records, Box 32, 220224, f. 11
Westminster – *Monasticon*, I (1817), 282–3
Improvement – Fischer 1929, 145; *Monasticon*, V (1817–30), 371

140 London – Harvey 1975.B, 41; Welch 1900, 14
Leicester – *Records of the Borough of Leicester*, ed. M. Bateson, II (1901), 246, 250
Cambridge – A. Gransden, *Historical Writing in England c. 550–c. 1307* (1974), 339 note 162; I am grateful to Mr L. S. Colchester for this reference and the next
Wells – HMC, *Wells*, II (1914), 108–9
Westminster – WAM 18908
Cambridge – Willis & Clark 1886, I, 27, 569–71; II, 56

Eltham – E. J. Priestley 1973 (above, note to p. 87), 301
Westminster – Taylor 1953, 21; Amherst 1895, 89; WAM, Lease Registers I–III (1485–1555)
Norwich – Amherst 1895, 11
Radley – Berkshire Record Office, D/EP.1.M.15

142 Hildebert – Migne, CLXXI (1854), 1235

Appendix One Some Royal Gardeners
The lists are based mainly on CPatR and CClR, with material from account rolls already quoted; for Windsor see also Hope 1913

155 *Forme of Cury* – R. Warner ed., *Antiquitates Culinariae* (1791), 1–35

Appendix Two Friar Henry Daniel
The quotations are taken from BL, Arundel MS. 42, and Additional MS. 27329

161 John de Sancta Maria – CPatR 1367–70, 91; 1381–5, 366; CClR 1374–7, 147; 1377–81, 162, 409
Charles le Convers – CPatR 1388–92, 430
See also M. Adler, *Jews of Medieval England* (1939).

ADDENDA

p. 16 *Tree-planting.* Further examples of planting forest trees are at Maidstone (Kent) in 1300, where 22 elms for planting were bought for 4s. (Lambeth Palace, roll 658); and in 1303 at Billingham (Durham), where ash trees were planted in the garden (Durham, muniments of the Dean & Chapter, Enrolled Manors 1299–1303, m.3d), instances which I owe to the kindness of Professor P. D. A. Harvey.

p. 21 *Columella and Palladius.* Concerning manuscripts of Columella *De agricultura*, R. A. Mynors pronounced that 'the work itself was not known here' (in D. J. Gordon ed., *Fritz Saxl* (1957), 209. R. N. Thomson in *Manuscripts from St. Albans Abbey 1066–1235* (Woodbridge: Brewer, 1982), 40, quotes R. H. Rodgers as to 'how common Palladius' work was in 12th-century libraries, including those of England'.

p. 86 *Lambeth Palace.* For comparison, the Abbot of Westminster in his garden at La Neyte (by Ebury Bridge, Westminster) was growing skirrets (*eskiriwitas*) in 1275–6 (WAM 26850); and in 1327 seeds were bought of onion, leek, parsley, beet, orach, 'spinach', borage, cresses, worts, hyssop, fennel, chervil, violet, coriander and langdebefe (*lingua boum*) at low prices from $\frac{1}{2}$d. to 6d., but no amounts are stated. A larger quantity of hemp seed was brought for 1s. (WAM 26873).

p. 120 *Liquorice.* At Halsham in east Yorkshire the hall of the manor-house stood next to 'le Licorescegarth' in 1349 (CIpm, IX, p. 220).

p. 121 *Carrot.* The Bury St Edmunds herbal of c 1120 (Oxford, MS. Bodley 130, f. 23v) has a naturalistic picture of a carrot plant with an orange-coloured root.

p. 126 *Frankfurt Paradise painting.* Mr Anthony Huxley considers that 'Borage' is really Germander Speedwell; 'Sage' some other labiate plant; and 'Snowdrop' really a Snowflake (*Leucojum vernum*). In the last case I certainly agree, but feel there is some doubt in the others.

p. 131 *Chelsea Manor.* In c 1537 a purchase of 4 bundles of 'Osyerse for the Erbor' was made for 2s. 8d. for St James's; and for Chelsea 20 cherry and 5 filbert trees for 7s. 8d.; 5 damson and 2 red peach trees, 2s. 4d.; 200 'Dammaske Roses', 2s.; 11,000 sets of 'Whyte thorne' for £3 13s. 4d. and 64,000 sets of 'prevett' for £16 (BL Royal MS 14 B.iv.A) This extensive use of privet is noteworthy.

p. 136 *Palace gardens.* At Raglan Castle, Gwent, early in the 15th century 'there were orchards full of apple trees and plums, and figs and cherries and grapes, and French plums and pears, and nuts and every fruit that is sweet and delicious' (MS. of Iolo Morganwg, Llanover, Gwent, kindly communicated by Mrs Elisabeth Whittle).

p. 164 *Cabbage.* At Leeds Priory (Kent) c 1505, 2s. was spent 'in Cabbeges and sedes to sowe in the garden and for oynons' (Oxford, Bodleian MS Top. Kent d.4 (R).)

APPENDIX ONE

Some Royal Gardeners

SEVERAL OF THE ENGLISH gardeners in charge of the royal gardens have been mentioned in the text, but in most cases they are shadowy figures. Some of them, however, were evidently men of standing and actively concerned both with horticulture and the supply of plants. At the chief gardens they follow one another in a fairly regular succession, although few were actually appointed by patent. In general they were allowed regular wages and also robes, besides being termed 'Master' in a few instances. In the hope that publication of outline lists may encourage further biographical research, the series of names are set out below for London (Westminster and the Tower), Windsor Castle, Eltham and Sheen.

While the earlier gardeners were certainly in direct charge of the growing of plants and trees, or skilled in the management of vines, the later holders of office seem often to have had only a nominal responsibility and to have exercised their offices by deputy. This presumably was the case with those styled 'esquire' in the fifteenth century, and perhaps also with men who had parallel careers as, for example, Groom of the Sadlery or King's Footman. Only exhaustive search through all surviving accounts is likely to disentangle such anomalies.

It is probable that some of the gardeners moved from one estate to another, not only from Westminster to the Tower of London, but also to Windsor as in the case of John le Gardener who died in 1337. Robert le Vynour was undoubtedly in charge both in London and at Windsor in the 1360s, but there is nothing to show whether he was identical with the Robert Gardiner at Sheen who held office before William Rokyngham and died on 29 May 1387. At Windsor the Master Vinedresser or Keeper of the King's Vine may have been distinct from the Keeper of the Great Garden, but the two offices were sometimes at least held together, as by Adam Goodale, a yeoman of the Crown, who was also Porter of the Outer Gate in the 1460s.

In the latter part of the fourteenth century there were two or possibly three of the royal gardeners named John. It is not inconceivable that one of them may have been the 'Mayster Jon Gardener' who compiled the famous treatise. In the comparable instance of the *Forme of Cury*, the royal cookery book, we are explicitly told that it was compiled by the 'chief masters cooks' of King Richard the Second. Though perhaps too early to qualify as a candidate for the authorship, John de Standerwyk, who was a Yeoman of the Chamber and also Gardener at Westminster and the Tower, had gardens at Westminster from which his crops were stolen in 1335, and other property at Staines. No doubt he came from the little Somerset village near Beckington.

LONDON (Westminster Palace and the Tower of London)

William the Gardener	3d. a day	(1262–1278)
Roger le Herberur	2¼d. a day	(1268–1307)
in 1286 received a robe as a 'valet'		
Maurice de la Grave		(1312–1313)
also 'Master Maurice' the gardener		
John le Gardener	(at Windsor in 1325)	(died 1337)

John de Standerwyk	grant during good behaviour	3 July 1337
granted office of sealing woolsacks 1343		(died 1345)
James des Armes	grant for life	16 Mar. 1345
Robert le Vynour	writ of aid	4 May 1353
grant during pleasure of 8d. a day as tender of the King's Vine at Westminster etc., and also 4d. a day to supervise the vines at Windsor and other manors and to inform and teach two men to cut, keep and maintain the vines		3 Apr. 1363 (–1366)

   It is not certain that the Roger who appears as a royal gardener from 1268 to 1307 was one and the same man, nor that he was the Roger, son of William le Gardener, who had property in Westminster in 1251; he or another Roger le Gardener of Westminster, with his wife Christina, was buying land in Fulham in 1281.

   The John de Turri (of the Tower) who flourished in 1275–78 may have been a royal gardener, or a nurseryman. In 1307–08, probably under Master Maurice, there were two under-gardeners at Westminster Palace, Roger de Wicham and Roger de Fulham. In 1328 there was one William the gardener of the King at Westminster in charge of the vines; and before 1365 John Gardyner 'of Westminster' had done good service for which he was granted a pension at St German's in Cornwall, which he held until 1400. By 20 Feb. 1405 he was dead, being described as John Pennalowe, 'gardyner'.

WINDSOR CASTLE

Emo or Edmund the Gardener	2½d. a day	(1256–1277)
had grants of robes		
Fulk le Provincial	2½d. a day, robes	(1268–1277)
Adam the Gardener	2½d. a day	(1296–1327)
Gardener of the King's Garden without the Castle		
John the Gardener	2½d. a day	(1325, 1327 –1337)
also King's Gardener at London		(died 1337)
John de Wyndesores	grant during good behaviour	20 Jan. 1336
	grant for life	24 Feb. 1338
	2½d. a day	4 Nov. 1338
	mentioned as gardener	1350
Alexander Allet	grant at will	12 Apr. 1349
gardener until the Great Garden was granted to College		1351
[Henry Gardiner	for the Canons of Windsor	1362–1366]
John Roche	Master of the Vines	(1359–1361)
Robert le Vyneour	at Westminster	1353
granted 4d. a day to supervise the vines at Windsor and other manors etc.(see London		3 Apr. 1363
John Bremond	6d. a day	(1377–1382)
The King's Vinedresser at Windsor		
removed from office after a fatal assault with a knife, but pardoned		12 Oct. 1383
John Prince		(1382–1387)
The King's Vinedresser at Windsor		
granted 2d. a day for life		7 Jan. 1384
with John Lynde, to maintain the Queen's vines at Windsor		16 Feb. 1387

Thomas the Gardener	3d. a day	(1384–1388)
John Heydon	granted 6d. a day for life	8 July 1390
Keeper of the King's Garden at Windsor		
grant confirmed by Henry IV		3 Nov. 1399
Robert Bolley, esq.	Keeper of the Great Garden	(–1446)
William Bolley,	son of Robert Bolley	(1446–1452–)
	grant for life	1 June 1446
	grant for life	18 Jan. 1452
Adam Goodale	6d. a day	(1461–1468)
Keeper of the King's Great Garden at Windsor and Keeper of the King's Vineyard by Windsor Castle		
grant for life (from 6 March)		5 July 1461
John Pend	6d. a day for life	(1485–)
Master Viner or Keeper of the Garden called 'the Vinery' by Windsor Castle		
John Whitewell	6d. a day during pleasure	16 Mar. 1499
Keeper of the Great Garden adjoining Windsor Castle		
	grant, during pleasure	4 Nov. 1509
William Rutter	£4 a year	(1528–1532)
The King's Gardener of Windsor		

ELTHAM PALACE

William Gascoigne	3d. a day	(1384–1388)
father of John Gardyner, below		(died 1397)
John Gardyner	grant, as held by his father	30 Dec. 1397
repeated confirmations of grant, 1400–1431		(died 1445)
William Parker	jointly with John Gardyner	18 June 1440
joint grant confirmed		18 June 1441
Robert Palmer	grant for life (from 22 Oct. 1485)	11 Nov. 1486
superseded for non-attendance		23 Sep. 1487
Robert Hart	grant, during pleasure	23 Sep. 1487
one of the King's footmen	grant for life	20 May 1490

NOTE: Many of the gardeners with regular fees below the normal living wage for craftsmen at the time undoubtedly received their board as household servants in addition. Many, if not all, of them had houses provided by the Crown, and some of them received special rewards, notably in the time of Henry VII and Henry VIII, beyond their pay.

SHEEN (later RICHMOND PALACE)

Thomas Wyghts	3d. a day	(1363–1366)
Robert Gardiner		(1384–1387)
held office before William Rokyngham		(died 29 May 1387)
William Rokyngham, a Groom of the Sadlery		(1387–1403)
	grant during good behaviour, as Robert	3 June 1387
	grant for life	19 July 1391
	grant confirmed for life	10 Nov. 1399

John du Pont	appointment	17 July 1417

Surveyor of the King's Gardens of his Manor of Sheen, to take fruitbearing and other trees and herbs for the gardens and account for them

	warrant under signet of Henry V, on board ship at Portsmouth, as above	26 July 1417
Thomas Barton, a Serjeant of the Pantry	grant for life, for good service	8 June 1457
Robert Skerne, esq.	grant	23 Sep. 1486

Keeper of the Manor and Garden, Park etc. of Sheen

Thomas Fysshe, Serjeant of the Pantry, and Richard Brampton, Yeoman of the Pantry, grant in survivorship of offices of Keeper of the Manor, Gardener of Sheen, the Park etc.   29 Nov. 1486

John Lovell		(Head Gardener at Greenwich Palace 1519)
Head Gardener to Richmond Palace, 2d. a day		(1528–1550)
father of John Lovell junior		(died 1550)
John Lovell junior	grant for life	27 Aug. 1550

Keeper of the Orchard within the Manor of Richmond and Keeper of the Queen's Garden and Lodge there, with £6 1s. 8d. a year

	grant of £4 a year for weeding etc.	2 Dec. 1555

The will of John Lovell senior has survived (Greater London Record Office, DW/PA/5, Archdeaconry of Surrey), dated 11 Dec. 1549 and describing him as yeoman, of Richmond, Surrey (proved 27 March 1550). He left his dwelling house to his wife Katheryn Lovell with remainder to John Lovell his youngest son, then to George Lovell his eldest son, then to Ann Lovell his daughter and lastly to the heirs of his other daughter Joan Yannynge.

APPENDIX TWO

Friar Henry Daniel, Botanist and Gardener

IT HAS LONG BEEN a commonplace to describe William Turner (c 1508–1568) as 'the Father of English Botany.' We may with equal justice describe Henry Daniel, who lived some two centuries earlier, the Grandfather of the science in England. Living as he did before the invention of printing, his work has survived in a twilight world from which he begins to emerge as a pioneer. Like almost all serious botanists of the Middle Ages, he approached the study of plants as a medical man in search of simples, but he differs from most of his predecessors and contemporaries in that he has left evidence of strictly horticultural as well as botanical interests. He is also exceptionally vocal in respect to the aesthetic interest of plants, their sweetness of perfume and their beautiful appearance. He was, like Turner, interested in names and collected many synonyms, as indeed did his contemporary the physician John Bray (died 1381). He was, however, more concerned with variation in nomenclature, noting for example that Hemlock (*Ameos*, Homeloc) 'in some countries' (i.e. counties or districts) 'is called "Kex", in some countries "Wodewhistel."'

Daniel had an enquiring mind and consulted learned masters of the subject as well as the standard written texts such as the 'Platearius abridged' which was his main standby for medicinal virtues and prescriptions. From him we learn that the influence of site and soil was already being discussed in relation to the distinction between forms. Were two similar plants to be regarded as species or as mere varieties? Of two sorts of *Acus muscatus* (Cranesbill, belonging to the modern genera *Geranium* and *Erodium*) he wrote:

> one that is mickle like to that is said now, save mickle like in flower to *Flos Campi* [Campion], but not azurish nor so full of great stalks, and groweth in the same manner, soil and site; and some suppose that it is the same that is said right now, but diversity of soil and site maketh it to grow diversely.

Another point, both of botanical and garden interest, was the fact that certain plants set no seed but could only be increased by cuttings or bulbs. So of *Bulbus squylliticus* or Squylle (*Urginea maritima* (L.) Bak.), already introduced from the Mediterranean to English gardens, he noted that:

> It is wonder like Leek, save greater and higher and flowered wonder like, but it seedeth not but dwineth away. It multiplieth only ... in root as doth Saffron

and similarly in his description of *Centumcapita major* (Chives; *Allium schoenoprasum* L.):

> Herb common among us. It groweth not but set. It keepeth himself in ground over winter. It is ... as young 'Oynenet' [Scallions] and in his top but one flower, red purple, shape most like the top of the 'Sowkle' [Honeysuckle in the sense of Red Clover] save more fair, and no seed but dwineth away. We call it Chives ...

The garden Carrot 'groweth not but set of seed'; in the case of Fennel, 'many say, and namely good gardeners, that if it be sown or set in waning of the moon' the plant will succeed. Other plants were easy to increase by setting of cuttings, slips or divisions, as in the case of Southernwood (*Abrotanus*; now *Artemisia abrotanum* L.), which does not

> spread far in ground no more than Rue; gladly it groweth both root and 'slyvyng' [cutting].

The plants of the medicinal 'Gentian' (*Allogallica, Genciana*; now *Meum athamanticum* Jacq.) 'grow of setting gladly enough'; and various native plants too were brought into cultivation, such as Agrimony, Betony, Mallows and Spurge. On the other hand Daniel had had to learn how to shelter Rosemary from the drying blasts of midwinter, and had difficulty in keeping Sweet Marjoram alive, though he had better success with Germander and was able to grow but not to fruit the Pomegranate (*Cicius, Inbalausion, Malus granatus, punicus, pomus granatus*, Pomgarnet tre):

> It is a very bush with many boughs and branches and starts, leaves shaped mickle toward leaves of Almond tree save more short and more small [narrow] and more white green and more shining. It groweth among us gladly and in plenty but it beareth not, for we cannot fare therewith.

In the 'Aaron Danielis' manuscript is a shorter version:

> It is a bush full of branches, leaves like Almond tree somewhat. It is of man height and half, or tway at most. It will have all the sun and covering from every frost and snow and cold air.

Apart from the detailed treatise on the cultivation of Rosemary, Daniel's keen interest in the minutiae of gardening shows to best advantage in his long section on *Cucurbita*, 'Gowrde' (the Bottle Gourd, *Lagenaria vulgaris* Ser.), which as we know was being grown at Lambeth in 1322 from seed presumably obtainable in London shops:

> We set in clean ground, what ground so it be, and long it is ere it come up; and when it cometh up most like young Foalfoot [Coltsfoot, *Tussilago farfara* L.] or young Borage, two little leaves thick and nearhand round, and so it stand long ere it launch. When it beginneth it launcheth good speed. As soon as it cometh up we lay all about a good space from him, a foot or two ... dust or ashes or else barley chaff ... This is done ... for snails smell it from far, as hound trace of hare or nose (a) sweet thing and eat it all that they may get thereof above the ground ... so me thirl [I perforate] an earthen pot a small hole in the bottom and hang it full of water on a crooked stick with a feather in the hole that the water may [fall] thereon to water it. Water not but at even or else long after the sun is past therefrom. ... at their navels grow out flowers whitish, then fade and dwine and form like small phials or cruets and wax into pots, some of quart, some of gallon, some more, some less. Then some let them run on boughs or such, or set sticks or such to bear them from the ground, or else take stones broad and thin ... and set the pots thereon, and after dew and rain wipe away the wet with hands or with clout and dry the bottoms and the places where it stand, and set them again soft and easily for bruising. When it have lost greenhood and are of such colour like the gourds that thou seest palmers [pilgrims] bring from beyond [sea] cut them off and hang or set up to drying and hardening out moisture and air as in a bakehouse or so. When it are full dry thou mayst hear the seed rattling within, then with a hooked stick or such a thing, hew out that is therein.

Friar Daniel was not without a trace of quiet humour, as when he remarks in his section on *Anesum*, Carloc (i.e. Charlock, (*Sinapis arvensis* L.): 'many use it in mustard, meddling that and mustard seed together, and say it is mustard.' He could also relate a tall story for what it might be worth without expressing any opinion on it:

> Thus said me a Jew new turned to the faith: 'Lunary hath leaves round like the Bean, growing like Trefoil; juice yellow; root red as madder; it hath 15 leaves waxing and waning after the Moon. It groweth in mountains that are bushy, and in such it will grow great plenty.'

This myth of the plant that waxed and waned with the moon was rapidly embroidered. Before the end of the century the compiler of the Latin original of the 'Agnus Castus' herbal (British Library, Sloane Ms. 2498) had confused 'Lunaria' with 'Luminaria', one of the names for the great Mullein, and produced a fantasy:

> *Asterion* is a herb that grows among stones and in rough places. This herb shines by night and he who sees it unexpectedly says that he has seen a ghost; it is mostly found by shepherds. Now this herb has yellow flowers, entire and round like a cymbal or a bell or like the flowers of 'foxegloue'; but its leaves are of a blue colour and have the mark of the moon in the middle like clover and are bigger than clover leaves and round as a penny; it has one stalk and a red trunk and smells like musk and has a yellow juice. The herb grows at the new moon without leaves, putting out a leaf every day as the moon waxes for 15 days, and then through another 15 days during the waning of the moon it loses a leaf [daily] and so it grows and declines with the moon. Wherever it grows it does so in great quantity.

The mullein with its tall stalk and yellow flowers might indeed seem like a phantom at night, and would appear to shine, but has nothing to do with the mysterious plant of the legend, which is generally supposed to be the fern *Botrychium lunaria* (L.) Swartz., Common Moonwort.

Friar Daniel's story also raises the question of the identity of the Jewish convert. He was probably one of two Jews from Spain who came to England soon after the Black Prince's Nájera campaign on behalf of his friend Pedro I of Castile, whose friendship with Muslims and Jews was notorious. The defeat and murder of Pedro by his bastard brother Enrique de Trastamara produced a new crisis in relations between the three religions of Spain and it is not surprising that at least two Jews were tempted by the handsome alms offered by the King of England in the House of Converts in Chancery Lane (on the site of the Public Record Office). So on 25 February 1368 John de Sancta Maria in Ispannia, newly converted, had a grant for life of the accustomed pension and accommodation 'with the profits of the gardens belonging thereto'; and on 6 December 1369 a similar grant was made to Laurence de Sancto Martino of Spain, 'with the profits of a garden.' Presumably both were physicians skilled in herb gardening; both were still living in 1380 and in 1384 John de Sancta Maria had a new grant, and continued to cultivate the gardens until he died in 1405. On 11 June 1391 a special protection for five years was issued to Charles le Convers (i.e. a convert), physician and surgeon, who had come into England to practice his art, along with his servants. Much earlier two other converts from abroad, Janettus of Spain in 1344–46, a Jew, and in 1348 Theobald de Turkie, a convert but possibly a Muslim, had received pensions. Such individuals may well have brought with them exotic seeds and plants and knowledge of their cultivation.

Daniel himself had probably travelled abroad, for in giving a translation from Albertus Magnus he refers to his works in these terms: 'as I find written of his books at "Boloygne" (Bologna)'. It is, however, his journeys in England which provide the most intriguing scraps of information, for Friar Daniel was one of the very first botanists to record precise find-spots for plants and to comment on habitats in what we must call ecological terms:

> *Barbastus Tapsus*, Moleyne [Common Mullein, *Verbascum thapsus* L.] groweth by his own and namely in gardens and in closes that be not over mickle weed grown, and not but nigh man.

> 'Hardowe' [presumably Knapweed or Hardheads, *Centaurea nigra* L., or perhaps Cornflower, *C. cyanus* L.] is an herb that groweth also in fields at lands' ends and by high ways and on meres [boundary balks] and under woods' sides, with a stalk right hard and tough and twists, and in every top fair flowers azurish …

> *Acus muscata* (a blue Cranesbill, presumably *Geranium pratense* L.] … called of some *tronus*

salomonus, and *tronaria magna*, Salamonys trone and the great Tronary ... It groweth in woodish and high places toward the south it groweth of his own and where he groweth in wild place that long before was tilled, he will be high and 'tronish' as is said; on other place not so bold; he groweth not only but the good earth is and clean ground ...

Daniel's scraps of topographical botany include the mention of *Anacrocus* [Meadow Saffron, *Colchicum autumnale* L.] 'in the West country of England in a mead a little from Bruton'; Juniper 'in many places in Kent under wood sides and bushes and namely in east Kent near a town they call Chatham by south-east, there thou mayst go a mile and more by used cartway, and there right nought groweth but that and grass'; and a Mallow (probably *Malva neglecta* Wallr.) which 'nowhere groweth but in woods ... and about the midst of England in the forest of Rockingham between Stamford and 'Cleve' [King's Cliffe] in the right hand of the high way under bushes ...' The most detailed of these stations is given for a kind of *Caculus*, a 'wild carrot' which seems from his description to be *Caucalis latifolia* L., the Great Bur Parsley, an uncommon casual:—

Might I never find this herb [*Caculus azininus, Daucus azininus*] but only in Lincolnshire within a mile from Stamford town on the left hand toward Lincoln; on the right hand is Water Mead. ... (It) is nothing like to the other two [tame and wild Carrot] but it is more fair and wonderful to the sight: root little more stiff, and more high, nearhand as wheat. About the midst of the stalk come out branches some 3 or 4 or 5 in greatness of a stalk of Cockle (*Agrostemma githago* L.) and out the midst of those branches come as many branches, and so in to the crop, most like a curious candlestick; and so in the top of every branch a flower, dim red, mickle toward a Cockle flower. And therefore some call it *Candelabrum Moisy*, the Moses' Candlestick.

APPENDIX THREE

Plants of the Middle Ages: a Dated List

THE FOLLOWING LIST displays both the variety and the limitations of the garden flora of north-western Europe between AD 800 and 1540. Most of the available plant-lists have been used but not all the plants in every list are included. What is left consists of over 250 species, roughly as many as Friar Henry Daniel grew in his garden at Stepney in the middle of the fourteenth century. Well over half this total, some 150 species, are unquestioned natives of Great Britain. Within the limits of date set by the occurrence of plants in the English lists this provides a basis for the reconstruction of historic gardens; other certainly native plants may be added (see below, p. 164). Such a claim has to be qualified in respect of the varieties grown, for only a minority of mediaeval garden plants had yet been improved. Generally it is the type of the wild species that is to be understood, though there is evidence for the existence of doubles and of colour varieties by 1500 in the cases of Buttercup (Crowfoot), Columbine, Cornflower, Daisy, Heartsease (Pansy), Hollyhock, Hyssop, Pink (*Dianthus* spp.), Rose, Stock and Violet.

 The list is in alphabetical order of English names, but scientific names have been added: those for British natives taken from the nomenclature edited by Douglas H. Kent in W. Keble Martin's *The Concise British Flora in Colour* (1965); the rest are as far as possible in agreement with the *Dictionary of Gardening* of the Royal Horticultural Society (2nd edition 1956, corrected 1965). There is room for doubt over precise identification and botanists should assume that the names are aggregates used in the widest sense. Several different species or hybrids may occur under a single name (notably Kidney Bean, Birch, Bramble, Burdock, Calamint, Campion, Centaury, Cinquefoil, Clover, Crowfoot, Dock, Elm, Fern, Flax, Hawthorn, Hellebore, Linden, Mercury, Mint, Mullein, Mustard, Oak, Orach, Orchis, Peony, Poplar, Rose, St John's Wort, Savory, Sedge, Spurge, Stonecrop, Thistle, Willow). The cereal crops: Barley, Millet, Oats and Wheat have been excluded, as well as the weeds Cleavers (*Galium aparine* L.) and Dodder (*Cuscuta* spp.). Other plants which cannot be satisfactorily identified have also been omitted: Long and Round Birthworts, Greater Centaury, White Hellebore and Liverwort. Patience (*Rumex patientia* L.) occurs only in very late lists but may be included under Dock; Rape cannot be marked off from Turnip, nor Scallions from Onion and Shallot; Osiers are included with Willow and Tare with Vetch.

 Difficulties arise where the same name is used for unrelated plants, as with *Helleborus* and *Rhamnus*. The 'Black' Hellebores are supposedly species of *Helleborus* while the 'White' Hellebores are the liliaceous *Veratrum*. In the Middle Ages, however, there is little evidence for the cultivation of *Veratrum*, and it is certain that 'Black Hellebore' often meant the wild *Helleborus viridis* contrasting with the white-flowered *H. niger*, now called the Christmas Rose. 'Rhamnus' strictly means the Buckthorn (*Rhamnus catharticus* L.), whose black purgative berries were a medicine; but the name was also applied to the Gooseberry (*Ribes uva-crispa*), to other Currants, and also to the Hawthorn and the Barberry. The herbs Anise ('Anisum') and Dill ('Anetum') were mistaken for one another; in England Dill was far more commonly grown than Anise. Orach is in theory *Atriplex hortensis* L. but the English and French names were applied to a whole range of related plants used for pottage and belonging to the modern genera *Amaranthus*, *Atriplex*, *Beta* and *Chenopodium*. Members of the Thistle group were used as physical herbs or grown as ornamental plants, but they were not only confused with one another but also with Teasel

('Carduus' with 'Cardo'). Two alien species were undoubtedly cultivated here: the Blessed Thistle (*Cnicus benedictus* L.) and Our Lady's Thistle (now Milk Thistle), *Silybum marianum* (L.) Gaertn.).

Attention has already been drawn (pp. 78, 118) to the deep-seated confusion over the cultivated sorts of *Brassica oleracea*, including not only what we think of as Cabbage, but also Colewort and Kale, as well as Cauliflower, Broccoli and Brussels Sprouts. Some varieties go back a long way, especially Cauliflower, cultivated in Islamic lands including Spain several centuries before it reached the North. Here are listed only Kale (including Colewort), plucked for pottage; and Cabbage, standing for all the heading sorts. By 1260 Albertus referred to headed (*caputium*) worts and in 1322 seed of 'caboche' was bought for Lambeth Palace as well as a whole gallon of colewort (*olerum*), but cabbage seems not to have been reliable. A miscellany of the mid-fifteenth century (BL Royal MS. 17 A.xxxii, f. 120v), after a tip 'to destroy moss that groweth upon apple trees' continues with: 'For to make round Cabbage'

> Take young Cabbages and set them in a ground that is greatly dunged, for in manner the ground where they shall be set cannot have too much dung, and let them be set every from other the space of the length of a yard; and always as they grow pluck off the lowest leaves, and so continue to the time that the leaves in the top begin to roll and to fold inwards, and then pluck no more of the leaves but let them grow, and they will grow round.

The *ravacaulos* of Charlemagne's list may not necessarily stand for Kohl-Rabi but rather for some other rooting kind of *Brassica*. On the other hand the Turnip seems to be accounted for by *napos* occurring elsewhere in the Capitularies.

Most of the lists suffer from mysterious omissions. It is certain from other evidence that highly ornamental plants that were well known and credited with medicinal virtues seldom appear in the inventarial lists: such are Wood Anemone, Bellflower (*Campanula* spp.), Cranesbill (*Geranium* spp.), Globe Flower (*Trollius europaeus*), Golden Rod (*Solidago virgaurea*), Jacob's Ladder or Greek Valerian (*Polemonium caeruleum*), Lady's Mantle (*Alchemilla*), Lily of the Valley (*Convallaria majalis*), Loosestrife both Purple (*Lythrum salicaria*) and Yellow (*Lysimachia vulgaris*), Marsh Marigold (*Caltha palustris*), Pasque Flower (*Pulsatilla vulgaris*) and Speedwell (*Veronica* spp.). We have seen (p. 29) that the decorative qualities of the Lily, Rose and Violet guaranteed them a place, and many of the plants that may primarily have been included for utilitarian reasons did double duty in pleasure gardens. For this reason the present list has not been subdivided: for a comparable selection of plants grown in England in the fourteenth century, arranged in categories, see *Early Nurserymen* (1975), Appendix II.

Certain types of plant may, however, be considered. Evergreens were uncommon, but omitting the rare Fir and Pine and the Rosemary of late introduction, there was a useful muster: the trees Bay, Box, Holly and Yew; the smaller shrubs Butcher's Broom, Juniper, Rue, Savin and Spurge Laurel; Ivy as a climber and Periwinkle for ground cover. Climbing plants for covering arbours began with the Grapevine and some kinds of wild Rose, though these were all single. Some pictures indicate double flowers on climbing roses Pl. VI; 30, for which Richard Gorer suggests the ingenious explanation of multiple grafting and budding onto native stocks. The budded growths might not have a very long life but they could have been repeated indefinitely. Other climbers abundantly evidenced are Woodbine (*Lonicera periclymenum*) and Bindweed (*Calystegia sepium*), but White Bryony was also grown as 'wild vine', and the Garden Pea is a plant of great and delicate beauty recognized by Bourdichon and other illuminators. The enterprising gardener grew Bottle Gourds and could also have made use of the native red Wild Pea (*Lathyrus sylvestris*) and the Vetches (*Vicia cracca* and *V. sylvatica*) to add colour to hedges.

From the accounts for planting royal gardens it is clear that the main flowering trees were Pear, Apple and Cherry, but there was a supporting cast of Medlar, Quince and Plum, as well as the less common Almond, Peach and Service. There were the native Buckthorn, Elder, Hawthorn, Rowan and Sloe, and finally the magnificent shrubs Broom and Gorse. Other trees were gradually introduced over a long period. Crescenzi by 1300 was compiling his list of non-fruiting trees, notably Box, Broom, Cypress, Dogwood, Guelder Rose, Laburnum, Rosemary, Spindle and Tamarisk, and this was soon to exercise an important influence on royal gardens, as in Paris, Tours, London and Windsor. In 1501–07 Bourdichon's exquisite pictures include Broom, Gorse, Guelder Rose, Myrtle, Pomegranate, Privet

(*Ligustrum vulgare* L.), Bladder Senna (*Colutea arborescens* L.), Spindle (*Euonymus europaeus* L.), Tamarisk, Wayfaring Tree (*Viburnum lantana* L.) and Whitebeam (*Sorbus aria* Crantz.). He also shows the Common Jasmine (*Jasminum officinale* L.), the earliest conclusive proof of its presence in north-western Europe, though we know from Turner that by 1548 'it groweth communely in gardines bout London.'

Bourdichon is also our first informant regarding several bulbous, herbaceous and annual flowers. He painted two Bellflowers (*Campanula medium* L. and *C. rapunculus* L.), Candytuft (*Iberis umbellata* L.), Cockscomb (*Celosia cristata* L.), three varieties each of Columbine and Cornflower, two each of Daisy and Hyssop, two Grape Hyacinths (*Muscari comosum* and *M. racemosum*), the Orange Lily (*Lilium bulbiferum* L. var. *croceum*), two Marigolds (*Calendula*), two Mulleins, an improved Pansy as well as a wild Heartsease, Pasque Flower, St Bernard's Lily (*Anthericum liliago* L.), four species of Speedwell, two colours of Stock (*Matthiola incana* R. Br.), Sweet William, Venus' Looking Glass (*Specularia speculum* A. DC.), and a purple and a white Violet.

The lists used are those of Palladius (*c* AD 380), Charlemagne (*c* 800), the St Gall plan (*c* 820), Walafrid (*c* 840), Aelfric (*c* 995), 'Macer' (*c* 1050), Hildegard (*c* 1150), Neckam (before 1200), Garlande (*c* 1225), Bartholomew (*c* 1240), Albertus Magnus (*c* 1260), the Harleian Ms. 978 (*c* 1265), Crescenzi (1305), Daniel (*c* 1375) with additions from the list of Bray and the illustrations of Arderne, the Bourgeois of Paris (1393), Jon Gardener (*c* 1400), *Promptorium Parvulorum* (*c* 1440), the Mayer MS. (*c* 1450), the Fromond List (*c* 1500), Bourdichon's paintings in the Hours of Anne of Brittany (1501–07), the Ashmole MS. 1504 (*c* 1520) from the original (the edition by Clare Putnam, *Flowers and Trees of Tudor England*, 1972, is incomplete), and William Turner (1538) from the edition by W. T. Stearn for the Ray Society (1965). In regard to some dates, see Note below.

The Carolingian lists have an immense literature, but the little of it that is horticultural suffers from preconceptions such as that of 'literary classicism' (see e.g. W. Metz, *Das karolingische Reichsgut* (Berlin, 1960), 36–41; W. Horn & E. Born, *The Plan of St Gall* (3 vols., University of California Press, 1979), II, 212). It has to be stressed, however, as by Fischer-Benzon in 1894 (see p. 28) that many (in fact 29 out of 89) of the plants in the Capitulare cannot be found in classical sources or the Hermeneumata (Glossaries), an adequate proof that the list did express contemporary facts of the reign of Charlemagne. The St Gall gardens, too, are still discussed against the background of the old negative dogma that there were no ornamental or pleasure gardens before the Renaissance and that there are no mediaeval sources from which an adequate picture of the garden flora can be obtained (e.g. D. Lauenstein, *Der deutsche Garten des Mittelalters bis um das Jahr 1400* (Göttinger Dissertation, 1900); W. Sörrensen in J. Duft ed., *Studien zum St. Galler Klosterplan* (St Gallen, 1962), 193–277). Consideration of the great diversity between successive lists, and the increasing number of fresh introductions, will serve as a corrective and show how far the lists were from being stereotyped copies.

The column for *c* 1375 is not a single list but a compilation; that of *c* 1450 (the Mayer MS.) was printed in Wright & Wülcker 1884, 710–18; the plants depicted by Bourdichon in the Hours were identified by Jules Camus in *Journal de Botanique*, VIII (1894).

Note: Recent research suggests that the date of the list of plants compiled by Jon Gardener is more probably *c* 1350 than *c* 1400; and that of the Fromond list *c* 1520 or even somewhat later.

NOTES TO THE LIST

A few of the entries call for particular comment:

ALKANET The evidence refers to the dye-plant. Although Evergreen Alkanet (*Pentaglottis sempervirens* (L.) Tausch.) is hardy in England and has strayed from gardens in the last four centuries, there is no evidence for its cultivation here or for its English name before the late sixteenth century.

CUMIN Well evidenced in the lists and as a commodity, but there is little direct evidence of cultivation.

DITTANY Almost all the entries rest under some suspicion in that several different plants may be meant (p. 30), apart from occasional confusion with Dittander.

GITH The names *git*, *gith*, *gitto*, were applied not only to the ancient crop-plant 'Black Cumin' (*Nigella sativa* L.) but also to the cornfield weed Cockle (*Agrostemma githago* L.) and to the grass Darnel (*Lolium temulentum* L.); great caution is required in establishing a firm identification.

GOURD Much confusion exists because the Latin *cucurbita*, the classical word for a gourd (notably *Lagenaria vulgaris* Ser.) was applied by Linnaeus to a genus of plants now known to be exclusively American in origin. The bottle-gourd (*Lagenaria*) was mainly grown for the dried shells of its fruit, but one form is edible and another so bitter as to have been used as a substitute for Colocynth. The latter (not included in the present list) is *Citrullus colocynthis* Schrad., a tropical plant far too tender to have produced fruit in Charlemagne's empire. The inclusion of *coloquentidas* in addition to *cucurbitas* in the Capitulare, therefore, presents a problem. Since *coloquentidas* has elsewhere been found used of the substitute bitter-gourd, it may be that the two names mean, respectively, the edible and the bitter forms of *Lagenaria vulgaris*. Another possibility, suggested to me by Richard Gorer, is that *coloquentidas* meant the Water Melon (*Citrullus vulgaris* Schrad.)

HOLLYHOCK Daniel in the fourteenth century makes it clear that the name was applied to other large Mallows (perhaps more especially to *Lavatera arborea* L.), but his description of the red and white 'Winter Roses' leaves no doubt as to the introduction and acclimatization of the true *Althaea rosea* Cav. (*Alcea rosea* L.) before his time. It may have been preceded by *Althaea cretica* Weinm. brought back from the Levant by crusaders and pilgrims.

HORSETAIL Shavegrass, Scouring or Dutch Rush, commonly called Paddock's (= Toad's) Pipe in the Middle Ages, 'is a rough herb with the which men polish combs, bows and cups' (John Bray, BL Sloane MS. 282, f. 169); it was also much used for burnishing armour.

SAFFRON Besides the true Saffron, always a decidedly difficult plant to crop in England, two other species were formerly grown: *Crocus nudiflorus* Sm. and *C. purpureus* Weston (*C. vernus* auct.). This last, unlike the other two, flowers in spring. I am most grateful to Miss F. E. Crackles, F.L.S., for a great deal of help over saffron.

SPEEDWELL Several native species of *Veronica* seem to have been cultivated as ornamental plants, for their beauty and their long flowering season. Germander Speedwell (*V. chamaedrys* L.) was known as Forget-me-not before the name was applied (after the middle of the sixteenth century) to species of *Myosotis*.

SPINACH *Spinacia oleracea* L. was not known to the Greek or Roman writers, nor does it appear in the earlier Arabic sources. According to Berthold Laufer (*Sino-Iranica*, Chicago, 1919, 392–8) the name is Persian and there was cultivation in Persia from the 6th century A.D. Chinese sources state that it came to China from Nepal in A.D. 647. It is mentioned in the 'Nabataean Agriculture' of al-Kaldani (10th century) but seems first to have been grown as a main crop in Spain, where Ibn Hajjaj (fl. 1074) wrote a monograph on it. Ibn Bassal then gave full details of its cultivation; so did Ibn al-'Awwam a century later. Turner writing in England in 1538 notes that *Atriplex hispaniensis* (Spanish Orach) seems to be our *spinachia*. Gerard (1597) calls it *Hispanicum olus* (Spanish worts) and it seems certain that north-western Europe got it from Spain.

There is difficulty in identifying the plants called *spinacia* etc. at intermediate dates. Albertus (*c* 1260) said that 'spinach is like borage, prickly (*spinosa*) and its seeds very prickly; its flower like that of borage'. Crescenzi in 1305 probably meant the real thing; but what was the Archbishop of Canterbury's 'spynhach' at Lambeth in 1322? John Bray, generally a trustworthy writer, says that 'spynnache' bears an ind(igo) blue flower and identifies it with 'linoyse', apparently *linozo(s)tis*, elsewhere given as a synonym for Mercury. The drawing of 'spinoke' in the Arderne MS. (BL Add. 29301, f. 52v), however, might well represent an erect Toadflax, as if by confusion between 'linoyse' and e.g. *Linaria purpurea* (L.) Mill. Daniel provides the equation: '*spinacule, byngly, bxury, spintichea*, spynache.' If 'byngly' is read 'byugly', it may be '*bigula*, browne bugill, silfe hele' in the herbal of 1373 translated by John Lelamoure of Hereford (BL, Sloane MS. 5, f. 16v); and this leads on to 'Tabulae Botanicae' (Winchester College MS. 51, B.8) where *prunella* (Selfheal) is 'spigurnell'; *Alphita* (ed. J. L. G. Mowat, Oxford, 1887, 174) has: 'spigurnelle, freydele [? miscopied for 'selfhele'] has an ind(igo) flower in the midst of its stalk: Eng. spinagre.'

On the other hand, 'Tabulae Botanicae' also gives '*spynache, spinachia, spinacea, spinargia*' as synonyms for 'caule imperal' which some call 'unplanted kale', also described as *brasica, caulus non plantatus, c. romanus, c. imperialis, krambi* etc., all appearing to indicate the Wild Colewort (*Brassica oleracea* L.). The Bourgeois of Paris (*c* 1393) refers to spinach as ready in February, 'with a long leaf crenellated like an oak leafe', growing in tufts and requiring to be blanched and well cooked. 'It has longer leaves, thinner and greener' that those of the common Beet (i.e. Spinach Beet). The Fromond MS. of *c* 1525 includes 'spynache' and places it among the pot-herbs.

In the list of the approximate dates heading each column are given for identification. The occurrence of a plant is indicated by '×', capitalized '×' in the English lists. The English names are printed in three type-faces:—

(1) thus, Agrimony, indicates a plant generally accepted as native to Britain;

(2) thus, *APPLE*, in italic capitals, to indicate a species or form unlikely to be native, but probably introduced before A.D. 1100;

(3) thus, ASPARAGUS, in Roman capitals, to mark the introductions of the period 1100–1538.

Where the symbol is placed in brackets: (×) (×) there is some doubt as to identification or the entry refers to an allied species; more serious doubt is marked with ?

Square brackets, [×], are used to indicate plants added from related sources, such as those in the Carolingian inventories and in other sections of the Capitularies; and those casually referred to by Walafrid. An asterisk, *, in the margin indicates that the plants so marked, although botanically considered natives of Britain, are alien forms. This applies to Apple, Asparagus, Beet, Cabbage, Carrot, Celery, Sweet Cherry, Chives, Kale, Linden and Pear.

168

Plant	Palladius 380	Charlemagne 800	St Gall 820	Walafrid 840	Aelfric 995	'Macer' 1050	Hildegard 1150	Neckam 1200	Garlande 1225	Bartholomew 1240	Albertus 1260	Harleian 978 1265	Crescentiis 1305	Daniel etc. 1375	Bourgeois 1393	Jon Gardener 1400	Promptorium 1440	Mayer MS 1450	Fromond 1500	Bourdichon 1505	Ashmole 1504 1520	Turner 1538
Agrimony — *Agrimonia eupatoria* L.		[x]		x	x		x				x	x		x		x	x	x	x			x
Alder — *Alnus glutinosa* (L.) Gaertn.	x	x		[x]	x						x		x	x			x				x	
Alexanders — *Smyrnium olusatrum* L.		x			x?			x	|			x		x		x	x		x			x
ALKANET — *Alkanna tinctoria* (L.) Tsch.	x	x	x		|	|	|	|	|	|	x						x				x?	
ALMOND — *Prunus dulcis* (Mill.) Webb	x	x	x	[x]	x		x	x		x	x		x	x				x	x	x	x	
ANISE — *Pimpinella anisum* L.	x	x	x		x			x		x	x	x	x	x	x	x	x		x	x	x	x
*APPLE — *Malus domestica* Borkh.	x																					
Archangel — *Lamium album* L.		x																		x		x
ARTICHOKE — *Cynara scolymus* Pers.	x					x	x	x	x	x	x		x	x		x	x	x	x	x	x	x
Asarabacca — *Asarum europaeum* L.	x						x	x	x	x	x			x							x	x
Ash — *Fraxinus excelsior* L.																						
*ASPARAGUS — *Asparagus officinalis* L.												x	x	x		x	x	x	x		x	x
Aspen Poplar — *Populus tremula* L.					x	x	x		x	x	x		x	x	x					x	x	x
Avens — *Geum urbanum* L.														x	x							
BALM — *Melissa officinalis* L.					x		x	|	x		x		x	x					x	x	x	
Barberry — *Berberis vulgaris* L.													x	x							x	
BASIL — *Ocimum basilicum* L.	x				x		x	x	x	x	x		x	(x)	x		x	x	x	x	x	x
BAY, LAUREL — *Laurus nobilis* L.	x	x	x				x	x		x	x		x	x							x	
BEAN, BROAD — *Vicia faba* L.	x	x	x				x	x	x	x	x		x	x						x	x	
BEAN, KIDNEY — *Vigna* spp.	x	x	x				x	x		x	x		x	x						x	x	

		×	×		×		×			×				×		×		×	×
	×		×	×	×	×		×				(×)			×	×			
×	×	×		×	×	×	×	×	×		×	×		×	×		×	×	×
	×	×			×					×	×			×	×	×	×	×	×
×	×	×		×	×	×	×			×	×	×			×				
×	×	×		×	×	×		×				×		×	×	×		×	
	×		×		×			×			×					×	×	
×	×	×	×	×	×	×	×	×		×	(×)	×	×		×	×	×	×	×
×		×	×	×	×		×				×		×	×	×	×		×
	×		×		×		×	×	×	×?	×		×	×		×	×	×	×
×	×	×		×	×						×		×	×	×	×	×
×	×		×		×			×				×		×			
	×			×	×			×	×			×			
×	×	×		×		×		×	×			×	×		×
×			×		×	×		×	×			×	×		×
	×					×			×				×		
×	×	×		×	×	×		×		×	×	×		×
	×											
×											×
×	[×]				×					×	×
×		×	×		×							

(Probably never cultivated)

Beech *Fagus sylvatica* L.
*BEET *Beta vulgaris* L.
Betony *Betonica officinalis* L.
Bindweed *Calystegia sepium* (L.) R. Br.
Birch *Betula* spp.
BORAGE *Borago officinalis* L.
Box *Buxus sempervirens* L.
Bramble *Rubus fruticosus* L. agg.
Brooklime *Veronica beccabunga* L. see also SPEEDWELL
Broom *Sarothamnus scoparius* (L.) Wimm.
Bryony, White *Bryonia dioica* Jacq.
Buckthorn *Rhamnus catharticus* L.
Bugle *Ajuga reptans* L.
BUGLOSS *Anchusa officinalis* L.
BULLACE *Prunus insititia* L.
Burdock *Arctium* spp.
Butcher's Broom *Ruscus aculeatus* L.
*CABBAGE *Brassica oleracea* L. var.
Calamint *Calamintha* spp.
Camomile *Chamaemelum nobile* (L.) All.
Campion *Silene* (*Melandrium*) spp.
CARAWAY *Carum carvi* L.
*CARROT *Daucus carota* L.

Plant	Palladius 380	Charlemagne 800	St Gall 820	Walafrid 840	Aelfric 995	'Macer' 1050	Hildegard 1150	Neckam 1200	Garlande 1225	Bartholomew 1240	Albertus 1260	Harleian 978 1265	Crescentiis 1305	Daniel etc. 1375	Bourgeois 1393	Jon Gardener 1400	Promptorium 1440	Mayer MS. 1450	Fromond 1500	Bourdichon 1505	Ashmole 1504 1520	Turner 1538
Catmint *Nepeta cataria* L.		×		×	×	×	×	×			×	×		×		×	×		×			×
Celandine, Greater *Chelidonium majus* L.	×	×	×		×	×	×	×	×	×	×	×	×	×			×	×		×		×
*CELERY *Apium graveolens* L. var.		×			×	×		×		×	×	×	×	×	×	×	×	×	×	×		×
Centaury, Lesser *Centaurium* spp.	×	×	×	×		×	×	×		×			×	×	×					×		
CHERRY, MORELLO *Prunus cerasus* L. vars.	×	×	×		×		×	×	×	×	×		×	×	×			×	×		×	
*CHERRY, SWEET *Prunus avium* L. vars.	×	×	×		×			×	×		×		×	×						×		
CHERVIL *Anthriscus cerefolium* (L.) Hoff.	×				×			×	×				×	×				×		×		
CHESTNUT *Castanea sativa* Mill.		×												×			×				×	×
CHICKPEA *Cicer arietinum* L.		×			×		×	×			×		×	×			×		×	×		×
Chickweed *Stellaria media* (L.) Vill.														×								×
Chicory *Cichorium intybus* L.		×					×							×			×		×			
*CHIVES *Allium schoenoprasum* L.	×	×			×		×				×			×	×		×			×		
Cinquefoil *Potentilla reptans* L. etc.				×			×					×	×	×	×	×			×	×	×	×
CLARY *Salvia sclarea* L.	[×]				×		×					×		×		×	×		×		×	×
Clary, Wild *Salvia pratensis* L.												×		×		×	×				×	×
Clover *Trifolium* spp.					×		×							×				×		×	×	×
Cockle *Agrostemma githago* L.							×		×		×			×			×					
Coltsfoot *Tussilago farfara* L.					×		×							×			×	×	×	×	×	×
Columbine *Aquilegia vulgaris* L.														×			×			×	×	×
Comfrey *Symphytum officinale* L.					×?							×	×	×		×	×		×	×	×	×

	×			×	×	×		×			×	×	×		×	×	×	×		×	×		×
		×			×				×	×	(×)					×							
×		×	×			×			×	×				×		×		×	×				×
×	×		×			×	×			×	×	×	×	×		×			×	×	×		
×		×			×		×	×		×	×	X?		×		×	×	×	×			×	
		×	×	×		×			×	×	X?		×	×	×			×	×	×			
×		×	×		(X)			×	×	×	×	×				×		×					
	×	×									×		×					×					
×		×	×	×	● ×	×	×	X?	×	×	×	×	×	×	×	×	×	×	×	×	×		
×			×		×	×		×	×		×		×	×	×	×	×	×	×				
×		×					×	×	×		×		×	×			×		×		×		
×			×	×	x?	×	×	×	×		×		×	×	×	×	×						
×						×		×	×		×	X?		×	×	×	×						
										×						×							
×	×		×		×		(X)	×		×	X?		×	×	×	×							
	×		×	(×)	×		×		×	×	×		×			×			×				
	×	x?	×			×		×		×	×		×		×								
×	×	×	×		×		×		×	×	X?		×		×	×	×						
		[×]											×										
	×	×				×		×					×	×									
	×	×	×		×		×		×		×		x?		×	×	×						
×		×		×		×		(×)	×		×				×	×	×	×					

CORIANDER
  Coriandrum sativum L.
COSTMARY
  Chrysanthemum balsamita L.
Cowslip
  Primula veris L.
CRESS
  Lepidium sativum L.
Crowfoot
  Ranunculus spp.
Cuckoopint
  Arum maculatum L.
CUCUMBER
  Cucumis sativus L.
Culrage
  Polygonum hydropiper L.
CUMIN
  Cuminum cyminum L.
CYPRESS
  Cupressus sempervirens L.
Daffodil
  Narcissus pseudonarcissus L.
Daisy
  Bellis perennis L.
DILL
  Peucedanum graveolens Benth.
Dittander
  Lepidium latifolium L.
DITTANY
  Origanum dictamnus L.
Dock
  Rumex spp.
DRAGONS
  Dracunculus vulgaris Schott
Elder
  Sambucus nigra L.
Elecampane
  Inula helenium L.
Elm
  Ulmus procera Salisb. etc.
ENDIVE
  Cichorium endivia L.
Fennel
  Foeniculum vulgare Mill.
FENUGREEK
  Trigonella foenum-graecum L.
Fern (Bracken)
  Pteridium aquilinum (L.) Kuhn etc.

171

Plant	Palladius 380	Charlemagne 700	St Gall 820	Walafrid 840	Aelfric 995	'Macer' 1050	Hildegard 1150	Neckam 1200	Garlande 1225	Bartholomew 1240	Albertus 1260	Harleian 978 1265	Crescentiis 1305	Daniel etc. 1375	Bourgeois 1393	Jon Gardener 1400	Promptorium 1440	Mayer MS. 1450	Fromond 1500	Bourdichon 1505	Ashmole 1504 1520	Turner 1538
FEVERFEW *Chrysanthemum parthenium* (L.) Bernh.					×	x?		×				×		×			×			×		×
FIG *Ficus carica* L.	×	×	×		×		×	×	×	×	×		×	×	×			×				
FIR, SPRUCE *Picea abies* (L.) Karst.		[x]			×		×						×					×				
FLAX *Linum usitatissimum* L. etc.	×									×	×		×	×			×			×	×	
Fleabane *Pulicaria dysenterica* (L.) Bernh.								×			×	×	×	×			×			×		
Fumitory *Fumaria officinalis* L.							×			×	×	×	×	×			×			×		
Gale, Sweet *Myrica gale* L.	×	×	×			×	×	×	×	×	×	×	×	×	×	×	×	×	×	×		×
Galingale *Cyperus longus* L.						×							×									
GARLIC *Allium sativum* L. see also RAMSONS	×	×			×	×		×	×	×	×		×	×			×			×		
GENTIAN *Gentiana lutea* L.			×				×				×		×									
GERMANDER *Teucrium chamaedrys* L.	×	×				×	×	×			×			×			×	×	×	×		×
GITH *Nigella sativa* L.				×				×	×	×	×	×	×	×			×		×	×		×
Gooseberry *Ribes uva-crispa* L.	×				(X)				×	×	×	×	×	×	(x)	×	×		×	×		×
Gorse *Ulex europaeus* L.					×									×	×		×		×	×		×
GOURD *Lagenaria vulgaris* Ser.	×	×	×																			
Gromwell *Lithospermum officinale* L.					×	×	×	×				×		×	×	×	×		×	×	×	×
Groundsel *Senecio vulgaris* L.					×						×			×		×	×		×			
Hartstongue Fern *Phyllitis scolopendrium* (L.) Newm.														×		×	×		×			
Hawthorn *Crataegus monogyna* Jacq. etc.								(X)	×	×	×	×	×	×		×	×	×	×	×		

172

	×		×	×	×	×	×	×		×		×	×		×	×	×	×	×
	(×)		×	×		×					×	×		×	×		×	×	
×	(×)		×		×	×	×		×	×	×	×		×		×		×	
	×			×			×			×					×	×	(×)		
×		×		×						×					×	×	×		
×	×	×		×	×	×			×		×	×				×	×		
×				×		×		×		×	×					×	×		
×	×	×	×	×	×	×		×	×	×	×	×	×	×	×	×	×		
×	×		×	×		×	×	×		×		×	×		×	×			
×	×	×		×			×	×		×		×			×		×		
×	×	×		×		×	×		×	×		×	(×)	×	×				
×	×			×						×	×	×	×	×					
	×									×					×				
			×		×		×		×	×	×		×						
	×	×		×		×?		×		×	×			×	×		×		
	×	×		×				×?		×				×					
	×	×		×	×		×				×								
						×			×										
	×							×		×				×					
	×	[×]								×		×							
×		×										×	×	×					

Hazel
Corylus avellana L.

HELLEBORE, BLACK
Helleborus niger L. etc.

Hemlock
Conium maculatum L.

HEMP
Cannabis sativa L.

Henbane
Hyoscyamus niger L.

Holly
Ilex aquifolium L.

HOLLYHOCK
Althaea rosea Cav.

HOP
Humulus lupulus L.

Horehound, White
Marrubium vulgare L.

HORSERADISH
Cochlearia armoracia L.

Horsetail
Equisetum hyemale L.

Houndstongue
Cynoglossum officinale L.

Houseleek
Sempervivum tectorum L.

Hyacinth, Wild
Endymion non-scriptus (L.) Garcke

HYSSOP
Hyssopus officinalis L.

IRIS, PURPLE
Iris germanica L.

IRIS, WHITE
Iris florentina L.

Iris, Yellow
Iris pseudacorus L.

Ivy
Hedera helix L.

Juniper
Juniperus communis L.

*KALE, COLEWORT
Brassica oleracea L.

Langdebefe
Picris echioides L.

LAVENDER
Lavandula spica L.

173

Plant	Palladius 380	Charlemagne 700	St Gall 820	Walafrid 840	Aelfric 995	'Macer' 1050	Hildegard 1150	Neckam 1200	Garlande 1225	Bartholomew 1240	Albertus 1260	Harleian 978 1265	Crescentiis 1305	Daniel etc. 1375	Bourgeois 1393	Jon Gardener 1400	Promptorium 1440	Mayer MS. 1450	Fromond 1500	Bourdichon 1505	Ashmole 1504 1520	Turner 1538
LEEK *Allium porrum* L.	×	×	×		×	×	×	×	×	×	×	×	×	×	×	×	×	×	×	×		
LENTIL *Lens esculenta* Moench	×				(X)	×	×	×		×	×		×					(X)				
LETTUCE *Lactuca sativa* L.	×	×	×	×	×	×		×		×	×	×	×	×		×	×	×	×	×	×	×
LILY *Lilium candidum* L.	×	×	×		×	×	×	×	×	×	×		×	×		×	×	×	×	×	×	×
*LINDEN *Tilia* spp.										×	×			(X)			×	×				
LIQUORICE *Glycyrrhiza glabra* L.	×	×	×	×	×	×	×	×	×		×	×	×	×			×			×	×	×
LOVAGE *Levisticum officinale* Koch	×	×			×			×					×	×			×		×	×		
LUPIN *Lupinus albus* L.		×				×			×		×			×								
MADDER *Rubia tinctorum* L.	×				×	×	×	×	×	×	×	×	×	×		×	×	×	×	×	×	×
Mallow *Malva sylvestris* L.	×				×			×		×	×	×	×	×			×	×	×	×		
MANDRAKE *Mandragora officinarum* L.					×		×	×		X?	×	×		×			×		×			
Maple *Acer campestre* L.		×			×	×		×	×	×	×	×	×	×	×		×	×	×	×	×	×
MARIGOLD *Calendula officinalis* L.	×				×		×	×			×	×		×			×		×	×	×	×
MARJORAM *Origanum majorana* L. see also ORIGAN		×			×		×	×	×			×	×	×								
Marsh Mallow *Althaea officinalis* L.					×							×		×								
Mayweed *Anthemis cotula* L.					×		×	×			×	×		×								
Meadowsweet *Filipendula ulmaria* (L.) Maxim.					×		×	×				×		×								
MEDLAR *Mespilus germanica* L.	×	×	×					×	×		×		×	×	×			×	×	×		×
MELON *Cucumis melo* L.	×	×		×				×					×	(X)			(X)	×				

175

Species																							
Mercury *Mercurialis* spp.	×			×			×	×	×			×	×			×			×		×			
Mint *Mentha* spp.		×		×			×			×	×	×	×				×							
Mint, Horse *Mentha aquatica* L., etc. see also PENNYROYAL	×	×	×	×			×	×	×		×	×	(×)	×		×	×	×	×					
Mistletoe *Viscum album* L.	×	×	(×)		×					×			×			×		×			×	×		
Monkshood *Aconitum napellus* L.		×					×	×		×	×		×	×	×					×				
Mouse-ear *Hieracium pilosella* L.	×	×	×		×	×	×	×	×		×	×	×	×	×	×			×		×	×		
Mugwort *Artemisia vulgaris* L.		×			×		×	×		×		×			×				×	×				
MULBERRY *Morus nigra* L.		×						×				[x]	×											
Mullein *Verbascum thapsus* L. etc.	×	×	×	×	×	×	×	×	×	×	×	×	×	(×)	×	×	×	X?	×	(×)	×			
Mustard *Sinapis alba* L. etc.	×	×	(×)		×		×	×	×	×	×		×	×	(×)	×	×	×	×					
Nettle *Urtica dioica* L.	×	×	×				×	×	×	×	×		×	×		×	×	×	×					
Nightshade, Black *Solanum nigrum* L.		×	×		×		×	×	×	×	×		×	×	×	×	×	×	×					
Nightshade, Deadly *Atropa bella-donna* L.			×		×		×	×		×	×			×	×		×		×					
Oak *Quercus robur* L. etc.	×		×			×		×		×	×		×	×	×	×	×	×						
Onion *Allium cepa* L.	×			×		×		×	×	×	×		×			×	×	×	×					
ONION, WELSH *Allium fistulosum* L. see also SHALLOT			×	×				×	×	×	×		×	×	×	×	×	×	×					
ORACH *Atriplex hortensis* L. etc.			×				×	×	×	×	×		×	×	×	×			×					
Orchis *Orchis mascula* (L.) L. etc.	×	×	×	×			×	×	×	×	×	(×)	×	×	×	×			×		×			
Origan *Origanum vulgare* L. etc. see also MARJORAM		×		[x]			×	×	×	×	×		×	×	[x]	×			×		×			
Orpine *Sedum telephium* L.	×	×	×		×		×	×	×	×	×	(×)	×	×	×	×	×	×	×					
PARSLEY *Petroselinum crispum* (Mill.) N.	×	×	×		×		×	×	×	×	×		×	×	×	×	×	×	×		×	×		
PARSNIP *Peucedanum sativum* Benth.	×	×	×		×		×	×	×	×	×		×	×	×	×	×	×	×		×	×		

	Palladius 380	Charlemagne 800	St Gall 820	Walafrid 840	Aelfric 995	'Macer' 1050	Hildegard 1150	Neckam 1200	Garlande 1225	Bartholomew 1240	Albertus 1260	Harleian 978 1265	Crescentiis 1305	Daniel etc. 1375	Bourgeois 1393	Jon Gardener 1400	Promptorium 1440	Mayer MS. 1450	Fromond 1500	Bourdichon 1505	Ashmole 1504 1520	Turner 1538
PEA *Pisum sativum* L.	×	×					×	×			×		×	×	×					×	×	
PEACH *Prunus persica* Batsch.	×	×	×	[x]	×		×	×	×	×	×	×	×	×	×	×	×	×	×	×	×	×
*PEAR *Pyrus communis* L.	×	×	×		×		×	×	×		×		×	×		×	×	×		×		×
Pellitory *Parietaria diffusa* Mert. & Koch	×	×	×	×	×		×	×	×	×	×	×	×	×		×	×	×	×	×		×
Pennyroyal *Mentha pulegium* L.					×	×	×	×			×	×	×	×	×		×		×	×		×
Peony *Paeonia* spp.			×		×	×	×	×	×	×	×	×		×	×	×	×	×	×	×		
PERIWINKLE *Vinca minor* L.			×		×	×	×		×		×	×		×			×		×	×	×	×
Pimpernel *Anagallis arvensis* L.								×													×	
Pine *Pinus sylvestris* L. etc.			×		×		×	×	×	×	×	×	×	(×)	×		×	×	×	(×)	×	×
PINK *Dianthus caryophyllus* etc.														×								×
PLANE *Platanus orientalis* L.								(×)		(×)	(×)		×				×	×				×
Plantain *Plantago media* L.								×		×	×	×	×	×	×		×			×		
Plantain, Ribwort *Plantago lanceolata* L.					×	×	×	×	×	×	×	×	×	×	×	×	×	×	×	×	×	×
Plantain, Waybread *Plantago major* L.	×	×	×		×	×	×	×		×	×	×	×	×	×	×	×	×	×	×	×	×
PLUM *Prunus domestica* L.				[x]					×	×	×	×	×	×	(×)	×	×	(×)		×	×	×
Polypody *Polypodium vulgare* L.			×			×		×	×	×	×	×	×	×			×	×	×	×		
POMEGRANATE *Punica granatum* L.	×	×	×	×	×	×	×	×	×	×	×	×	×	×			×	×	×	×	×	×
Poplar *Populus* spp. see also ASPEN																						×
POPPY *Papaver somniferum* L.																						
Poppy. Wild *Papaver rhoeas* L.			×		×			×			×	×	×	×				×		×		×

176

177

×	×	×	×			×	(×)	×							×	×	×		
				×			×	×		×	×	×	×						×
	×	×	×		×		×		×		×		×		×	×	(×)	×	×
×	×	×	×	×		×		×		×		×	×		×	×	×		
×		×			×	×				×	×	×		×	×		×		
×	×		×	×	×		×		×	×		×	×	×	×		×	×?	
×		×			×				×	×	×		×	×					
		×								×		×							
×	×	×	×	×	×	×	×	×	×	×	×	×	×	×	×	×	×	×	×
	×	×	×	×	×	×		×	×		×		×	×	×	×			×
			×		×					×	(×)		×		(×)				
	×	×	×	×	×			×	×	(×)		×							×
		×		×	×				×							×			
	×							×			×						×	?	
	×	×		×		×		×			×	×							
×	×	×				×		×		×	×					×			
	×			×		×		×		×									
		×	×	×		×	×	×	×		×			×	×?				
	×			×		×		×		×									
	×	×		×		×		×		×					×				
	×	×	×	×	×	×	×	×		×				×					×

Primrose *Primula vulgaris* Huds.
PURSLANE *Portulaca oleracea* L.
QUINCE *Cydonia oblonga* Mill.
RADISH *Raphanus sativus* L.
Ramsons *Allium ursinum* L. see also GARLIC
Reed *Phragmites communis* Trin.
ROCKET *Eruca sativa* Mill.
ROCKET, SWEET *Hesperis matronalis* L.
ROSE *Rosa gallica* L. etc.
ROSEMARY *Rosmarinus officinalis* L.
Rowan *Sorbus aucuparia* L.
RUE *Ruta graveolens* L.
Rush *Juncus conglomeratus* L.
SAFFRON *Crocus sativus* L.
SAGE *Salvia officinalis* L.
St John's Wort *Hypericum perforatum* L. etc.
SAVIN *Juniperus sabina* L.
SAVORY *Satureia hortensis* L. etc.
Scabious *Knautia arvensis* (L.) Coult. etc.
Sea Holly *Eryngium maritimum* L.
Sedge *Carex* spp.
Selfheal *Prunella vulgaris* L.
SERVICE *Sorbus domestica* L.

178

Plant	Palladius 380	Charlemagne 800	St Gall 820	Walafrid 840	Aelfric 995	'Macer' 1050	Hildegard 1150	Neckam 1200	Garlande 1225	Bartholomew 1240	Albertus 1260	Harleian 978 1265	Crescentiis 1305	Daniel etc. 1375	Bourgeois 1393	Jon Gardener 1400	Promptorium 1440	Mayer MS. 1450	Fromond 1500	Bourdichon 1505	Ashmole 1504 1520	Turner 1538
SHALLOT *Allium ascalonicum* L. see also ONION		×	×				×						×	×	×			×		×		
SKIRRET *Sium sisarum* L.		(×)				×	×							×			×			×		
SOAPWORT *Saponaria officinalis* L.								×					×	×						×		
Solomon's Seal *Polygonatum multiflorum* (L.) All.	×	×		×	×	×	×	×			×	×	×	×	×	×	×	×	×	×		×
Sorrel *Rumex acetosa* L.								×				×	×	×		×	×		×	×		×
SOUTHERNWOOD *Artemisia abrotanum* L.	×											×	×	×	×	×	×	×	×	×		×
Sowthistle *Sonchus oleraceus* L.											?			×					X?	×	×	
Spearwort *Ranunculus lingua* L.											×		×	×	×		×			×		
Speedwell *Veronica chamaedrys* L. etc.		×			×		×				×	×	×	(×)?		×	×	×	×	×	×	×
SPINACH *Spinacia oleracea* L.?	×									×	×		×	×					×	×		
Spurge *Euphorbia spp.*		×								×	×		×	×	×		×	×	×	×		×
Spurge Laurel *Daphne laureola* L.											×		×	×								
SQUILL *Urginea maritima* (L.) Baker					×						×		×	×		×	×		×	×		×
STAVESACRE *Delphinium staphisagria* L.										×	×		×	×			×			×		
STICKADOVE *Lavandula stoechas* L. see also LAVENDER													×	(×)								
Stitchwort *Stellaria holostea* L.													×	×		×			×	×		×
Stonecrop *Sedum anglicum* Huds. etc.		×			×							×		×		×	×	×	×	×	×	×
Strawberry *Fragaria vesca* L.					×							×		×	×	×	×	×	×	×	×	×
Tansy *Chrysanthemum vulgare* (L.) Bernh.			×?	×?	×		×					×		×	×	×	×	×	×	×	×	×

×						(×)	×			×	×	×	×	×		×	×		
×	×				×			×	×		×							×	
×	×		×					×	×	×		×		×			×	(×)	×
	×	×		×			×	×		×	×	×	(×)						
×	×	×		×			×		×	×	×	×	×		×			×	
	×						×	×		×		×	×	×	×	×		×	×
×		×		×	×		×			×		×	×	×			×	×	×
		×						×		×									
×	×	×	×	×	×		×	×	×	×	×	×	×	×	×	×	×	×	×
×	×	×	×	×		×			×		×	×	×						
×			×			×			×						×	×	×	×	
×		×		×			×	×	×		×		×	×	×				×
	×	×		(×)			×	×		×	×			×					
	×						×	×		×				×	×				
	×	×				×	×	×					x?		×				
	×	×			×		×	(x)		×		×	×						
		×		×			×							×					
×	×		×	×		×	×	×		×	×	×	×		×	X?	×	×	
			[x]	[x]															
						×													
×		[x]				×													
×	×	×			×	×	×			×				×					

Teasel *Dipsacus fullonum* L.
Thistle *Carduus* spp. etc.
THYME *Thymus vulgaris* L.
Thyme, Wild *Thymus serpyllum* L. etc.
TURNIP *Brassica rapa* L. etc.
Tutsan *Hypericum androsaemum* L.
Valerian *Valeriana officinalis* L.
Vervain *Verbena officinalis* L.
Vetch *Vicia sativa* L.
VINE *Vitis vinifera* L.
Violet *Viola odorata* L.
WALLFLOWER *Cheiranthus cheiri* L.
Wallwort *Sambucus ebulus* L.
WALNUT *Juglans regia* L.
Watercress *Rorippa nasturtium-aquaticum* (L.) Hayek
Waterlily, White *Nymphaea alba* L.
Waterlily, Yellow *Nuphar lutea* (L.) Sm.
Willow *Salix* spp.
Woad *Isatis tinctoria* L.
Woodbine *Lonicera periclymenum* L.
Woodmarch. (Sanicle) *Sanicula europaea* L.
Woodruff *Galium odoratum* (L.) Scop.
Wood Sage *Teucrium scorodonia* L.

	380 Palladius	800 Charlemagne	820 St Gall	840 Walafrid	995 Aelfric	1050 'Macer'	1150 Hildegard	1200 Neckam	1225 Garlande	1240 Bartholomew	1260 Albertus	1265 Harleian 978	1305 Crescentiis	1375 Daniel etc.	1393 Bourgeois	1400 Jon Gardener	1440 Promptorium	1450 Mayer MS.	1500 Fromond	1505 Bourdichon	1520 Ashmole 1504	1538 Turner
Wood Sorrel *Oxalis acetosella* L.					×									×		×	×		×			×
Wormwood *Artemisia absinthium* L.				×		×	×	×		×	×	×	×	×		×	×	×	×	×		×
Yarrow *Achillea millefolium* L.					×		×	×				×		×		×	×	×		×		×
Yew *Taxus baccata* L.					×		×	×		×	×		×	×			×	×				×

180

Index

Numerals in *italics* are principal references; those in **bold Roman**, thus: **Pl. III.A**, refer to the colour plates; those in **heavy type** are the figure numbers of black and white illustrations. The usual abbreviations are used for the ancient counties; also abp, archbishop; bp, bishop; L indicates plants included in the alphabetical List in the Appendix. Plants are mostly referred to by their English names. Note that there are collected entries for: Books and Journals cited; named Gardeners; and Tools and Utensils.

Aachen, Germany 28, 34, 37
Abbasid caliphate 37
Abdarrahman III, caliph of Cordova 38
Abele – *see* Poplar, White
Aberg, Mr F. Alan xvi
Abingdon Abbey, Berks. 86–7, 92, 114, 123, 140
Ablaqueatio 52, 79
Abraham ibn Ezra, astronomer 43
Abu Bakr, first caliph 37
Abu Hanifah al-Dinawari, botanist 38
Acanthus 67
    False – *see* Hogweed
Adalbert, abp of Bremen 54
Adam as a gardener **Pl. I**
Adarasca, hellebore 130
Adelard of Bath, scientist 43, 78
Aelfric, grammarian 3–4, 52, 122, 123, 165
Aeneas Silvius – *see* Pius II
Aesthetics 2, 4, 10, 16, 17, 29, 34, 42, 44–5, 50, 67, 79, 80, 82, 88, 92–3, 119, 126, 134, 159; **2, 6, 18** *see also* Design
Agrimony 29, 32, 34, 73, 120, 132, 160, L
Aix-en-Provence 135
Albertus Magnus, scientist xv, 6, 8, 17, 21, 22, 45, 48, 74, 75, 76, 123, 161, 165, 166; **5**
Albolote (Granada), Spain 40
Albrecht, duke of Austria 75
Alcuin, scholar 21, *27–8*
Alder 34, 80, 122, L
Alençon, Normandy **83**
Alexanders 23, 31, 32, L
Alexandria, Egypt 40
Alfonso I, king of Aragon 43
    VI, king of Castile 50
    X the Learned, king of Castile 43, 106
Alfred, king of Wessex 27, 34–5, 60
Al-Ghafiqi, botanist 43
Al-Harrani, Yunus ibn Ahmad 38
Al-Jazari, Ibn al-Razzaz, inventor 106
Al-Kaldani, Ibn al-Wahshiyya, horticulturist 38, 166
Al-Kamil, sultan of Egypt 43
Alkanet 166, L
Al-Ma'mun, sultan of Toledo 40
Al-Maqqari, historian 38
Almeria, Spain 44
Almond 22, 23, 32, 41, 66, 120, 122, 160, 164, L
Al-Mu'tamid, sultan of Seville 40
Alps, mountains, xiv 76
Al-Tignari, Abu 'Abd Allah 40
Alton Priors, Wilts. *13*, 17, 110
Alvechurch, Worcs. 12, 103
Amalfi, Italy 50
Amaranth, Wild 41

Amaranthus 163
Ambrosia, ? tansy 34
Ambulacris, walks 140
    see also Deambulatoria
American plants 30, 121, 166
Amherst, Hon. Alicia xiv, 2, 84, 118, 127
Ammi 31
Anachota, sweet bay 124
Anatolia, Turkey 43
Anemone 70, 164
Angers, France 135
Anglo-Saxon plant-names 3–4, 52
Aniane Abbey, Languedoc 28
Animals – *see* Menageries
Anise 31, 41, 163, L
Annappes (Nord), France 32
Anne of Bohemia, queen of England 87, 131
    of Brittany, queen of France 45, 124
Antioch, Turkey 43, 54
Antwerp, Belgium xii, 1, 118
Apple 6, 12, 24, 27, 29, 32, 34, 35, 41, 54, 58, 60, 64, 72, 73, 75, 78, 79, 82, 84, 87, 92, 93, 122, 132, 140, 142, 164, 167, L; **Pl. VIII; 36, 63**
    Blandurel 78
    Costard 82
    Crab 122
    Paradise 93
    Pearmain 54
Apricot 41, *122*
Apuleius, Herbal of 58
Arabs, Arab civilization xiv, 20, 37, *38–50*
    see also Islam; Moors
Arbour 142; **44, 76**
    see also Dome-arbour; Tunnel-arbour
Arbutus 41
Archaeological evidence 23, 35, 44, 78, 86, 125, 142
Archangel (*Lamium album*) L
Arderne, John, surgeon 86, 115, 165
Aristotle 44
Armstrong, Mr J. Roy xvi, 151 (p. 79)
Artemisiam, feverfew, mugwort 67
Artichoke, Globe 29, 31, 42, *120–1*, L
Arum 30
    see also Cuckoopint; Dragons
Arundel Castle, Sussex 11
Arundel, Thomas, abp of Canterbury 103
Asarabacca 32, L
Ascalon, Palestine 31
Ascalonicas 31
Ash 13, 16, 41, 58, 66, 73, 79, 122, 140, 154 (p. 16), L
Ashmole MS 1504 165
Asia Minor 38
Asparagus 24, 120, 167, L

Aspen – *see* Poplar
Assyria 37
Atriplex 163
Aubergine – *see* Egg-plant
Audley, Sir James 87
Auger, Mr Timothy xvi
Augsburg, Germany 134, 135
Augustine, St, abp of Canterbury 18
Auricula, ? primrose 34
Auslasser, Vitus, herbalist 135
Austria 28
Auxerre, France 10
Avens 127, L
Avenues 142
Aviaries 88, 103, 106, 135
Avicenna (Ibn Sina), scientist 76
Avignon, France 76, 103
Avranches, Normandy 54
Azarole 42
Azedarach 41

Babylonia x, 18, 37
Bacon, Roger, scientist 78
Badsey, Worcs. 16
Baghdad, Iraq 20, 28, 37, 48, 60
Balm 30, 41, 120, 131, L
Balsam Garden 60; **33**
Bamberg, Germany 134
Bamburgh Castle, Northd. 123
Banana 42
Bane, Mrs xvi
Banqueri, J. A., Arabist xiv
Banquet house 45, 106
Banwell, Som. 136
Barantyne, Sir William 136
Barba jovis, stickadove 67
Barbari, Jacopo de', cartographer **54**
Barbastro, Spain 54
Barberry 163, L
Barcelona, Spain 38
Bardfield, Essex 87–8, 110, 112
Barley 32, 75, 163
Barmecides 37
Barnwell Priory, Cambs. 58, 140
Bartholomew the Englishman – see Glanville
Basel, Switzerland 135; **73**
Basil 6, 41, 107, 120, L
Baskets x; **8, 26**
Basset, Sir Ralph of Drayton 103
Batey, Mrs Mavis xvi
Bathsheba **19**
Batty, Miss Joyce xvi
Baudri, abp of Dol 58
Baugé, France 135
Bay, Sweet (Laurel) 6, 29, 30, 32, 41, 66, 73, 93, 95, 122, *124*–5, 132, 136, 164, L
Bean, Broad 23, 29, 31, 32, 35, 72, 75, 78, 121, L
 green 87, 121
 Kidney 30, 32, 120, 121, 163, L
Bearpark, Durh. 16
Beating down fruit 64; **36**
Beauchamp, Richard 107
Beaufort, Jane, queen of Scotland 96, 98; **46**
Beauvais, Vincent of, encyclopaedist 21, 75

Becket, Thomas, abp of Canterbury 66, 122
Beckington, Som. 155
Bede, the Venerable 21, 27
Beds, garden 32, 44, 61, 88, 95, 112; Pl. VII.A; **11, 23, 24, 35, 48, 54, 56, 66**
 chequered 98; Pl. IV.B; **15, 52**
 raised 44; Pl. VII.A; **23, 43, 50, 51, 60, 62, 64, 65, 66**
 sunk 44
Beech 8, 73, 122, L
Beere, Richard, abbot of Glastonbury 136, 142
Beet 22, 23, 29, 31, 32, 73, 78, 154 (p. 86), 167, L
Bekynton, Thomas, bp of Bath and Wells 136
Belgium 28
Bellflower 130–1, 133, 164, 165
Belvedere 106
Benches, turf 6, 94, 98, 103, 112; Pl. III.A; **12, 13, 17, 24, 39, 42, 46, 51, 56, 60, 66, 74, 76**
 round trees 112; **47.A, B, 63**
Benedict, St 26
Benedict, St, abbot of Aniane 28
Benedictine Order 34, 50, 58
Benediktbeuren Abbey, Germany 58
Bengeworth, Worcs. 73
Bening, Simon, miniaturist **42**
Benno, bp of Meissen 54
Bernard, St 8
Beta 163
Betony 23, 29, 32, 34, 120, 127, 160, L
Bicester Priory, Oxon. 92
Bigod, Roger, 5th earl of Norfolk 12
Billingham, Durh. 92, 154 (p. 16)
Bindweed 41, 42, 112, 132, 164, L
Bingen, Germany 66
Binks, Thomas, carpenter 135
Birch 122, *123*, 163, L
Birds 60; Pl. III.B, VII.A, VIII
 see also Aviaries, Peacock, Pheasant, Swan
Birthwort, Long 163
 Round 163
Bisham, Berks. 54
Bishop Auckland, Durh. 12, 136
Bistort 67
Blackberry 73, 122
Bladder Senna 165
Blite 29, 32, 41
Blois, Peter of, archdeacon of Bath 103
Bluebell (*Endymion non-scriptus*) 127, 133, L
Bluebottle – see Cornflower
Blunt, Mr Wilfrid 34
Boccacio, Giovanni, poet 51
Bodmin, Cornw. 73
'Bois de Duc', France 92
Bologna, Italy 50, 76, 161; **5**
Bond, Mr C. James xvi
Bonfini, Antonio 134
Boniface, St 27
Bonn, Germany 75
Books xiv–xv
 classical 20–22
Books and Journals cited:
 Aaron Danielis (Daniel) 118–19, 126, 127, 160
 Agnus Castus 115, 118, 161
 Alphabetum Herbarum (Daniel) 119

INDEX

Alphita 126
Andalusian Georgics (Ibn Luyun) 44
Arboricultural Journal 13
Blostman (Alfred) 34–5
Book of Agriculture (Ibn al-'Awwam) xiv, 41
Book of Agriculture (Ibn Bassal) 40–1
Book of Hours (Kerver) **63.A**
Book of Hours of Isabella of Portugal **62**
Book of Mechanical Devices (Al-Jazari) 106
Book of Plants (Al-Dinawari) 38
Book of Simples (Ibn Wafid) 43
Canterbury under the Angevin Kings (Urry) 64
Chronicle (Baker) 73
Chronicle (Florence and John of Worcester) **28**
The Churle and the Bird (Lydgate) 112
Circa instans (Platearius) 50, 127, 159
Clavis sanationis (Januensis) 50
The Concise British Flora in Colour (Martin) 163
De Arboribus (Daniel) 118, 125
Decameron (Boccacio) 51
De Herbis, de Aromatibus, et de Gemmis (Huntingdon) 58
De Laudibus Divinae Sapientiae (Neckam) 66–7
De Naturis Rerum (Cantimpré) 75
De Naturis Rerum (Neckam) 66–7
De Ornatu Mundi (Laverdin) 142
De re Herbaria (Daniel) 118
De re Rustica (Cato, Varro, Columella, Palladius) 20–1
Description of England (Harrison) 115
Description of London (FitzStephen) 66
De viribus herbarum ('Macer') 52
Dictionarius (Garlande) 73
Dictionary of Gardening (R. H. S.) 163
Duodecim graduum (Constantine) 50
Early Nurserymen (Harvey) 122, 164
Elements (Euclid) 43
Erec (von Ouwe) 70
The Feate of Gardening (Jon) 115, 118
Fleta 75
The Flower and the Leaf 123, 132
Forme of Cury 155
The Frankeleyns Tale (Chaucer) 95
Glossarium Helmstadtiense 60
Grimani Breviary **23, 34**
Hennessy Book of Hours **42**
Herbal (Apuleius) 58; **38**
Herbal (Rufinus) 50
Herbarius (Auslasser) 135
Histoire de Charles Martel 74–76
History of the British Flora (Goodwin) 2, 124
Hortulus (Walafrid) 25, 34
Hours of Anne of Brittany (Bourdichon) 121, 124, 126, 131, 165; **47**
Hours of Turin 98; **45**
Husbandry (Henley) 78
L'instruction d'un jeune Prince **56**
Journal de Botanique 165
Das karolingische Reichsgut (Metz) 165
The Kingis Quair (James I) 96
The Knightes Tale (Chaucer) 124
Legend of Good Women (Chaucer) 94
Life and Miracles of St Godric (Reginald) 60
Livre du Cuer d'Amours espris 13

Mai und Beaflor 70
The Marchantes Tale (Chaucer) 94–95
Materia Medica (Dioscorides) 37–8
Meier Helmbrecht (Wernher) 72
Le Ménagier de Paris 118
Nabataean Agriculture (Al-Kaldani) 38, 41, 42, 75, 166
Die Nachtigall 70
Naturalis Historia (Pliny) 21
Der naturen bloeme (Maerlant) 75
New Herball (Turner) 124
On the Popular Names of British Plants (Prior) 131–2
Opus pandectarum medicinae (Silvaticus) 50
Outlaw's Song of Trailbaston 124
Paradis d'amour (Froissart) 131
Pharmacopoeia (Harpestreng) 75
Pharmacopoeia (Ibn al-Baitar) 43
Philobiblon (Bury) 86
Pierce the Ploughman's Crede 95
The Plan of St Gall (Horn and Born) 165
Plants and Trees of Andalusia (Ibn Amr) 43
Promptuarium Parvulorum 124, 165
Quaestiones naturales (Adelard) 43, 76
Regimen Sanitatis Salerni 50
Roman de la Rose (Lorris) 72, 87; **Pl. III.B; 9, 60, 61**
Roman de Renaud de Montauban **Pl. VII.B; 57**
Ruralium Commodorum Liber (Crescenzi) 3, 76; **55, 68**
Sino-Iranica (Laufer) 166
Somnium Viridarii 21
Studien zum St Galler Klosterplan (Duft) 165
Tale of Beryn 95
Tractatus de colleccione herbarum 72
Tractie de Conseil **58**
Treatise on Rosemary (Daniel) 118
Trees and Woodland in the British Landscape (Rackham) 2
Très Riches Heures du Duc de Berry 98; **Pl. IV.A, B**
Troy Book (Lydgate) 95–6
Utrecht Psalter **27**
Valerius Maximus **66**
Walewein 70
Borage 67, 73, 78, 86, 87, 120, 126, 132, 154 (p.86), 160, L;**16**
Bordeaux, France 3, 93
Borders, garden **Pl. III.A, V; 13, 31, 48, 52, 66, 83**
Botanic gardens – see Garden
Botfield, Beriah, bibliographer 78
Boulogne, France 51
Bouquets of flowers 86
Bourchier family 67
Bourdichon, Jean, painter 121, 122, 124, 126, 127, 164, 165; **47**
Bourgeois of Paris 118, 165, 166
  see also Books and Journals: *Ménagier de Paris*
Bouts, Dirk, painter **52**
Bowls, game of xiv; **7**
Box 4, 23, 41, 73, 122, 124, 125, 126, 132, 164, L
Boxgrove Priory, Sussex 112; **63.B, C**
Boys, William, abbot of Evesham 17
Bradbourne, Derbys. 16
Bramble 73, 163, L
  see also Blackberry
Bray, Henry de, landowner 16
  John, physician 86, 115, 131, 159, 165, 166

Brent, East, Som. 136
Breuil, France 26
Briar 73, 122
　see also Rose, Dog; Sweetbriar
Brick edgings **51, 55**
Bristol 103, 110, 119, 121, 125
Brithnoth, abbot of Ely 35
Britlas, chives 29
Brittany 26
Broccoli 164
Brogden, Dr W. xvi
Bronsil Castle, Herefs. 107
Brooke, Prof. Christopher xvi
Brooklime 132, L
Broom 122, 132, 164, L
Broughton Castle, Oxon. 106
Brown, Lancelot 'Capability' 142
　Prof. R. Allen xvi
Bruges, Belgium 76; **14, 23, 68**
Brussels, Belgium 135
Brussels Sprouts 164
Bruton, Som. 162
Bruynseels, Mr Dominic 151 (p. 87)
Bryony, White 164, L
Buckingham, 3rd duke of – see Stafford, Edward
Buckthorn 73, 122, 163, 164, L
Bugle L
Bugloss 73, 78, L
Bullace 73, 122, L
Burdock 30, 31, 163, L
Burgh, Elizabeth, lady of Clare 87
　Hubert de, earl of Kent 12
Burgundy 10, 28, 114, 135; **1, 3.A, B, 74–76**
Burladores, water-jokes 106
Burnel, Robert, chancellor 82
Burnet 73
Burstwick, Yorks. 84
Bury, Richard of, bp of Durham 86
Bury St Edmunds Abbey, Suff. 12, 58, 136; **38**
Butcher's Broom 40, 164, L
Buttercup 126, 132, 163; **Pl. VIII**
Butts for archery 140; **25**
　see also Sports
Byland Abbey, Yorks. 21

Cabbage 22, 41, 66, 78, 86, 118, 121, 154 (p. 164), 164, 167, L
　Roman 41
　see also Colewort, Kale
Caen, Normandy 54
Caernarvon Castle, North Wales 84
Cairo, Egypt 48, 60
Calamint 163, L
Calendar 26, 34
Cambridge 107, 140
　Corpus Christi College 107
　King's College 140
　King's Hall 107
　Pembroke College 107
　Peterhouse 107, 140
　Queens' College 140
　St Giles 140
Camomile 41, 98, 126, 132, L; **38, 42**
Campion 126, 127, 132, 159, 163, L

Canals 8
Candytuft 165
Cannock Forest, Staffs. 64
Canterbury, Kent 12, 66
　Archbishop of 86, 92, 98
　Archbishop's Palace 66, 123
　Cathedral Priory 64; **Pl. I**
　　Le Gloriet 106
　　plan of 64; **37**
　St Augustine's Abbey 21
Canterbury Bells (*Campanula medium*) 133, 135
Cantimpré, Thomas de 75
Caper Spurge 32
Capitulare de Villis 28–32, 120, 131, 165
Caraway 31, 41, 120, L
Cardones 29, 31
Cardoon 29, 31
Carlisle, Cumb. 64
Carlos III, king of Navarre 45
Carnation 48, 126, 135; **Pl. VII.A, B; 13, 16, 24, 26, 50, 55, 74**
Carob 42
Carrot 29, 32, 34, 41, 118, *121*, 154 (p. 121), 160, 162, 167, L
carvitas, carrots 34
Castor-oil Plant 132
Catherine of Aragon, queen of England 135
Catmint 32, L
Cato the Elder 20, 21, 24, 76
Cauliflower 41, 121, 164
Causton, Alice, alewife 131
Caxton, William 114
Cecil, William, lord Burleigh 13
Cedar 4, 41, 51, 67
Celandine, Greater 41, 73, L
Celery 31, 32, 42, 78, 121, 167, L
Celsus maior – see Mulberry
Cemetery 34; **18**
Ceneda, Italy 27
Centaury, Greater 163
　Lesser 30–1, 86, 163, L
Cepas 31
Cerdic, King of Elmet 20
Cereals 32
　see also Barley; Millet; Oats; Rye; Spelt; Wheat
Chahar bagh, 'four gardens' 60, 106, 148 (p. 6)
Charageat, Mlle Marguerite 106
Charbuy (Yonne), France 10
Charlemagne, emperor of the Franks 25, *27–30*, 32, 52, 120, 131, 165
Charles IV, emperor 51
　V, emperor 45, 106
　V, king of France 76, 92
　VI, king of France 92–3
Charles II of Anjou, King of Naples and Sicily 76
　prince of the Franks 34
　the Bold, duke of Burgundy **56**
Charlock 160
Chatham, Kent 119, 162
Chatsworth, Derbys. x
Chaucer, Geoffrey xv, 72, 86, 87, 94–5, 96, 115, 122, 124, 125, 131
Cheiranthus, wallflower 34
Chelsea Manor, Middx. 131

Chenar – *see* Plane
Chenopodiaceae, 24
Chenopodium 163
Chequered beds – *see* beds
  paving **62**
Cherbourg, Normandy 45
Cherry 22, 23, *24*, 29, 32, 34, 41, 58, 73, 75, 78, 79, 82, 92, 93, 122, 126, 140, 154 (p. 131), 164, 167, L
  sour 23, *24*, L
  sweet 23, *24*, L
Cherry-laurel 124
Chertsey, Surrey 16
Chervil 32, 154(p. 86), L
Chester Castle 64, 84
Chestnut, Sweet *16*, 22, 23, 32, 41, 54, 73, 84, 122, 123, L
'Chibol', Welsh Onion 31, 73
Chick-pea 32, 67, L
Chickweed 35, L
Chicory 29, 30, 31, 32, 41, 67, 73, 120, 127, L
Chilbolton, Hants. 79, 110, 114
Childebert I, king of Paris 27
China x, 18
Chiriton, William, abbot of Evesham 16
Chives 29, 31, 32, 66, *121*, 159, 167, L
Cholet, kale seed 72
Christmas Rose 30, 132
Chufa 42
Churchyard trees 79
  see also Yew
Cinquefoil 163, L
Cistercian Order 54–8, 75
Cîteaux, Burgundy 58
Citron 41; **31**
Citrus fruit 22, 41, 45–8
Clairvaux, Burgundy 8
Clare Castle, Suff. 87–8, 92, 110, 121
Clarendon Palace, Wilts. 11, 79, 80
Clary 29, 32, 86, 120, 131, L
  Wild L
Cleavers 163
Clement V, pope **73**
Clere, Hants. 72
  see also Highclere
Climate 2, 26, 42, 67, 86
Climbers 24, 164
  see also Grapevine, Vine
Cloisters in gardens 11, 80, 112; **68**
  see also Galleries
Clotaire I, king of the Franks 27
Clover, Trefoil 70, 78, 96, 127, 159, 163, L; **Pl. VI**
Cocharelli manuscript **32**
Cockle (*Agrostemma githago*) 126, 162, 166, L
Cockscomb 165
Codesley Park, Durh. 103
Codex Vindobonensis of Dioscorides 38
Coimbra, Portugal 48
Colchester Abbey, Essex 110
  Castle 21
Colchester, Mr L. S. xvi, 153 (p. 140)
Colchicum 66, 70, *162*
Colerne, William of, abbot of Malmesbury 12
Colewort, Worts 22, 24, 32, 35, 64, 66, 72, 73, 78,

79, 84, 86, 107, *118*, 121, 154 (p. 86), 164, 166
College gardens 107, 110
Collocasia 50
Colocynth 28, 29, 30, 31, *166*
Cologne, Germany 75, 135
  archbishop of 75
  Cathedral 58
Coltsfoot 160, L
Colubrina 67
Columbine 6, 60, 66, 73, 126, 131, 132, 163, 165, L; **13, 16, 17, 51, 56, 71**
Columella, agriculturist 21, 24, 44, 76, 154 (p. 21)
Comfrey L
Constance, Germany 28
Constantine VII Porphyrogenitus, Byzantine emperor 38
  the African, physician 50
  Greek monk 52
Constantinople 38, 54
Convers, Charles le, physician 161
Conway, North Wales 84
Coppice 114, 122
Cordova, Spain 38, 42, 44, 48
Corfe Castle, Dors. 106
Coriander 24, 32, 41, 154 (p. 86), L
Cork Oak – *see* Oak
Cornel, Cornelian Cherry, 'Whippeltree' 66, 73, 122
Cornflower, Bluebottle 131, 132, 161, 163, 165
Costmary 31, 32, 34, 120, L
Costus hortensis, ? costmary 34
Cotton 41, 42
Coulson, Mr Charles 107
Coutances, Normandy 8, 10, 22, 50
Cowslip 126, 127, 132, L
Cox, Mr E. H. M. xv
Crab – *see* Apple
Crackles, Miss F. E. xvi, 151, (p. 78), 166
Cranesbill *119*, 127, 133, 159, *161*, 164
Cranmore, Lincs. 16
Crediton, Devon 27
Cremona, Gerard of 42
Crescenzi, Pietro de (Petrus de Crescentiis) xv, 3, 8, 17, 22, 44, 75, 76, 123, 131, 134, 135, 164, 165, 166; **5, 8, 55, 64, 68**
Cress 30, 32, 86, 107, 118, 121, 154 (p. 86), L
Crisp, Sir Frank xiv, xv, 3
Crocus 70
  see also Saffron
Cromwell, Richard 125
Crosswort 120, 127
Crowfoot 163, L
  see also Buttercup
Crowland Abbey, Lincs. 58
Crowland, Godfrey of, abbot of Peterborough *12–13*, 16, 88, 112
Crudwell, Wilts. 12
Crusades 22, 50, 54, 82, 124
Cuckoopint, Wild Arum L
Cucumber 24, 29, 31, 32, 86, 121, L
Cucurbitas, gourds 30
Culrage L
Cultivation 74–5, 115, 118
Cumin 31, 32, 41, *166*, L
  Black 31, 32, 41

Currant, Red 123, 163
Custance, Dr Roger xvi
Cuttings 125
Cuxham, Oxon. 17, 79
Cypress 6, 41, 45, 67, 120, *125*, 132, 164, L; **3.B**

Daffodil 127, 132, L
Daisy *94*, 98, 126, 127, 131, 132, 142, 163, 165, L;
    Pl. VI, VIII; **39**, **42**, **60**, **61**, **83**
    see also Marguerite
Dalton, Durh. 114
Damascus, Syria 38, 43, 48
Damerham, Wilts. 73
Dami, Luigi 76
Damson 35, 154 (p. 131)
Dandelion **39**
Daniel, Henry, physician ix, 44, 67, 86, *118–19*,
    120, *122*, 123, 124, 125, 126, 127,
    130–1, *159–62*, 163, 165, 166
Dark Ages x, 2, 22–3, 25
Darnel 166
Dartington Hall, Devon 106
Date-palm 41, 67; **31**
David, Gerard, painter **2**
Day Lily (*Hemerocallis*) **16**
Deambulatoria, walks 92
    see also Ambulacris
Deer 8, 10, 87, 142
Delisle, Léopold xv, 54, 75, 121
Demesne farming 2, 76–8
Denmark 58, 75
Deschamps, Eustache, poet 87
Design of gardens 22, 41, 44, 50, 136, 142
    see also Aesthetics
Desmond, Mr Ray xvi
Déville, Normandy 92
Dewberry 122
Dickie, Dr James 44
Dieppe, Normandy 92
Diet 61
Dill 24, 31, 32, 42, 118, 163, L
Dioscorides 38, 43
Diptamnum 30
Diseases of plants 40
Dissolution of monasteries 136, 140
Ditching 110
Dittander 30, 32, 66, 67, L
Dittany 30, 66, 73, *166*, L
    False 30
Diyarbakir, Turkey 106
Dobson, Prof. R. B. xvi, 153 (p. 124)
Dock 163, L
Dodder 163
Dogwood 66, 122, 164
Dol, Brittany 26, 58
Dome-arbour 98; **Pl. IV.A**
Domesday Book 54
Dominican Order 6, 8, 78, 118
Dorothy, St 26
Dourdan, Château de, France 98; **Pl. IV.B**
Dover Castle, Kent 16
Dover, Richard, abp of Canterbury 103
Dragantea, dragons; tarragon 30
Dragons 30, 31, 42, 67, L

Dunblane, Scotland 124
Dunning, Dr R. W. xvi
Dunstable, Beds. 10, 61
    Priory 16, 112
Durham 16
    bishop of 17, 136
    Cathedral Priory 92, 103, 106, 112, 114, 115
Dyer's Greenweed – see Woodwax
Dye-stuffs 31, 32, 35, 41, 42, 73, 86, 87

Eadfrith, abbot of St Albans 35
East, the ancient x, 18, 37
Ebersberg (Bavaria), Germany 135
Ebony 67
Ecology, 161
Eden, Garden of 1; **Pl. I**
Edessa – *see* Urfa
Edgings, boarded **65**
    brick **51**, **55**
Edith-Matilda, queen of England 8
Edward the Confessor, king of England 23
    I, king of England 3, 17, 43, 78, 79, 82, 86, 106,
        115, 130
    III, king of England xii, 2, 86, 106, 115, 119
    IV, king of England 76, 135; **68**
    the Black Prince 112, 115, 161
Edwin, king of Northumbria 20
Egg-plant, Aubergine 41
Egypt x, 18, 37, 40
Elder 122, 164, L
Eleanor of Castile, queen of England ix, 78, 87, 106,
    127
    of Provence, queen of England 3, 70, 74, 87
Elecampane 42, 120, L
Elephant 28
Elizabeth I, queen of England 136
Elm 13, 16, 41, 66, 98, 122, 135, 136, 140, 154
    (p. 16), 163, L
    Wych 122
Elmet, kingdom of 20
Eltham Palace, Kent 87, 110, 114, 140, 155, *157*
Ely, Cambs. 12, 35, 73
Empire, Holy Roman 86
Enclosure 110
    see also Ditching, Fences, Hedges, Walls
Endive 29, 31, 32, 120, 121, L
Enford, Richard of, prior of Winchester 13
Engelbert II, abp of Cologne 75
Enrique de Trastamara, usurper of Castile 161
Environmental influences 159
Erfurt, Germany 134
Esculus, ? service 73
Esher, Surrey 88
Eskilsø Abbey, Denmark 58
'Estrade' – *see* Shrub, Trimmed
Etheldreda, queen of Northumbria 35
Ethelwold, St, bp of Winchester 35
Evergreens *124–5*, 131, 140, 164; **50**
Eversley, Geoffrey, king's clerk 42
Evesham Abbey, Worcs. *16–17*, 73
Evreux, Normandy 45, 75, 121
Experimental science 43, 76
Eye, Northants. 13, 73, 119
Eye, Suff. 119

Fahrnau, Germany 92
Falconry **1**, **34**
　see also Westminster, Charing Cross Mews
Famine 3, 86
Fasiolum, 'kidney bean' 30
Feast in a garden **Pl. VIII**
Febrifugiam 30
Fécamp, Normandy 58–60
Feckenham, John, abbot of Westminster 136
Fence, boarded 72, 87, 98, 110; **Pl. III.A; 1**
　trellised – see Trellis; see also Railing
　wattled 12, 64; **36, 65, 67**
Fennel 24, 29, 31, 32, 42, 58, 73, 78, 120, 127, 133, 154 (p. 86), 160, L
　seed 84
Fenugreek 31, 32, 42, 120, L
Ferdinand I, king of Aragon 45
Ferme ornée, 10
Fern 163, L
Feverfew 30, L
Fiacre, St 26
Fig. 4, 22, 23, 24, 32, 40, 41, 73, 118, 122, 154 (p. 136), L; **32**
Figueras, Spain 48
Filbert 123, 154 (p. 131)
Finchale Priory, Durh. 60, 92
Fir 122, *125*, 132, 164, L
Fischer, Herman, botanist xv, 28, 30, 34, 66
Fischer-Benzon, R. von, botanist 28, 30, 31, 165
Fishbourne, Sussex 23
Fishing 88, 98, 106, 114; **Pl. IV.B**
Fishpond 8, 12, 103, 110, 114, 133, 135, 136
FitzBaldwin, William 64
FitzStephen, William 66
FitzWalter, William 10
Fladbury, Worcs. 17
Flag, Purple (German Iris) 29, 32, 34, 66, 93, 119, 126, 131, 132, 135, 142, L; **12, 16, 17, 31, 48, 51**
　White (Orris) L
　Yellow 26, 132, L
　see also Iris
Flanders xii, xiv, 126, 140
Flax 32, 35, 41, 75, 163, L
Fleabane L
Fleur-de-lis – see Flag
Floras, local 43
Florence, Italy 48, *50–51*, 120
　Medici Palace **Pl. II**
Florence, Council of 134
Flower-pot – see Tools and Utensils
Flowers 31, 34, 38, *41–2*, 44, 48, 51, 58, 86, 92, 96, *119*, *126–33*, 161–2, *164–5*
　see also Aesthetics
Forcing 24
Forestry 2, 13, 35, 88, 114, 122
　see also Planting; Pruning; Trees; Woodland
Forest trees 8; **2**
　see also named species
Forget-me-not (*Myosotis* spp.) 126, 132
Fountains (baths, cisterns, conduits) 11, 88, 114; **1, 11, 12, 15, 19, 32, 34, 42, 44, 60, 83**
　see also Water
Foxglove 130, 132

France xii, xiv, 3, 18, 27, 28, 42, 43, 45, 48, 50, 54, 82, 92–3, 118, 126, 135, 136
Francis of Assisi, St 26
Franciscan Order 8
François I, king of France **83**
Frankfurt-am-Main, Germany 126, 134, 154 (p. 126)
　Feast of Guild of Archers **Pl. VIII**
Frankincense 34
Fraxinella 30
Frederick I Barbarossa, emperor 60
　II, emperor 70
Frisk, Gösta 54
Froissart, Jean, writer 87, 131
'Fromond' list ix, 121, 125, 126, 165
Fruit, reserved from lease 103
Fulham, Middx. 112, 156
Fumitory L
Furniture, garden 45; **21, 22.C, D**

Gaillon, Normandy 54, 131
Gale, Sweet 67, L
Galingale L
Galleries 106, 135, 140; **69, 83**
　see also Cloisters
Ganzenmüller, W. 70
García Ramírez, king of Navarre 50
Garden 2
　balcony **53**
　botanic 40, 51
　enclosed (*Hortus conclusus*) xii, 60, 95; **34, 44**
　'hanging' 45, 70
　large 76
　physic 27, 51; **18**
　pleasure 4, 6, 8, 10, 13, 38, 44, 48, 60, 73, 74, 76, 87, 92, 103, 106, 120, 135, 136, 140
　public 50–51, 66, 92, 140
　roof **53**
　small 48, 142
　sports 51; **25**
　terrace **48**
　walled 95; **44, 47.B, 50, 54, 55.A, 56, 57, 60–2, 74, 75, 77–82**
　window-box x; **4**
'Garden of Paradise' painting 126; **Pl. V**
Gardeners, master 80–2, 155–8; **69**
　Spanish 78
　for individuals, see below
Gardeners, Nurserymen, Seedsmen etc.:
　Adam the Gardener (fl. 1296–1327) 156
　Aleyn, John (fl. 1351) 115
　Allet, Alexander (fl. 1349–51) 156
　Armes, James des (fl. 1345) 156
　Barton, Thomas (fl. 1457) 158
　Basing, Robert (fl. 1335), monk-gardener 92
　Bishop, John (fl. 1388), hedger 110
　Bolley, Robert (fl. 1446) 157
　　William (fl. 1446–52) 157
　Bremond, John (fl. 1377–83) 156
　Bury, J. (fl. 1393), of Esher 88
　Chapman, Peter (fl. 1296–1300), seedsman 79
　Coventre, Robert (fl. 1358) 115
　Cuvreur, Nicholas le (fl. 1279) 82
　Devenyssh, William (fl. 1358) 115
　Emo, ? Edmund, of Windsor (fl. 1256–77) 82, 156

Florence, Angelo of (fl. 1350) 51
Florentyn, William (fl. 1259–78), painter 11
Fruter, John le (fl. 1275) 82
Fulham, Roger de (fl. 1307–08) 156
Fulk le Provincial – see Provincial
Fysshe, Thomas (fl. 1486) 158
Gardener, John ('Jon') (fl. *c* 1345) ix, 115, 118, 155
Gardiner, Alan (fl. 1358) 115
    Robert (fl. 1384–d. 1387) 157
Gardyner, John – see Pennalowe
    John (fl. 1397–d. 1445) 157
Gascoigne, William (fl. 1384–d. 1397) 157
Geoffrey son of Ralf (fl. 1200) 61
Gilot (fl. 1307–16) 13
Goodale, Adam (fl. 1461–68) 157
Grave, Maurice de la (fl. 1312–13) 155
Hart, Robert (fl. 1487–90) 157
Henry (fl. 1362–66) 156
Herberur, Roger (fl. 1268–1307) 80, 82
    see also Roger
Heydon, John (fl. 1390–99) 157
John (fl. 1325–d. 1337) 155, 156
John of the Tower (fl. 1275–78) 82, 156
Le Nôtre, André (1613–1700) 142
Lezcano, Semén (fl. 1390) mason, 45
Lovell, John senior (fl. 1519–d. 1550) 158
    John junior (fl. 1550–55) 158
    Nicholas (fl. 1353) 115
Palmer, Robert (fl. 1485–87) 157
Parker, William (fl. 1440–41) 157
Pend, John (fl. 1485) 157
Pennalowe, John (fl. 1365–1400) 115
Persant, Philippart (fl. 1380) 92
Peter (fl. 1278) 82
Pont, John du (fl. 1417) 158
Prince, John (fl. 1382–87) 156
Priour, John (fl. 1388) hedger, 110
Provincial, Fulk le (fl. 1268–77) 78, 156
Raby, Philip (fl. 1353) 64
Ralf son of Salomon (fl. 1170) 61
Roche, John (fl. 1359–61) 115, 156
Roger (fl. ? 1250–1307) 80, 82
    see also Herberur, Roger
Roger of Lambeth (fl. 1322) 86
Rokyngham, William (fl. 1387–1403) 157
Russell, Henry (fl. 1539–d. 1549) 131
Rutter, William (fl. 1528–32) 157
Salomon (fl. 1130) 61
Sapt, William (fl. 1283) 79
Sattifer, Geoffrey (fl. 1283) 79
Skerne, Robert (fl. 1486) 158
Spicer, John (fl. 1296–1300), seedsman 79
Standerwyk, John (fl. 1337–d. 1345) 155, 156
T. of Chester (fl. 1302) 84
Thomas (fl. 1384–88) 157
Thomas, Bartholomew (fl. 1351), ? fruiterer 88
Vynour, Robert le (fl. 1353–66) 155, 156
Whitewell, John (fl. 1499–1509) 157
Wicham, Roger de (fl. 1307–08) 156
William of Bardfield (fl. 1343) 87
    of Clare (fl. 1343) 87
    of Lancaster (fl. 1226–50) 73
    the Gardener (fl. 1262–78) 80, 82, 155
    (fl. 1328) 156

Wolf, John (fl. 1538–47) 122
Wyghts, Thomas (fl. 1363–66) 157
Wynde, John (fl. 1520) 136; **77**
Wyndesores, John de (fl. 1336–50) 156
Garden labourers 58; **28, 47.C, 58, 64, 65, 66, 68**
Gardener's house 34, 80, 110, 112
Gardening, processes of 110–15
Gardinarius 73
Gardinum 4, 82
Garetta, ? gazebo 87
Garite, ? gazebo 92
Garlande, John de 73, 131, 165
Garlic 31, 32, 41, 73, 75, 87, 107, L
Garofilus, carnation 126
Gateley, Norf. 16
Gazebo 87, 92, 106, 140
Genoa, Italy 50, 121
Gentian 160, L
Gerald the Welshman 10
Gerard, abp of York 8
Gerard, John, herbalist 166
Germander 66, 70, *127*, 160, L
Germany xii 27, 28, 34, 50, 54, 58, 60, 66, 123, 126, 134
Gertrude, St 26
Ghent, Belgium xii; **23**
Giovanetto, Matteo di, painter 76
Gith (*Nigella sativa*) 120, 166, L
Gladiolus communis, 'hyacinth' 34
Glanville, Bartholomew de, encyclopaedist 4, 6, 8, 17, 21, 48, 67, 74–5, 76, 122, 124, 165; **5**
Glasshouse 75, 88, 92, 106
    see also Hothouse
Glastonbury Abbey, Som. 73, 118, 136; **79–82**
    Sharpham Park 136
Globe Flower 164
Gloriet 44, 76, *103*–6; **Pl. IV.B; 1, 19, 22.A, 33, 56, 57, 62**
Glorieta 106
Gloucester 10
    Abbey 58
    Castle 11, 58, 80, 84–6
    Kingsholm 83
    see also Lanthony
Glynde Place, Sussex 103
'Godfrey upon Palladius' 21, 124
Godmanchester, Hunts. 79
Godric, St 60
Godwin, Sir Harry 2, 124, 131
Golden Rod 164
Gooseberry *82*, *122–3*, 163, L
Gorer, Mr Richard xvi, 42, 44, 164, 166
Gorse 73, 164, L
Gothein, Marie Luise xv, 51
Gothic art x, 23, 76
Gourd 29, 30, 31, 86, 121, *160*, 164, *166*, L; **23**
Gozbert, abbot of St Gall 32
Gozzoli, Benozzo, painter **Pl. II**
Grafts, grafting 22, 64, 72, 75, 78, 79, 80, *82*, 164
Grammont, Normandy 125
Granada, Spain 1, 38, 44, 45, 48
Grapevine 2, 6, 22, 24, 34, 35, 41, 45, 75, 93, 98, 114, 142, 164; **29, 32**
    see also Vine

INDEX

Graphic records xii; **Pl. IV.A, B; 59, 83**
Grass 6, 35, *74*, 93, 132; **13, 52, 69**
  see also Lawn
Gravel 112; **Pl. VII.B; 51, 52**
  see also Sand
Great Bur Parsley (*Caucalis latifolia*) 162
Greece, Greeks 18, 37, 50
Greenwich, Kent 135
Gregory XIII, pope 26
  of Tours 26
Gromwell L
Groundsel 35, L
Guadix, Spain 40
Gualtherus, physician 51
Guelder Rose 30, 164
Guildford Manor, Surrey 11, 79, 80, 112
Guiscard, Robert 8
Gwyn, Mr Peter J. xvi

Hadfield, Mr Miles xii, 3, 13, 124
Hadloub, Johans, poet 70
Haito, abbot of Reichenau 32
Hampstead Marshall, Berks. 12
Hare, Thomas le 11
Harewell, ? Berks. 114
Harfleur, Normandy 122
Harlestone, Northants. 16
Harley Ms. 978, 165
Harper, John the 88
Harpestreng, Henry, herbalist 75
Harran, Turkey 38
Harrison, William, topographer 88, 115
Hartstongue L
Harun al-Rashid, caliph of Baghdad 28, 37
Harvey, Prof. Paul D. A. xvi, 79, 148 (p. 12), 149 (p. 17), 151 (p 87), 153 (p. 123), 154 (p.16)
Haseley, Little, Oxon. 136
Haughmond Abbey, Salop. 84
Havering-atte-Bower, Essex 10, 61, 64, 80
Hawkweed 73
Hawthorn 73, 75, 80, 88, 96, 98, 110, 122, 132, 140, 154 (p. 131), 163, 164, L
Hazel 10, 13, 16, 32, 41, 73, 86, 92, 122, L
Heartsease 60, 132, 163, 165
  see also Pansy
Heather 119
Hedges 11, 12, 13, 16, 17, 61, 72, 74–5, 87, 88, 98, 110, 140, 142; **15, 33, 43, 48, 62**
Heidelberg, Germany x
Hellebore 130, 163, L
  White 163
  see also Christmas Rose
Helmond Castle, Netherlands 92
Hemlock 159, L
Hemp 24, 32, 75, 79, 87, 154 (p. 86), L
Henbane 41, L
Henley Manor, Surrey 87
Henley, Sir Walter of 78
Henna 41
Henri IV, king of France 40
  d'Albret, king of Navarre **83**
Henricus Anglicus, herbalist 127
Henry I, king of England 10, 11, 43, 50, 58, 61, 103; **28**
II, king of England 2, 11, 48, 50, 58, 64, 70
III, king of England 3, 11, 67, 74, 78, 79, 80, 132
IV, king of England 45, 115, 124; **6**
V, king of England 106, 134
VI, king of England 134, 135
VII, king of England 115, 135, 157
VIII, king of England 23, 119, 122, 131, 136, 157
Henslow, George, botanist 132
Heraldic beasts **15, 75**
Herbals, illustrated 25; **38**
Herbarium 4, 13, 60, 64, 80; **37.A, Б**
  see also Herber
Herber 4, 11, 12, 13, 80, 82, 84, 87, 88, 94, 95, 96, 98, 103, 107, 110, 112, 127, 140, 142; **11, 33, 34, 42, 43, 47.B, 55, 60, 64, 66, 67, 69, 74, 83**
'Herberur' 80, 82, 132
Herbores, ? arbours 112
Herbs, *passim* L
  gathering 72
  physical 31, 32
  pot 32, 78
  salad 32
Herbularius, physic garden 32
Hereford Castle 80
Hermann of Brandenburg 75
Hermitage, garden **10**
Hesdin, France 50, 106; **10, 59**
Hesperis, Dame's violet 34
Hexham, Northd. 54
Hibiscus rosa-sinensis 42
Highclere, Hants. 72, 88, 114
  see also Clere
High Easter, Essex 123
Hildegard, abbess of Bingen 66, 131, 165
Hildesheim Cathedral, Germany 70
Hindolveston, Norf. 16
Hindringham, Norf. 16
Hisham II, caliph of Cordova 38
Historical verisimilitude **72**
Hogweed, False Acanthus 67
Holand, John, earl of Huntingdon 106
Holbein, Hans the younger, painter **16**
Holland 28
  see also Netherlands
Holly 122, 124, 132, 133, 164, L
Hollyhock 41, 42, 126, 127, *130*, 133, 163, *166*, L; **16**
Holmes, Dr George A. xvi
Honeysuckle (*Lonicera* spp.) – see Woodbine
Hops 27, 35, 120, L
Horehound, White 34, L
Hornbeam 66, 122
Horseradish L
Horsetail 166, L
Hortolanus, ortolanus, gardener 73
Hortus, ortus 4, 66, 67
Hortus, kitchen garden 32
  conclusus – see Garden, enclosed
Hothouses 24, 45
Houlme – see Le Houlme
Houndstongue L
Houseleek 32, 67, L
Hovedø Abbey, Norway 75
Howel Dda, king of Wales 35, 60

INDEX

Howlett, Dr D. R. xvi, 151 (p. 84)
Huesca, Spain 43
Hull, Yorks. 136
Humbert II, dauphin of the Viennois 76
Humlonarias, hop-grounds 27
Hundred Years War 45, 86, 106
Hungary 28
Hunting 106
Huntingdon 79
Huntingdon, Henry of 58
Hurst, Mr Henry R. xvi
Hussites 51
Hyacinth 34
  Grape 165
  Wild – *see* Bluebell
Hyams, Edward, writer 3, 66
Hydraulic science 40
Hyssop 30, 73, 78, 86, 95, 131, 132, 154 (p. 86), 163, 165, L: **51**

Ibn al-'Awwam, botanist xiv, *41–2*, 43, 166
Ibn al-Baitar, botanist 43
Ibn al-Suri, botanist 43
Ibn Amr, geographer 43
Ibn Bassal, horticulturist *40–1*, 42, 43, 44, 121, 166
Ibn Farah, Muhammad ibn 'Ali, botanist 40
Ibn Hajjaj, Abu-l-Jayr, botanist 42, 166
Ibn Juljul, physician 38, 43
Ibn Khallikan, writer 148 (p. 6)
Ibn Luyun al-Tujibi, Abu 'Uthman, poet 44–5
Ibn Sina – *see* Avicenna
Ibn Wafid, physician 40, 42, 43
Illustration, botanical 43, 58, *115*, *126*
Impyard, etc., nursery 58, 92, 114
  see also Nursery
Inda (Kornelimünster), Germany 28
India x
Indigo 42
Ingelheim, Germany 28
Introductions 22, 37, 38, 41, 42, 72, 94, 115, 135
Ireland 118
Iris 6, 29, 31, 32, 40, 42, 66, 70, 93, 132, L
  see also Flag
Isaac, rabbi, physician 78
Isabel, princess of England 87
Isabella of France, queen of England 86
  the Catholic, queen of Spain Pl. VII.A; 43
Isidore, St, bp of Seville 26
  metropolitan of Russia 134
Islam 22, 37, 106
  see also Arabs, Moors
Island 114, 140
  see also Naight
Islay, Scotland 125
Italy xiv, 3, 8, 22, 23, 24, 28, 40, 48, 50, 51, 74, 76, 82, 103, 120, 121, 134; **Pl. II; 10, 31, 32, 70**
Ivy 41, 42, 164, L

Jachenau Abbey, Germany 58
Jacob's Ladder (*Polemonium*) 131, 164
James I, king of Scotland 96, 98, 142, 152 (p. 96); **40, 46**
Janettus of Spain, convert 161
Januensis, Simon, physician 50

Japan x
Jasmine 40, 41, 42, 51, 165
Jean, duc de Berry **Pl. IV**
Jerusalem **3.A**
  patriarch of 34
  Sepulchre, Holy 88
Jewish converts 161
  physicians 43, *78*, 161
Joan of Navarre, queen of England 45
John, king of England 58, 61, 73
  duke of Bedford 135
  of Gaunt, duke of Lancaster 96, 106
  (Johannes), illuminator 98; **Pl. III.A**
Jones, Dr A. C. xvi
  E. W., botanist 124
'Jon Gardener' 115, 118, 165
Joret, Charles xiv, 75, 76, 86
Jourdain le Balistaire 75
Jousting 106
Jovis barba, houseleek 67
Judaism 43
Judas Tree 42
Jujube 42
Jumièges Abbey, Normandy 75
Juniper 96, 119, 125, 132, 162, 164, L

Kale 22, 24, 29, 64, 72, 73, 164, 167, L
  see also Cabbage, Colewort
Kaufmann, Alexander xiv
Kellaway, Mr William xvi
Keller, F. xiv
Kempe, Margery 103
Kempton, Middx. 11, 12, 80
Kenilworth Castle, Warwicks. 98, 106, 112, 152 (p. 107); **22.A**
  Pleasance in the Marsh 106
Kennington, Surrey 87, 112
Ker, Mr Neil 21
Kerver, Theilman, engraver **63.A**
Kettering, Northants. 112
Kew Gardens, Surrey 119
Khorasan, Persia 40
King's Cliffe, Northants. 119, 162
Kingston, Dors. 123
Kirkstead Abbey, Lincs. 75
Knapweed (*Centaurea*) 161
Knots 80, 112, 135; **54, 77**
  see also Labyrinth; Maze
Kohl-Rabi 29, 32, 164
Königssaal (Aula Regia) Abbey, Bohemia 51
Kornelimünster – *see* Inda

Labour, cost of 115
Laburnum 164
Labyrinth 92
  see also Maze
Lady's Mantle 164
Lake – *see* Water
Lambert of Ardres, chronicler 70
Lambeth, Surrey 160
  Palace 12, 86, 88, 98, 103, 121, 164, 166
  Park 88

Lancaster Castle, 73
Landscape 58, 96; Pl. II, Pl. IV, Pl. VII.A; **14, 15, 55.A, 58, 59, 70.A**
Landulf, bp of Cremona 50
Langdebefe (*Picris echioides*) 154 (p. 86), L
Langley, King's, Herts. 78, 84, 112, 114
    Marish, Bucks. 84
Langres, Burgundy 58
Lanthony, Glos. 10, 58, 80, 84
Laon, France 43
Lapis specularis, ? mica 24
La Rochelle, France 87
Laserwort 30
Latham, Mr Ronald E. xvi, 151 (pp. 79, 84)
Latin language xiv, 37
    names for plants 22, 30
Lauingen, Germany 6
Laurel – *see* Bay
Laurustinus 30
Lavender 29, 42, 66, 92, 120, 131, 133, L; **Pl. VII.A; 51**
    French – *see* Stickadove
Laverdin, Hildebert de, bp of Le Mans 142–3
Law of gardens 26–7, 34, 35, 60
Lawn xiv, 6, 11, 12, 13, 45, 51, 60, 61, 74, 80, 98, 110, 112, 132, 142; **Pl. III.A, Pl. IV.B, Pl. VII.A; 5, 7, 42, 43, 44, 60, 61, 72, 83**
Lawrence, Dr C. H. xvi, 148 (p. 12)
Leadwort 41
Leasehold 92, 103
Leases, to plant trees 92, 140
Lebanon 43
Ledbury, Herefs. 107
Leeds Castle, Kent 106
Leek 29, 31, 41, 72, 73, 75, 79, 84, 86, 87, 107, 115, 154 (p. 86), 159, L
Legal records 26–7, 34, 35, 72–3
Leicester 140
Le Houlme, Normandy 75, 125
Leighton (? Lixtune), Chesh. 54
Lemmon, Mr Ken xvi
Lemon 42, 67
Lentil L
Lentiscus, birch 123
Leo III, pope 28
Leonora of Castile, queen of Navarre 45
Les Ponts-de-Cé, France 135
Lettuce 22, 24, 29, 32, 41, 78, 121, L
Liédet, Loyset, miniaturist **74–76**
Ligustra, bluebell 127
Lily 6, 21, 22, 23, 26, 27, 28, 29, 31, 32, 34, 35, 41, 42, 60, 66, 70, 73, 82, 93, 96, 126, 131, 132, 135, 142, 164, L; **16, 31, 34, 48**
    Orange 165
    St Bernard's 165
Lily of the Valley 126, 131, 164; **12, 72**
Limbourg, Pol de, painter xii, 98; **Pl. IV**
Lincoln 119, 162
    Cathedral xii
    palace 12
Lincoln, earl of 84, 123
Linden, Lime-tree 66, *70*, 73, 122, 123, 163, 167, L
Linum catharticum 35
Liquorice 58, 120, 154 (p. 120) L

Lists of plants 3–4, 27–30, 32, 34, 41, 42, 52, 66, 73, 120, 165, 168–80
Literacy 22
Liutgart of Wittigen, St 60
Liverwort (*Marchantia*) 118, 130
    (? *Salvia*) 18, 130–1, 163
Llandaff, Wales 45
Lochner, Stefan, painter **Pl. VI; 24**
London 1, 17, 54, 94, 119, 120, 131, 135, 160, 164, 165
    Baynard's Castle 6
    Bridge House 103
    Charterhouse 125
    Cheapside 106
    Dominican Friary (Blackfriars) 61
    Ely Place 98, 103, 112
    Fleet Street 87
    Franciscan Friary 16
    Garden Market 61
    Grocers Company 140
    Holborn 84, 98, 103, 112, 123
    London Wall garden 103
    Pewterers Company 140
    St Augustine, Watling Street 61
    St Mary at Hill 126
    St Mary, Woolchurch-haw 16
    St Michael Queenhithe 103
    St Nicholas Shambles 16
    St Olave, Southwark 103
    St Paul's Churchyard 61
    St Stephen Walbrook 125
    Southwark 79
        palace (Winchester House) 72
    Suffolk Garden 87
    Tower of 3, 11, 61, 79, 80, 82, *155–6*
    Tower Hill 80
    Wall, King's Garden 87
    see also Westminster
Loosestrife 133, 164
    Purple 164
    Yellow 164
Lorraine 28
Lotus (*Celtis australis*) 42
Louis, emperor of the Franks 34
    IX, St, king of France 3
    XII, king of France 45
Lovage 31, 32, L
Lovell, George 158
Lucerne 42
Lucullus 24
Luini, Bernardino, painter **71**
'Lunary' – *see* Moonwort
Lupin 42, 120, L
Lychnis, Scarlet 126
Lydgate, John, poet 95–6, 103

McDonnell, Dr K. G. T. xvi
'Macer Floridus', herbalist 52–4, 165
McGarvie, Mr Michael xvi
Machaut, Guillaume de, poet **20**
Mackreth, Mr Donald F. xvi, 16
Mackworth-Young, Sir Robert xvi, 152 (p. 96)
MacMichael, Mr Nicholas H. xvi
Madder 31, 32, 41, 73, 86, 87, L

Madrazo, Pedro de, topographer xiv, 45
Madrid, Spain 51, 66
Maerlant, Jacob van, poet 75
Magones, ? carrots 34
Mainz, Germany 134
Malden, Surrey 110
Malling, South, Sussex 79
Mallow 23, 29, 32, 42, 73, 120, 126, 127, 160, 162, L; **13**
Malmesbury Abbey, Wilts. 12, 52
Malmesbury, William of, historian 8, 35
Mandeville, Geoffrey de, earl of Essex 54
Mandrake 4, 67, 120, L
Manorbier, Pembrokes. 10
Manuring 79, 92, 110
Manydown, Hants. 92
Maple 122, 124, L
Maps: Western Europe 19; Britain 55; Venice 54
 see also Plans
Margaret of Anjou, queen of England 114, 135; **33**
Marguerite 96, 98, 126; **83**
 see also Daisy
Marguerite d'Angoulême **83**
Marienlebens, Meister des, painter **39**
Marigold (*Calendula*) 4, 30, 66, 67, 73, 131, 132, 165, L; **17**
Marjoram 30, 41, 92, 131, 133, 160, L
Marlborough Castle, Wilts. 11
Marseilles, Provence 4
Marshmallow 29, 32, 41, 120, 127, L
Marsh Marigold 164
Martagon lily 23, 67
Martial, poet 24
Martin, Mrs Janet xvi
Mary I, queen of England 136
Massys, Quentin, painter **15**
Masterwort (*Peucedanum ostruthium*) 35
Mayer MS. 124, 165
Mayweed L
Maze 112
 see also Labyrinth
Mead – see Turf
Meadowsweet L
Meare Manor, Som. 136
Measuring 88, 110
Meaux, France 26
Meaux Abbey, Yorks. 84
Mecca, Arabia 40
Medina Azahara, Spain 38
Mediterranean 1, 22, 43, 123, 126, 159
Medlar 23, 32, 42, 73, 78, 122, *123*, 132, 164, L
Megenberg, Konrad von 107
Melilot 41
Mells Manor, Som. 136, 140; **79–81**
Melon 29, 31, 32, L
Memling, Hans, painter **Pl. VII.A; 43**
Menageries 10, 28, 50, 87, 103; **Pl. III.B**
Menéndez Pidal, Ramón 54
Meon, West, Hants. 72
Mercury 73, 163, 166, L
Meriet, Sir John de 103
Merriott, Som. 17, 103, 114
Merton, Walter of, chancellor 82
Mesopotamia 20

Methley, Yorks. 114
Metz, Guillebert de 86
Meung-sur-Loire, France 52
Mexico x
Mice 112
Michael the carpenter 88
Michelmarsh, Hants. 114
Miélot, Jean, miniaturist 106
Milan, Italy 27, 50, 51
Millet 32, 163
Milton, Kent 16
Mint 29, 31, 32, 58, 78, 163, L
 Horse 32, L
 Wild 32
Mistletoe L
Mithradates VI Eupator, king of Pontus 24
Mitrovica (*Sirmium*), Yugoslavia 24
Moat 12, 13, 80, 83, 84, 85, 88, 106, 107, 110, 114; **9, 62, 78**
Mohammed, prophet 37
Moles 112
Monasteries 26, 34, 50, 54, 58, 72, 74, 76, 78, 118, 136; **18, 37**
Monastic libraries 21
Monkshood, L
Montbray, Geoffrey I de, bp of Coutances 8, 22, 50
Monte Cassino Abbey, Italy 50
Montpellier, France 1, 28, 40, 50
Moon, influence of 75
Moonwort, 'Lunary' (*Botrychium*) 161
Moors xiv, 28, 31, 44, 45, 48, 54, 106
 see also Arabs, Islam
More, Sir Thomas 131, 136; **16**
Moricandia moricandioides 42
Morimond Abbey, Burgundy 58
Morley, Daniel de, scientist 42
Morocco 20, 40
Mortain, count of 8
Moshe Sephardi – see Petrus Alfonsi
Moss, gathering 114–15, 164
Mostaert, Jan, painter **53**
Motte, mount 114
Mount 88, 112, 114, 135, 136; **79**
Mountain Ash – see Rowan
Mounter, William the 64
Mouse-ear L
Mowing 110, 112, 115, 132; **28**
Mugwort 34, 35, L
Muhammad III al-Nasir, sultan of Morocco 40
 V, sultan of Granada 44
Mulberry (Black) 22, 23, 32, 66, 73, 122, *123*, 124, L
Mullein 127, 130, 133, 161, 163, 165, L
Multiple uses 2, 110
Murcia, Spain 38
Mustard 24, 32, 73, 79, 160, 163, L
Myrtle 48, 67, 164
Myrtus 67
'Mystical Marriage of St Catherine' **44**

Naight, islet 86, 87
 see also Island
Nájera, Spain 161
Naples, Italy 50, 54, 135
Napos, turnip 164

INDEX

Narbonne, France 43
Narcissus 41, 42, 67; **16**
National styles in gardening xii-xiv
Naturalism in art xii
Navagero, Andrea 48
Navarre, Spain 45
Neale, Mrs Frances xvi, 152 (p. 103)
Neckam, Alexander, scientist 4, 21, 28, 66–7, 121, 122, 124, 165
Netherlands xii, 28, 125, 134
   see also Belgium, Holland
Nettle 34, 35, 73, L
Newberry, Percy xiv
Newton, Canon Henry de 16
Nice, France 76
Nightshade 73
   Black L
   Deadly L
Nonsuch, Surrey 124
Norden, John, surveyor 76; **40**
Norman Conquest 8, 38, 50, 54, 67
Normandy xv, 8, 54, 75, 121
Normans in Sicily 48–50
Northampton Castle 84
Northolme, Northants. 16
Northumbria 20, 28
Norton Priory, Chesh. 125
Norwich 78, 84, 103
   Cathedral and Priory 16, 115, 140
Norwood, Surrey 98
Notker Labeo 4
Nottingham Castle 11, 79–80
Noyers, Hugh de, bp of Auxerre 10
Nuns, nunneries 8, 27, 58
Nuremberg, Germany 70, 134, 135
Nursery, *noresirie* 17, 58, 103, 114
   see also Impyard
Nursery trade 17, 58, 80, 82, 84, 110, 140
   see also Seedsman's trade
Nutmeg 67
Nuts 78, 79
   see also Hazel, Walnut

Oak 8, 13, 16, 58, 66, 72, 73, 79, 114, 122, *126*, 140, 163, L
   Cork 67
   Holm 41
   Kermes 126
Oats 32, 75, 163
Observation posts 106
   see also Gazebo, 'Standing'
Oculus Christi, clary 131
Odiham Castle, Hants. 87
Odo Magdunensis, physician 52
Oeillet, carnation 48
Oleander 41
Oleaster 4
Olite (Navarre), Spain xiv, 45
Olive 4, 22, 24, 26, 37, 41, 67; **34**
Omayyad caliphate 38
Ombersley, Worcs. 17
Ombresley, John, abbot of Evesham 17
Onion 29, 31, 32, 41, 72, 75, 78, 79, 87, p. 86, 154 (pp. 86, 164), 163, L

sets 87
   Welsh 31, L
Orach 29, 32, 154 (p. 86), 163, L
Orange 40, 41, 45, 51, 67; **31, 32**
Orchard 4, 8, 10, 11, 12, 13, 22, 25, 26, *27*, 32, 34, 35, 37, 52, 54, 58, 60, 61, 73, 76, 78, 79, 95, 103, 132, 134, 136, 140, 142, 154 (p. 136); **36, 37.A, 40**
Orchis 163, L
   Spotted 132
Origan (*Origanum vulgare*) L
Orléans, France 52
Orosius, historian 35
Orpine L
Ortolanus, Ortus, – *see* Hortolanus, Hortus
Osier 75, 154 (p. 131), 163
Outdoor meals 70, 87; **56, 57, 59, 70.A, 76**
Ouwe, Hartman von, poet 70
Oxford 79, 84, 86, 107
   Christ Church 124
   Merton College 17
   New College 107

Padua, Italy 6, 40, 51
Painshill, Surrey **10**
Paintings 126
Palermo, Sicily 44, 48
Palestine 3, 43
Palladius 21, 22, 30, 76, 120, 154 (p. 21), 165
Palliser, Dr David xvi, 153 (p. 123)
Palm 4, 37; **3.A, B**
'Palm', ? yew 82
'Palma Christi' 132
Palm-branch 3–4
Pamplona (Navarre), Spain 45
Pansy 126, 132, 163, 165; **16, 17**
   see also Heartsease
Paradise 1, 34, 35, 50, 103, 142–3; **Pl. III.B; 20**
Parduna, ? burdock 30
Paris, France 1, 4, 27, 51, 58, 73, 94, 107, 112, 121, 124, 131, 135, 164
   Louvre xii, 75, 92
   Palais 98; **Pl. IV.A**
   Pré aux Clercs 51
   Sainte Chapelle 3
   St-Germain-des-Prés 27, 51
   St-Pol garden 92–3, 135
   Tournelles, Palais de 135
Paris, Matthew, historian 12
Parish, Robert, ironmonger 103
Park 1, 8, 10, 11, 12, 22, 28, 48, 50, 60, 64, 70, 72, 87, 88, 92, 96, 98, 103, 136, 142; **Pl. III.B; 19, 33, 34, 47.A, 55.A, 58, 67**
Parma, Italy 51
Parsley 31, 32, 73, 78, 86, 107, 154 (p. 86), L
Parsnip 29, 32, 118, 121, L
Paseo, recreational walk 66
Pasque Flower 164, 165
Paths, Walks 32, 44, 61, 88, 92, 106, 112, 140; **Pl. VII.A; 11, 43, 44, 48, 50, 55, 57, 69, 83**
   paved **49, 62, 66**
Patience, Monk's Rhubarb 120, 163
Patron saints of gardens 26

Pavilions 44, 45, 48, 76, 87, 92, *103–6*, 107, 135, 140; **22, 56, 57, 58**
    see also Gloriet
Payne, Mr Raef 34
Pea 24, 29, 31, 32, 35, 72, 75, 121, 164, L
    Everlasting 132
    Green 72, *121*
    Rounceval 121
    Wild 164
Peach 22, 23, 29, 32, 34, 41, 54, 73, *82*, 122, 124, 154 (p. 131), 164, L
Peacock 28, 92, 133; **Pl. VII.A; 1, 42, 44, 48, 74**
Pear 6, 23, 24, 27, 29, 32, 41, 54, 72, 73, 75, 78, 79, *80*, 82, 84, 87, 92, 93, 122, 132, 140, 164, 167, L
    Cailhou, Kayl' 80, *82*, 84
    Gilefr' 82
    Martin 82
    Pesse-pucelle 82
    St-Regle, Rewl 82
Pecham, John, abp of Canterbury 79
Pedro I, king of Castile 45, 161
Pellitory 67, 73, L
Pellitory-of-Spain 35, 130
    False 35, 67
Peninsula, Iberian xiv, 31, 38, 48, 78, 135
    see also Portugal, Spain
Pennyroyal 32, L
Peony *82*, 126, 127, 131, 132, 135, 163, L; **16, 41**
Pepin the Short, king of the Franks 27
Pepper, Indian 34
    Sudan 41
    White 67, *121*
Pepperwort 67
Percy, Henry Algernon, 5th earl of Northumberland 136
Perfume 6, 34, 74, 95, 96, 127, 131, 142, 159
Pergola 41, 44, 87; **Pl. VI; 39, 53**
Periwinkle 126, 131, 132, 164, L
Perselle, ? cornflower 131
Persia, Iran 1, 18, 20, 37, 123
Perspective, optical xii, 2
Peterborough, Northants. 16, 119
    Abbey 12, 88
Petrarch, Francesco, poet 51; **17**
Petrus Alfonsi (Moshe Sephardi), physician 43
Petygrew, butcher's broom 40
Pever, Peyvre, Sir Paulin 12
Pheasant 88
Philip the Good, duke of Burgundy **1**
Philippa of Hainault, queen of England 87, 88, 118, 119, 126, 127, 131
Physic garden – *see* Garden
Picnic – *see* Outdoor Meals
Pigott, Mr C. D. 23
Pilgrims 22, 42, 58, 70, 132, 160
Pimpernel (*Anagallis*) L
Pine 23, 34, 41, 45, 73, 122, *125*, 132, 164, L
    Stone 28, 32, 34, 125
Pink (*Dianthus* spp.) 126, 163, L; **13, 17, 24, 50, 51**
    see also Carnation
Pipe Rolls 61, 72
Pisa, Italy 40
Pisan, Christine de, poetess **46**

Pistachio 22, 41, 123
Pius II (Aeneas Silvius), pope 134
Plague 86
Plane (*Platanus orientalis*) 42, 67, 122, *123–4*, L
Plans 32, 64; **18, 40.A, B**
    St Gall Abbey **18**; Canterbury Priory **37**; Windsor **40.A, B**; Gloucester 83; Peterborough Abbey 85; Kenilworth 107
    see also Maps
Plantain L
    see also Ribwort, Waybread
Planting, plantations 2, 13–17, 50, 79, 103; **1, 2, 3, 8, 9, 20, 58, 59, 60, 61, 83**
Platearius, John and Matthew, physicians 50, 127, 159
Pleaching 110
'Pleasance in the Marsh' 107; **1**
    see also Hesdin, Kenilworth
Pleasure garden – *see* Garden
Pliny the Elder 21, 24, 29
Plum 18, 20, 23, 29, 32, 35, 41, 73, 75, 78, 93, 122, 132, 140, 164, L
    see also Damson, Sloe
Poetic records 27, 70, 72, 94–6
Poitiers, France 27
Pollarding 140; **14**
Polypody L
Pomegranate 6, 22, 34, 38, 40, 41, 45, 67, 88, *160*, 164, L; **31, 32**
Pomerium, orchard 4, 10, 12, 13, 27, 66
Pond – *see* Fishpond, Water
Pontefract, Yorks. 58
Pontoise, John of, bp of Winchester 78
Pool – *see* Fishpond, Water
Poplar 41, 73, 122, 163, L
    Aspen 73, 122, L
    White 70
Poppy 29, 31, 32, 35, 41, L
    Opium 24, L
Porreta, ? spinach-beet 73
Portugal xiv
Pot – *see* Tools and Utensils: Flower-pot
Prague, Bohemia 51
Prato, Italy **31**
Prices of plants and seeds 17, 35, 72–3, 76, 79, 82, 86, 92–3, *110–15*
Priestley, Mr E. J. 151 (p. 87)
Primrose 34, 132, L
Prior, R. C. A. 131–2
Privet 154 (p. 131), 164–5
Probus, Roman emperor 24
Provençal language 40
Provence 4, 76, 118, 135
Pruning 52, 79, 92, 107, 114; **27**
Pugh, Prof. R. B. xvi, 153 (p. 124)
Pulteney, Richard, botanist xiv
Pumpkin 30
Purslane 41, 66, 78, *121*, L
Purton, Wilts. 12
'Pyne appull' – *see* Pine
Pyrenees, mountains xiv, 45

Quickset – *see* Hawthorn
Quince 32, 41, 73, *82*, 84, 122, 132, 164, L

Rackham, Dr Oliver xvi, 2, 13, 16, 114, 152 (p. 110)
Radegunda, queen of the Franks 27
Radish 22, 24, 29, 31, 32, 41, L
Radley, Berks. 140
Radmore, Staffs. 64
Raglan Castle 154(p. 136)
Railings **15, 35, 41, 45, 52, 60, 66, 72, 74**
  see also Rails, Trellis
Rails 88, 95, 96, 98, 110, 112, 135, 140; **13, 24, 41, 50**
Raisin 122
Ramsey Abbey, Hunts. 58
Ramsons L
Ranulph III, 6th earl of Chester 64
Rape (*Brassica napus*) 163
Ravacaulos, ? kohl-rabi 164
Ravenna, Italy 27
Raymund, carpenter 76
Reed L
Reformation 134
Reginald the monk of Durham 60
Reichenau, Germany 28, 34
Religious records 26
Renaissance gardens x, xii, xiv, 22, 48, 50, 74, 76, 106, 120, 134, 140, 165
René of Anjou, king of Naples 135; **62**
Rhamnus 163
Riat, Georges xiv
Ribston, Yorks. 124
Ribwort 73, L
Richard I, Coeur-de-Lion, king of England 61, 64, 67, 70
  II, king of England xii, 74, 84, 86, 95, 106, 131, 134, 155; **6**
Richmond Palace, Surrey 135, 140, 158
  see also Sheen
Rigg, Mr A. G. 115–18
Rimpton, Som. 79
Ripon, Yorks. 79
Robert of Anjou, king of Naples 31
  duke of Normandy 50
  II, count of Artois, 106
  de Venys, abbot of Malmesbury 58
  the carpenter 88
Robertet, Jean, miniaturist **14**
Robur minor, box 126
Rocket 32, 67, *121*, L
  Sweet 42, 126, *127*, 133, L
Rockingham Forest 119
Rock Rose 30
Roger II, king of Sicily 48, 50
Rogers, J. E. Thorold 17, 79, 86
Rohde, Eleanour Sinclair xv
Rolbant, Miss Mimi xvi
Roller, lawn 11
Roman Empire 18
  villa gardens 22, 23
Romanesque style 23, 37
Rome, Italy xiv, 1, 8, 25, 27, 35, 37, 50, 54, 122
  Gardeners Company of 50
Rome, Mr Alan M. xvi
Romsey, Hants. 8, 58
Romulus Augustulus, Roman emperor 25
Rosa foetida bicolor 42

Rosamund's Bower 11, 110
  see also Woodstock, Everswell
Rose xiv 4, 6, 21, 22, 23, 26, 28, 29, 30, 31, 32, 34, 41, 42, 48, 51, 60, 66, 70, 73, 75, 76, 82, 84, 86, 92, 93, 96, 98, 122, 126, 131, 132, 135, 142, 154 (p. 131), 163, 164, L; **9, 12, 13, 15, 17, 24, 31, 34, 41, 46, 47.B, 60, 70–73**
  'cabbage' **71**
  climbing 61, 70, *164*; **Pl. VI; 30, 39, 76**
  Dog 70, 127, 132
  Golden **73**
  improved **70.B, 73**
  Musk 48
  wild 132
  see also Briar; Sweetbriar
Rosemary 28, 29, 31, 32, 34, 92, 115, 118, 120, 125, 131, 132, 135, 160, 164, L; **13, 51**
'Rose of Spain', hollyhock 127
Rose-water 75
Rotherhithe Manor, Surrey 114, 115
Rouen, Normandy 54
  archbishop of 92, 121, 122, 125, 131
  St-Ouen Abbey 75
Rowan, mountain ash 164, L
Rowley, Mr Trevor xvi
Rows of trees 13, 16, 98, 103, 122; **14, 62**
  see also Avenues
Rozmital, Leo von, traveller 48, 135
Rue 6, 29, 31, 32, 34, 41, 164, L; **51**
Rufinus, herbalist 50
Runham, Norf. 54
Rush, L
Russel, John 103
Russell, Prof. J. C. 2
Rutherwyk, John, abbot of Chertsey 16
Rye 32

Safflower 41, 121
Saffron 21, 41, 86, 107, 118, 121, 159, *166*, L
Saffron Walden, Essex 86
Sage 6, 29, 31, 32, 34, 73, *82*, 92, 95, 118, 126, 130, 154 (p. 126), L
St Albans, Herts. 35
  Abbey 12, 35, 122, 123
St Blasien, Germany 92
St Davids, Wales 10
St-Denis Abbey, France 27
St Edmunds, Walter of, abbot of Peterborough 73
St Gall Abbey, Switzerland xiv, 4, 28, 32, 165; **18**
St German's, Cornw. 115
St Gudule, Master of, painter 51
St Ives, Hunts. 79
St John's Wort 163, L
St Victor, Hugh of, theologian 4
Salads 32, 78
Salas, Dr Xavier de xvi
Salerno, Italy 43, 50
Sales, Mr John xvi
Salic Law 26
Saliunca, ? gorse 73
Salzman, L. F. 16
Samson, bp of Dol 26
Sancta Maria, John de, convert 161
Sancto Martino, Laurence de, convert 161

INDEX

Sand 88, 112, 135, 140; **Pl. VII.A**
   see also Gravel
Sandal Castle, Yorks. 87
Sanecki, Mrs Kay xvi
Sanicle 73
   see also Woodmarch
Saragossa, Spain 38
Saumur, France 135
Savin 31, *125*, 132, 164, L
Savory 29, 32, 34, 42, 163, L
   Summer 34
   Winter 34
Saxony, Germany 4
Saye and Sele, Lord and Lady xvi, 152 (p. 106)
Scabious L
   Devil's Bit 35
Scaife, Mr Rob xvi, 153 (p. 125)
Scale, proportionate 142
Scallion 73, 159, 163
   see also Onion; Shallot
Scandinavia xiv, 8
Schongauer, Martin, painter **41**
Scientific enquiry 78
Scotland xv, 79, 140, 142
Sea Holly (*Eryngium* spp.) 119, L
Sebesten 41
Sedding, John Dando, architect 114
Sedge 163, L
Seed, bought 78
   gathering *72*, 110
Seed-growing 134
Seedsman's trade 79, 84, 110
   see also Nursery trade
Segmenta, ? cuttings, ingredients 27
Selfheal 166, L
Selwood, John, abbot of Glastonbury 136
Sensibility 44
Service 32, 41, 73, 120, 122, 164, L
Sesame 41
Severus, priest 26
Seville, Spain 1, 40, 42, 45, 48
Shaftesbury, Dors. 119
Shaking and beating down of fruit 64; **36**
Shallot 29, *31*, 32, 72, 163, L
Shea, Miss Paula xvi
Sheen Palace, Surrey 86, 87, 112, 114, 155, *157–8*
   see also Richmond
Sherburn-in-Elmet, Yorks. 20
Sheringham Manor, Norf. 103
Shrewsbury, earl of **33**
Shrubs, shrubbery 34, 61, 98; **Pl. VII.A; 3.A, B, 11, 15, 31, 52, 58, 64**
   trimmed, 'estrade' **Pl. VII.A; 15, 23, 43, 47.A, 50, 51, 53, 55, 56, 57, 62, 66**
Sicily xiv, 3, 8, 40, 43, 48, 50, 54
Siena, Italy 51
Sileris, brook willows 72
Silesia 58
Silkstead, Hants. 13, 79, 84, 92, 110
Silum 30
Silvaticus, Matthaeus, physician 50
Singer, Charles 66, 78
Sirmium – see Mitrovica
Skirret 30, 32, 41, 86, 121, 154 (p. 86), L

Sloe 35, 122, 164
Smallage 31, 78, 121
Smith, Miss Verena 112; **63**
Snowdrop 132
Snowflake (*Leucojum*) **72**, 126
Soapwort L
Solomon, rabbi, physician 78
Solomon's Seal 132, L
Solothurn, Switzerland 126
Solsequium, chicory, marigold 67, 73
Somersham, Hunts. 12
Sops in wine 127
Sorrel 35, 42, L
Southernwood 29, 31, 160, L
Southwark – see London
Southwell, Notts. 12
Sowthistle, L
Spain x, xiv, 28, 31, 38, 40–45, 48–51, 82, 103, 121, 161, 164
Spalding, Lincs. 13
Spearwort L
Spectaculi, ? gazebo 140
Speedwell (*Veronica* spp.) 126, 132, 154 (p. 126), 164, 165, 166, L
Spelt (*Triticum spelta*) 32
Spices, exotic 67
Spinach 24, 41, 78, 86, 120, 121, 154 (p. 86), 166, L
   -Beet 41, 73, 166
Spindle (*Euonymus*) 164, 165
Spooner, Herman, botanist, xvi
Sports xiv, 135, 140; **7, 25**
   see also Bowls; Butts
Spring (copse, plantation) 17, 114
Spruce 125
Spurge 29, 120, 160, 163, L
   -Laurel 164, L
'Spyhouse', ? gazebo 106
Squills 31, 159, L
Stafford, Edward, 3rd duke of Buckingham 136; **77**
Staines, Middx. 155
Stairs, steps **Pl. IV.A; 43, 48, 52, 58, 75**
Stakes for vines 84, 87, 88, *114*; **8, 29**
Stamford, Lincs. 119, 162
Standerwick, Som. 155
'Standing' 98, 106
Stavesacre L
Stearn, Dr W. T. 150 (p. 7), 165
Stepney, Middx. 119, 127, 163
Stickadove, French lavender 29, 67, L; **13**
Stirling, Scotland 123, 142
Stitchwort L
Stock 41, 42, 126, 163, 165; **13, 16, 17**
Stoke-by-Nayland, Suff. 114
Stonecrop 163, L
Stourton, Lord 136
Strassburg, Gerhard of, ambassador 60
Strawberry 24, 34, 122, 123, 126, 132, L; **Pl. VI; 39, 41, 57, 72**
Strozzi, Filippo 120
   Lorenzo 48
Studham Manor, Beds. 16
Studley Royal, Yorks. x
Stury, Sir Richard 87
Subiaco, Italy 26

Suffolk, earl of 87
Sugar Cane 42
Sumach 42
Sumeria 37
Summerhouse **Pl. VII.A**; 10, 25, 43, 56, 57
   see also Gazebo; Gloriet; Pavilion
Sunderland, Mrs Clare xvi
Swan 133; **Pl. VII.A; 1**
Sweetbriar 132
Sweet William 165
Switzerland 28, 31
Sycamore (*Acer pseudoplatanus*, etc.) 122, 123, *124*, 132
Synonyms, lists of 119
Sypesteyn – *see* Van Sypesteyn
Syria 43

Tafalla (Navarre), Spain xiv, 45; **22**
Talbot, Dr C. H. xvi
Talworth, Surrey 72
Tamarisk 164, 165
Tannhäuser, minnesinger 70
Tansy 29, 32, 34, L
Tapestry of garden 6
Tare 163
Tarragon 30
Tarring, Sussex 122
Tarsus, Turkey 43
Tatto, abbot of Reichenau 28
Taunton Castle, Som. 72
Teasel 29, 31, 32, 41, 87, 163, L
Tegernsee Abbey, Germany 58
Teilo of Llandaff, St 26
Tendring Hall, Suff. 114
Terebinth 67
Teynham Manor, Kent 103
Thacker, Dr Christopher xvi
Theophrastus, botanist 31
Theory and practice 74
Thionville, France 32
Thistle 73, *163*–4, L
Thomas, Mr Graham S. xvi, 150 (p.70)
Thorn – *see* Hawthorn
Thornbury Castle, Glos. 136, 140; **77**
Thorney, Cambs. 35
Thyme 78, L
   Wild L
Tiles, blue-glazed 48
Toddington, Beds. 12
Toledo, Spain 1, 38, 40, 42, 48
'Tomb' in garden 88
Tools and Utensils 114
   for individual tools see below:
     Apron 114; **26**
     Auger 114
     Axe 114
     Billhook 98; **pl. III.A; 47.C, 58**
     Bushel-measure 114
     Flower-pot 42; **Pl. VII.B; 6, 16, 23, 56, 65, 66, 71, 74**
     Hawk, mason's 114
     Ladder 114; **36**
     Mallet 114; **5**
     Pitchfork 114; **28**
     Rake 114; **64**
     Rope 114
     Saw 114; **35**
     Scythe 114; **28**
     Seed-basket 114
     Shears 114
     Shovel 114; **65**
     Sickle 114
     Sieve 114
     Spade 114; **Pl. I; 28, 58, 64, 66, 67, 68, 69**
     Trowel 114
     Water-pot 114; **23**
     Wheel-barrow 58; **26, 35**
Topiary 136, 142
   see also Shrubs, trimmed
Tortworth, Glos. 123
Tours, France 28, 42, 124, 164
   St-Martin, Abbey of 28
Translation of classical works 37
   of Arabic works 43–4, 50
   vernacular 44, 76
Transplanting 22, 86, 118
Transportation of plants 38, 42, 45, 54, 58, 87, 118; **8**
Trees 122–6, 154 (p. 16); **Pl. IV.B, Pl. V; 2, 3, 9, 10, 11, 13, 14, 15, 18, 19, 20, 25, 31, 32, 42, 43, 44, 45, 46, 52, 58, 59, 60, 61, 62, 67, 69**
   Fruit 29, 80, 82; and see individual species
   see also Orchard, Rows, Shrubs, Woodland
Trees, non-fruiting 76, 140
Trefoil – *see* Clover
Trellis 41, 42, 61, 80, 92, 98, 110, 112; **Pl. IV.B; Pl. VII.A; 13, 17, 34, 37, 42, 45, 46, 47.B, 60, 69, 71, 74, 76, 83**
Tremayne, Lawrence J. xvi
Trent, Castello **70**
Trevisa, John, translator 4, 44, 74
Trier, Germany 34
Trieux (Moselle), France 32
Trumpington, William of, abbot of St Albans 12
Tunnel-arbour 87, 92–3, 98, 112, 114, 140, 142; **Pl. IV.A, B; 13, 30, 42**
Turf, 61, 80, 82, 84, 87, 92, 94, 98, 110, 112, 140; **Pl. III, Pl. IV, Pl. VI; 5, 13, 41, 57, 60, 61**
   flowery, 'flowery mead' **Pl. VI, Pl. VII.B, Pl. VIII; 31, 39, 44, 46, 49, 50, 60, 61, 72, 83**
Turkie, Theobald de, convert 161
Turner, T. Hudson xiv, 21, 82
   William, dean of Wells 30, 120, 123, 124–5, 131, 134, 159, 165, 166
Turnip 32, 41, 78, 118, 163, 164, L
Tutsan, L
Tyre, Lebanon 43
Tyrol, Austria 135

Ulleskelf, Yorks. 136
Ulm, Germany 135
Ultrogotha, queen of Paris 27
Umbellifers 31
Uniones 31
Urfa (Edessa), Turkey 38, 43
Urry, Dr William xvi, 64

Valencia, Spain 40, 45–8, 78
Valerian L
   Greek 131, 164

Valla, Lorenzo 45
Van Eyck, Hubert, painter xii, 98; **3.A, B**
    Jan, painter xii; **3.A, B; 12, 48**
Van Sypesteyn, C. H. C. A. 4
Varro, agriculturist 20–1, 76
Vase, ornamental **6, 16, 56, 71, 74**
    see also Tools and Utensils: Flower-pot
Vaughan, Prof. Richard xvi
Vauxhall Gardens, Surrey **25**
Vegetables ix, 61, 86, 92, *115*, 118
Venantius Fortunatus, poet 27
Venice, Italy 27, 51; **54**
Venus' Looking Glass 165
Veratrum 163
Vergier 12, 66, 87
Vernacular translations 4, 21, 44, 74, 76, 118
Vernon, Normandy 16
Versailles, France x, 45
Vervain 24, 132, L
Vetch 24, 75, 107, 120, 163, 164, L
Vienna, Austria 1, 51, 134; **13**
Vikings 35
Vincennes, France xii
Vine 6, 23, 24, 27, 28, 35, 40, 61, 72, 73, 78, 80, 82, 84, 87, 92–3, 107, 114, 132, 135, 140, 155, L; **Pl. IV.B; 8, 27, 29, 39, 53, 59, 83**
    see also Grapevine
Vineyard 8, 10, 12, 13, 27, 28, 34, 52, 54, 60, 73, 84, 87, 107, 112, 114, 134; **8, 37.A**
    of pleasure 135
Violet 4, 6, 21, 22, 23, 27, 29, 34, 41, 42, 60, 66, 70, 73, 119, 126, 131, 132, 154 (p. 86), 163, 164, 165, L; **Pl. VI; 57, 72**
Virectum 4
Virgultum 4, 8, 12, 17, 48, 66, 73, 114, 136
Viridarium 4, 8, 10, 11, 48, 92
Visconti, Azzo, lord of Milan 51
Viterbo, Italy 76
Vivaria, ponds 103
Voltaire, F. M. A. de 25

Walafrid Strabo, monk 25, 28, 34, 131, 165
Wales, North 84
Waleys, Sir William 103
Walks – see Paths
Wallflower 41, 42, 60, 92, 119, 126, 127, 132, L; **41**
Walls, garden 13, 110, 112, 142; **Pl. IV.B; 20, 55.A, 79, 80, 82**
Wallwort L
Walnut 6, 23, 32, 41, 54, 66, 73, 84, 122, *123*, L
Walters, Mr S. M. 23
Waltham Abbey, Essex 21
Wandelbert of Prüm, monk 34
Ward, Mrs G. A. xvi, 151 (p. 87)
Warenne, earl of 87
Warentiam, madder 31
Warfare, Arab methods of 37
Water (lakes, ponds, pools, rivers, streams, wells) 6, 8, 10, 11, 12, 13, 17, 35, 38, 41, 44, 45, 50, 51, 60, 80, 82, 84, 87, 88, 95, 96, 98, 103, 106, 107, 110, 114, 136, 140, 142; **Pl. II, Pl. III.B, Pl. IV.B, Pl. VII.A; 1, 2, 9, 11, 20, 21, 33, 40.B, 43, 44, 48, 49, 51, 55.A, 60**
    see also Fishpond, Fountain, Moat
Waterbeach, Cambs. 140
Watercress 118, L
Water-engines 106
Watering 84, 160
    -pot 114
Water Lily 42, 66, 133
    White L
    Yellow L
Water Melon 166
Watkin, Dom Aelred xvi
Waton, Mr Paul V. xvi
Watson, Anthony 124
Waybread L
Wayfaring Tree 165
Weeding 110, 115
Weedon, Bucks. 110
Weld (*Reseda luteola*) 73
Wellingborough, Northants. 79
Wells, Som. 16, 92, 123, 140
    Cathedral 16, 103
Wenceslaus, king of the Romans 86
Wernher the Gardener, poet 72
Werrington, Northants. 16
Westminster 61, 74, 82, 140, 142, 155
    Abbey 3, 78, 80, 84, 88, 110, 112, 115, 136, 140, 154 (p. 86); **78**
    Charing Cross, Mews 11, 106; **34**
        St Mary Roncesvalles Hospital 121
    Dean's Yard 140
    Jewel House 112; **78**
    Palace xii, 11, 61, 74, 79, 80, 112, 155–6; **7, 78**
Weyden, Rogier van der, painter **49, 50**
Whaddum, Canon John 140
Wheat 32, 75, 162, 163
'Whippeltree' – see Cornel
Whitebeam 165
White Ladies Aston, Worcs. 84
Whiting, Richard, abbot of Glastonbury 136, 142
Whortleberry 119
William I, king of England 8, 54
    II Rufus, king of England 8, 142
William of Holland, king of the Romans 75
    I, king of Sicily 48, 50
    II, king of Sicily 48
    VIII, duke of Aquitaine 54
    of St Genevieve, abbot of Eskilsø 58
Willis, Robert xiv
Willow 4, 41, 42, 58, 66, 72, 73, 75, 82, 122, 140, 163, L
Wilton Diptych 131
Winchester, Hants. 13, 35
    bishopric of 72
    Castle 11, 79, 80
    Cathedral and Priory 13, 79, 84, 92, 106, 110
        Sacrist's garden, 'Paradise' 34
    College 88, 110, 114
Window box x; **4**
Winds 45
Windsor, Berks. 78, 82, 164; **40**
    Castle xii, 10, 11, 54, 76, 79, 80, 87, 96, 112, 114, 115, 155, 156–7; **40**
    Great Garden 10, 76, 80, 96, 98, 125, 135, 142, 152, (p. 96), 156–7; **40, 46**

Park 13; **40**
  Vineyard of pleasure 135
Wine 2–3, 24, 28, 54
'Winesour' plum 20
Winter Cherry (*Physalis alkekengi*) 66
Woad (*Isatis tinctoria*) 42, 73, L
Wolsey, Thomas, cardinal 136
Wolsingham, Durh. 17
Woodbine, Honeysuckle (*Lonicera* spp.) 61, 96, 122, 127, 132, 133, 164, L
Woodland xii, 10, *13*, *16–17*, 60, 73, 79, 86, 92, 103, 107; **83**
Woodmarch (Sanicle) L
  see also Sanicle
Woodruff L
Wood Sage 130, L
Wood Sorrel L
Woodstock, Oxon. 10, 50, 64, 79, 80, 87, 103, 114
  Everswell 11, 50, 80, 106
Woodwax (*Genista tinctoria*) 119
Wootton St Laurence, Hants. 92
Worcester 73
  bishop of 17, 84
  Cathedral 21

Worcestre, William, antiquary 112, 125
Worms, Germany 8
Wormwood 34, 41, L
Worts – *see* Colewort
Wressle Castle, Yorks. 136
Wright, Thomas, antiquary xiv, 70
Würzburg, Germany 134
Wykeham, William of, bishop of Winchester 88, 106, 114

Yarmouth, Great, Norf. 54
Yarrow L
Yeats-Edwards, Mr Paul xvi
Yeveley, Henry, mason 112; **78**
Yew 4, *82*, 122, *125*–6, 132, 164, L
York 8, 12, 20, 27, 28, 35, 84, 123
  archbishop of 8, 16, 54
  Old Baile 16
Yusuf I, sultan of Granada 44

Zouche, Lady 88, 119, 130
  William, 2nd lord 119

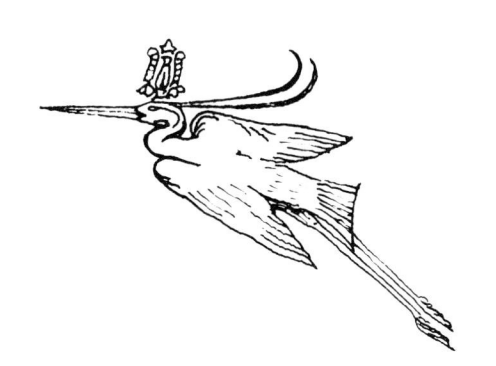